IMMIGRATION LAW IN THE EUROPEAN COMMUNITY

IMMIGRATION AND ASYLUM LAW AND POLICY IN EUROPE

Volume 2

Editors

Elspeth Guild
Kingsley Napley Solicitors, London,
Centre for Migration Law, Katholieke Universiteit, Nijmegen

Jan Niessen
Migration Policy Group, Brussels

The series is a venue for books on European immigration and asylum law and policies where academics, policy makers, law practitioners and others look to find detailed analysis of this dynamic field. Works in the series will start from a European perspective. The increased co-operation within the European Union and the Council of Europe on matters related to immigration and asylum requires the publication of theoretical and empirical research. The series will contribute to well-informed policy debates by analysing and interpreting the evolving European legislation and its effects on national law and policies. The series brings together the various stakeholders in these policy debates: the legal profession, researchers, employers, trade unions, human rights and other civil society organisations.

The titles published in this series are listed at the end of this volume.

Immigration Law in the European Community

by

ELSPETH GUILD

KLUWER LAW INTERNATIONAL

THE HAGUE / LONDON / BOSTON

A C.I.P. Catalogue record for this book is available from the Library of Congress.

ISBN 90-411-1593-5

Published by Kluwer Law International,
P.O. Box 85889, 2508 CN The Hague, The Netherlands.

Sold and distributed in North, Central and South America
by Kluwer Law International,
101 Philip Drive, Norwell, MA 02061, U.S.A.
kluwerlaw@wkap.com

In all other countries, sold and distributed
by Kluwer Law International, Distribution Centre,
P.O. Box 322, 3300 AH Dordrecht, The Netherlands.

Printed on acid-free paper

Printed in the Netherlands.

CONTENTS

Preface   ix

Table of Cases   xi

Introduction   1

Part I: THE COMMUNITY LAW FOUNDATION

CHAPTER 1
The Foundations of the Community's Immigration Laws   7

1.1. Member State Discretion and Movement of Persons   7
1.2. Community Criteria: Conditions Excluding Discretion   21
1.3. Securing Member State Obedience   32
1.4. Conclusions   36

CHAPTER 2
Non-discrimination and Obstacles   37

2.1. Introduction   37
2.2. The Contours of Non-discrimination   40
2.3. Direct and Indirect Discrimination on the Ground of Nationality   45
2.4. Obstacles and their Classification   55
2.5. Conclusions   59

Part II: THIRD COUNTRY NATIONALS PRIVILEGED
           UNDER AGREEMENTS WITH THE EC

CHAPTER 3
An Overview of Third Country Agreements   65

3.1. Introduction   65
3.2. The Agreements and Community Law   71
3.3. The Court of Justice and its Competence   78
3.4. The Principles of Interpretation: Direct Effect   82

3.5. The Principles of Implementation: Where Direct Effect is Lacking   92
3.6. Conclusions   94

CHAPTER 4
The Early Agreements, their Developments and Beneficiaries   95

4.1. Introduction   95
4.2. The Agreements and Provisions on Labour   98
4.3. The Agreements, their Councils and Subsidiary Legislation   100
4.4. Yaounde to Lomé IV   105
4.5. The Maghreb Agreements   110
4.6. Conclusions   117

CHAPTER 5
Interpretation of the Turkey Agreement:
National Discretion and Community Law Coherence   121

5.1. Introduction   121
5.2. The Approach of the Legislator   124
5.3. The Concept of a Worker   145
5.4. The Treatment of Family Members   154
5.5. The Meaning of Public Policy and the Loss of Status   161
5.6. Conclusions   169

CHAPTER 6
Immigration Lessons: The Central and Eastern Europe Agreements   173

6.1. Introduction   173
6.2. Format of the Agreements   177
6.3. People and Pressure to Emigrate   178
6.4. Movement and Rights of Workers   182
6.5. The Right of Establishment   190
6.6. Discrimination, Obstacles and Coherence   201
6.7. Conclusions   209

Part III: THE TREATY AND THIRD COUNTRY NATIONALS:
            THE IMPETUS TOWARDS COMPETENCE AND COHERENCE

CHAPTER 7
The Drive Towards Completing the Internal Market:
Divided Loyalties   213
7.1. Introduction   213
7.2. The Economic Incentive: Creating the Internal Market   219
7.3. Pulling in Different Directions: The Competence Challenge   233
7.4. Persons, Borders and Discretion   240
7.5. Conclusions   249

CHAPTER 8
Pillar Talk: The Maastricht Treaty Compromise   255

8.1. Introduction   255
8.2. The New Immigration Regime in the EC Treaty   268
8.3. Visas and Community Law   273
8.4. Individual Rights in the Light of White, Grey and Black Lists   279
8.5. Physical Presence and Legal Presence   290
8.6. Conclusions   292

CHAPTER 9
The Search for Objectives: The Amsterdam Treaty   295

9.1. Introduction   295
9.2. The EC Treaty and Third Country Nationals: After Amsterdam   296
9.3. The Internal Market and an Area of Freedom, Security and Justice 305
9.4. Temporary Protection: The Commission's Proposal During the
      Negotiations   311
9.5. Immigration Policy: The Commission's Proposal at the Time
      of the Negotiations   324
9.6. Legally Resident Third Country Nationals:
      A Testing Ground of Rights   326
9.7. Conclusions   334
      Annex   336

CHAPTER 10
Conclusions   341

BIBLIOGRAPHY   355

INDEX   367

PREFACE

"The aim is an open and secure European Union fully committed to the obligations of the Geneva Refugee Convention and other relevant human rights instruments, and must be able to respond to humanitarian needs on the basis of solidarity. A common approach must also be developed to ensure the integration into our societies of these third country nationals who are lawfully resident in the Union."

With these fine words the European Council set out its strategy towards the development of an European immigration and asylum law at its Summit in Tampere, Finland, October 1999. The Tampere Summit is not the subject of this book, rather the story which begins in 1957 with the signature of the Treaty of Rome and finds a new impetus in the declarations of the European Council at Tampere.

The new powers which the Amsterdam Treaty's entry into force on 1 May 1999 had transferred to the Community in the field of immigration and asylum now need to be exercised. The powers themselves are very wide and permit many different and conflicting approaches. The purpose of this study is to look at the history of immigration law in the European Community, from the Community's conception in 1957. Can we discern the framework and principles from this history which will be needed for the next step of the Community's development in this field? With this underlying concern I began work on this dissertation in June 1997 as the Member States finalised and signed the Amsterdam Treaty. My greatest thanks in this endeavour for their help, insight, generosity and patience must be to Professors Kees Groenendijk and Roel Fernhout who guided me throughout. Without their great kindness this work would never have been completed.

To others too, however, I am indebted for their assistance and encouragement: first to my jury, Professor Deirdre Curtin and Professor Pieter Boeles; secondly to all the participants of the Centre for Migration Law at the University of Nijmegen (including Hannie van de Put); to those experts who were so generous with their expertise, Denis Martin, Steve Peers and Aleidus Woltjer, and to Helen Staples without whose practical assistance I could not have finished. For his constant support and affection it is a special pleasure to thank Didier Bigo. Finally, I owe gratitude to everyone in the immigration department at my office at Kingsley Napley in London for their help and patience.

Elspeth Guild

TABLE OF CASES

INTERNATIONAL COURT OF JUSTICE

Nottebohm Case (Liechtenstein v Guatemala) ICJ Reports 1955   22
Mavrommatis Palestine Concessions Case PCIJ Series A No 2
   (1924)   204
Panevezys-Saldutiskis Railway Company Case PCIJ Series A No 76   204
   (1939)

EUROPEAN COURT OF HUMAN RIGHTS

Abdulaziz, Cabales and Balkandali [1985] Ser. A No. 95   75
Berrehab [1988] Ser A 138   26
Moustaquim [1991] Ser A 193   26
Vilvarajah [1991] Ser A 215   1
Beldjoudi [1992] Ser A 234A   26
Gül European Court of Human Rights Reports 1996 – I   1, 75
Chahal European Court of Human Rights Reports 1996 – V   1
Amuur v France, 25 June 1996, 17/1995/523/609   291
D v UK, 2 May 1997, 146/1996/767/964   291
Matthews v UK, 18 February 1999, 24833/94   318

EUROPEAN COURT OF JUSTICE

26/62 Van Gend en Loos [1963] ECR 1   15
75/63 Hoekstra (née Unger) [1964] ECR 177   29
90 & 91/63 Commission v Luxembourg & Belgium [1964] ECR
   625   33
6/64 Costa v ENEL [1964] ECR 585   16, 71
15/69 Ugliola [1969] ECR 363   131, 185
1/72 Frilli [1972] ECR 457   42
44/72 Marsman [1972] ECR 1243   185
152/73 Sotgiu [1974] ECR 153   37, 50, 52, 185
167/73 Commission v France [1974] ECR 359   56
181/73 Haegeman [1974] ECR 449   81, 84
2/74 Reyners [1974] ECR 631   61, 90, 102,
   191, 197, 223

8/74 *Dassonville* [1974] ECR 837   206
36/74 *Walrave* [1974] ECR 1405   27
41/74 *Van Duyn* [1974] ECR 1337   28, 46, 47, 60,
                                                                     162

67/74 *Bonsignore* [1975] ECR 297   28
32/75 *Cristini* [1975] ECR 1085   52
36/75 *Rutili* [1975] ECR 1219   28, 48
43/75 *Defrenne* [1976] ECR 455   33
48/75 *Royer* [1976] ECR 497   16, 28, 167,
                                                                     184, 204

87/75 *Bresciani* [1976] ECR 129   81, 83, 84
118/75 *Watson & Belmann* [1976] ECR 1185   14, 48, 204
33/76 *Rewe* [1976] ECR 1989   35
40/76 *Kermachek* [1976] ECR 1669   55
8/77 *Sagulo* [1977] ECR 1495   60
30/77 *Bouchereau* [1977] ECR 1999   60, 162
65/77 *Razanatsimba* [1977] ECR 2229   109
175/78 *Saunders* [1979] ECR 1129   58
207/78 *Even* [1979] ECR 2019   131
149/79 *Commission v Belgium SNCB I* [1980] ECR 3881   50
157/79 *Pieck* [1980] ECR 2171   13, 262
270/80 *Polydor* [1982] ECR 329   83, 198
53/81 *Levin* [1982] ECR 1035   29, 60, 145,
                                                                     189, 193, 291

104/81 *Kupferberg* [1982] ECR 3641   79, 82
115-116/81 *Adoui & Cornaille* [1982] ECR 1665   48, 161
36/82 *Morson* [1982] ECR 3723   154
286/82 *Luisi & Carbone* [1984] ECR 377   22, 27
237/83 *Prodest* [1984] ECR 3135   33
238/83 *Meade* [1984] ECR 2631   22
267/83 *Diatta* [1985] ECR 567   58, 131, 155,
                                                                     156

293/83 *Gravier* [1985] ECR 593   42
41/84 *Pinna* [1986] ECR 1   52, 53, 140, 185
137/84 *Mutch* [1985] ECR 2681   52
205/84 *Commission v Germany* [1986] ECR 3793   194
59/85 *Reed* [1986] ECR 1283   16, 52
66/85 *Lawrie-Blum* [1986] ECR 2121   30, 31, 60, 61,
                                                                     145, 146, 151

139/85 *Kempf* [1986] ECR 1741   60, 145
225/85 *Commission v Italy* [1987] ECR 2625   185
281/85, 283-85/85, 287/85 *Germany and Ors v
    Commission* [1987] ECR 3203   131, 234, 235,
                                                                     236, 237

39/86 *Lair* [1988] ECR 3161   31, 151
12/86 *Demirel* [1987] ECR 3719   73, 79, 80, 84,
                                                      89, 90, 91, 119,
                                                      195, 199, 200

249/86 *Commission v Germany* [1989] ECR 1263   75, 154
20/87 *Gauchard* [1987] ECR 4879   58
143/87 *Stanton* [1988] ECR 3877   54, 57
181/87 *Daily Mail* [1998] ECR 5483   193
186/87 *Cowan* [1989] ECR 195   42
196/87 *Steymann* [1988] ECR 6159   30, 149, 192,
                                                      193

235/87 *Matteucci* [1998] ECR 5589   109
344/87 *Bettray* [1989] ECR 1621   145, 149
389 & 390/87 *Echternach* [1989] ECR 723   54, 68, 142, 146
9/88 *Lopes da Veiga* [1989] ECR 2989   169
171/88 *Rinner-Kühn* [1989] ECR 2743   14, 146
C-228/88 *Bronzing* [1990] ECR 531   53
C-297/88 *Dzodzi* [1990] ECR I-3763   154
C-68/89 *Commission v Netherlands* [1991] ECR I-2637 224, 274
C-113/89 *Rush Portuguesa* [1990] ECR I-1417   68
C-192/89 *Sevince* [1990] ECR I-3461   79, 83, 84, 85,
                                                      87, 88, 92, 100,
                                                      125, 167, 168,
                                                      174, 188, 199

C-221/89 *Factortame* [1991] ECR I-3905   192
C-292/89 *Antonissen* [1991] ECR I-745   22, 27, 55, 151
C-357/89 *Raulin* [1992] ECR I-1059   31
C-363/89 *Roux* [1991] ECR I-273   27
C-3/90 *Bernini* [1992] ECR I-1071   31
C-6, 9/90 *Francovich* [1991] ECR I-5357   93
C-10/90 *Masgio* [1991] ECR I-1119   56
C-18/90 *Kziber* [1991] ECR I-199   7, 55, 79, 85,
                                                      89, 93, 101,
                                                      104, 108, 112,
                                                      114, 119, 153,
                                                      174, 184, 186,
                                                      200, 202

C-295/90 *Parliament v Council re Students* [1992] ECR I-4193   42
C-369/90 *Micheletti* [1992] ECR I-4239   24
C-370/90 *Singh* [1992] ECR I-4265   46, 58, 68, 164,
                                                      345

Opinion 1/91 [1991] ECR 6079   32
C-27/91 *Le Manoir* [1991] ECR-5531   146

C-237/91 *Kus* [1992] ECR I-6781   79, 144, 148,
                                                              157, 161, 167,
                                                              323
C-312/91 *Metalsa* [1993] ECR I-3751   83
C-20/92 *Hubbard* [1993] ECR I-377   44
C-118/92 *Commission v Luxembourg* [1994] ECR I-1891   41
C-272/92 *Spotti* [1993] ECR I-5185   185
C-398/92 *Mund & Fester* [1994] ECR I-467   44
C-419/92 *Scholz* [1994] ECR I-505   25
C-12/93 *Drake* [1994] ECR I-4337   108
C-43/93 *Van der Elst* [1994] ECR I-3803   68, 343
C-58/93 *Yousfi* [1994] ECR I-1353   114
C-280/93 *Germany v Commission* [1994] ECR I-4973   107
C-279/93 *Schumacker* [1995] ECR 225   54
C-308/93 *Issarte-Cabanis* [1996] ECR I-2097   55
C-355/93 *Eroglu* [1994] ECR I-5113   88, 138, 142,
                                                              161, 171, 195
C-415/93 *Bosman* [1995] ECR I-4921   14, 16, 59, 202,
                                                              344
C-434/93 *Bozkurt* [1996] ECR I-1475   87, 151, 169
C-469/93 *Chiquita Italia SpA* [1995] ECR I-4533   107
Opinion 1/94 (WTO) [1996] ECR I-5267   72, 77
Opinion 2/94 [1996] ECR I-1759   75
C-7/94 *Gaal* [1995] ECR I-1031   160
C-55/94 *Gebhard* [1995] ECR I-4165   32, 61, 192,
                                                              194, 203
C-103/94 *Krid* [1994] ECR I-719   114
C-116/94 *Meyers* [1995] ECR, I-2131   186
C-206/94 *Paletta* [1996] ECR I-2357   164
C-214/94 *Boukalfa* [1996] ECR I-2253   33
C-227/94 *Olivieri-Coenen* [1995] ECR I-301   108
C-237/94 *O'Flynn* [1996] ECR I-2639   52, 53, 202
C-277/94 *Taflan-Met* [1996] ECR I-4085   92, 93, 105
C-302/94 *R v HM Treasury ex p British Telecommunications PLC*
   [1996] ECR I-1631   17
C-336/94 *Dafeki* [1997] ECR I-6761   165
C-4 & 5/95 *Stöber* [1997] ECR I-511   53, 59, 202, 203
C-13/95 *Süzen* [1997] ECR I-1257   69
C-43/95 *Data Delecta* [1996] ECR I-4671   42, 43, 344
C-53/95 *Kemmler* [1996] ECR I-703   194
C-65/95 & C-111/95 *Radiom and Shingara* [1997] ECR I-3343   28, 47, 49
C-107/95 *Asscher* [1996] I-3089   32, 193
C-126/95 *Hallouzi-Choho* [1996] ECR I-4807   114

C-171/95 *Tetik* [1997] ECR I-329   55, 140, 151,
                                                        170

C-266/95 *Merino Garcia* [1997] ECR I-3279   53, 203
C-285/95 *Kol* [1997] ECR I-3069   165
C-351/95 *Kadiman* [1997] ECR I-2133   88, 155, 157
C-392/95 *Parliament v Council* [1997] ECR I-3213   169, 273, 282
C-36/96 *Günaydin* [1997] ECR I-5143   147, 149, 150,
                                                        151, 166

C-57/96 *Meints* [1997] ECR I-6689   54
C-64/96 & C-65/96 *Uecker & Jacquet* [1997] ECR I-3171 49, 69, 131
C-85/96 *Martinez Sala* [1998] ECR I-2691   49, 146, 151
C-98/96 *Ertanir* [1997] ECR I-5179   151, 168
C-170/96 *Commission v Council* [1998] ECR I-2763   286, 288, 289,
                                                        290, 291

C-262/96 *Sürül* [1999] ECR I-2685   88, 93
C-348/96 *Calfa* [1999] ECR I-11   50
C-350/96 *Clean Car* [1998] ECR I-2521   344
C-416/96 *El Yassini* [1999] ECR I-1209   85, 86, 89, 100,
                                                        112, 113, 184,
                                                        187, 198, 254

C-1/97 *Birden* [1998] ECR I-7747   147, 148, 150,
                                                        151, 348

C-113/97 *Babahenini* [1998] ECR I-183   114
C-210/97 *Akman* [1998] ECR I-7519   68, 85, 138,
                                                        139, 142, 143,
                                                        161

C-234/97 *Bobadilla* [1999] ECR I-7555   15
C-230/97 *Awoyemi* [1998] ECR I-6781   22, 68, 69, 70,
                                                        343

C-340/97 *Nazli* [2000] ECR I-4903   88
C-378/97 *Florus Ariël Wijsenbeek* [1999] ECR I-6207   231, 232
C-37/98 *Savas* judgment: 11.5.2000   90
C-65/98 *Eyup* judgment: 22.6.2000   141, 159
C-179/98 *Mesbah* [1999] ECR I-7955   22, 23, 112, 159
C-63/99 *Gloszczuk* pending   198
C-239/99 *Kondova* pending   198
C-257/99 *Barkoci and Malik* pending   198
C-268/99 *Jany and Ors* pending   198
T-115-94 *Opel Austria v Council* [1997] ECR II-39   81

INTRODUCTION

"As the Court has observed in the past, Contracting States have the right, as a matter of well-established international law and subject to their treaty obligations including the European Convention on Human Rights, to control the entry, residence and expulsion of aliens."[1]

International law contains only limited obligations on states to respect the choices of individuals as to the country in which they live. The three major exceptions in international law to national sovereignty are primarily based on characteristics of the individual's personal status or relationship of the individual to his or her state over which the individual generally has limited control. First, the principle of admission to the state of which one is a national is well established and contained, *inter alia* in Protocol 4 European Convention on Human Rights (ECHR). Secondly, the enjoyment of family life can found a claim to remain, at least, on the territory of a state of which an individual is not a national contained, *inter alia*, in Article 8 ECHR.[2] Thirdly, persons are entitled to remain on the territory of a state of which they are not nationals if the only alternative is to return them to a place where they fear inhuman and degrading treatment or punishment[3] or persecution on defined grounds.[4] Within these parameters the crossing of external borders is generally considered, in international law, a reserve of national sovereignty.

Further in the application of the limiting principles, a wide margin of appreciation is permitted to the state to decide whether the claims of, for instance, family relationships[5] or inhuman or degrading treatment[6] are sufficiently strong to warrant entry into or residence on the territory of the state.[7] In the concept

---

1 Chahal European Court of Human Rights Reports 1996-V.
2 Other sources include Article 26 International Covenant on Civil and Political Rights.
3 Article 3 ECHR and Article 3 UN Convention against Torture.
4 UN Convention on the status of refugees 1951 and Protocol 1967.
5 See for example Gül European Court of Human Rights Reports 1996 - I.
6 See for example Vilvarajah [1991] Ser A 215.
7 Within the system of the European Convention on Human Rights the judgments of the Court of Human Rights are of course final but those judgments generally leave a wide margin of appreciation to the state. This wide discretion which the Court has inferred has, in some cases been criticized by observers, for instance, P. van Dijk and G.J.H. van Hoof, *Theory and Practice of the European Convention on Human Rights*, 2nd Edition, Kluwer Law and Taxation Publishers, Deventer, 1990 pp. 585-606. The argument is that this concept permits a differentiation in the application of the Convention. The uniformity and clarity which the Convention promises to the individual (and the state as regards its

of state sovereignty is inherent the right to exercise discretion in immigration policies. In so far as the state reserves its discretion over entry, residence and expulsion of individuals, those individuals have little power in determining as a matter of choice what country they live in. They can choose the country they would like to live in but then it is the state which selects. This is the guiding principle of immigration policies primarily of developed countries.

The immigration law of the European Union is characterised by a different relationship between the state and the individual as regards movement across national borders. The contours of this relationship will be examined in this study through a consideration of the scope of discretion available to a Member State and degree of choice available to the individual.

Through amendment of EC Treaty, subsidiary legislation and agreements with third countries the Community has assumed an expanding competence in respect of all aspects of migration. The most dramatic change has occurred with the amendments of the Treaty which took effect on 1 May 1999 when the Amsterdam Treaty came into force. The premise to be examined here is whether in the exercise of that competence certain principles can be discerned which inform the division of power and choice between the state and the individual.

First, as regards Community nationals who are migrant workers in a host Member State, it is now an uncontroversial statement that the discretion and choice whether to move or not is given to the individual with only minor interference permitted by the State. However it is important to see how this state of affairs came into being. Was it self evident when the EC Treaty came into force in 1958 or was there an incremental development to this state of affairs? How important in this context is the right to non-discrimination and the assimilation of a very wide concept of worker, benefits for workers and obstacles to movement? Secondly, when the Community began to incorporate into agreements with third countries provisions relating to workers and subsequently persons, can the principles applicable to Community national migration as regards the extent and limitations on state discretion be discerned? Thirdly, what principles applied when the Member States began to coordinate their national policies on admission of third country nationals in general? Finally, what lessons does the history of the Community and migration provide for the implementation of the Community's new powers over third country national immigration?

---

obligations) is diluted through the concept of a margin of appreciation if allowed to extend too far.

This analysis may be useful in a Europe which is now seized with a fear of foreigners increasingly depicted as huddling on the borders struggling to get in. What can be learned from this European experience in allocation of the right of initiative or choice between the state and the individual in terms of actual choices made by individuals has some surprising aspects. For instance, in 1985 1.4% on average of the population of the Member States consisted of nationals of other Member States. In 1993 this percentage had changed to 1.5%. In fact, the percentage hit 1.5 in 1987 and has stayed there.[8] The acquisition of citizenship in the Member States, on average including both acquisition of citizenship by Community nationals[9] and third country nationals exhibits slightly greater variation: 1.4% of the foreign population acquired citizenship in 1985, 1.5% in 1993 but 1989 was a busy year – 1.9% acquired citizenship.[10]

Whether an immigration law is a success or failure depends on its objectives and who is looking: different assessments may result from the state's point of view, from the individual's point of view or in the case of the European Community, its point of view. The three perspectives do not necessarily coincide. For instance, the state may have as a goal to discourage unemployed foreigners from joining the local labour market, the individual may have as a goal finding a better job with more pay; the Community has as an objective: the ever closer union of the peoples of Europe. Where the Community has competence it will be interesting to consider how through the laws it chooses to make to achieve its goal, set out in the EC Treaty itself, individuals and the Member States reconcile themselves.

The consideration of the area will follow the law – from the adoption of the initial EC Treaty to the Amsterdam Treaty amendments looking exclusively at movement of persons. Many of the decisive steps along this path took place in completely different areas of Community law but benefited, developed and indeed in some cases formed rights of free movement of persons as an unintended by-product of other activities. Nonetheless in the building of the Union, the symbolic value of free movement of persons has been substantial. Particular emphasis will be placed on the decisions of the Court of Justice. This is inevitable in view of the tremendous importance of the Court in the creation of an enduring and binding supra-national framework.[11] Its role as

---

8 Migration Statistics 1997, Eurostat, Luxembourg 1998.
9 Though it should be noted that nationals of the Member States often do not apply for citizenship of another Member State where they may be resident.
10 There was a substantial jump in acquisition rates in Finland, Netherlands, UK and Italy in 1989. Migration Statistics 1995, Eurostat, Luxembourg, p 16.
11 "For educated observers of European affairs, whether friends or foes of a strong Community, the magnitude of the contribution made by the Court of Justice to the

ultimate arbiter between the national official anxious to retain national discretion, the Community *fonctionnaire* charged with implementing Community
rules effectively and the individual seeking to move has been decisive.

The purpose of this study, then, is to look at an interesting legal structure on
immigration and see whether it in fact bucks the trend in the Western world of
ever tighter control of administrative discretion by avoiding the concept of
selection implicit in that discretion[12] or achieves the same result by other means.
If this structure were to be expressed as a diagram it would appear as a triangle:
what is the relationship between the individual as a migrant and the Member
State to which he or she wishes to go; the relationship between the Member
State and the Community regarding the power to regulate that prospective or
actual movement; and that between the individual and the Community as
regards the nature and quality of the agreement between the Community and
the Member State:

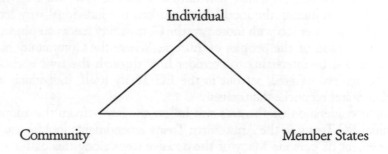

 _____

integration of Europe has almost become a by-word." G. F. Mancini, The Making of a
Constitution for Europe CMLRev 26:595 (1989).
12 "in addition, it must be recognised that, given the kinds of restrictions we currently place
on immigration, the kind of decision made by an immigration official necessarily
involves subjective elements. In addition, the restrictions we place on immigration
generally involve some kind of subjective national judgment on why and in what
situations we want to restrict access to membership in our community. While we want
the officials who make the ultimate decisions as to who is admitted into membership in
our community to be 'discriminating', we want them to discriminate on the basis of an
applicant's merits or capacities, and not on the basis of irrelevant considerations such as
the grounds prohibited by section 15 of the [Canadian Human Rights] Charter. M.
Dobson-Mack, Independent Immigration Selection Criteria and Equality Rights:
Discretion, Discrimination and Due Process, Les Cahiers de Droit 34: 549-572 (1993).

PART I

THE COMMUNITY LAW FOUNDATION

Chapter One

The Foundations of the Community's Immigration Laws

1.1. Member State Discretion and Movement of Persons

Migrants as Economic Actors

It is often said that within the Community context, free movement of persons arose as a manifestation first and foremost of movement of labour and secondarily of management (or the self-employed).[1] Most of us are economic actors of one sort or another for some period of our lives[2] and for most of us that period is the majority of our lives.[3] Therefore the adoption of a free movement criterion based on the individual as an economic actor (present or former) rather than on some other criterion, for instance, liability to persecution or

---

1   Report of the High Level Panel on the Free Movement of Persons chaired by Mrs Simone Veil, European Commission, 18 March 1997.

2   "16. The question which I shall now consider is whether a person like Kziber is to be regarded as a member of the family of a worker of Moroccan nationality living with him within the meaning of Article 41(1) of the [EEC-Morocco Cooperation] Agreement.
    The German Government disputes this, pointing out that it emerges from the decision making the reference to the Court that Kziber's father is a pensioner and that he can therefore not be regarded as a 'worker of Moroccan nationality' who is 'employed' in one of the Member States of the Community within the meaning of that provision so that Kziber herself is not a member of the family living with such a worker. This assertion amounts to claiming that a person in receipt of a pension is no longer a worker and cannot claim the benefit of the non-discrimination rule established by the Agreement, something which, in my opinion, cannot have been the intention of the Contracting Parties. I therefore consider that Article 41 cannot be interpreted in the sense that persons of Moroccan nationality who have worked in the Community and have subsequently been receiving a retirement pension are excluded from the scope of Article 41." Opinion, A-G Van Gerven as approved by the Court: "27. As regards the concept of 'worker' in Article 41(1) of the Agreement, it encompasses both active workers and those who have left the labour market after reaching the age required for receipt of an old-age pension or after becoming victims of the materialization of one of the risks creating entitlement to allowances falling under other branches of social security." C-18/90 *Kziber* [1991] ECR I-199.

3   The current participation rate in Europe is 55.3% of the population, which does not include persons seeking work or retired from the labour force, Statistics in Focus 1997, Eurostat, Luxembourg, 1998.

family membership, to refer to some of the most common other criteria[4] currently in play at the national level as regards movement of persons, is inclusive rather than exclusive.

At the time of the negotiation of the EC Treaty, the movement of labour in Europe was dominated by South to North labour migration, primarily from Italy towards Germany, the Benelux and to a less extent France.[5] The first migratory movement was initially dominated by intra EC workers. Post WWII, the flows of persons in Europe are frequently categorised as falling into three waves: labour in the 1950s and 1960s, family in the 1970s and refugees in the 1990s. Migration was, in the 1950s and 1960s, labour-oriented which meant that the spectre of recession in the early 1970s led to political statements regarding stopping labour migration.[6] While such a policy was theoretically possible as regards third country nationals it was no longer so as regards Community nationals and their family members. Their rights were by this time enshrined in the EC Treaty and its subsidiary legislation which deprived the Member States acting individually, of the right to limit or prevent access of migrant workers, nationals of other Member States, from entering, working and residing in any Member State.

The regulation of migrant labour had been the subject of international agreement from the beginning of the century. Under the auspices of the International Labour Organisation (ILO) Recommendation No 2 adopted at the General Conference of 1919 provided for admission of migrant workers on the basis of reciprocity. In 1939 the ILO produced the Migration for Employment Convention governing the same area after which as migration increased so did international treaty regulation.

While the European Community was developing its law on migration, in the international arena similar activities were taking place.[7] None of them however resulted in a system of directly effective rights for individuals in the way

---

4   One could add also, place of birth, nationality or residence but these criteria apply in different sorts of circumstances. What is under consideration here is the right of access to a country of a national of another country where the individual has no previous link of residence, birth or citizenship with the prospective host country.

5   S. Castles, The Guestworker in Western Europe, International Migration Review 1986, Vol. 20, No 3, pp 761-778. S. Castles and M. Miller, The Age of Migration, 2nd Edition, Macmillan, London, 1998, pp. 67-104.

6   H. Zlotnick, Identification of Migration Systems, in M. Kritz, L. Lean Lim, and H. Zlotnik, *International Migration Systems: A Global Approach*, Clarendon Press, Oxford, 1992, p. 31.

7   From the 1950s, the regulation of employment migration in Europe was also governed by bilateral agreements such as the one between Germany and Italy, 1955. Vereinbarung zwischen der Regierung der Bundesrepublik Deutschland und der Regierung der Italienischen Republik über die Anwerbung und Vermittlung von Italienischen Arbeitskraften nach der Bundesrepublik Deutschland 20.12.1955.

Community law would develop. However, the contents and approach of these international agreements provide a background against which Community law must be understood. The most important international background for the development of migration law of the EC was and continues to be the Council of Europe which I will deal with first and secondly the UN, both through its treaty making powers and through the agency of the International Labour Organisation. Finally, the WTO very recently has created a new framework for economic immigration through the General Agreement on Trade in Services (GATS) to no small extent the result of European Community commitment. However, the scope of this new development is beyond this book.

International Treaties Relating to Labour Migration: 1949 – 1999

Measure	UN/International Labour Organisation (ILO)	Council of Europe
Convention 97 on Migration for Employment	1949 parties[8] (EU): 8[9]	
European Convention on Establishment		1955 parties (EU): 12[10]
European Social Charter (original)		1961 parties (EU): all[11]
Convention 117 on Social Policy	1962 parties (EU): 3[12]	
Convention 143 concerning Migrant Workers	1975 parties (EU): 3[13]	
European Convention on the Legal Status of Migrant Workers		1977 parties (EU): 10[14]
UN Convention on the Protection of the Rights of All Migrant Workers; not yet in force; not ratified by any EU Member State	1990	

The interest of the wider Europe to regulate either labour migration or the conditions of residence and employment of migrant workers on a multilateral basis had its main impetus between 1961 and 1977. The instruments adopted during that period enjoyed a reasonable degree of support, ratification was normal.

Three times the Council of Europe opened for ratification instruments which regulate migrant workers. The first was the Convention on Establish-

---

8   Parties here means countries which have signed the relevant instrument. Signature/ratification: where an instrument has been ratified the date of ratification is included. If it has only been signed that date is then included. R. Plender, *Basic Documents on International Migration Law*, 2nd Ed. Martinus Nijhoff, The Hague, 1997.
9   Belgium, 1953; France, 1954; Germany, 1959; Italy, 1952; Netherlands, 1952; Portugal 1978; Spain, 1967; UK, 1951.
10 Austria, 1957; Belgium, 1962; Denmark, 1961; France, 1955; Germany, 1965; Greece, 1965; Ireland, 1966; Italy, 1963; Luxembourg, 1969; Netherlands, 1969; Sweden, 1971; UK 1969.
11 The European Social Charter only covers migrants tangentially. Its main concern is the securing of economic and social rights for persons on the territory. All the EU Member States are parties.
12 Italy, 1966; Portugal, 1981; Spain, 1973.
13 Italy, 1981; Portugal, 1978; Sweden, 1982.
14 Belgium, 1978; France, 1983; Germany, 1977; Greece, 1977; Italy, 1995; Luxembourg, 1977; Netherlands, 1983; Portugal, 1979; Spain, 1980; Sweden, 1978.

ment which relates mainly to the treatment of nationals of other Parties residing on the territory of one Party. Article 2 provides that the Parties should facilitate to the extent permitted by their economic and social conditions the prolonged or permanent residence of nationals of other Parties on their territory. It regulates the grounds of expulsion of persons residing on the territory but in the main it provides for equal treatment in a wider variety of fields such as working conditions and social rights of nationals of one Party resident on the territory of another. The next instrument, the European Social Charter, insofar as it relates to migrants, does not seek to regulate movement of persons but rather their treatment when moving to and on the territory of the Parties. Again the key to the rights is equal treatment with workers nationals of the host Party in social and economic spheres. The last instrument was the Council of Europe's Convention on the Legal Status of Migrant Workers for which the decision to draft dates from 1966.[15] In contrast with the others, it includes detailed provisions on the recruitment of migrant workers as well as their treatment on the territory. The regulation of recruitment is premised on the idea that the state will itself carry this out. Therefore an active selection role of the state is fundamental to the instrument. This limits its use as a precedent for the European Union in drafting an instrument on primary immigration, even though it is signed by most of the Member States. The nature of labour migration in 2000 is dominated by corporate recruitment and movement of employees balanced against state certification. However, importantly the principle of equal treatment in social and economic rights arises here as well. From the record of ratification, it appears that European states prefer European multilateral instruments to international ones. This may be not least because the European agreements generally limit the benefit of rights for migrant workers to those who are nationals of other contracting parties.

The ILO was also involved in the preparation of instruments to regulate movement of labour following WW II. Its Convention on migration for employment No 97 of 1949 came at the beginning of substantial labour migration in Europe. Besides a duty to facilitate the departure, journey and reception of migrants for employment, the Convention places a duty on its Parties to assure equal treatment after entry onto the territory. It also places limits on expulsion of migrant workers after long residence and in the case of industrial accident leading to long term incapacity. By Annexes to it, the Convention sets standards for Government sponsored recruitment of labour migration. To this extent it too has been marginalised by the occupation by companies of that territory which previously had been the domain of state bodies.

---

15 E. Guild, *The European Convention on the Legal Status of Migrant Workers (1977) An Analysis of its Scope and Benefits*, Council of Europe, Strasbourg, 1999.

The second ILO Convention, on migrant workers, No 143, has enjoyed very little support from European states. Only three have become parties. It focuses on the suppression of clandestine or illegal migration whether for employment or otherwise. Thereafter, the convention creates or reinforces existing obligations to ensure equal treatment for migrant workers.

All of these conventions depend on the willingness of the signatories to implement their provisions and none requires the devolving of rights to individuals. They provide standards for state activity. A defining feature of all these initiatives is the scope of discretion allowed to the receiving state.[16] The adoption of the criterion of economic activity in particular as a worker, accordingly, followed both existing precedent and pressing economic need. The situation changed after the 1973 oil crisis and the exercise of discretionary control became ever increasingly apparent through the tightening of criteria for labour migration.

By 1990, the discourse on access to the territory was almost uniformly by reference to the exceptions where access is permitted rather than a norm when rejection is unusual. Today lawyers advising potential immigrants to Europe often resort to an explanation of ways to immigrate on a long term basis along the same lines as the classic waves but in a different order: there are three gates: first, you come within the class of specified family members eligible to admission to the state on that ground – gate 1 – family reunification; secondly, there is a real risk that you will be persecuted on specific grounds in your country of origin if you are not allowed to stay in this country of refuge – gate 2 – asylum status; thirdly, you qualify for admission on employment/investment grounds – gate 3 – economic activity. Of the three gates, the first is not particularly amenable to individual action which will render the person able to enter (other than marriage). The second gate is, in general, resistant to individual initiative – either the state of origin will protect a person or it will not.[17] The third gate provides the greatest flexibility for the individual.

The third gate was the defining choice of the Community in its immigration law. Before long the first gate was added as a derived right to those passing

---

16 For a more detailed history of international provisions relating to labour migration see K. Lewin, The Free Movement of Workers CMLRev 300 (1964/65); W.R. Böhning, *The Migration of Workers in the United Kingdom and the European Union*, OUP, London, 1972; S. Castles and G. Kosack, *The Function of Labour Immigration in Western European Capitalism*, in P. Braham, *Discrimination and Disadvantage in Employment: the experience of black workers*, Harper & Row, London, 1981; M. Piore, *Birds of Passage: Migrant Labour and Industrial Societies*, CUP, Cambridge, 1979; R. Cohen, *The New Helots*, Ashgate, Aldershot, 1987.

17 This is a deliberate oversimplification: there is a serious discussion about the extent to which the definition of a refugee is capable of manipulation both by states and individuals.

through the third gate but has never taken on a fully independent existence.[18] The second gate has fallen, until recently, outside the material scope of Community law. What is interesting in the development of the password to enter through the third gate is that at the same time that ever more complicated and restrictive rules were devised at national level to transfer from the individual to the Member State authorities the power to regulate passage,[19] at the Community level the opposite development was occurring.

The Individual as King

The Community, in developing its immigration law, consistently removed from the Member State authorities the power to decide who to admit. Instead the process was transformed into one increasingly characterised by the power of the individual to choose.[20] This process was characterised in 1976 by the Court

---

18 One curious exception is Article 3 Regulation 1251/70 which grants a right to remain permanently for family members of a Community migrant worker when under the specified circumstances the worker acquires that right (basically retirement) and after the worker's death. It is not entirely clear whether such a right of permanent residence can find expression in Community secondary legislation where it is not apparent in the Treaty itself. The new power in Article 63(4) EC introduced by the Amsterdam Treaty on rights and conditions of residence of third country nationals may change this.

19 It was in the exercise of sovereignty that states allowed a wide margin of choice to the individual in labour migration in, for instance, the 1960s when the demand for labour could not be filled from the domestic market, which choice was subsequently clawed back as the supply of labour domestically exceeded demand.

20 The ever-tighter limitations on national discretion resulting from decisions of the Court of Justice did not go unnoticed. Even supporters of the Community occasionally had difficulty with the principle: "Further, the Court clearly holds that point of entry inquiries may not be used in order to establish whether an otherwise qualified individual may be refused entry under the public policy provision [157/79 Pieck [1980] ECR 2171 at p. 2185 para 9]. The Court has given no guidance as to how the authorities may then determine if an individual does indeed constitute a threat to public policy. If the individual is admitted to the country, he may prove to be a danger to public policy before inquiries may be made about him, or before the machinery for deportation can be put into effect... By strictly limiting point of entry requirements, and at the same time leaving unsolved the way in which inquiries into an alien's right to enter and remain should be pursued, the Court has created a major problem for the immigration authorities of the Member States. Finally, it should be emphasized that for countries such as the United Kingdom, where no form of compulsory registration of residence in a community is known, and where the system of issuing identity cards is not practiced, the problems posed by Pieck are especially serious." D. O'Keeffe, Practical Difficulties in the Application of Article 48[39] of the EEC Treaty CMLRev 19:35-60 (1982).

of Justice on the right of free movement for economic purposes (Articles 39-55)[21] as follows:

> "Articles 48 [39] to 66 [55] of the Treaty and the measures adopted by the Community in application thereof implement a fundamental principle of the Treaty, confer on persons whom they concern individual rights which the national courts must protect and take precedence over any national rule which might conflict with them."[22]

The process has been so successful not least in acknowledging the diversity of economic activity and recognizing as economic actors those with only a marginal or tenuous connection with the labour market[23] that by 1990 the Member States agreed on an extension of a right of residence to anyone who did not seem likely to be a burden on the social assistance system of the state.[24] Of course, there was an additional pressure: the completion of the internal market and the intended abolition of intra-Union border controls on 31.12.92[25] meant that the Member States were conscious of the need to "complete" the movement rights for nationals of the Member States. The right of movement disassociated from economic activity was subsequently transformed into a right of residence attendant on citizenship of the Union.[26] This immigration law which empowers the individual to make the choice whether to move or not by reducing to a minimum the discretion of the state to interfere with the choice has been rewarded by the experts with 'declassification'.[27] The flexibility itself has apparently disguised the fact that what is at issue is indeed law.

---

21 All references to Articles of the EC Treaty are according to the numbering in force after 1 May 1999. In respect of references in direct quotes from decisions of the Court or the writing of others, the numbering is kept as it appears in the original followed by the new numbering in square brackets.

22 118/75 *Watson & Belmann* [1976] ECR 1185.

23 The Court held that although the character of the work must be genuine and effective (53/81 *Levin* [1982] ECR 1035) that does not exclude employment for just 10 hours per week (171/88 *Rinner-Kühn* [1989] ECR 2743) nor indeed does the employer even need to be an undertaking, all that is required is the existence of, or the intention to create, an employment relationship (C-415/93 *Bosman* [1995] ECR I-4921).

24 Directive 93/96 on students, Directive 90/365 on pensioners and Directive 90/364 on anyone else who is economically inactive but self-sufficient.

25 Article 14 EC.

26 Article 18 EC.

27 For example: C. Wihtol de Wenden, CERI, Paris, Les obstacles à une politique communautaire de l'immigration Third ECSA-World Conference, Brussels, 19-20 September 1996; P. Henson and N. Malhan, Domestic Politics and Europeanisation in the German Migration Debate: The Elusive Search for a European Migration Policy Third ECSA-World Conference, Brussels, 19-20 September 1996.

Inadvertence: the development of the right of choice

EC immigration law would not have developed into one where the individual has the maximum choice had not two principles been established as character- istics of Community law: first, the concept of direct effect, and secondly supremacy of Community law over national law. Recently the remedy of damages against the state for failure to implement correctly Community law is developing into a powerful tool at the disposal of the individual to enforce rights. It has yet to become a standard pleading in the field of free movement of persons but may well. It is important to bear in mind that some of these principles arose in other contexts and in response to challenges outside the field of free movement of persons.

First, – direct effect:[28]

"The conclusion to be drawn from this is that the Community constitutes a new legal order of international law for the benefit of which the States have limited their sovereign rights, albeit within limited fields, and the subjects of which comprise not only Member States but also their nationals. Independently of the legislation of Member States, Community law therefore not only imposes obligations on individuals but is also intended to confer upon them rights which become part of their legal heritage. These rights arise not only where they are expressly granted by the Treaty, but also by reason of obligations which the Treaty imposes in a clearly defined way upon individuals as well as upon the Member States and the institutions of the Community."[29]

As regards free movement of workers, this direct effect applies not only vertically between the state and individual but also horizontally between indi- viduals:[30]

"The Court has held that the abolition as between Member States of obstacles to freedom of movement for persons and to freedom to provide services[31] would be compromised if the abolition of state barriers could be neutralised by obstacles resulting from the exercise of their legal autonomy by associations or organisations not governed by public law (see 36/74 *Walrave* [1974] ECR 1405).

---

28 See P. Pescatore, The Doctrine of Direct Effect: An Infant Disease in Community Law, ELRev 8:155 (1983).

29 26/62 *Van Gend en Loos* [1963] ECR 1.

30 The full extent of so-called horizontal direct effect, that is the application of Community law between private individuals, is a complex question. The Court has recently given an indication of the breadth which may apply: "The Court has already held that a Member State may leave the implementation of the objectives pursued by Community directives to social partners through collective agreements, but the State is still responsible for fulfilling its obligation to ensure that the directives are fully implemented by adopting such provisions as may be appropriate." C-234/97 *Bobadilla* [1999] ECR I-7555.

31 By extension this must also apply to the right of establishment Article 49 EC.

It has further observed that working conditions in the different Member States are governed sometimes by provisions laid down by law or regulation and sometimes by agreements and other acts concluded or adopted by private persons. Accordingly if the scope of Article 48 [39] of the Treaty were confined to acts of a public authority there would be a risk of creating inequality in its application."[32]

Secondly, – supremacy of Community law:[33]

"By contrast with ordinary international treaties, the EEC Treaty has created its own legal system which on entry into force of the Treaty, became an integral part of the legal systems of the Member States and which their courts are bound to apply. By creating a Community of unlimited duration, having powers stemming from a limitation of sovereignty, or a transfer of powers from the States to the Community, the Member States have limited their sovereign rights, albeit within limited fields, and have thus created a body of law which binds both their nationals and themselves."[34]

Limited fields can, when fully revealed, be rather larger than originally anticipated. This is certainly the case with free movement of workers. Although the Court of Justice has insisted that the rights of workers under the Treaty are either explicit or implicit in Article 39 EC[35] itself, nonetheless, the fact that their full effect has been slowly revealed through a series of judgments over more than 30 years has made their accommodation by the Member States easier. For instance, the right of a Community worker to be accompanied by an unmarried partner to a host Member State where such a provision applies to nationals of the host State is a social advantage protected by Community law.[36] The fact that the Member States were unaware of this and therefore did not need to accommodate it until the matter was clarified for them by the Court in 1985 no doubt made this unexpected pill easier to swallow. This results primarily from the unravelling of the full consequences of the right to equal treatment with nationals of the host State. It is in this area of national treatment that the Member States have seen the more unexpected consequences of the Community's immigration policy.

Third, – damages:

"It should be recalled, as a preliminary point, that the principle of State liability for loss and damage caused to individuals as a result of breaches of Community law for which the State can be held responsible is inherent in the system of the

---

32 C-415/93 *Bosman* [1995] ECR I-4921.
33 See F. Snyder, The Effectiveness of European Community Law: Institutions, Processes, Tools and Techniques MLR 56:19 (1993).
34 6/64 *Costa v ENEL* [1964] ECR 585.
35 48/75 *Royer* [1976] ECR 497.
36 59/85 *Reed* [1986] ECR 1283; Article 7(2) Regulation 1612/68.

Treaty (judgments in joined cases C-6 & 9/90 *Francovich* [1991] ECR I-5357) and joined cases C-46 & 48/93 *Brasserie du Pecheur & Factortame* [1996] ECR I-1029). It follows that that principle holds good for any case in which a Member State breaches Community law."[37]

Again, for a Treaty signed in 1957 it is noteworthy that the inherent liability of the state for damages to individuals harmed by its failure to implement or implement correctly the Treaty only manifested in 1991.

The consequences for individuals exercising or seeking to exercise free movement rights are enormous. Only through the creation of these principles could the discretionary power of the Member States be limited genuinely and effectively. This will become even more apparent when I later turn to the extension of the concepts and principles of the Community's internal immigration law to third country agreements. The initial choices of the Community regarding the components of migration law have resulted in an extremely enduring structural approach to the issue increasingly at variance with developments at the national level.

Moving the Goal Posts

When, in 1986 the Member States decided to extend the scope of the Community to include the abolition of intra-Member State border controls on persons two conceptually irreconcilable systems of migration came into conflict. The Member States had come to accept, and in a very short period of time, their loss of discretion over the movement of Community nationals. However, the prospect of the loss of such discretionary power over all persons proved more difficult to digest.[38] The unravelling of the principle of abolition of intra-Member State controls led to some interesting assumptions: first the Member States needed to agree who could pass through the external frontiers in common as once within the Community persons would be free to move as they wished. This assumption disregarded completely the experience of two of the three European control free travel areas: the Nordic Union and the Common Travel Area (the third, the Benelux did involve agreement on co-ordination of external frontiers). In respect of all three no effective provision on harmonisation of external border controls was inserted into the legal mechanisms of their creation. It was not an issue. In the European Community context, however, the issue of borders and border crossing became tangled in the question of police powers and security. Very quickly the security issues

---

37 C-302/94 *R v HM Treasury ex p British Telecommunications PLC* [1996] ECR I-1631.
38 See, D. O'Keeffe, Union Citizenship, and C. Closa, Citizenship of the Union and Nationality of the Member States, in D. O'Keeffe and P. Twomey, (eds.) *Legal Issues of the Maastricht Treaty*, Chancery Law Publishing, Chichester, 1994.

came to dominate the free movement discussion.[39] Following this thread through to its natural conclusion results in the need for agreement on the main aspects of immigration control.[40]

Secondly, asylum policy needed to be agreed at least, so they claimed in 1986,[41] in so far as which state would be responsible for which asylum seekers. However, this principle unravels too: unless the same criteria are used to determine an asylum application and agreed standards on procedures and appeal rights apply the division of state responsibility will not be fair as the applicant will not have an equivalent chance in every Member State. This issue which was not politically hot in 1986 became so quickly particularly as the Soviet Union came to an end and the numbers of asylum seekers in the Community began to rise.[42]

In approaching these issues, national policy of the Member States was (and continues to be) based on the principles of selection, exclusion and national discretion. The framework established for the Community was ill equipped to incorporate such principles and so the Member States established a new forum where the foundations mirrored those of national law.[43] The framework contained two elements, what became the Third Pillar of the TEU (before the Amsterdam Treaty amended it) and the Schengen arrangements – starting with the original Schengen Agreement 1985 to abolish border controls *inter alia* on

---

39 D. Bigo, The Landscape of Police Co-operation, in E. Bort and R. Keat, (eds.) *The Boundaries of Understanding*, ISSI, Edinburgh, 1999.
40 The Palma Document, basis of the Member States' intergovernmental discussions on flanking measures for the implementation of Article 14 EC first published as Annex 5 Report of the House of Lords Select Committee on the European Communities 1992: Border Control of People Session 1988-9, 22nd Report (HL Paper 90).
41 There is also a very substantial degree of political expedience in this development; see for instance Declaration 31 to the Maastricht Treaty on time limits (and Chapter 8).
42 Asylum Seekers in the European Union 15: 1985-1994.

Year	Number of applications
1985	159,176
1986	191,020
1987	163,471
1988	209,841
1989	289,114
1990	403,496
1991	514,428
1992	674,056
1993	516,710
1994	306,532

43 Initially the Ad Hoc Group Immigration from 1985-93 then Title VI, Justice and Home Affairs of the Treaty on European Union (TEU) popularly known as the Third Pillar.

persons between five Member States. The experiment did not work.[44] The latest changes to the EC Treaty introduced by the Amsterdam Treaty provide the power to introduce into Community law general rules on immigration of third country nationals. Whether the exercise of that power will result in the delegation to national authorities in their capacity as implementing tools of Community law of a selective discretion remains to be seen.[45]

Overriding Interests of an Institutional Nature

The challenge of establishing an effective supranational legal order lies in persuading the executives, administrations and courts of the Member States that within the material scope of the new legal order, they as public officials, are the manifestation of and servants for the order itself. Their role is therefore transformed.[46] For instance, when an official in a national immigration office is looking at an application by a third country national to come to the state from a third state to work, that official is the servant of national law. However, when he or she turns to the next file, relating, for instance, to the third country national child of a Community worker, that official is acting as an official of the supranational legal order.[47] So, similarly is the judge at national level.[48]

---

44 European Commission Report to the Intergovernmental Conference, Brussels, 1996.

45 This is the subject of Chapters 7-9.

46 "One of the great advantages of the 177 [234] procedure over 169 [226] lies in the fact that under 177 it is a national court which renders the final decision – in many cases holding in effect that a Member State is in default of its obligations under the Treaty. Whereas, in the final analysis, a Member State may disregard a decision of the Court under the 169/171 [226/228] procedure, it is far more difficult to disregard the decisions of its own courts." J.P. Jacque and J.H.H. Weiler On the Road to European Union – A New Judicial Architecture: An Agenda for the Intergovernmental Conference, CMLRev 27: 185-207 (1990). Another advantage is the relative absence of political pressure which may distort the decision whether to proceed with an action. Under Article 226 EC, the Commission has power to take one or more Member States to Court for a failure to implement Community law but the Commission can be too sensitive to political concerns of the Member States.

47 "However, it is submitted that if the rules and procedures underpinning the free movement of workers are to function as they were intended to function, the key to their success lies in their administration, and that at the lowest levels. The education of immigration officers, their knowledge of the protections afforded by Community law and the manner of their contacts with members of the public remain decisive in the vast majority of cases. Immigration officers typically follow domestic procedures devised by the Member States and circulated to them in the form of practice directions. In some Member States, the impression of a discretionary authority with regard to immigration is perpetuated, such as by the Immigration Rules for Control on Entry in the United Kingdom, by the administrative insistence in the Netherlands on the production of proof of medical insurance." D. O'Keeffe, Practical Difficulties in the Application of Article 48

Thus the challenge for the Community, not just in this field but in the whole range of its competences, was to convince the national administration, government, courts, etc, that Community law, within its own domain must be given priority over contrary national law. This very practical problem found its expression in the development of the duty of good faith. It is in achieving this goal of obedience that the concept as a key reveals itself.[49] It is a matter of State commitment whether one international legal order works to create real and applied effects in the national order. The Community legal order in particular works because it was given from the beginning the tools to do so.

It may be argued that the development of migration rights which leave a very wide discretion to the individual at the expense of the State in the context of the Community is exceptional and explicable in view of the longer term objective:[50] turning aliens, nationals of the Member States, into citizens of the Union; or in more orthodox terms, the goal of assimilating the position of nationals of the Member States to that of own nationals. However such a perspective presents two problems. First the idea of citizenship of the Union is a very modern one, having entered the EC Treaty in 1993. Secondly, it cannot accommodate the EC agreements with third countries which govern questions of access to the territory and continuing rights of residence for the purpose of economic activities for nationals of the other contracting party in the extension of the same principle of limiting national discretion. The migration law itself is based on the principle of privileged treatment (free movement and non-discrimination) for foreigners on the basis of inter-state agreements.

---

[39] of the EEC Treaty, CMLRev 19:35-60 (1982). Since that article both UK and Dutch law have been changed and practice now conforms generally to Community law. Nonetheless, this is a central issue. Too often the mindset of the officials entrusted with the application of Community law is so entrenched in national perspectives as to blind the official as regards his/her Community function.

48 "Les institutions communautaires doivent donc atteindre les objectifs du traité notamment par l'intermédiaire des Etats membres ou plus précisément par l'intermédiaire des autorités de ces Etats. Il se crée ainsi une relation directe entre institutions communautaires et autorités nationales qui distingue la Communauté d'autres organisations internationales. Cette relation particulière est encore soulignée et renforcée par le système de renvois préjudiciels prévus à l'article 177 [234]" Dr O. Due, Conference Robert Schuman sur le Droit Communautaire à Florence, le 17 Juin 1991.

49 "Member States shall take all appropriate measures, whether general or particular, to ensure fulfilment of the obligations arising out of this Treaty or resulting from action taken by the institutions of the Community. They shall facilitate the achievement of the Community's tasks. They shall abstain from any measures which could jeopardize the attainment of the objectives of the Treaty." Article 10 EC.

50 Inherent in the preamble to the Treaty of Rome: the ever-closer union of the peoples of Europe.

The limitation of discretionary power of national authorities may be seen as a necessary step in the process of reconfiguring those national authorities into, at least partial, tools of Community law. It remains to be seen, though, whether, once that process has been accomplished and nationals of the Member States transformed into citizens of the Union with equal rights, those authorities will again be entrusted with discretionary, selection powers in respect of third country nationals, on the basis of power delegated from the Community. This possibility is explicit in the changes following the Amsterdam Treaty and will be considered in Chapter 9. Such a development may result from Community immigration law: i.e. from one based on rights arising from nationality (and economic activity) of a specific state (through the EC Treaty or a third country agreement) to a policy designed to process migrants of any nationality on a discretionary assessment of the individual's characteristics. In the current climate of anxiety about immigration flows in Europe it may be difficult indeed to maintain the right of individual choice if the incremental approach inherent in third country agreements (i.e. only nationals of the privileged state enjoy the right not any third country national) is abandoned. Nonetheless, the inclusion of a right of entry, economic activity and residence for third country nationals in Community agreements with third states concluded from 1991[51] onwards which right embodies the same principles of self selection and choice as have been outlined above indicates historic as well as structural coherence.

1.2. COMMUNITY CRITERIA: CONDITIONS EXCLUDING DISCRETION

The EC Treaty originally employed two main criteria to devolve the right of choice to the individual. As long as the individual fulfilled those two criteria he or she was entitled, subject to a public policy, security and health proviso, to move. The first criterion was nationality of a Member State, the second economic activity, at first active and subsequently passive (i.e. economic self-sufficiency).

Nationality of a Member State

The legal framework of nationality of a Member State has three facets. First, it is the definition of the relationship of participation of the individual and the state.[52] To this extent it is a fundamental expression of sovereignty. Secondly, that sovereignty is bracketed by international law which places restrictions on

---

51 The agreements with the Central and Eastern European countries: See Chapter 6.
52 T.H. Marshall, *Class, Citizenship and Social Development*, Garden City, NY, Doubleday, 1964.

how a state treats its nationals (i.e. Protocol 4 ECHR), and more importantly for this discussion, a state's right to define its relationship with an individual. The second layer, the international framework, places restrictions on the first. In international law, other states are not necessarily required to give effect to one state's conferral of citizenship on an individual. The International Court of Justice has permitted an investigation into the "social fact of attachment" before international recognition must be accorded.[53] Thirdly, the Community law regime provides that nationality of a Member State is the preserve of the Member State which within its own domain cannot be challenged as fundamentally as in international law, but gives not only an entitlement to rights such as free movement but also a "parasitic" citizenship of the Union.[54]

The EC Treaty originally made provision for individuals to move in three situations: to take employment (extended to seeking employment as well[55]), Article 39, to engage in self employment – Article 43, and to provide services (extended to include receiving services[56]) Article 49. The latter two provisions are clearly worded to apply only to Community nationals. Article 39, however, refers only to movement of 'workers'. This led to much discussion as to whether the concept of workers also includes third country nationals resident in the Member States. The Court of Justice in its decision of 1984[57] is often quoted as proof that third country nationals are excluded though in fact the case was limited on its facts to social security and the Court's comments do not necessarily carry the interpretation imputed to them.[58] However, more recently,

---

53 *Nottebohm Case (Liechtenstein v Guatemala)* ICJ Reports 1955 p. 4.
54 The Evolving Concept of Community Citizenship: From the Free Movement of Persons to Union Citizenship, S. O'Leary, Kluwer Law International, The Hague, 1996; European Citizenship Practice: Building Institutions of a Non-State, A. Wiener, Westview Press, London, 1997. It is curious that in the commentary on citizenship of the Union, the issue which actually has arisen before the ECJ is not among those dealt with extensively. A Moroccan national acquired citizenship of a Member State, Belgium. He sought a social security benefit which he was refused on the grounds of national law. As he was a Community national who had not exercised his free movement right, under Community law his situation was classified as wholly internal and therefore outside the material scope of Community law. However, were he to be treated as a Moroccan national, then Community law would protect him on the basis of the equal treatment provision of the EEC Morocco Co-operation Agreement 1976. The Court held that he was not entitled to rely on his Moroccan nationality against the Belgian state of which he was a national, and that as a Belgian national who had not exercised a free movement right he was not entitled to rely on Community law, all in all a rather harsh decision as regards its effects. C-179/98 *Mesbah* [1999] ECR I-7955.
55 C-292/89 *Antonissen* [1991] ECR I-745.
56 286/82 *Luisi & Carbone* [1984] ECR 377.
57 238/83 *Meade* [1984] ECR 2631.
58 In fact, Regulation 1408/71 on the co-ordination system for social security expressly includes some third country nationals it its scope

the Court of Justice came down more firmly interpreting Article 38 as applicable only to workers who are nationals of a Member State.[59]

It is a matter for the Member States by declaration to state who are their nationals for the purposes of Community law. Nervousness appears to have beset the Member States on this issue in 1991 when they created citizenship of the Union.[60] That citizenship is defined: "every person holding the nationality of a Member State shall be a citizen of the Union". Just in case there might be some question on the point, the Member States added Declaration (Number 2) clarifying that the question whether a person possesses the nationality of a Member State shall be settled solely by reference to the national law of the Member State concerned. This clarification was then elaborated by a new declaration agreed subsequent to the first Danish referendum again underlining the ephemeral nature of the concept of citizenship of the Union in comparison with nationality of a Member State. In the Amsterdam Treaty Article 17 EC was amended to state "Every person holding the nationality of a Member State shall be a citizen of the Union. Citizenship of the Union shall complement and not replace national citizenship".

In 1979 the Court had already clarified that Member States could not treat a national of another Member State differently depending on the time or manner in which he or she had acquired that citizenship.[61] In 1988 the Court went further in limiting Member States' discretion as regards recognition of citizenship. However, in the event of a conflict of rights which arise from the fact of holding different nationalities, Member States are only required to recognise those attendant on nationality of a Member State.[62] Accordingly, an incremental development or perhaps more accurately a gradual revelation can be perceived of the absence of host State control over any question of citizenship to the benefit of the State of origin.

Between the two amending treaties (the Maastricht Treaty and the Amsterdam Treaty) the Court of Justice had held that while the rules of acquisition and loss of citizenship rest, in accordance with international law, within the competence of each Member State, that competence must be exercised with

---

59 C-230/97 *Awoyemi* [1998] ECR I-6781.
60 Article 17 EC.
61 "There is no provision in the Treaty which, within the field of application of the Treaty, makes it possible to treat nationals of a Member State differently according to the time at which, or the manner in which they acquired the nationality of that State, as long as, at the time at which they rely on the benefits of Community law, they possess the nationality of one of the Member States and that, in addition, the other conditions for the application of the rule on which they rely are fulfilled." 136/78 *Auer* [1979] ECR 437.
62 C-179/98 *Mesbah* [1999] ECR I-7955.

respect for Community law.[63] The Court went on to state that a Member State may not restrict the effects of the grant of the nationality of another Member State by imposing additional conditions (such as a habitual residence requirement of the person on the territory of the Member State in question) for recognition of that nationality with a view to the exercise of a fundamental freedom of the Treaty.

Nationality for the purposes of Community law requires intra-party recognition of nationality on an absolute basis of another party's assertion subject only to its exercise with respect for Community law. As pointed out by Hall, the source of this obligation must be Article 10 EC.[64] This means that within the Community legal order non-recognition by one Member State of citizenship accorded by another Member State could only be justified if the Member State by according its citizenship had failed to take all appropriate measures whether general or particular, to ensure the fulfilment of the obligations arising from the Treaty, facilitate the Community's task or abstain from any measures which could jeopardise the attainment of the objectives of the Treaty. This Community definition of citizenship in effect turns inside out the first legal order. For Community law purposes, the exclusive domestic jurisdiction applies subject only to the limits of Community law.[65]

What happens where one Member State withdraws its citizenship from someone who is in the process of exercising Treaty rights? Such a situation could arise under the German citizenship law adopted in 1999. Young people born in Germany to foreign national parents who have resided there for eight or more years, acquired German citizenship at birth but only retain it by declaration made between the ages of 18 and 24. So for example, if a young Turkish girl is born in Germany to parents who have lived there for over 8 years, she will be a German national. Say at the age of 16 she moves, as she is entitled to, to another Member State and studies, takes employment or otherwise settles down there exercising her rights as a Community national. She forgets to register between the ages of 18-24 her wish to remain German and (because she is still holding Turkish citizenship) therefore loses her citizenship.

---

63 C-369/90 *Micheletti* [1992] ECR I-4239.
64 S. Hall, *Nationality, Migration Rights & Citizenship of the Union*, Martinus Nijhoff, The Hague, 1995, p. 63.
65 Which at least in theory include human rights obligations "Furthermore it is well settled that fundamental rights form an integral part of the general principles of law whose observance the Court ensures. For that purpose the Court draws inspiration from the constitutional traditions common to the Member States and from the guidelines supplied by international treaties for the protection of human rights on which the Member States have collaborated or of which they are signatories. Respect for human rights is therefore a condition of the lawfulness of Community acts." Opinion 2/94 [1996] ECR I-1759.

What is her position, that of the host Member State and that of Germany? The simple solution would be that the individual on ceasing to be a national of a Member State immediately loses any Treaty rights derived from that status and her continued residence and economic activities become dependent on national law of the State where she may be. This may not be entirely satisfactory in terms of legal certainty for the host Member State. It may be exceedingly unsatisfactory for the individual who, by exercising Treaty rights and living in another Member State, may have lost the legal basis for a claim to continued residence in the State, the nationality of which she had held. The position of Germany would undoubtedly be uncomfortable. First, the host Member State will be unhappy about the turn of events which has resulted in it acquiring the responsibility to expel to Turkey the young woman. Secondly, the Community is unlikely to be particularly sympathetic with a situation which was clearly foreseeable on the adoption of the law. Would such a situation constitute a breach of the good faith duty of Article 10? That would be for the Court of Justice to determine though in my view it is certainly not outside the scope of the provision to provide a solution in conjunction with Articles 17 and 18 EC, citizenship of the Union.

A solution appears tempting from the Court's decision in *Scholz*.[66] In this case an Italian national who had acquired that citizenship on marriage, having been born a German national sought relief against discrimination in employment on the basis that her experience in the German civil service was excluded from consideration in a civil service competition in Italy for the post of canteen worker. The Court held that the fact that she had acquired Italian nationality has no bearing on the application of the principle of non-discrimination. However it went on to state:

> "Any Community national who irrespective of his place of residence and his nationality has exercised the right to freedom of movement for workers and who has been employed in another Member State falls within the scope of the aforesaid provisions."

In the example of the former German national, as she would no longer be a Community national this finding is not, perhaps, so useful. Indeed the difficulty here leads back to the definition of a worker for the purposes of Article 39 EC as nationals of the Member States. For this limitation means that the individual in the example will always fall outside the personal scope of the Treaty as regards freedom of movement, unless the person's 'second' nationality is also that of a Member State.

Whether, then, loss of citizenship might come within the domain of Community law depends on the effect of Article 17 EC, citizenship of the Union.

---

66   C-419/92 *Scholz* [1994] ECR I-505.

The act of withdrawing citizenship of a Member State has the consequence of depriving the individual of citizenship of the Union. The result may be that the individual has no basis for residence in either the Member State of origin or the host Member State. He or she may be required to go to some country elsewhere in the world where he or she may have no links other than formal nationality leaving behind in the Union all close family members. In such a case a question of respect for family and private life under Article 8 of the European Convention on Human Rights (ECHR) arises.[67] Article 7 TEU states "the Union [which includes the Community] shall respect fundamental rights, as guaranteed by the [ECHR] and as they result from the constitutional traditions common to the Member States as general principles of Community law." Whether in view of these provisions, the Court would find that the withdrawal of citizenship under such circumstances would come within the field of application of Community law is uncertain.

Some commentators have suggested that the ICJ's effective link test for international recognition of nationality might be useful in Community law.[68] This is questionable. It would introduce exactly that element which the Court of Justice has excluded: a subjective assessment by the host State in which national discretion must be exercised. It may well be preferable to rely on the good faith basis of the duty to give effect to the grant of citizenship. Such a basis allows a latitude to the Member States (or the Community institutions) to exercise an *in extremis* control over citizenship laws of any Member State. For instance, if a Member State chose to confer its citizenship on a very large number of third country nationals having no link whatsoever with the state and who were liable, if induced to enter the Community labour market, to cause severe disruption, other Member States or the institutions could object on the basis of Article 10 EC. In practice, however, Member States have taken a very cautious approach to citizenship both their own and others. The recognition of German citizenship to a significant number of *Aussiedler* by the German Government has been subject to only limited public debate by the other Member States.[69] Similarly the practice of one Member State to confer its citizenship on any person who invests a specified amount of money in the state[70] has not led to public censure.

---

67 *Beldjoudi* [1992] Ser A 234A; *Moustaquim* [1991] Ser A 193; *Berrehab* [1988] Ser. A 138.
68 S. O'Leary "Nationality Law and Community Citizenship: A Tale of Two Uneasy Bedfellows" (1992) 12 Yearbook of European Law 353.
69 K. Groenendijk, Regulation of ethnic immigration: the case of the Aussiedler, New Community 23(4) 461, 1997.
70 I.e. Ireland.

Economic Activity

Three types of economic activity merit specific provision as regards free movement of persons in the EC Treaty: workers, Article 39,[71] establishment, Article 43 and provision of services, Article 49.[72] Establishment and provision of services do not necessarily require movement of persons. Establishment of a commercial presence in another Member State can be carried out by engaging only local staff. Much service provision within the Union does not involve the movement of persons – for instance cross border television broadcasts. At the time of the negotiation of the Treaty of Rome (pre 1957) the overwhelming consideration of the Member States as regards movement of persons for economic purposes related to labour migration from South to North.[73] Accordingly the defining consideration was movement of "workers". The self-employed were of less practical and political importance. Article 43 EC was designed to be used by persons exercising economic activities in the liberal professions. The programme contained in Article 47 EC on the cross recognition of diplomas is a clear indication of the original thinking on this provision. In the economic climate of 1957 there did not seem to be a particularly pressing need for the Treaty to devote many words to the situation of a Mr Agnelli moving to Germany to set up a Fiat production company. The categories, however, are not tidy – they overlap in all sorts of unhelpful ways. Already by 1974 the Court itself had started to avoid determining which provision is applicable to a set of facts on the basis that the same rules apply to them all.[74]

It is in the context of the meaning of "worker" that the tension between Member State discretion and individual choice found an early expression. The end of the transitional period as regards free movement of workers came in 1968 which necessitated the adoption of subsidiary legislation to complete

---

71 Which includes work seekers C-292/89 *Antonissen* [1991] ECR I-745.
72 Which includes recipients of services 286/82 *Luisi & Carbone* [1984] ECR 377.
73 See above at Section 1 of this Chapter.
74 "The activities referred to in Article 59 [49] are not to be distinguished by their nature from those in Article 48 [39], but only by the fact that they are performed outside the ties of a contract of employment." 36/74 *Walrave* [1974] ECR 1405; "[22] The third question is whether the applicable Community rules require the Member State to issue a residence permit to a national of another Member State where it is not disputed that the person concerned is carrying on an economic activity, the only point at issue being whether it falls to be classified as employment within the meaning of Article 48 [39] of the Treaty or activity as a self-employed person within the meaning of Article 52 [43] of the Treaty. [23] On that point it should be observed that Articles 48 [39] and 52 [43] of the EEC Treaty afford the same legal protection and that therefore the classification of an economic activity is without significance." C-363/89 *Roux* [1991] ECR I-273.

implementation of the free movement right.[75] Transitional provisions had already been in place since 1961[76] which formed part of the implementation programme. These will be of interest specifically when looking at the development of the subsidiary legislation under the EEC Turkey Association Agreement 1963 and its 1970 Protocol in Chapter 5. For the moment, though, I will focus on the end of the transitional period for workers under the EC Treaty.

The timing of the end of the transitional period was significant – the heyday of high employment in Northern Europe was not yet over. The oil crisis and the concomitant rise of unemployment were still four years away. Whether the implementing regulation and directive would have achieved the same degree of consensus among the Member States had the transitional period occurred after 1973 is an interesting but academic question.[77] Certainly it was not until 1974 that the Court of Justice was first faced with a case where the balance of individual choice against state discretion in movement of persons had to be determined.[78] This was rapidly followed by two cases in 1975,[79] and a continuous stream of cases thereafter. The Court came down unequivocally in favour of the individual's right to choose to move for an economic activity.[80] All of these cases exhibit a common theme: the Member States apply domestic law to the Community concept of movement of workers – in the first case, refusal of admission to the territory on grounds of public policy,[81] in the next two expulsion on public policy grounds.[82] It is interesting that the Court applied the same principles to these situations which within the legal order of some Member States are highly differentiated.[83] The Court resisted arguments by the Member States that national concepts of public policy prevail.[84]

Further, it held that a residence permit has only declaratory effect.[85] By finding that a residence permit only evidences the exercise of a right which a

---

75 Regulation 1612/68 and Directive 68/360.
76 Regulation 15/61.
77 Italy's role was critical as the sole immigrant sending country. Its interests were substantially to protect the position of its nationals in other Member States.
78 41/74 *Van Duyn* [1974] ECR 1337.
79 67/74 *Bonsignore* [1975] ECR 297; 36/75 *Rutili* [1975] ECR 1219.
80 Though in *Van Duyn* the Court was much criticized for its failure to give full effect to the equal treatment right of the migrant worker – G. F. Mancini, The Free Movement of Workers in the Case Law of the European Court of Justice in *Constitutional Adjudication in European Community and National Law, Essays for the Hon. Mr Justice T. F. O'Higgins*, D. Curtin, D. O'Keeffe (eds.), Butts, Dublin, 1992.
81 *Van Duyn, supra.*
82 *Bonsignore, supra.*
83 See for instance C-65/95 & C-111/95 *Radiom and Shingara* [1997] ECR I-3343.
84 36/75 *Rutili* [1975] ECR 1219 para 27.
85 48/75 *Royer* [1976] ECR 497.

Community worker enjoys by virtue of the Treaty itself, the Court gave to all Community workers self-determining power at the expense of Member State control. It is interesting that in these cases the Court carried out this task while reaffirming the legitimacy of the interest of the State to have knowledge of the resident population and its right to maintain sanctions for breaches of its immigration laws. In the next Chapter I will look at the Member States' arguments in favour of discretionary control and the Court's reply. This reasoning of the Court was invariably aimed towards the realisation of rights and therefore the discussion belongs along side the developing concepts of non-discrimination and obstacles to free movement.

It is apparent, in particular, from the Opinions of the Advocates General in the early expulsion cases[86] that the Member States had enjoyed a regular practice of expelling Community workers on national law grounds. Only after the sanction of expulsion had been circumscribed on the grounds of public policy, public health and public security by the Court did the next discretionary practice of the Member States become apparent. How is a worker to be defined and who gets to do so? Surprisingly this issue did not reach the Court for a further six years.

The Court considered the relevance of a lack of definition in the Treaty of the term worker in particular depth in 1982.[87] Some Member States argued that the term must be understood within the context of national law.[88] They suggested that in the absence of any provisions on hours of work and remuneration in Community legislation, it is necessary to have recourse to national criteria for the purpose of defining both minimum wage and minimum hours of work to determine the content of the concept of worker. The Court rejected the argument, building on an earlier decision of 1964[89] that the terms "worker" and "activity as an employed person" may not be defined by reference to the national laws of the Member States but have a Community meaning.[90]

---

86 See in particular *Bonsignore*, Opinion of A-G Maryas.

87 53/81 *Levin* [1982] ECR 1035.

88 For example, 53/81 *Levin* [1982] ECR 1035, the Danish Government argued "the term migrant worker covers persons who acquire the means to provide for their own needs and those of their family, whether they have employment which is not merely sporadic or pursue some other activity. The term also implies that the persons concerned work a normal number of hours, which in Denmark is a minimum of 30 hours per week." The Dutch Government followed a similar line of reasoning.

89 75/63 *Hoekstra (née Unger)* [1964] ECR 177.

90 "If that were not the case, the Community rules on freedom of movement for workers would be frustrated, as the meaning of those terms could be fixed and modified unilaterally, without any control by the Community institutions, by national laws which would thus be able to exclude at will certain categories of persons from the benefit of the Treaty". 53/81 *Levin* [1982] ECR 1035.

The reasoning of the Court is interesting not least for the blunt language impugning the Member States' good faith and the explicit statement that national discretionary power is inimical to free movement of workers. The result of the Court's finding is that the margin of discretion of the national authorities to determine who may claim to be a worker is highly circumscribed.

In the same case the Court was asked to consider the relevance of motive of a worker in moving to another Member State. It was argued that the plaintiff, a British national married to a South African who had been refused asylum and any other basis of residence in the UK, had chosen to move to the Netherlands not because she wished to work there but because she wished only to live there. Her interest in working was purely marginal and ancillary to her wish to reside with her husband (a right she could not enjoy in her country of origin). In other words, she expressed an interest in working so that she would be allowed to take up residence on the basis of Community law (as it then stood) but this was a sham. Again the Court chose to exclude from the equation any power of the national authorities to make subjective investigations into the intentions and motives of Community migrants.

> "[Article 39(3) EC, Regulation 1612/68 and Article 2, Directive 68/360] merely give expression to the requirement, which is inherent in the very principle of freedom of movement for workers, that the advantages which Community law confers in the name of that freedom may be relied upon only by persons who actually pursue or seriously wish to pursue activities as employed persons. They do not, however, mean that the enjoyment of this freedom may be made to depend upon the aims pursued by a national of a Member State in applying for entry upon and residence in the territory of another Member State, provided that he there pursues or wishes to pursue an activity which meets the criteria specified above, that is to say, an effective and genuine activity as an employed person.
>
> Once this condition is satisfied, the motives which may have prompted the worker to seek employment in the Member State concerned are of no account and must not be taken into consideration."

The Court retained for the Member States an appreciation of whether work is actually genuine and effective[91] but circumscribed this assessment to a narrow band. For instance, it found that low productivity is not a bar to the genuineness and effectiveness of work. In a high water mark in this line of cases, the Court found that a member of a religious or spiritual community who undertakes various jobs, such as plumbing, housekeeping and participates in the external economic activities of the community qualifies as a worker.[92]

---

91 66/85 *Lawrie-Blum* [1986] ECR 2121.
92 196/87 *Steymann* [1988] ECR 6127.

There are exceptions, for instance workers who become students. By virtue of Article 7(2) Regulation 1612/68 a worker is entitled to non-discrimination in social advantages. These include student grants where there is a relationship between the employment and studies.[93] Community nationals who are students foremost do not enjoy non-discrimination in social advantages and therefore are not entitled to student grants. An appreciation is therefore open to the Member States as regards the intentions of students who apply for grants. In respect of this latter consideration, the Court accepted that abuse was a possibility and where proven excluded the benefit of Community law.[94] However, this distinction may be justified on grounds of the Court's holding that to qualify as a worker the activity must be genuine and effective.

More recently, the guidance given by the Court on how national courts (and therefore national administrations as well) should interpret genuine and effective leaves a slightly wider margin:

"The national court may, however, when assessing the effective and genuine nature of the activity in question take account of the irregular nature and limited duration of the services actually performed under a contract for occasional employment, the fact that the person concerned worked only a very limited number of hours in a labour relationship may be an indication that the activities exercised are purely marginal and ancillary. The national court may also take account if appropriate of the fact that the person must remain available to work if called upon to do so by the employer."[95]

The Court provided the basic elements for the determination of whether a person is a worker: the essential feature of an employment relationship is that for a certain period of time a person performs services for and under the direction of another person in return for which he or she receives remuneration.[96] When considering self employment the Court indicated that the same framework applies, the critical difference is that the self employed are not

---

93 39/86 *Lair* [1988] ECR 3161; Subsequently the Court confirmed this relationship and indeed expanded it in 1992 "A migrant worker who voluntarily ceases employment in the host State in order to devote himself, after the lapse of a certain period of time, to full-time studies in the country of which he is a national, retains his status as a worker on condition that there is a relationship between his previous occupational activity and the studies pursued." C-3/90 *Bernini* [1992] ECR I-1071.

94 "In so far as the arguments submitted by the three Member States in question are motivated by a desire to prevent certain abuses, for example, where it may be established on the basis of objective evidence that a worker has entered a Member State for the sole purpose of enjoying after a very short period of occupational activity, the benefit of the student assistance system in that State, it should be observed that such abuses are not covered by the Community provisions in question." 39/86 *Lair* [1988] ECR 3161.

95 C-357/89 *Raulin* [1992] ECR I-1059.

96 66/85 *Lawrie-Blum* [1986] ECR 2121.

subordinated.[97] Service providers are defined by reference to the transient nature of their economic activity.[98] But all are Community definitions and all persons exercising economic rights are entitled to free movement and residence subject to the public policy, security and health provisos which I will consider in more depth in the next Chapter.

1.3.   SECURING MEMBER STATE OBEDIENCE

Good Faith

"The EEC Treaty, albeit concluded in the form of an international agreement, nonetheless constitutes the constitutional charter of a Community based on the rule of law".[99] The Community is based on a constitutional foundation deeper than the reciprocity inherent in international agreements. This is notwithstanding the fact that the instrument establishing the Community is a traditional multilateral treaty. The development of the legal tools which have effected this transformation has been well documented elsewhere.[100] Among the most important, though, is that of good faith. It is worth bearing in mind here that the development of the concept of good faith in Community law took place in fields widely different from free movement of workers. Indeed, it may well be that had the Treaty been limited to matters relating to workers its development would have been far less wide reaching. The success of such agreements in the ILO and Council of Europe regulating the position of migrant workers referred to in Section 1 above is instructive. While starting from reciprocity, the Treaty includes such an extraordinary array of subject matters, it very quickly became impossible for any Member State to weigh up the benefits and detriments of membership. The package and its value became a matter of political faith. The legal container into which the complex mix was poured was entitled "good faith" and attached to Article 10 EC.

The use of the concept of pre-emption, however is valuable to understanding the process.[101] It defines the scope available to the national authority in

---

97 C-107/94 *Asscher* [1996] ECR I-3089.

98 C-55/94 *Gebhard* [1995] ECR I-4165.

99 Opinion 1/91 Draft Agreement between EEC and EFTA [1991] ECR 6079.

100 G.F. Mancini, The Making of a Constitution for Europe, CMLRev 26:595-614 (1989).

101 "Supremacy and direct effect are usually regarded as two of the three principal doctrines encapsulating the judicial constitutionalism of the Treaty. The third notion is pre-emption, which may be dealt with very briefly. A familiar notion to American lawyers, pre-emption plays a decisive role in the allocation of power and it is an essential complement of the supremacy doctrine" G.F. Mancini, The Making of a Constitution for Europe, *supra.*

"competition" with the Community in any particular area. It determines whether a whole policy area has been actually or potentially occupied by the central authority (in this case the Community) so as to influence the intervention of the States in that area.[102] In a field such as free movement of workers the Community occupies fully the territory.[103] This in turn means that national rules purporting to regulate that movement can only have validity where they are in conformity with Community law.

Having occupied the full area of free movement of workers the Community rules constitute a legal order greater than that which would apply under a reciprocity duty. There can be no suspension of duties of one or more Member States as a result of the default of another.[104] Moving from the duty of Member States to one another, the default of the Commission equally does not relieve Member States of the duty to fulfil their obligations under the Treaty.[105] From the Treaty itself, the basis for this duty is found in Article 10 EC.

This article, commonly known as the good faith article, can strike dread into the heart of even the most stout-hearted national administrator in view of the breadth of its interpretation. It demands of all authorities in the Member States not just compliance with the letter of Community law but with its spirit as defined by the Court of Justice. As a common recourse of national authorities when faced with a condemnation of national legislation or court rulings is to give the most limited interpretation to the condemnation so as to restrict as far as possible its effects, such a positive duty of candour is quite unwelcome. Article 10 applies to all Member State authorities. In other words it encompasses all state actors including the courts. It applies within the territorial scope[106] but binds only the parties to it. The duty of good faith is owed, as a result of the constitutional character of the Treaty, to the individuals to whom the benefit accrues. The pre-emptive position of Community law in fields

---

102 A. Cappelletti, T. Seccombe and J.H.H. Weiler, A General Introduction, in A. Cappelletti, T. Seccombe and J.H.H. Weiler, *Integration Through Law*, Vol. 1 Book 1, De Gruyter, Leiden, 1986.

103 At least in so far as Community nationals are concerned, see *supra*.

104 43/75 *Defrenne* [1976] ECR 455.

105 90 & 91/63 *Commission v Luxembourg & Belgium* [1964] ECR 625.

106 For the purpose of Article 39 EC the territorial scope is perhaps wider than might be imagined. For instance activities which are carried out outside the territory of the Community may still qualify the worker as such to protection under the Article. The key is whether the employment relationship retains a sufficiently close link with the Community 237/83 *Prodest* [1984] ECR 3135. For example, a Belgian national resident in Algeria was recruited to work for the German consulate in that country. She was employed under a contract which stipulated that it was governed by Algerian law (to be interpreted though by a German Court). She claimed the benefit of Article 39 EC. Her claim succeeded, the Court found that the employment relationship retained a sufficiently close link with the Community to qualify. C-214/94 *Boukalfa* [1996] ECR I-2253.

which are within its exclusive competence means that no question can be permitted to arise as to the validity of independent national action in the relevant sphere. And, as a result Community rights are enforceable by the beneficiaries directly against the State through the national courts.[107] The duty of good faith arising from the Treaty and binding on the national courts reinforces the duty on them to ensure consistency of interpretation of the rights through use of the preliminary reference procedure contained in Article 234 EC to seek clarification from the Court of Justice. Therefore, in a sense the duty of good faith to the principles of the Community (as opposed to any particular party) and binding on all state actors constitutes a sort of glue which fixes the applicability and effectiveness of Community law at every level.

There are two aspects to the good faith duty which are important in the field of free movement of persons. First the territorial scope: by limiting the duty to a specified number of states there is a greater sense of security for the state as to control of persons.[108] In 1957 when the explosion of demand for labour in Western Europe was getting under way, protection of the domestic labour market from foreign workers was not an overwhelming concern. National policies on admission of foreign labour were relaxed in comparison with 1999. However strict control over population movement and registration of foreign workers was maintained complemented by wide national powers on expulsion. An experiment in free movement of labour controlled as to the number of states to which it applied appeared manageable. From the perspective of 1999 and the atmosphere of mistrust of foreigners, the outcome of that experiment is reassuring. It should also not be underestimated that the original six Member States, notwithstanding their bloody history of the 20th century, nonetheless have and in 1957 enjoyed a sense of commonality.[109] While familiarity may

---

107 For instance, the right cannot be restricted as a result of an act by the individual's state of origin or the Commission. For example, at the outbreak of the Gulf War Iraqi nationals resident in a number of Member States were subject to measures including expulsion which had no relation to their personal actions but to the act of their state of nationality. With respect to Union citizens, the expression of inter-state tension in this way is excluded not least through the duty of good faith.

108 "Une des plus grandes difficultés sur laquelle la Conférence de Paris en 1929 échoua était non pas l'octroi aux étrangers du traitement égal à celui des nationaux, mais précisément le refus des pays occidentaux de reconnaître dans tous les cas le principe du traitement national comme une règle fondamentale du droit commun international, sans aucune garantie quant à la portée et le contenu de ce traitement." J.L.F. van Essen, La Convention Européene d'Établissement NTIR 1956, p. 135.

109 The overwhelming consideration at the time was how to maintain peace in Europe: the proposal of Mr R. Schuman, the French Foreign Minister on 9 May 1950 for the fusion of the coal and steel industries of France and Germany was intended to be "the first concrete foundation for the European Federation which is indispensable for the preser-

breed contempt, envy and a variety of other unpleasant reactions, it also engenders a sense of similarity. One of the underlying purposes of the Treaty was to foster that sense of interdependence and from the very beginning lead to the ever closer union of the peoples of Europe.

Secondly, with the Community concept of good faith came the creation of directly applicable rights for individuals and the duty of national courts to give effect to those rights even against the State.[110]

> "Applying the principle of co-operation laid down in Article 5 [10] of the Treaty, it is the national courts which are entrusted with ensuring the legal protection which citizens derive from the direct effect of the provisions of Community law."[111]

An interesting contrast is discernible with the European Convention on Establishment. That convention, concluded under the auspices of the Council of Europe in 1955, aims to facilitate the entry of nationals of the states parties onto the territory of the other parties for temporary or permanent stay.[112] Therefore like the EC Treaty it contains the same controlled approach of benefiting only a circumscribed number of people on the basis of reciprocal obligations.

The Establishment Convention provides that "Each Contracting Party shall, to the extent permitted by its economic and social conditions, facilitate the prolonged or permanent residence in its territory of nationals of the other Parties."[113] However, in comparison with Article 39 EC, the Parties are permitted to derogate on "cogent economic or social" grounds.[114] Even though the wording of the provision appears mandatory, all force is removed from it by the admission of economic or social reasons to prevent access to the labour market or self employment.[115] In other words, the provision gives such a large

---

vation of peace" see D. Wyatt and A. Dashwood, *European Community Law* (3rd ed.) Sweet & Maxwell, 1993, p. 3.

110 John Temple Lang, Community Constitutional Law: Article 5 [10] EEC Treaty, CMLRev 27:645-681 (1990).

111 33/76 *Rewe* [1976] ECR 1989.

112 Articles 1 & 2; see also P. Boeles, *Fair Immigration Proceedings in Europe*, Martinus Nijhoff, The Hague, 1997, chapter 13.

113 Article 2.

114 It is of course debatable the extent to which the Member States actually considered that Article 39(3) EC in fact differed from Article 10 of the Establishment Convention. It took the detailed consideration of Article 39(3) EC by the Court of Justice to clarify just how much difference the choice of wording makes.

115 As the Council of Europe's own Commentary on the Convention states: "The scope of Article 10 is considerably curtailed by the restrictions there provided for. Cogent economic or social reasons can be invoked for a country's refusal to treat a national of

margin of appreciation to the Parties within which they may exercise their discretion as to prove virtually worthless for individuals.

1.4. CONCLUSIONS

In this chapter I have looked at the development of a system of law on migration based on a triangular relationship of rights and duties which empowers the individual to chose to migrate or not. The traditional relationship in international law of the individual alien subject to the control of the State, limited only in exceptional circumstances, no longer applies within the European Union. Based on the individual's characteristics as a national of a Member State and his or her economic position, a direct legal relationship is created with the European Community. On the basis of that legal relationship the individual is entitled to make choices irrespective of the preference of the Member State. If the Member State wishes to interfere with the individual's choice it must justify that interference within the parameters of its legal relationship with the Community in accordance with the Community's rules regarding the individual's rights. The history of this development is one tied fundamentally to a much wider objective of economic integration. The tools which I have considered in this chapter as regards the achievement of enforceable rights for individuals are:

1. Fundamental criteria: nationality and economic activity;

2. Good faith: the insertion of a positive duty on States to achieve goals;

3. The legal relationship of the individual with the supranational body which enjoys sufficient force to require State compliance.

In the next chapter I will look at the development of the tools of equality: non-discrimination and the abolition of obstacles and what they have meant for migrant workers in the territory of the Union.

---

another Party on an equal footing with its own nationals." Commentary on the European Convention on Establishment, Strasbourg 1980, para 48.

CHAPTER TWO

NON-DISCRIMINATION AND OBSTACLES

2.1. INTRODUCTION

Free movement of workers could not be accomplished without the abolition, on the one hand, of discrimination on the basis of nationality and on the other of obstacles to free movement within the Union. Article 39 EC itself gives a primary place to non-discrimination in subparagraph 2. However, achieving free movement involves another step – the abolition of obstacles to the exercise of the right contained in the objective of the Community, Article 3(c) EC. The relationship between these two concepts as regards the free movement of persons is important but not always entirely clear. The Community legislator in 1961 on adopting Regulation 15/61 which implemented Article 39 during the transitional stage, stated in the preamble that the objective "comporte l'élimination des délais et autres restrictions faisant obstacle à la libération des mouvements de travailleurs". Further by the end of the transitional period according to the preamble "toutes les entraves à la circulation des travailleurs seront abolies".[1]

At the end of the transitional period the legislator, to give full effect to Article 39, adopted Regulation 1612/68 where the preamble provides as regards the relationship between the two concepts: "the right of freedom of movement, in order that it may be exercised, by objective standards, in freedom and dignity, requires that equality of treatment shall be ensured in fact and in law in respect of all matters relating to the actual pursuit of activities as employed persons and to eligibility for housing, and also that obstacles to the mobility of workers shall be eliminated in particular as regards the worker's right to be joined by his family and the conditions for the integration of that family into the host country". The integration right is attached to the concept of obstacles rather than equal treatment, though equal treatment is also fundamental to its achievement.

The Court quickly recognised the dual aspects of the concept of discrimination: direct as contrasted to indirect or covert discrimination.[2] Exceptions have been recognised by the Court on the basis of imperative reasons relating to the general interest primarily for the second type. The concept of obstacles to free

---

1   "Includes the elimination of time limits and other restrictions which are an obstacle to the free movement of workers"; "all obstacles to movement of workers will be abolished".
2   152/73 *Sotgiu* [1974] ECR 153.

movement of workers has not always been clearly separated from discrimination.[3] Johnston and O'Keeffe argue the Court has, in the first half of the 1990s, demonstrated "a more open hostility towards national measures which although not discriminatory, are capable of hindering the free movement of workers. This has led it to adopt a more liberal policy towards reverse discrimination... ".[4] In the second half of the 1990s the concept of obstacles to movement of persons has become central to the Court's reasoning though it remains to be seen whether a *rapprochement* between the concepts of non-discrimination and obstacles is underway.

The relationship between the Community concepts of discrimination and obstacles is important not only in order to understand the principal tools of economic integration in Community law but also, in the wider context of this investigation, in order to plot the rights of different groups within the Union. These two principles are foundations of the free movement of migrant workers in the Community. They form the floor of rights below which no Member State may fall in the treatment of foreign workers, nationals of another Member State. As the Community has slowly been given competence over third country nationals attention is warranted to the way in which the principles developed for Community nationals, extend or are limited in respect of this new category. The coherence of Community law is in question – can the comprehensive interpretation of these principles be maintained in the extension of rights to third country nationals?

Before looking at the legal position it may be helpful to start with a snapshot of whom we are talking about. 1.5% of the total population of the European Economic Area (EEA)[5] live in an EEA state other than that of their nationality.[6] This means that of a total population in the region of 370 million in the European Union, only about 5.5 million are registered as living in another Member State. The largest number of EU citizens living in another Member State are Italian, at under 1.2 million of whom approximately 0.5 million live in Germany, 0.25 million in France and slightly over 200,000 in Belgium. The total population of Italian nationals in Italy is in the region of 57 million.

---

3   E. Johnston and D. O'Keeffe, From Discrimination to Obstacles to Free Movement:
     Recent Developments Concerning the Free Movement of Workers 1989-1994 CMLRev
     31:1313 (1994).
4   E. Johnston and D. O'Keeffe, From Discrimination to Obstacles to Free Movement:
     Recent Developments Concerning the Free Movement of Workers 1989-1994 CMLRev
     31:1313 (1994).
5   The Member States of the European Union plus Iceland, Liechtenstein and Norway.
6   Unless otherwise indicated, the source of all statistics in this section is: Migration Stat-
     istics 1995, Eurostat, Luxembourg, 1996.

The next highest number of Community nationals living in a state other than that of their nationality are Portuguese. Out of a total population of 10.5 million 875,600 live in other Member States. Well over half of these people live in France and slightly under 100,000 in Germany. Next in the numbers of nationals living elsewhere in the Union comes Spain, somewhat less that 0.5 million nationals out of a total population of just under 40 million of whom over 200,000 live in France and approximately 134,000 in Germany. Then comes Greece with 427,700 nationals out of a population of 10.5 million of whom the vast majority live in Germany, and finally the United Kingdom with 425,000 out of a population of over 55.5 million with 100,000 in Germany and over 50,000 in each of Ireland, Spain and France. As a percentage of the total population these figures indicate very different rates of migration.

In general, the population of EEA nationals resident in other Member States or parts thereof equals or exceeds 3% of the population only in South East England, the Paris area, Southern France, parts of Germany and Sweden.

EU Citizens in Selected Host States

Host country → Country of nationality ↓	Belgium: Population 9,294,370	France: Population 53,375,726	Germany: Population 74,840,955	Spain: Population 39,136,069
Greece: Population 10,577,738	19,987	6,091	345,902	474
Italy: Population 57,212,100	217,534	252,579	557,709	13,580
Portugal: Population 10,618,675	20,495	649,714	98,918	28,631
Spain: Population 39,136,069	49,459	216,047	133,847	
UK: Population 55,626,205	24,866	50,422	107,130	53,441

The numbers are surprising because they are so low. The highest absolute numbers are Italians in Germany who account for less than 1% of all Italians in Europe and constitute much less than 1% of the population of Germany. The heat of debates surrounding migrant workers seems disproportionate to the actual numbers involved. In 1997, the Commission produced a High Level Panel Report[7] on the problems encountered by Community nationals seeking to exercise their free movement rights and an Action Plan for Free Movement of Workers[8] to attack obstacles to movement of persons. In light of the very steady and low percentage of migrants resident in a Member State other than that of their nationality, it is striking that Member State authorities should continue to perpetuate obstacles to the exercise of the right to such an extent as to incur this activity from the Commission. If for no other reason than administrative cost, this seems counterproductive. In the last section of this chapter I will set out the reasons which the Member States have given to the Court of Justice for their position. I will then also set out the Court's answer to those arguments. However, from the perspective of the migrant, discrimination and obstacles are inimical to freedom. As expressed so eloquently in the preamble to Regulation 1612/68 what is a stake for them is the exercise of the right not only in freedom but with dignity.

2.2. THE CONTOURS OF NON-DISCRIMINATION

The Treaty Sources of Non-Discrimination on Grounds of Nationality

The source of the non-discrimination right arises from the Treaty and subsidiary legislation. In the Treaty, first Article 12 EC:

> "Within the scope of the application of this Treaty, and without prejudice to any special provisions contained therein, any discrimination on grounds of nationality shall be prohibited ... "

Secondly, as regards workers, Article 39 EC:

> "1.   Freedom of movement for workers shall be secured within the Community.
>
> 2.   Such freedom of movement shall entail the abolition of any discrimination based on nationality between workers of the Member States as regards employment, remuneration and other conditions of work and employment."

Thirdly, as regards the self employed and service providers, the non-discrimination right is tied to the treatment afforded to own nationals – Articles 43 and 49 EC.

---

7   Report of the High Level Panel on the Free Movement of Persons, chaired by Mrs Simone Veil, presented to the Commission 18.3.97.
8   Communication from the European Commission COM (97) 587 final of 12.11.1997.

Fourthly, in subsidiary legislation, as regards workers: Regulation 1612/68 Article 7:

> "1. A worker who is a national of a Member State may not, in the territory of another Member State, be treated differently from national workers by reason of his nationality in respect of any conditions of employment and work, in particular as regards remuneration, dismissal, and should he become unemployed, reinstatement or re-employment.
>
> 2. He shall enjoy the same social and tax advantages as national workers.
>
> 3. He shall also by virtue of the same right and under the same conditions as national workers have access to training in vocational schools and re-training centres.
>
> 4. Any clause of a collective or individual agreement or of any other collective regulation concerning eligibility for employment, employment, remuneration and other conditions of work or dismissal shall be null and void in so far as it lays down or authorises discriminatory conditions in respect of workers who are nationals of the other Member States."

As regards the self employed and service providers, Directive 73/148 gives effect to Articles 43 and 49 EC. Although it does not contain a non-discrimination provision the Court of Justice, applies by analogy Article 7(2) of Regulation 1612/68.[9]

The Scope of the Non-Discrimination Prohibition

The concept of non-discrimination can cover a multitude of situations. Depending on how it is interpreted and used it can provide more or less effective protection for migrants against differential treatment. In the field under consideration here only one ground of discrimination is expressly prohibited: that based on nationality. Further the prohibition is limited to the field of application of Community law – in other words it can only apply where the Community has competence. It is important here to look carefully at the meaning of discrimination on the basis of nationality in Community law as it is one of the keys to understanding the Community's approach to third country nationals particularly through third country agreements. Unless there is clarity about the extent and application of the principle in Community law it will not be possible in the next chapter to unravel its application to third country nationals.

Non-discrimination on the basis of nationality must be understood in the wider context of the Community's approach to unequal treatment in general. Throughout the EC Treaty discrimination based on nationality is prohibited in

---

9   C-118/92 *Commission v Luxembourg* [1994] ECR I-1891.

the fields of application of Community law, of which the provisions set out are the most important for migrants. There are other grounds of prohibited discrimination such as on the basis of sex as regards pay.[10]

The Court was slow to recognise a semi-autonomous nature to Article 12 EC. Flynn argues[11] that prior to the *Phil Collins* judgment of 1993, the Court had made it clear that "the scope of the Treaty" within which discrimination is prohibited by Article 12 EC did not extend to non-economic activity although this concept was liberally interpreted in *Cowan*[12] and *Gravier*.[13] *Gravier* may in fact be more fundamental to the change. However, A-G La Pergola in *Data Delecta and Forsberg*[14] notes that as early as 1972 decisions were slipping through which did not conform to this strict interpretation of the general non-discrimination prohibition.[15] While the principle of *specialia generalibus derogant* still applies to Article 12 – the prohibition on discrimination contained there serves the purpose of closing off the system of non-discrimination and enables any lacunae in the Community legal order to be bridged.[16] It is to that extent ancillary to the non-discrimination protection contained in other provisions of the Treaty. It may be a sufficient legal base for subsidiary legislation when in an area of mixed Community and Member State responsibility.[17]

Quite rightly, the Court has found that the constitutional limit of Community law, in other words its field of application, is also the limit of the scope of the prohibition contained in Article 12: "in prohibiting 'any discrimination on grounds of nationality', Article 6[12] of the Treaty requires perfect equality of treatment in the Member States of persons in a situation governed by Community law and nationals of the Member State in question".[18] O'Leary draws together the consequences of Article 12 in different aspects of the individual's interface with Community law not least pointing out the shortcomings which the problem of scope creates for the principle.[19] Where the

---

10 Barnard has analysed the meaning of equality juxtaposing it against the concept of non-discrimination by reference to the sex discrimination jurisprudence of the Court: C. Barnard, The Principle of Equality in the Community Context: P, Grant, Kalanke and Marshall: Four Uneasy Bedfellows, Cambridge Law Review, July 1998 Volume 57.2, p.352.

11 L. Flynn, Joined Cases C-92/92 and C-326/93 *Collins*, CMLRev 32: 997-1011 (1995).

12 186/87 [1989] ECR 195.

13 293/83 [1985] ECR 593.

14 C-43/95 [1996] ECR I-4671.

15 A-G La Pergola refers in particular to 1/72 *Frilli* [1972] ECR 457 and the better-known case of 186/87 *Cowan* [1989] ECR 195.

16 A-G La Pergola in *Data Delecta supra*.

17 C-295/90 *Parliament v Council re Students* [1992] ECR I-4193.

18 C-43/95 *Data Delecta* [1996] ECR I-4671.

19 S. O'Leary, The Principle of Equal Treatment on Grounds of Nationality in Article 6[12] EC a Lucrative Source of Rights for Member State Nationals? In A. Dashwood

right to non-discrimination is tied to the limits of competence of the Community as expressed in the Treaty, the individual certainly does not get comprehensive protection.

The need for a wide interpretation of the nationality discrimination prohibition arose from the reluctance or inability of the Member States to accept that preferential treatment of their own nationals in comparison with other Community nationals is contrary to the Treaty. The subject matter of the *Data Delecta* case is instructive: security for costs in judicial proceedings. The case, the first reference to the Court of Justice from a Swedish court, involved a British national who was required to provide security for costs in order to pursue an action in court against a Swedish defendant. Under Swedish law a foreign national, not residing in Sweden, or a foreign legal person intending to bring an action in a Swedish court against a Swedish national or legal person must, on application by the other side, furnish security for such costs of the judicial proceedings as the foreign national or foreign legal person may be ordered to pay on delivery of final judgment.[20] Clearly this constitutes discrimination on the basis of nationality in comparison with own nationals. But does it come within the scope of the Treaty? The Court of Justice found that it does on the basis that such a rule "is liable to affect the economic activity of traders from other Member States on the market of the State in question. Although it is, as such, not intended to regulate an activity of a commercial nature, it has the effect of placing such traders in a less advantageous position than nationals of that State as regards access to its courts".[21] It appears to me that this creates a contingent, indefinite subject matter which in the presence of nationality discrimination becomes crystallised into the scope of the Community. Without the element of discrimination it would remain outside the scope of Community law.[22] Once that finding is established, then clearly the discrimination is direct, an issue to which I will return later.

Twice before the Court had been faced with similar issues: security for costs in legal proceedings which impose a heavier burden on bringing an action for

---

and S. O'Leary, (eds.) *The Principle of Equal Treatment in E.C. Law*, Sweet & Maxwell, London, 1997, p. 105.

20 See paragraph 5 of A-G's Opinion in the judgment.

21 C-43/95 *Data Delecta* [1996] ECR I-4671.

22 "Mais au-delà, de celles-ci [the specific non-discrimination provisions] l'égalité de traitement vaut comme principe général de droit communautaire dont le contenu est unique à travers toutes ses applications, malgré des apparences multiples dues aux fonctions diverses assumées par ce principe." K. Lenaerts, L'égalité de traitement en droit communautaire – un principe unique aux apparence multiple, Cahier de droit européen 1991, p. 3.

nationals of other Member States than for own nationals.[23] In the earlier cases, the Court's solution was to tie the right to non-discrimination on the basis of nationality enshrined in Article 12 to another provision of the Treaty.[24] In *Data Delecta* this approach appears finally to have been abandoned in favour of an interpretation which allows unification of the concept of nationality discrimination within the scope of Community law: national legislative provisions which fall within the scope of application of the Treaty are, by reason of their effects on intra-Community trade in goods and services, necessarily subject to the general principle of non-discrimination laid down by the first paragraph of Article 12 of the Treaty, without there being any need to connect them with the specific provisions of the Treaty.

This does not remove the need to determine the scope of Community law for the purposes of the application of the principle but it does indicate an increasingly relaxed approach to that scope for the purposes of determining the application of the non-discrimination principle. Further, the wider the scope of the Treaty, so wider too is the scope of the non-discrimination principle's application. This then leads to the next step.

The wider the scope of the principle of non-discrimination on the basis of nationality is therefore, the narrower the margin of discretion available to the Member States either to prevent nationals of other Member States from participating in benefits available to own nationals or, from the other perspective, to favour own nationals to the exclusion of nationals of other Member States. As is now clear, the scope of Article 12 is determined by reference to the overall scope of Community law. Therefore every time the Council exercises Community powers to realise potential competences the scope of Article 12 is broadened. For instance, with the new competences of the Community inserted into the EC Treaty by the Amsterdam Treaty on 1 May 1999, it is arguable that the non-discrimination principle now applies in those fields. In this sense the scope has been widened. Indeed, the Amsterdam Treaty's amendments to the EC Treaty could, potentially at least, change the meaning of the ground of prohibited discrimination – nationality. As the Treaty now, in Title IV, specifically refers to third country nationals and their treatment, does this then have consequences for how "nationality" must be understood in Article 12? It is too early yet to make even tentative conclusion about such a possibility. In those new areas where the Council must exercise its new powers before the competence becomes effective, the Council's act will have the effect of "turning on the power" for the specific Article, and potentially at least, extending the scope of Article 12.

---

23 C-20/92 *Hubbard* [1993] ECR I-377; C-398/92 *Mund & Fester* [1994] ECR I-467.
24 In *Hubbard* to Articles 49 and 50 on freedom to provide services; in *Mund & Fester* to Article 293 the power to enter into agreements *inter se*.

As of 1 May 1999, the Treaty has a new power to prohibit discrimination on a variety of grounds: sex, racial or ethnic origin, religion or belief, disability, age or sexual orientation.[25] With it comes a new approach to non-discrimination. Unlike Article 12 EC which starts with the statement "within the scope of application of this Treaty ... " the new article begins "without prejudice to the other provisions of this Treaty and within the limits of the powers conferred by it upon the Community". Between these two wordings a gulf may exist – the second may, on an expansive interpretation have the consequence of extending Community powers to all matters relating to discrimination on these grounds or, it may be only an alternative wording to the first. Bell poses two possible interpretations: a scope which in fact goes no wider than that of Community law, or an autonomous power subject only to the procedural requirements of the Treaty.[26] In my view the new provision's scope is limited to that of Community law. I take this position not least in the light of the drafting history. From the first published draft in the Dublin II proposal, the changes to the wording of the provision were always designed to limit the scope of the provision. As the Dublin II wording followed that of Article 12, which is limited to the scope of Community law, it becomes very difficult to argue a wider scope was intended by the legislator in the final version.

When, in the next section, I come to consider third country nationals, this issue of scope will dominate. While discrimination on the basis of nationality may be identically interpreted, the question of the scope of its application is disputed. For example, in the context of the EEC Turkey Association Agreement and its subsidiary legislation, discrimination on the basis of nationality against Turkish workers enjoying the protection of the legislation is prohibited as regards remuneration and working conditions. However, does the scope of the concept of "worker" or "working conditions" in that agreement cover the same territory as in the EC Treaty?

2.3. DIRECT AND INDIRECT DISCRIMINATION ON THE GROUND OF NATIONALITY

Discrimination is a notoriously difficult concept to pin down in law. First there must be some way of assessing what is equal treatment. All too often situations are inherently different and inherently the same depending on the point from which one is looking at them. In trying to get at this problem Community law has divided nationality discrimination into direct and indirect and prohibited

---

25 Article 13 EC.
26 M. Bell, EU *Anti-Discrimination Policy: From Equal Opportunities Between Women and Men to Combatting Racism*, European Parliament, Brussels/Luxembourg LIBE 102 EN02-1998.

both. This approach is justified by the emphasis of the legislator on attacking both discrimination in law and in practice (see for instance Article 3(1) Regulation 1612/68). Unless the tool of indirect discrimination is available it may be difficult to reach discrimination in practice.

Direct Discrimination

Non-discrimination in general requires that similar situations are not treated differently unless the differentiation is objectively justified nor different situations similarly. Direct discrimination is in principle easy to identify within the area of Community free movement of persons as it involves an explicit nationality limitation. In other words, direct discrimination is discrimination in law – it is the national law (or regulation) itself creates the discrimination. For instance, in the legislation under consideration in the *Cristini (Fiorini)* case, fare reduction rail cards for family members were only available to own nationals of the host State. In that case the discrimination was clear, the question which arose was whether the field of application of the discrimination came within Community law (it did).

Testing Direct Discrimination I: Expulsion

As a test of Community law on direct discrimination against nationals of other Member States expulsion or exclusion from the territory represents a high water mark. Article 39(3) guarantees the free movement right only subject to the public policy, public security and public health provisos. However, in the exercise of those provisos to what extent does the non-discrimination right play a role? In expulsion/exclusion matters the assessment of the appropriate comparator is the key to the extent and value of the non-discrimination right. In the first case the Court considered on the public policy proviso it recognised that "it is a principle of international law, which the EEC Treaty cannot be assumed to disregard in the relations between Member States, that a State is precluded from refusing its own nationals the right of entry or residence".[27] This prohibition was again recognised, (though not in relation to expulsion or exclusion) with specific reference to Article 3(1) Protocol 4 ECHR in 1992.[28]

The Community legislator introduced the non-discrimination principle directly into expulsion issues by Article 8 Directive 64/221 providing that "the persons concerned shall have the same legal remedies in respect of any decision concerning entry, or refusing the issue or renewal of a residence permit, or ordering expulsion from the territory, as are available to nationals of the state

---

27 41/74 *Van Duyn* [1974] ECR 1337.
28 C-370/90 *Singh* [1992] ECR I-4265.

concerned in respect of acts of the administration." Conceptually, this intention to approximate the procedural requirements through non-discrimination to situations fundamentally dissimilar creates a tension difficult to resolve. In view of the privileged position in international law recognised in the Community legal order of admission of own nationals, there was no alternative to the finding that "the remedies available to nationals of other Member States [in respect of exclusion on public policy grounds] cannot be assessed by reference to the remedies available to nationals concerning the right of entry".[29]

How then, can the application of exclusion/expulsion specifically permitted on grounds of public policy, public health and public security in the Treaty be reconciled with the right to non-discrimination?[30] A first attempt was to consider the underlying subject matter of the expulsion/exclusion decision. In what Mancini, rightly in my opinion, described as a false step[31] the Court rejected this approach in 1974.[32] In *Van Duyn*, a Member State refused admission to a national of another Member State who was seeking to take up employment with a religious organisation of which the host Member State disapproved but which was not proscribed by law. It was argued that exclusion on the basis of economic (and religious) activities with a religious organisation where no penalty accrues to own nationals for such activities constituted prohibited discrimination on the basis of nationality. The Court rejected that argument and found that the Member State could justify exclusion on the grounds of public policy even for activities in respect of which own nationals were under no restriction without violating the principle of non-discrimination. The Court's reasoning was:

"Where the competent authorities of a Member State have clearly defined their standpoint as regards the activities of a particular organisation and where, considering it to be socially harmful, they have taken administrative measures to counteract these activities, the Member State cannot be required, before it can rely on the concept of public policy, to make such activities unlawful, if recourse to such a measure is not thought appropriate in these circumstances."[33]

---

29 C-65/95 & C-111/95 *Radiom & Shingara* [1997] ECR I-3343.

30 This problem is, of course not unique to Community law. Article 16 of the UN Convention relating to the Status of Refugees also provides for free access to the courts – how can this be provided on a non-discriminatory basis where there is a fundamental difference of status between the two groups to be treated equally, the non-national and the national? For a consideration of this wider issue see P. Boeles, *Fair Immigration Proceedings in Europe*, Martinus Nijhoff, The Hague, 1997 p. 71 *et seq.*

31 G. F. Mancini, The Free Movement of Workers in the Case Law of the European Court of Justice" in *Constitutional Adjudication in European Community and National Law, Essays for the Hon. Mr Justice T. F. O'Higgins*, D. Curtin, D. O'Keeffe, (eds.) Butts, Dublin, 1992.

32 41/74 *Van Duyn* [1974] ECR 1337.

33 41/74 *Van Duyn* [1974] ECR 1337.

This interpretation of the non-discrimination principle, indicated a great sensitivity to Member State's appreciation of the social consequences of a migration
right. The difficulty was that such an interpretation blocked the effectiveness of
the non-discrimination tool.[34] However, in the following year the Court at least
in part rejected this limitation on the principle and found that only where
penalties are applicable to own nationals for the behaviour upon which the
expulsion decision is based could penalties be applied to Community nationals
for similar behaviour.[35] The Court set out its reasoning:

> "Although Community law does not impose upon Member States a uniform
> scale of values as regards the assessment of conduct which may be considered
> as contrary to public policy, it should nevertheless be stated that conduct may
> not be considered as being of a sufficiently serious nature to justify restrictions
> on the admission to or residence within the territory of a Member State of a
> national of another Member State in a case where the former Member State
> does not adopt, with respect to the same conduct on the part of its own
> nationals, repressive measures or other genuine and effective measures intended
> to combat such conduct."[36]

This, of course, is only a partial solution to the problem. Where penalties are
applicable in national law against own nationals for offences which approximate
to those of migrant workers (for example in respect of formalities on free
movement) there will still be discrimination against Community nationals if
expulsion is an option. The Court had to deal with such an issue in 1976:

> "Among the penalties attaching to a failure to comply with the prescribed
> declaration and registration formalities, deportation, in relation to persons
> protected by Community law, is certainly incompatible with the provisions of
> the Treaty since, as the Court has already confirmed in other cases, such a
> measure negates the very right conferred and guaranteed by the Treaty".[37]

This is not to suggest that a real solution has been found for the conundrum of
expulsion and non-discrimination. More recently the Court has again considered the balance between an individual right to non-discrimination and the
State's right to exclude persons on the ground of public security. It affirmed
the margin of discretion available to the State:

> "whereas in the case of nationals the right of entry is a consequence of the
> status of national, so that there can be no margin of discretion for the State as
> regards the exercise of that right, the special circumstances which may justify

---

34 G. F. Mancini, the Free Movement of Workers in the Case Law of the European Court
    of Justice, in *Constitutional Adjudication in the European Community and National Law, Essays
    for the Hon. Mr Justice T F O'Higgins*, D. Curtin, D. O'Keeffe, (eds.) Butts, Dublin, 1992.
35 *36/75 Rutili* [1975] ECR 1219.
36 115-116/81 *Adoui* [1982] ECR 1665.
37 118/75 *Watson* [1976] ECR 1185.

reliance on the concept of public policy as against nationals of other Member States may vary over time and from one country to another, and it is therefore necessary to allow the competent national authorities a margin of discretion."[38]

The decision post-dates the introduction of citizenship of the Union in 1993 which concept could have been deployed in the reasoning. Indeed the lack of any reference to citizenship of the Union in the context of expulsion is perhaps an indication of a missing characteristic in the make up of that concept. Article 17 EC which creates citizenship of the Union does not directly indicate that expulsion is acceptable notwithstanding "citizenship". The ambiguous phrase contained in Article 18 EC regarding the right of residence of citizens of the Union "subject to the limitations and conditions laid down in this Treaty and by measures adopted to give it effect" may include the restriction of a residence right on the basis of public policy, public health and public security. However, such an interpretation would have fundamental consequences for the concept of citizenship itself. It would be a clear statement of the legal division between the concepts of nationality and citizenship. Only the former, even in Community law, gives an unfettered right of access to the territory. The latter does not have this quality. The approach of the Court when addressing Article 18 EC directly indicates a similar caution towards the concept. It held that citizenship of the Union is not intended to extend the scope *ratio materiae* of the Treaty so as to include situations internal to a Member State and which have no link with Community law.[39] This position was maintained in the *Martinez Sala* [40] decision. Here a Spanish national sought a social security benefit in Germany which she was refused as she lacked German nationality, a residence or establishment permit, the three qualifying requirements in national law. The authorities refused to issue her a residence permit as the basis of her presence was the Council of Europe's Convention on Medical and Social Assistance which only inhibited her expulsion. The Court referred to Article 18 but did not rely on it. Instead it held that as she was lawfully resident in Germany she was entitled to rely on Article 12, the non-discrimination provision. In her otherwise useful case report on the *Sala* judgment, O'Leary does not pick up on the importance of the residence right based on a convention outside EC law as founding in effect a scope strong enough to apply Article 12, non-discrimination.[41] It is noteworthy that the right to non-discrimination in Community law therefore appears capable of attaching to a residence right

---

38 C-65/95 & C-111/95 *Radiom & Shingara* [1997] ECR I-3343.
39 C-64 & 65/96 *Uecker & Jacquet* [1997] ECR I-3170.
40 C-85/96 *Martinez Sala* [1998] ECR I-2691.
41 S. O'Leary, Putting Flesh on the Bones of European Union Citizenship, European Law Review, 1999, Vol. 24, No 1 p.86-79.

which is not derived from Community law at all but from a Treaty to which the Member State is a party with no reference to Community law.

In *Calfa*, the Court held that citizenship of the Union was not relevant to the right of Greece to expel an Italian tourist on the basis of a minor drugs conviction. This decision seems decisive of the lack of additional protection from discrimination on the basis of "citizenship" in Community law.[42]

Testing Discrimination II: Public Sector Employment

A second testing ground between free movement and direct and indirect discrimination is access to the public service. The scope of Article 39(4) EC excluding the public service from the ambit of equal treatment of workers holds an important place in the development of the principle of non-discrimination for migrant workers. The opening up of the public service to nationals of other Member States and the corresponding limitation of the scope of Article 39(4) EC took place in two steps. First in 1974 the Court was faced with discriminatory practices against a national of another Member State who had already been admitted to the civil service of the host State. The Court found that the very fact that he had been employed by the civil service in itself meant that the interests which the exception contained in Article 39(4) allows a Member State to protect are not in issue and therefore cannot be a foundation for justifying an exception to the principle of non-discrimination.[43] In other words, once a person has been admitted to the public service the justification for discrimination on the basis of Article 39(4) is immediately circumscribed.

The second step took place approximately six years later. Member State authorities continued to apply Article 39(4) widely, excluding from all levels of the civil service nationals of other Member States. In view of the size of the civil service as a major if not the most important employer in every Member State this, in practice, meant that a large part of the labour market was excluded as far as nationals of other Member States were concerned. The Court was asked to give a specific definition to "employment in the public service". The Court chose to limit its meaning to those posts which involve the direct or indirect participation in the exercise of powers conferred by public law and in the discharge of functions whose purpose is to safeguard the general interests of the State or of other public authorities and which therefore require a special relationship of allegiance to the State on the part of the persons occupying them. Further, the post must require reciprocity of rights and duties which form the foundation of the bonds of nationality.[44] The Court's reasoning is

---

42   C-348/96 *Calfa* [1999] ECR I-11.
43   152/73 *Sotgiu* [1974] ECR 153.
44   149/79 *Commission v Belgium* SNCB I [1980] ECR 3881.

important to understanding the relationship between free movement and exception. The Court recognised that the principle of free movement of workers is one of the foundations of the Treaty. Accordingly, the right of workers to move and in so doing enjoy equal treatment must be given a purposive interpretation. Therefore any express limitation on the right as a derogation from the principle must be restrictively construed. The burden is firmly placed on the Member States where seeking to rely on the derogation to justify the post on the basis of direct or indirect participation in the exercise of powers conferred in public law or duties designed to safeguard the general interests of the State or public authorities. This reasoning is the mirror image of national immigration law relating to third country nationals. In Community law exclusion is the exception which must be justified. In national law of the 1990s, admission is the exception which must be justified.

Indirect Discrimination

When first legislating for equal treatment for workers, the Community did not find it necessary to make any reference to indirect discrimination.[45] However, by 1968 and the end of the transitional period, the Commission and the Council did consider a reference to such discrimination advisable.[46] The problem of Member States' legislation and practice which have the effect of limiting access to nationals of other Member States while avoiding any direct reference to nationality was sufficiently acute to justify the provision. Indirect discrimination differs from direct discrimination in that it is the result which matters: is the effect of a law or regulation when applied in practice actually discriminatory against nationals of other Member States? If the answer is yes, indirect discrimination is at work.

Indirect discrimination was first identified by the Court in the field of persons in 1974. An Italian national employed by the German post office had family members resident in Italy and so was entitled under the relevant German legislation to a separation allowance. The authorities increased the amount

---

45 Regulation 51/61 Article 8(1) "Le travailleur ressortissant d'un État membre ne peut pas, en raison de sa nationalité, être traité différement des travailleurs nationaux. Il bénéficie du même traitement que les travailleurs nationaux pour toutes conditions d'emploi et de travail notamment en matière de rémunération et de licenciement." Reference was made in the implementation programmes for Articles 43 and 49 prepared by the Commission.

46 Regulation 1612/68 Article 3(1) "Under this Regulation, provisions laid down by law, regulation or administrative action or administrative practices of a Member State shall not apply: ... – where, though applicable irrespective of nationality, their exclusive or principal aim or effect is to keep nationals of other Member States away from the employment offered."

payable by way of a separation allowance for some workers, based on where they had been recruited but refused to increase the amount for others, like Mr Sotgui, who had been recruited abroad. The Court therefore was faced with a question of the indirectly discriminatory effect of criteria on eligibility for benefits. In that first judgment, it worked out a formula for identifying indirect discrimination: the rules on equal treatment both in the Treaty and subsidiary legislation forbid not only overt discrimination by reason of nationality but also all covert forms of discrimination which, by the application of other criteria of differentiation, lead in fact to the same result.[47] Objective differences, however, can justify differential treatment where situations are comparable. On this basis Mr Sotgui did not get the increased allowance.

The formulation of the indirect discrimination concept is not so far from that found in Article 3(1) of Regulation 1612/68 but is phrased more flexibly. Like the Regulation, it does not recognise the need for an investigation into the intention of the Member State in order to establish indirect discrimination. Unlike the Regulation, there is no need for the exclusionary effect to be "exclusive or principal". Under the Court's formulation, discrimination is equally unlawful where the unintended by-product of a Member State's practice. By providing Community law with a result-based assessment of discrimination the Court attacked the heart of national discretion. So long as a Community national ends up in a worse position than own nationals an issue of indirect discrimination will arise. This approach followed that of the Community legislator building in a consistent fashion on the clear intention of the Commission and Council. However, it provided one critical addition: objective assessment. The Court clarified the position in *O'Flynn* where it held:

> "Unless objectively justified and proportionate to its aim, a provision of national law must be regarded as indirectly discriminatory if it is intrinsically liable to affect migrant workers more than national workers and if there is a consequent risk that it will place the former at a particular disadvantage."[48]

The concern is to achieve substantial equality of treatment. In this area, indirect discrimination developed to a large extent through cases involving social security benefits for migrant workers and their families.[49] Some of the most interesting cases relate to "social advantages" though they are less numerous.[50] The issue of residence requirements for access to a benefit in particular has

---

47　152/73 *Sotgiu* [1974] ECR 153.
48　C-237/94 [1996] ECR I-2617.
49　For example, 41/84 *Pinna* [1986] ECR 1.
50　For instance fare reduction cards 32/75 *Cristini* [1975] ECR 1085; the right to require that criminal proceedings take place in a language other than that normally used in the court 137/84 *Mutch* [1985] ECR 2681; the possibility of obtaining permission for residence of an unmarried partner 59/85 *Reed* [1986] ECR 1283.

given rise to much wrangling. A residence requirement will of course apply equally to an own national and a national of another Member State but the question is to what extent will the consequence of that application be different for the two categories and can that difference of result properly come within the concept of indirect discrimination?

In so far as the Court chose to accept that "the fact that some members of his family should live in countries other than the one in which he is employed is in fact a normal effect of a worker's moving within the Community"[51] there are different consequences for migrant workers than own nationals in respect of territorially limited benefits. This conclusion was reached without reference to statistical data. Indeed, an Advocate General, writing in 1996 refers to statistics submitted to the Court on numbers of migrants affected by a particular benefit rule in a case which was decided in 1990.[52] Nor does the Court make mention of any factual evidence for the finding that a territorially limited benefit for children has greater consequences for a migrant worker than own nationals.[53] However, is that difference of consequence equivalent to nationality discrimination? For Community law the answer is yes:

> "The [authority] grants family benefit to any person habitually or normally resident in the territory to which that law applies, where his dependent children are habitually or normally resident in that territory. Accordingly, that law treats nationals who have not exercised their right to free movement and migrant workers differently, to the detriment of the latter, since it is primarily the latter's children who do not reside in the territory of the Member State granting the benefit in question. In so far as the case files contain no material capable of providing objective justification for that difference in treatment, it must be regarded as discriminatory and hence incompatible with Article 52 [43] of the Treaty."[54]

More dramatically, the Court held:

> "It is not necessary in this respect to find that the provision in question does in practice affect a substantially higher proportion of migrant workers. It is sufficient that it is liable to have such an effect. Further, the reasons why a migrant worker chooses to make use of his freedom of movement within the Community are not to be taken into account in assessing whether a national provision is discriminatory. The possibility of exercising so fundamental a freedom as the freedom of movement of persons cannot be limited by such considerations, which are purely subjective."[55]

---

51 41/84 *Pinna* [1986] ECR 1.
52 C-228/88 *Bronzing* [1990] ECR 531.
53 C-4/95 *Stöber* [1997] ECR I-511.
54 C-4/95 *Stöber* [1997] ECR I-511, C-266/95 *Merino Garcia* [1997] ECR I-3279.
55 C-237/94 *O'Flynn* [1996] ECR I-2639.

One view of prohibited discrimination is that it must relate to immutable or intrinsic characteristics of the individual. In a case of a territorial limitation on benefits, the discriminatory effect on the individual arises from the failure to fulfil the territorial requirement (e.g. the children are not resident in the host Member State) notwithstanding the right in Community law for the family members to fulfil the requirement.[56] It does not arise directly from the nationality of the individual nor is it immutable. Of course there may be many important reasons why family members continue to reside in their country of origin, for instance continuity of the children's schooling might be an important factor, or one spouse may be employed in the state of origin and unwilling or unable to find employment in the host State. However, these are not immutable characteristics – they are choices made by the worker and his or her family.

In Community law the "immutable characteristics" approach to prohibited discrimination has not been adopted as regards movement of nationals of the Member States. The purposive interpretation which aims to facilitate free movement is preferred, expressed in terms of "an interpretation which gives the free movement rule a wide significance". Any rule whether based at Community level[57] or in national legislation[58] which places Community nationals at a disadvantage[59] in the exercise of their right to free movement in comparison with own nationals comes within the definition of indirect discrimination. For example, a German frontier worker cannot be refused an allowance which constitutes a social advantage but eligibility for which is subject to the person living in the state of employment solely on the ground that he does not live on the correct side of the border.[60] Similarly, a student who has been studying and living with his parents in a host Member State returned to his state of origin as did his parents. He then wished to rely on his right to non-discriminatory access to education contained in Article 12 of Regulation 1612/68 to return to the host Member State to finish his vocational training. The Court held that he was entitled to return (without his parents) to the host State to complete his education.[61] Such choices could not survive an immutable characteristics test.

With such a wide definition of discrimination on the ground of nationality both direct and indirect it is worth returning briefly to the material scope on which it bites in free movement of persons. As set out above, it has proved problematic in the field of expulsion. However, on narrowing the public service proviso it has proved effective in principle if not in practice. The category of

---

56 Article 10 Regulation 1612/68.
57 For example as in the *Pinna* case.
58 For example in C-279/93 *Schumacker* [1985] ECR 225.
59 143/87 *Stanton* [1988] ECR 3877.
60 C-57/96 *Meints* [1997] ECR I-6689.
61 390/87 *Echternach* [1989] ECR 723.

indirect discrimination has proved useful in attacking differential treatment in the access to social advantages.

Community migrant workers and their third country national family members enjoy through Community law, protection from direct and indirect discrimination. The scope and limitations of each of the concepts for Community nationals and their families must also be the outer boundaries of these concepts for third country nationals within the Union. However discrimination is defined for the purposes of Community law, a wider definition for third country nationals would place them in a more advantageous position than Community nationals. This in turn would mean that the scope of Community law had been exceeded. Exactly this issue has been encountered at least twice so far in Community law where an interpretation given to a provision of a third country agreement appears at first sight to go father than the equivalent provision as regards Community nationals.[62] In some cases the Community law right has been clarified as encompassing the wider interpretation given to third country nationals.[63] However, for the purposes of this chapter, the important aspect is the positive effect that the clarification of rights of third country nationals has on the development of a comprehensive interpretation of discrimination applicable to Community nationals.

2.4. OBSTACLES AND THEIR CLASSIFICATION

The Treaty Source of the Abolition of Obstacles

Article 3 EC is the main source of the duty to abolish obstacles:

> "For the purposes set out in Article 2 above, the activities of the Community shall include, as provided for in this Treaty, and in accordance with the timetable set out therein: ... (c) an internal market characterised by the abolition, as between Member States, of obstacles to the free movement of goods, persons, services and capital;"[64]

---

62 C-18/90 *Kziber* [1991] ECR I-199 in relation to 40/76 *Kermachek* [1976] ECR 1669; C-171/95 *Tetik* [1997] ECR I-329 and C-292/89 *Antonissen* [1991] ECR I-745.

63 C-308/93 *Issarte-Cabanis* [1996] ECR I-2097 which makes it clear that the right of a family member to a social benefit is the same for Community nationals as in respect of Moroccans protected by their Co-operation Agreement with the Community.

64 In the original Treaty the concept of obstacles was present but the internal market had yet to become a focus of attention. The original wording is "the abolition as between Member States, of the obstacles to the free movement of persons, services and capital".

This basis is reflected in the preamble to Regulation 1612/68,[65] an implementing measure for Article 39 EC on the free movement of workers.[66] However, here the legislative trails ends. The concepts of prohibited discrimination and obstacles are not always clearly differentiated in the field of persons. The purpose of the discrimination prohibition is to put migrant workers in an equal position with own nationals. The aim is to eliminate disadvantage for those persons who exercise their right of free movement.[67] Obstacles relate to the exercise of the right of free movement as is clear from the preamble to Regulation 1612/68 "obstacles to the mobility of workers shall be eliminated". An obstacle is a provision or practice which precludes or deters a national of a Member State from leaving his or her country of origin [or going to or remaining in a host Member State] in order to exercise a right to freedom of movement.[68] The mischief in Community law is tied to the act of movement.

Beginning in 1974 the Court attached the two concepts to one another in this field:

> "It follows from the general character of the prohibition on discrimination in Article 48 [39] and the objective pursued by the abolition of discrimination that discrimination is prohibited even if it constitutes only an obstacle of secondary importance as regards the equality of access to employment and other conditions of work and employment".[69]

The difference between a provision which might cause discrimination and an obstacle is not so great. It is perhaps not surprising that the first whiff of prospective effect comes from an Article 226 EC proceeding – *Commission v France*.[70] Where the Commission brings an infringement action against a Member State for maintenance or introduction of legislation contrary to Community law it will normally rely on the likely effect of the legislation (whether prospective or otherwise) as such actions are not usually based on the circumstances of a particular individual. Therefore in handing down judgment in such

---

65 "... and also that obstacles to the mobility of workers shall be eliminated, in particular as regards the worker's right to be joined by his family and the conditions of integration of that family into the host country."

66 It also appeared in its predecessor, Regulation 15/61: "qui comporte l'élimination des délais et autres restrictions faisant obstacle à la libération des mouvements de travailleurs ... " and "toutes les entraves à la circulation des travailleurs seront abolis ... ".

67 G. de Burca, The Role as Equality in European Community Law, in A. Dashwood and S. O'Leary (eds.) *The Principle of Equal Treatment in E.C. Law*, Sweet & Maxwell, London, 1997, pp. 13-34. For a complete consideration of the issues involved see D Martin, "Discriminations" "entraves" et "raisons impérieuses" dans le traité CE: trois concepts en quête d'identité, Cahier de droit européen 1998 vols. 5-6, p. 561.

68 C-10/90 *Masgio* [1991] ECR I-1119.

69 167/73 *Commission v France* [1974] ECR 359.

70 167/73 [1974] ECR 359.

cases it is normal for the Court to make reference to the likely, though not necessarily realised, effect of national law when interpreting the meaning of Community law.

Where a prospective consequence is then applied to cases on specific facts referred by national tribunals under Article 234 of the Treaty, there is a natural extension of the principle. In the context of a set of specific circumstances in respect of which clarification of Community law is sought, the Court speculates about the potential effect of national legislation or practice on the willingness of Community nationals to exercise their free movement rights. This prospective consequence first arose in an Article 234 reference to the Court in the *Stanton* case.[71] Mr Stanton was employed by a British insurance company and acted as director of a Belgian company. Under Belgian law he was deemed to be self-employed and required to pay social security contributions. He also paid social security contributions in the UK as an employed person. He objected to having to pay contributions in two countries for the same type of insurance. He maintained he should, on a proper construction of Community law, be exempt from self-employed contributions in Belgium as he was paying employed contributions in the UK. The Court found that the Belgian law did not discriminate on the basis of nationality. Further, as no evidence was adduced to it that the disadvantage resulting from the legislation fell mainly or exclusively on foreign nationals it found that there was no indirect discrimination (a very different conclusion was reach on a similar point in 1997 in *Stöber* – see below). Thereafter the Court looked at the prospective effect of the Belgian law and found a prohibited consequence of "disadvantage".

What happens in the case of return of migrants to their state of origin where their treatment is that identical to others who share their nationality but they suffer discrimination in comparison with the rights they had been enjoying as "Community nationals"? Can the discrimination concept work to protect rights which have been acquired in the process of exercising Community free movement on return to the country or origin or is this an obstacle?

A British national returned to the UK after having exercised a free movement right and was refused permission to enjoy family life with her third country national husband.[72] Under Community law, if the worker, Mrs Singh, had been a national of any other Member State it would have been clear that she was entitled to have her husband resident in the host State with her.[73]

---

71 143/87 [1988] ECR 3877.

72 In fact not much family life was being enjoyed by the couple as they were separated. Nonetheless they were still married and the third country national husband wished to continue to reside in the UK where his wife was living having returned together from Germany.

73 Article 10 Regulation 1612/68; the fact that the couple were separated does not have a consequence on the right of the Community national to have her husband with her in

Under national law, which the Member State alleged it was entitled to apply as a result of the exclusive nationality of Mrs Singh, the husband was liable to expulsion as he was not living with his wife. The discrimination suffered by Mrs Singh therefore, if it can be said to be on the basis of nationality at all, was not between the migrant worker and own national as they shared a nationality and common restrictive national law but between an own national and "Community" national. The Member State argued that the situation was one wholly internal to the UK and therefore as regards Community rights relating to free movement outside the field of application of Community law.[74]

The Court disagreed: first the State's act was an obstacle to the exercise of free movement, secondly, it would have discriminatory consequences which might have the effect of discouraging a national of a Member State from exercising his or her free movement right. On the consequential deterrent effect of differential and disadvantageous national rules in comparison with Community ones, the Court stated:

> "This case is not concerned with a right under national law but with the rights of movement and establishment granted to a Community national by Articles 48[39] and 52[43] of the Treaty. These rights cannot be fully effective if such a person may be deterred from exercising them by obstacles raised in his or her country of origin to the entry and residence of his or her spouse. Accordingly, when a Community national who has availed himself or herself of those rights returns to his or her country of origin, his or her spouse must enjoy at least the same rights of entry and residence as would be granted to him or her under Community law if his or her spouse chose to enter and reside in another Member State".[75]

The 1995 judgment in *Bosman* provides some important clarification on obstacles: discrimination needs a basis, in Community law that is nationality; obstacles, need movement – they are encountered as a result of movement prospective or actual.[76] In the *Bosman* case, transfer payments between football

---

the host Member State. Only divorce extinguishes the spouse's claim to residence 267/83 *Diatta* [1985] ECR 567.

74 Community provisions relating to the free movement of workers and the self employed cannot apply to the situation of persons who have never exercised a free movement right within the Community 175/78 *Saunders* [1979] ECR 1129; 20/87 *Gauchard* [1987] ECR 4879.

75 C-370/90 *Singh* [1992] ECR I-4265.

76 "It is sufficient to note that, although the rules in issue in the main proceedings apply also to transfers between clubs belonging to different national associations within the same Member State and are similar to those governing transfers between clubs belonging to the same national association, they still directly affect players' access to the employment market in other Member States and are thus capable of impeding freedom of movement for workers. They cannot, thus, be deemed comparable to the rules on

clubs for players, (the subject matter) was clearly indistinctly applicable both as regards the nationality of the person seeking to exercise a free movement right and the exercise inter and intra State. The Court recognised the obstacle would apply whether the individual sought to work for another club within his own Member State or for one in another Member State. Its effect on free movement for the purposes of Community law only bites however in the latter case. The former situation is outside Community free movement law as it is wholly internal to a Member State. The latter situation is within the scope of Community law as it includes a cross-border element and an obstacle hindering movement. Where within the scope of Community law, then, such an obstacle was held to be unlawful.

In *Stöber* the problem could have been categorised in either way but the Court found an obstacle. Here a German national had worked in Ireland between 1965 and 1969 (in other words before Ireland joined the Community) then returned to Germany whence he did not sally forth again. While in Ireland he fathered a child which remained resident in Ireland with her mother. Mr Stöber sought German child benefit on account of his child in Ireland which application was rejected on the basis that the child would have to be resident in Germany in order to qualify. Notwithstanding the indistinctly applicable nature of the child benefit rule the Court found:

> "A national ... could be deterred from leaving the Member State in which he resides ... [by the effect of the rule in question]. It follows that national legislation of the kind at issue in the main proceedings constitutes an obstacle to freedom of movement for workers... it is therefore unnecessary to consider whether there is indirect discrimination on the grounds of nationality... An assessment of whether a measure is an obstacle should take place before any assessment of whether it is indirectly discriminatory."[77]

Therefore, first, any rule which might prospectively result in discrimination between a migrant worker and an own national is unlawful. Secondly, any rule which actually discriminates either directly or indirectly must also be unlawful. Finally, rules which might deter movement must be abolished.

2.5. CONCLUSIONS

So far in this Chapter I have looked at the concepts of discrimination, both direct and indirect and obstacles to free movement of persons. As is clear, from the Community legislator and the Court of Justice, both these concepts were

---

selling arrangements for goods which in Keck and Mithuard were held to fall outside the ambit of Article 30 of the Treaty." C-415/93 *Bosman* [1995] ECR I-492.

77 C-4/95 *Stöber* [1997] ECR I-511.

given a wide meaning in this field with an increasing emphasis on getting tough with Member State laws which hinder exercise of free movement rights. The discretion of the Member States to apply legislation which (i) directly discriminates on the basis of nationality; (ii) applies residence or other criteria which result in differential access to benefits for migrant nationals and (iii) any other measures which make the exercise of a free movement right less attractive is continuously diminished. It is worth looking here at the Member State's arguments as to why they should enjoy such a margin of interpretation and the Court's reasoning against such interpretation.

The ground for discussion between the Member States, the Community legislator and the Court on the treatment on migrant workers, nationals of the Member States, took place within a framework of protection of the resident population against immigration rights. In favour of protection of the national territory the Member States argued:

(a) The Member States' assessment of undesirability of an immigrant is an expression of the right to protect its nationals. Even where the Member State does not make illegal an activity for its own nationals it is entitled to apply a different and discriminatory standard of public good when assessing foreign nationals' activities;[78]

(b) Differential penalties on foreigners for failure to comply with laws applicable to them cannot be equated with penalties applicable to nationals because foreigners are subject to expulsion;[79]

(c) Where a foreigner commits a criminal act it is for a Member State to determine whether it is sufficiently serious to justify expulsion as this is a measure to protect the national population (both nationals and foreigners);[80]

(d) The contents of definitions relating to free movement of persons must be determined by the Member States according to national law in order to protect both the labour market and working conditions in the Member State in question and also the migrant from indigence (i.e. the migrant is better off being indigent at the expense of his or her State of nationality than in the host State) and the public purse of the Member State.[81]

---

78 41/74 *Van Duyn* [1974] ECR 1337.
79 8/77 *Sagulo* [1977] ECR 1495.
80 30/77 *Bouchereau* [1977] ECR 1999.
81 53/81 *Levin* [1982] ECR 1035; *139/85 Kempf* [1986] ECR 1741; *66/85 Lawrie-Blum* [1986] ECR 2121.

The Court of Justice's response to these arguments is based on the creation of rights which entitle all Community nationals to the same level of protection whether they are nationals of one Member State or nationals of another Member State. Justification by the Member States based on the protection of one class of Community nationals (those who are nationals of one Member State) as against the protection of other Community nationals (those who are nationals of another Member State) was not acceptable. Accordingly, in answer to the Member States' arguments the Court consistently relied on the right to equal treatment as a fundamental part of the right of free movement. In one case the plaintiff specifically suggested that "a restricted interpretation of Article 48(1) [39(1)] would reduce freedom of movement to a mere instrument of economic integration ... ".[82]

It is interesting to note that the concept of integration is not relied upon by the Court of Justice until it comes to considering family members or the provisions of third country agreements. Instead, the Court's position is based on a right to free movement which is inimical to the exercise of discretion by a Member State to treat differently nationals of one Member State as opposed to nationals of another Member State. The Court considered the broad approach necessary in order to allow Community nationals to participate on a stable and continuous basis in the economic life of a Member State other than that of origin and thereby contribute to economic and social interpenetration.[83]

The underlying concept is that of equal participation in the full range of life in the host Member State. It is for this reason that the Court rejected the Member States claim to impose a discretionary definition and interpretation of free movement of persons. The logic is based on the right of economic integration but its expression is through an insistence on "rights" and their exercise.

In this Chapter I have looked at the Community concepts of discrimination, direct and indirect and obstacles to the exercise of Community rights. The definition of these concepts vis-à-vis Community nationals is important to the definitions in third country agreements and the provisions of the EC Treaty inserted by the Amsterdam Treaty as regards third country nationals. I have taken some time to explain the development of the concepts in Community law. It is important to remember that these definitions were a matter of dispute between the Member States and the Community. The same arguments which the Member States put forward in respect of Community nationals and the right to control the definition and meaning of discrimination, direct and indirect and obstacles would again arise in respect of third country nationals.

---

82 66/85 *Lawrie-Blum supra.*
83 2/74 *Reyners* [1974] ECR 631; C-55/94 *Gebhard* [1995] ECR I-4165.

PART II

THIRD COUNTRY NATIONALS PRIVILEGED UNDER
AGREEMENTS WITH THE EC

CHAPTER THREE

AN OVERVIEW OF THIRD COUNTRY AGREEMENTS

3.1. INTRODUCTION

This chapter will consider three questions relating to agreements between the European Community and third countries from the perspective of the development of a Community immigration law:

1. How are these agreements part of Community law and what does that mean?

2. To what extent does the Court of Justice have competence to interpret these agreements?

3. Do the same principles of interpretation applicable to the EC Treaty and its subsidiary legislation apply to these agreements?

There are a number of possible ways to categorise these agreements. I will consider here only those which include clear provisions on persons in chronological order commencing with the Greece and Turkey Agreements, then looking at the Maghreb Agreements, Yugoslavia and Lomé Agreements and finishing, in the next chapter with the agreements with the Central and Eastern European countries. The recent Machrek Agreements will be dealt with under the heading of the Maghreb Agreements because they follow the form of the former. In examining the agreements, I will focus on the elements which may constitute the foundations of an immigration law of the Community. In that examination, of key importance will be whether or not the approach of the Community towards third country nationals under the agreements is consistent with the legislative approach already adopted by the Community towards EU national migrants.

The EEC-Turkey Association Agreement[1] and the EEC-Greece Association Agreement were the first agreements to include provisions on labour. While Greece acceded to the Community before the provisions of its agreement on labour were the subject of litigation in the Luxembourg Court, the Turkey Agreement and its subsidiary legislation, through their interpretation by the Court have formed an important foundation of the Community's immigration law towards third country nationals. Of particular importance to this development are the positive rights relating to work and

---

1   Hereafter the Turkey Agreement.

residence contained in the agreement's subsidiary legislation. As has been discussed in Chapter 1, the fundamental feature of the Community's immigration law as regards Community nationals is the transfer of the issue of movement from one of selection and national discretion by the authorities of the state to a right of choice of the individual protected by the Community. This process was achieved by identifying a specific feature of an individual's life, economic activity, and making it the defining criterion for the right to migrate. By the wide interpretation given to economic activity and the narrow definition accorded to exceptions to the right, a genuine choice accrues to most nationals of the Member States. Are the same principles to be discerned in the Community's immigration law when it is extended to third country nationals through the third country agreements? In order to analyse this question first I must look at the status of the agreements. Are they subject to the same interpretative rules as Community law? If so, how then does the application of those rules which, as described in Chapters 1 and 2 include very strong enforcement mechanisms, apply to third country nationals who, under the terms of a third country agreement, enjoy positive rights in the Member States?

The 1976 Agreements with the Maghreb countries (Algeria, Morocco and Tunisia), the Yugoslavia Agreement and Lomé IV followed the Turkey Agreement by including labour provisions. The Morocco and Tunisia Agreements have been renegotiated and new agreements signed with Tunisia in 1995 (now in force) and Morocco in 1996. The provisions on migrant workers in the Member States remain largely unchanged, but there have been additions which reflect the development of Community migration policy in the intergovernmental framework. This group of agreements are important to the development of the Community's policy as they contain provisions on labour which promise the privileged third country nationals protected by the agreements equal treatment in limited fields. The question then arises as to the meaning and extent of the concept of non-discrimination on the basis of nationality in third country agreements in comparison with its meaning for the purposes of the EC Treaty. As has been seen in Chapter 2, the principle of non-discrimination on the basis of nationality has been given a very wide and purposive interpretation as regards Community national workers. How do those principles, developed in the context of Community nationals, transpose, if at all, to third country nationals privileged under an agreement between their state and the Community?

The agreements with the Central and Eastern European countries all include provisions which implicitly at least provide for access to the territory and economic activity for nationals of the privileged third country. They resemble the Greece and Turkey Agreements as they are intended to lead to accession of these states to the Union. All these agreements were entered into after 1990. In the light of the lessons which the Community learned in the earlier agreements what can be discerned from this development in particular as regards the intention of the legislator to use third country agreements to regulate immigration flows? These agreements stand out as the first to include provisions on labour giving a right of access to the territory from countries from which there is a perceived pressure to emigrate. Because of the very substantial gap in time and political context between these agreements with the Central and Eastern European countries and the other agreements, I will deal with them separately in Chapter 6, summing up what has been achieved.

A Short Overview of Community Competence over Third Country Nationals

Early in the history of the European Economic Community when it was still called such, it began to exercise its external competence *vis-à-vis* the rest of the world.[2] In accordance with Article 310 and procedures set out in Article 300 the Community was given competence to conclude with one or more States or international organisations agreements establishing an association involving reciprocal rights and obligations. It was similarly given powers to enter into third country agreements in respect of common customs tariffs under Articles 111 (now repealed) and 133 EC. Further, by a series of declarations to the original EEC Treaty it was clear that the Community was expected to enter into agreements at an early stage. Declarations of intention to enter into association were annexed in respect of the independent countries in the franc area, Libya, Somaliland, Surinam and the Netherlands Antilles, in other words former colonies of the original Member States. The resulting collective agreement would be enlarged to include more and more states and is now known as the Lomé Agreement.

The third country agreements concluded under Article 310 have proven important to the development of the Community's migration law as it is through provisions in those agreements that the Community exercised competence over third country national workers and subsequently the self-employed.[3] However, before moving to look at the competence provided under the agreements first a general outline of Community competence over third country nationals is appropriate.

Until 1999 Community competence over entry, stay, expulsion and economic activity of third country nationals was limited to derived rights of residence and economic activity first in respect of such family members of

---

2 For an analysis of this power see I. Macleod, I. Hendry & S. Hyett, *The External Relations of the European Communities*, Clarendon Press, 1996, Oxford; and D. McGoldrick, *International Relations Law of the European Union*, Longman, 1997, London.

3 See Chapter 6 on the agreements with the Central and Eastern European countries.

Community nationals exercising free movement rights.[4] These rights are dependent on the Community national and cease to exist in respect of the spouse when he or she ceases to reside in the Member State or otherwise ceases to come within the personal scope of Community law.[5] The children, however, retain a continuing right of access to the territory, employment and education.[6] Because of the divergence between national and Community law in fact a benefit has been created for Community nationals who move in respect of their family rights. Once a Community migrant has moved country to exercise his or her economic rights he or she is entitled to family reunion with spouses of any nationality, children under 21 and all dependent relatives in the ascending and descending lines.[7] If the Community national returns to his or her country of nationality, there is a right to those family members to accompany him or her.[8] In his analysis of the *Singh* decision,[9] Gutmann has described how the consequence of more restrictive family reunion provisions in national law is a positive incentive for nationals who cannot enjoy family reunion with third country national family members in national law to move to another Member State to do so. Subsequent to the genuine exercise of the economic activity in a host State they will be able to move home again with their family members, thereby defeating restrictive provisions of national law.

A second class of third country nationals also enjoy a derived right of movement and temporary residence in the Member States: third country national employees of Community enterprises posted to a Member State to carry out a contract for services of their employer.[10] Again in this case, the right "belongs" to the Community national employer as part of its right to provide services under Article 49 EC. The third country national can only enjoy the derived right so long as his or her employment relationship continues to exist and he or she is carrying out the employer's services. However, this derived right did not become apparent to the Member States until 1994 and

---

4   Article 10 Regulation 1612/68, Article 1 Directive 73/148.
5   For example, leaving aside the issue of rights attendant on citizenship of the Union, a Community national job seeker who no longer has a reasonable chance of finding employment will cease to be within the scope of Community law C-292/89 *Antonissen* [1991] ECR I-745; the only exception to this principle is contained in Regulation 1251/70 in respect of family members of a Community national who dies on the territory of the host Member State.
6   389,390/87 *Echternach* [1989] ECR 723; C-210/97 *Akman* [1998] ECR I-7519.
7   Article 10 Regulation 1612/68.
8   C-370/90 *Singh* [1993] ECR I-4265.
9   R. Gutmann, Discrimination against own nationals: a brief look at European and German immigration law, Immigration and Nationality Law and Practice, Vol. 9 No 3 1995, pp. 97-99.
10 C-113/89 *Rush Portuguesa* [1990] ECR I-1417; C-43/93 *Vander Elst* [1994] ECR I-3803.

implementing measures have only recently been proposed by the Community legislator.[11]

Of course Community social legislation such as Article 137 EC on health and safety or Article 141 on equal treatment between men and women as regards pay must apply generally to all members of the Community labour force irrespective of nationality. This position was confirmed albeit obliquely by the Court in the case of *Süzen*.[12] The case revolved around the correct interpretation of Directive 77/187 on the transfer of undertakings. The complainant worker, Mrs Süzen, was in fact a Turkish national. This fact was apparent from the record of proceedings of the referring court. In the Report of the hearing, Advocate General's Opinion and judgment no mention was made of the fact and it appears that it was accepted by the parties and intervenors (which included the German, UK and French Governments) that she was entitled to rely on the Directive notwithstanding that she was not a Community national.

However, conflicts arise between Community social and migration law as applied to third country nationals. While they enjoy the protection of the former, they are excluded from rights attendant on the latter. The problem was exemplified by the case of Mr Awoyemi. He was a Nigerian national who held a valid UK driving licence. He was stopped by the police in Belgium and was charged with driving a motor vehicle without being in possession of a Belgian driving licence. The case went to the Court of Justice on two questions: whether the Directive on cross-recognition of driving licences applied to Mr Awoyemi and secondly whether the Court's case law that Member States may not impose criminal penalties in this area so disproportionate to the gravity of the infringement as to become an obstacle to free movement of persons, applied to him and in particular to the sentence which he received on conviction.

The Court held that the relevant Directive "applies not only to nationals of Member States but also to holders of a driving licence issued by a Member State irrespective of nationality".[13] Therefore clearly Community law in fields such as transport and road safety apply to all persons within the Union whether or not they are Community nationals. However, the right not to suffer disproportionate penalties arises from the right to free movement of persons and:

> "a person such as Mr Awoyemi may not rely on that case law. ... a national of
> a non-Member country who finds himself in the same position as Mr Awoyemi

---

11 The Commission has recently proposed two Directives which would regularise the situation: OJ 1999 C 67/9.

12 [1997] ECR I-1259.

13 C-230/97 *Awoyemi* [1998] ECR I-6781.

may not effectively rely on the rules governing the free movement of persons which, according to the settled case law, apply only to a national of a Member State of the Community who seeks to establish himself in the territory of another Member State or to a national of the Member State in question, who finds himself in the situation which is connected with any of the situations contemplated by Community law (see for example case C-147/91 *Ferrer Laderer* [1992] ECR-I-4097, paragraph 7)."[14]

The benefit to third country national workers of Community social, consumer or environmental law (to name a few areas) is a by-product of legislation designed to protect all persons in the Union. This is the fundamental nature of the internal market, common rules must apply across the board to all participants in the market in all Member States. However, the perspective changes when Community immigration law is concerned. For instance, for third country nationals residing or seeking to reside and work in the Union the critical questions are of access to the territory, access to economic activities and security of residence and employment. These questions remained, until the entry into force of the Amsterdam Treaty, primarily within the hands of the Member States and subject to their discretion. Would the situation be different if Article 39 EC were interpreted as applying to third country nationals in their capacity as workers? As discussed above, the answer which Community law would give at the moment is "not necessarily". This situation reveals a dichotomy inherent in the system of Community law which has yet to be resolved: third country nationals are protected by Community law in so far as it relates to the fields outside immigration; Community nationals are entitled to the protection of Community law at home to the same extent as third country nationals but in order to access rights attached to free movement they must move country. This continues to be the case notwithstanding the creation of the concept of citizenship of the Union in Article 17 EC. At the moment the concept cannot be used to overcome the exclusion of the application of rights attached to free movement where a situation is found to be wholly internal to one Member State.[15]

The balance of competence between the Community and the Member States as regards the movement of third country nationals began to change after 1986 with the Single European Act. Through the drive to complete the Single Market and in particular Article 14 EC which provided for an area without internal frontiers for the movement, *inter alia*, of persons, a significant competence was ceded to the Community as regards third country nationals. With the amendment to the Treaty in 1992 by the Maastricht Treaty, provision was included at Article 140 for Community competence over "conditions of

---

14 C-230/97 *Awoyemi* [1998] ECR I-6781.
15 C-64, 65/96 *Uecker & Jacquet* [1997] ECR I-3170.

employment for third country nationals legally residing in Community territory". The Amsterdam Treaty amendments to the EC Treaty changed the balance fundamentally between the Member States and the Community as regards third country nationals. Those developments are the subject, however, of Chapters 7, 8 and 9. Although in time, the 1986 and subsequent consequences for Community competence over third country nationals often predate important decisions of the Court giving real effect to rights of third country nationals under the agreements, they represent a different strand of development in Community law which remained only tangentially influenced by the developing jurisprudence on the agreements. This is not to underestimate the influence on the legislator of the Court of Justice's rulings in respect of the agreements, but these developments come later.

3.2.   THE AGREEMENTS AND COMMUNITY LAW

The legal effects of agreements have been most firmly described recently as follows:

> "The legal effects of international agreements concluded by the Communities can be summarised by two principles. Such agreements are binding in international law and must be performed in good faith: *pacta servanda sunt*. And within the Community legal order, agreements form an integral part of Community law."[16]

Such an unequivocal statement by experts in Community law evidences just how completely the tale of third country agreements has unfolded. This does not, however, dispense with the need to review those agreements and Community competence as regards persons. The Community agreements with third states form an important part of the legal development of the Community not least as the expression of the external legal identity of the Community.[17]

Some agreements, such as the Turkey Agreement are mixed. This means that both the Community and the Member States are parties to them and share competence in relation to the agreements. As regards the competences which have been transferred to the Community, the Member States have relinquished sovereignty.[18] The doctrine of parallelism applies here. As the competence of

---

16   I. Macleod, I. Hendry & S. Hyett, *The External Relations of the European Communities*, Clarendon Press, Oxford, 1996.

17   J. Amphoux, Cour de Justice des Communautés européenes et Tribunal de première instance, Cahiers de droit européen, 1994, p. 92.

18   *Costa v ENEL* [1964] ECR 585.

the Community develops internally so it also extends externally.[19] However, the external competence is dependent on the extent to which authority has been granted and exercised by the Community internally. According to the Court of Justice in the absence of the internal exercise of a competence, a corresponding and exclusive, external competence to the Community only arises where it is necessary to achieve a Community objective or inextricably linked to the treatment to be afforded to Community nationals on a reciprocal basis.[20]

Generally, in respect of the Association and Cooperation Agreements, the fulfilment of obligations undertaken lies partly with the Community and partly with the Member States. There are at least three ways of considering such mixed competence:

1. There is a genuine sharing of competence between the Community and the Member States as some areas of the agreement fall outside even the potential scope of the EC Treaty;[21]

2. The powers of the Community and the Member States in respect of the field run in parallel – such as in respect of intellectual property, which is regulated by an agreement outside Community competence but touches inextricably on Community competence on free movement of goods and services;[22]

3. The Community has a potential exclusive competence which it has not exercised and so there is a residual competence to the Member States – as in respect of establishment and freedom for third country nationals to provide services.[23]

It also must be borne in mind that as the competences of the Community are enlarged and exercised internally so its external competences follow suit. Therefore what may have been a mixed field when an agreement was signed may subsequently and as a result of both the adoption of measures within Community law by the Council and the re-negotiation of the Treaty, now be an exclusive area of activity for the Community to the exclusion of the Member

---

19 D. McGoldrick, *supra*, p. 48.
20 *Opinion 1/94 (WTO)* [1994] ECR I-5267. In the light of the Community's new competence in Article 63(3) for repatriation of third country nationals, the question has arisen as to whether the power to conclude readmission agreements on third country nationals with third countries now rests exclusively with the Commission.
21 For example regular political dialogue provided for in the Agreements with the Central and Eastern European countries.
22 *Opinion 1/94 (WTO)* [1994] ECR I-5267.
23 *See Opinion 1/94 (WTO)* and Article 49 EC second paragraph.

States. In other words, there is no clear answer applicable to all situations in respect of provisions of mixed agreements. Consequently, as each agreement and its provisions are considered, this question of competence and responsibility arises. Further, the balance between responsibility of the Community and the Member States can vary over time. Accordingly, an issue which the Court of Justice may have held to be within the exclusive competence of the Member States, for instance, before ratification of the Maastricht or Amsterdam Treaties, and the adoption of measures under new fields, could now be open to question.

Competences and Their Exercise: An Example

The first case to come before the Court on the rights of workers under a third country agreement involved the question of whether the Turkey Agreement should be interpreted so as to entitle a Turkish worker to continue to enjoy family life with his wife, temporarily resident in a Member State, against the decision of the Member State that she should leave. The Court found that "there is at present no provision of Community law defining the conditions in which Member States must permit the family reunification of Turkish workers lawfully settled in the Community."[24]

This finding has been widely criticised. The grounds for the criticism cover two of the issues of concern in this chapter: to what extent are the agreements actually treated as Community law in the same way as the EC Treaty and secondly to what extent does the Court give a consistent interpretation to the agreements and the EC Treaty. Weiler considered:

> "It is correct that there is no positive provision of Community law defining the conditions in which Member States must permit the family reunification of Turkish workers lawfully settled in the Community. It is also true that the national rules at issue in this case did not have to directly implement a positive provision of Community law.
>
> But it does not strictly follow from the absence of positive provisions of Community law defining the conditions in which Member States must permit family reunification and requiring implementation, that this field is totally 'outside the scope of Community law'. Nor does it follow that the Member States are totally free under the Agreement, and thus under Community law (*Kupferberg* and new *Sevince* formula) to do whatever they want, including the violation of the fundamental human rights of migrants from Turkey.
>
> My contention is that even in the absence of positive Community law defining with precision many of the conditions of sojourn of migrants from Turkey, a situation which leaves much liberty to the individual Member States

---

24 12/86 *Demirel* [1987] ECR 3719.

in setting such conditions, the European Court of Justice retains jurisdiction (and a duty) to ensure that the fundamental human rights of such migrants, in relation to their rights of residence, should not be violated either by the Community or by its Member States."[25]

These comments address both questions – the scope of Community law for the purposes of the agreements and the Court's competence to interpret them.

Heldmann has also argued that there is more than ample competence for the issue of family reunification to be a Community matter taking into consideration the provisions of Association Council Decision 1/80 and the duty to be guided by the relevant articles in the EC Treaty. He concludes that the Court is capable of finding an equivalence of rights for Turkish workers with Community national workers in this area.[26]

Both these commentators raise the same issue in their criticism: what is the proper role of the legislator and what of the Court. Weiler argues that human rights principles should apply in such a way as to override the balance of powers (i.e. competences) between the Community and the Member States. However, as it is the fact of adherence to human rights instruments by the Member States which creates the compliance duty in Community law it is difficult to argue that the individual is better protected, as regards international human rights commitments, by the Community than by the Member State. If there is an international human rights duty to give Turkish workers family reunion rights in the Member States, then that duty bites first and foremost on the Member States who are signatories of the relevant instruments. The Community's compliance duty is a derived one from that of the Member States and only applies where the Member States competence in the field has been excluded. Here as regards family reunion for Turkish workers it has not. Heldmann's argument is slightly different, though results in the same problem. He argues that from the programmatic nature of Article 12 of the Turkey Agreement should be inferred an exercise of a potential competence, again with the help of Article 8 ECHR.

In my view, the argument of Weiler in particular is emotionally compelling but pays insufficient attention to the issue of the correct role of the legislator and that of the Court. The argument is that in the Court's finding it appears to abdicate its duty to ensure compatibility with, for instance, the ECHR by defining out of the scope of Community law family reunification for Turkish workers. However, first one must ask is there a fundamental human right to

---

25 J. H. H. Weiler, Thou Shalt Not Oppress a Stranger: On the Judicial Protection of the Human Rights of Non-EC Nationals, 3 EJIL (1992) 65.

26 H. Heldmann, Familiennachzug für Türken in Deutschland, in *Gastarbeiter – Einwanderer – Bürger?* (Hrsg) H. Lichtenburg/G. Linne/H. Gumrukcu, Nomos Verlag, Baden-Baden, 1994.

family reunification in the country of residence of one of the family members? Little support for this contention is to be found in the judgments of the European Court of Human Rights. When faced with this question in 1985, that Court was not persuaded that a migrant has a choice of where to reside with his or her family members under Article 8 ECHR,[27] which approach has been confirmed subsequently. So long as there is some country in which they can enjoy family life it is by no means clear that there is any duty on a Council of Europe country (provided it is not the only country where family life can be enjoyed) to facilitate or admit a family member.[28] However, even if there were, what would be the responsibility of the Court of Justice?

As regards Community law the Court has consistently held that:

> "It is well settled that fundamental rights form an integral part of the general principles of law whose observance the Court ensures. For that purpose, the Courts draws inspiration from the constitutional traditions common to the Member States and from the guidelines supplied by international treaties for the protection of human rights on which the Member States have collaborated or of which they are signatories. Respect for human right is therefore a condition for the lawfulness of Community acts."[29]

On this reasoning then, the act of the Community in settling a third country agreement should engage the duty of the Community to observe within the scope of that agreement all human rights obligations which have been recognised by the Member States. The right to family life as contained in Article 8 ECHR is such a right.[30]

However, the scope of the power in the agreement was not at issue. The Court was not faced with this question as there was no provision of Community law which for these purposes engages the law of the agreement on the issue. In other words, the Court has not held that there is no power for the Association Council to adopt a Decision on family reunion for Turkish workers. In respect of workers who have acquired rights under the agreement, specifically those who have worked for one year lawfully in a Member State, there is competence to the Association Council to do so.

It is quite another thing, though, to suggest that because there is a competence (or a potential competence) to adopt such a measure, that the legislative process can be dispensed with and the Court can move directly from a competence to a finding that in the absence of any exercise of the competence there is a breach of a fundamental human right. This leads back to the

---

27 *Abdulaziz, Cabales and Balkandali* [1985] Ser. A No. 95.
28 *Gül* 53/1995/559/645.
29 *Opinion 2/94* [1996] ECR I-1759.
30 *249/86 Commission v Germany* [1989] ECR 1263.

question of competence – until a competence has been exercised it remains mixed, and responsibility, for instance, in respect of family reunion for Turkish workers, stays within the sphere of the Member States.

As discussed above, the Community's competence in respect of third country agreements changes depending on its competence internally and its exercise. A new competence to the Community has been inserted by the Amsterdam Treaty at Article 63 EC: the Council shall adopt "measures on immigration policy within the following areas: (a) conditions of entry and residence, and standards on procedures for the issue by Member States of long term visas and residence permits, including those for the purpose of family reunion". From ratification of the Treaty until the Community exercises this competence it comes within the third category: a potentially exclusive competence which has not yet been exercised. Once the competence is exercised it will be exclusive to that extent. At that point the question of the rights of Turkish workers as regards family reunion under the agreement may be subsumed into a new more general power.

Potentially Exclusive Competences and Their Exercise: An Example

One of the most difficult aspects of the Community's competence under third country agreements in comparison with that of the Member States relates to mixed competences. Where the Community has a potentially exclusive competence because the Member States have agreed within the Treaty to extend such a power, but that competence has not yet been exercised, what happens? The jurisdictional issue may best be exemplified by an example.

A potentially exclusive competence which on account of the failure to exercise a power internally has resulted in the lack of an exclusive external competence is in respect of third country nationals established in the Community and seeking to provide services in another Member State. The Single European Act introduced a second paragraph to Article 49 EC permitting the provision's extension to third country nationals.[31] The Commission only put forward a proposal to give effect to the power in 1999.[32] In the negotiations of the General Agreement on Trade in Services annex to the World Trade Organisation Agreement, a dispute arose between the Member States and the Commission as to whether there was an exclusive competence to the Community as regards the negotiations.

---

31 "The Council may, acting by a qualified majority on a proposal from the Commission, extend the provisions of the Chapter [on freedom to provide services] to nationals of a third country who provide services and who are established within the Community."
32 OJ 1999 C 167.

The Council argued that the negotiating competence belonged to the Member States as the Community had not exercised its internal competence. The Commission argued that it was a Community competence as intrinsic to the operation of the internal market. The Court held:

"As the Court pointed out in the *ERTA* judgment (paragraphs 17 and 18) the Member States, whether acting individually or collectively, only lose their right to assume obligations with non-member countries as and when common rules which could be affected by those obligations come into being. Only in so far as common rules have been established at internal level does the external competence of the Community become exclusive."[33]

In other words, as the Community had not exercised its potentially exclusive competence over migration for service provision by third country nationals, it did not have an exclusive competence in the external sphere. However, of particular interest here is the reasoning of the Court. The Council had argued that there was no competence to the Community in respect of service provision and third country nationals except as contained in Article 49 second paragraph EC. The Court rejected this argument without making reference to Article 49 second paragraph. Instead it held that where there is a power to harmonise, that power is exercisable by the Community both in respect of own nationals and third country nationals:

"Although the only objectives expressly mentioned in the chapters on the right of establishment and on freedom to provide services is the attainment of those freedoms for nationals of the Member States of the Community, it does not follow that the Community institutions are prohibited from using the powers conferred on them in that field in order to specify treatment which is to be accorded to nationals of non-member countries. Numerous acts adopted by the Council on the basis of Articles 53 [44] and 56(2) [47(2)] of the Treaty – but not mentioned by it – contain provisions in that regard."[34]

In summary, therefore, the Community has decided that third country agreements form part of Community law. What is open for discussion is the effect of those agreements in relation to the competence of the Community under the EC Treaty. For the purposes of this consideration, the resolution of that question is critical to the development of the Community's immigration law.

---

33 *Opinion* 1/94 [1996] ECR I-5267.
34 *Opinion* 1/94 [1996] ECR I-5267. In the event, the Court held that as the internal competence of the Community over service provision by third country nationals had not been exercised the external competence was mixed between the Member States and the Community.

3.3. THE COURT OF JUSTICE AND ITS COMPETENCE

In respect of the third country agreements which contain provisions relating to workers, neither the Member States nor any of the Community institutions have challenged the power of the Community to enter into either the agreement or the inclusion of the relevant provisions. However, a number of Member States have sought to argue that the provisions relating to workers come within their competence rather than that of the Community and in particular the provisions are outside the jurisdiction of the Court.[35] The arguments which some Member States put forward to support their position were as follows:

(a) The movement of third country national workers falls within the exclusive jurisdiction of the Member States;

(b) The commitments under the agreements are under public international law and therefore are not acts within the meaning of the provisions on the Court's interpretative powers;[36]

(c) Implementation of the agreements is the responsibility of the Association Councils established under them and therefore the Community's role is excluded;

(d) Dispute resolution in respect of the agreements is already provided for under the agreements themselves which give this responsibility to the Association Councils. The Association Councils have the power to refer disputes to the Court of Justice. Therefore this is the route intended by the agreements by which their interpretation might be within the jurisdiction of the Court.

The Court countered with the following arguments:

1. The agreements are, as far as the Community is concerned, acts of one of the institutions of the Community;

2. Under the legal basis of Article 310 and 300 EC upon which the agreements are made, the Community is empowered to guarantee commitments towards non-member countries in the fields covered by the Treaty;

3. In ensuring respect for commitments arising from an agreement concluded by the Community institutions, the Member States fulfil, within the Community system an obligation in relation to the Community,

---

35 In particular the German and UK Governments in 12/86 *Demirel* [1987] ECR 3719 and the German Government in a number of subsequent cases.

36 Article 234 EC.

which has assumed responsibility for the due performance of the agreements.[37]

Some Member States also argued in the context of the interpretation of the decisions of the Association Councils that these could not be interpreted as part of Community law for the purposes of the interpretative function of the Court as they were not acts of the institutions of the Community.[38] The Court found this argument unpersuasive:

"Since the Court has jurisdiction to give preliminary rulings on the Agreement, in so far as it is an act adopted by one of the institutions of the Community (Case 181/73 *Haegeman* [1974] ECR 449), it also has jurisdiction to give rulings on the interpretation of the decisions adopted by the authority established by the agreement and entrusted with responsibility for its implementation."[39]

One Government continued to argue against the Court's jurisdiction until 1992.[40]

As agreements concluded by the Council under Article 310 EC, they are acts of one of the institutions of the Community within the meaning of Article 234(1)(b) EC, and as from their entry into force, the provisions of such agreements form an integral part of the Community legal order within the framework of which the Court of Justice has jurisdiction to give preliminary rulings concerning the interpretation.[41] The Member States fulfil, in respect of the agreements, an obligation of the Community which has assumed responsibility for the performance of the agreements.[42] Two types of obligation have been identified under the agreements:

(a) Those which contain a clear and precise obligation which is not subject as regards its execution or effects to the adoption of any subsequent act and which therefore have direct effect;[43]

(b) Those which require the contracting parties to take all appropriate measures, whether general or specific, to ensure the fulfilment of the obligations arising from the agreement. These obligations cannot dir-

---

37 12/86 *Demirel* [1987] ECR 3719.
38 C-192/89 *Sevince* [1990] ECR I-3573.
39 C-192/89 *Sevince* [1990] ECR I-3573.
40 The German Government finally abandoned the attempt to convince the Court of its lack of jurisdiction after the ruling in C-237/91 *Kus* [1992] ECR I-6781.
41 12/86 *Demirel* [1987] ECR 3719.
42 104/81 *Kupferberg* [1982] ECR 3641.
43 C-18/90 *Kziber* [1991] ECR I-199.

ectly confer on individuals rights which are not already vested in them by other provisions of the agreement.[44]

It is critical to the role of these agreements that in superseding national discretion they created duties shared between the Member States and the Community. In respect of other international agreements effectiveness of implementation can be uncertain. If these agreements constituted no more than acts of international law, the duty of reciprocity would apply alone. Implementation would be the obligation of each Member State individually.

The strength or weakness of implementation of international law from the perspective of the individual is a matter for national law and national implementation. For instance, in monist states the individual may well be able to rely directly on a convention's provision to establish a right enforceable nationally. Whether the provision of such an agreement has the characteristics which the national court considers necessary for it to be able to support an individual's claim is a matter of national law. This will not necessarily be uniform among even those signatory states which operate in a monist system: there is no guarantee that a national court in one signatory state will interpret the content of a provision of an international agreement in the same way as the national court of another signatory state.

In dualist systems, implementation through national law is generally required before an individual will be able to rely internally on a right which derives from an international agreement. Therefore, the individual in such dualist states will not be able to rely directly on the international agreement within the national legal system but only on the provision of national law which implements or purports to implement the obligation. As states do not consistently use the "copy out" form of transposition but rewrite provisions of international agreements to suit better their national legal structure, when an individual comes to rely on such a national provision and a national court is required to interpret it, what is under consideration is national law and therefore there is not necessarily the obligation to ensure the interpretation's uniformity with the international agreement whence it sprang.

Further, irrespective of the possibility for an individual to rely directly on provisions, there is generally no strong system to ensure consistent interpretation, such as is provided by the Court of Justice (the decisions of which must be applied by all levels of court and administration in all Member States). Many international agreements provide for dispute resolution committees to be established under the agreement but individuals rarely have access to such committees. In any event the decisions of such committees on interpretation of the agreement rarely have any specific standing in national law other than

_____

44 12/86 *Demirel* [1987] ECR 3719.

persuasive authority. Further, failure to implement international agreements can usually be pursued only by parties to the agreement through the usual international law channels winding up, *in extremis*, at the International Court of Justice.

The difference between the effectiveness of provisions of international agreements in general and the Community's international agreements resulted from the Court's involvement. In the first decisions on third country agreements in 1974[45] and 1976,[46] the Court took a strong position on the effects of such agreements:

> "As appears from Article 228(7) [300] of the EC Treaty, international Agreements concluded by the Community in conformity with the Treaty are binding on the institutions and the Member States. It is settled case-law that the provisions of such an Agreement form an integral part of the Community legal order once the Agreement has entered into force (see *Haegeman* [1974] ECR 449). It is also settled case-law that the provisions of such an Agreement may have direct effect if they are unconditional and sufficiently precise (*Bresciani* [1976] ECR 129; *Kupferberg* [1987] ECR 3641)."[47]

It was not necessarily clear at the time of the *Haegeman* judgment in 1974 what the full consequences of the applicability of agreements within the internal legal order of the Community would be for instance in the field of immigration. Indeed, if they had been fully apparent, it is not unlikely that the 1976 agreements with the Maghreb would have been differently configured.[48]

The position of the Court on the application of the agreements within the Community legal order was of course critical to the Court's own jurisdiction to interpret the agreements. But it was also critical to bringing into play the duty of good faith contained in Article 10 EC. For, by failing correctly to implement a provision of a third country agreement, a Member State could certainly in respect of a mixed agreement not only be in breach of its duties to the third state in international law but also would be in breach of its duty of good faith to the Community. As has been examined in Chapter 1, the duty of good faith goes beyond reciprocity in international law. It engages at every level of administration and court in the Member States the commitment not only to

---

45 181/73 *Haegeman* [1974] ECR 449.

46 87/75 *Bresciani* [1976] ECR 129.

47 *T-115/94 Opel Austria v Council* [1997] ECR II-39.

48 The interpretation of the Court of the right to equal treatment as regards social security in those agreements led the Member States, when settling the agreements with the countries of Central and Eastern Europe, to avoid any reference to equal treatment in that field – see D. Martin & E. Guild, *Free Movement of Persons in the European Union*, Butterworths, London, 1996.

carry out the letter of the law but to give effect to the spirit. It is for the Court to interpret the scope of the Member States' obligations under the agreements.

Therefore the Community becomes self-regulating as regards the implementation of obligations under the agreements. The steps taken or omitted by the third state whether in implementing its own duties or in seeking to pursue a Member State for non-implementation are irrelevant to the Member States' duty to the Community to comply. This is the consequence of such agreements:

> "By securing performance of the undertakings arising from an Agreement made by the Community institutions, Member States fulfil an obligation not only to the non-Member State concerned but also and above all to the Community which has assumed responsibility for due performance of the Agreement."[49]

In conclusion, then, notwithstanding arguments both political and legal put forward by the Member States that the Court should not be competent to interpret provisions on labour in third country agreements, the Court found it had competence for such interpretation. That competence is implicit in the fact that the same legal territory is covered in the EC Treaty. Therefore the source of the interpretative power of provisions on persons in third country agreements (at the very least) is the EC Treaty and the scope defined by reference to it.

3.4.   THE PRINCIPLES OF INTERPRETATION: DIRECT EFFECT

I have so far looked at the issues of the third country agreements as part of Community law and the power of the Court to interpret those agreements. I will now investigate the interpretation given to the agreements and their subsidiary legislation in respect of persons by the Court and the extent to which this is consistent with the interpretation which the Court has given to similar provisions of the EC Treaty and its subsidiary legislation in respect of Community nationals. However, before looking at the specific content and interpretation of provisions of the agreements, the first question is whether the same legal structural framework is applied by the Court to the interpretation of the agreements as is provided in respect of the EC Treaty. Are the principles developed in the sphere of the EC Treaty applicable to the interpretation of the third country agreements? In other words, is there a single and coherence legal framework in which both the EC Treaty and the third country agreements enjoy equal treatment as regards natural persons?

---

49   104/81 *Kupferberg* [1982] ECR 3641.

A first step is to look at what the purpose of the Court's jurisdiction over the third country agreements is. The Court gave an unequivocal answer that the purpose is the same as in respect of the EC Treaty to ensure uniformity of application:

> "The function of Article 177 [234] EEC [and the Court's consequential judgments] is to ensure the uniform application throughout the Community of all provisions forming part of the Community legal system and to ensure that the interpretation thereof does not vary according to the interpretation accorded to them by various Member States (see Case 104/81 *Kupferberg* [1982] ECR 3641; and Joined Cases 267-269/81 *SPI and SAMI* [1983] ECR 801)."[50]

Therefore the function of the Court in both cases is to ensure that the exercise of national discretion in the application and interpretation of provisions of the agreements or the Treaty is not permitted to interfere with the enjoyment of the rights conferred. The purpose of the interpretative power is the same. Of course while the purpose of the interpretative power was the same this does not mean that similar or identical provisions in third country agreements and in the EC Treaty must be interpreted identically.[51] What then about the status of the agreements and their subsidiary legislation – are these assimilated to the position of the Treaty and its subsidiary legislation?

For the individual, the most important question is whether the rights contained in the agreements and their subsidiary legislation are capable of having direct effect. Is the legal effect of the provisions comparable for the third country national and for the Community national? The problem was addressed in 1976 where the Court held that a rule in a decision of an Association Council could have direct effect.[52] First the Court qualified the question allowing for different answers to the same question in the future:

> "In order to determine whether an international treaty to which the European Community is a party is self-executing i.e. confers on those subject to Community law the right to rely on it in order to challenge a national legal provision, regard must be paid both to the spirit and to the general scheme and to the wording of both the treaty in question and the specific provision in it."

Then it gave an unambiguous answer to its own question:

> "The fact that the treaty does not provide for reciprocal obligations, but rather imposes significantly greater obligations on the Community than on the associated state, is inherent in the specific nature of that convention and therefore

---

50 C-192/89 *Sevince* [1990] ECR I-3461.
51 270/80 *Polydor* [1982] ECR 329; C-312/91 *Metalsa* [1993] ECR I-3751.
52 87/75 *Bresciani* [1976] ECR 129.

does not prevent recognition by the Community that some of its provisions have a direct effect within the Community."[53]

In that case, relating to customs duties on animal hides, not one Member State intervened. Only the Commission submitted observations to the Court. This is notwithstanding the fact that this was not the first case on third country agreements, and that in the case, two years earlier,[54] the Court had determined for the first time that it had jurisdiction to interpret these agreements. Apparently the Member States had no difficulty with the Court's finding on jurisdiction so long as this applied to commercial matters. The trouble started when the principles developed in that sphere began to be applied to provisions relating to workers in those agreements.

Gutmann has analysed the question of extension of principles to third country agreements with specific reference to the Turkey Agreement. As he demonstrates, in the context of that Agreement, the decisions of the Court of Justice in the early cases which had nothing to do with the rights of workers, created a framework within which it was unavoidable for the Court to find its jurisdiction on provisions regarding workers. The Member States' opposition to the application to workers of principles which they had argued in favour of in the earlier cases relating to other areas is better explained by political sensitivities in some Member States than coherence of the Community legal system.[55]

The first case relating to persons gave the answer to how direct effect is to be interpreted for the purposes of the third country agreements. The same formulation as in respect of Community law was used:

"A provision in an Agreement concluded by the Community with a non-member country is directly applicable when, regard being had to its wording and the purpose and nature of the Agreement itself, the provision contains a clear and precise obligation which is not subject in its implementation or effects, to the adoption of any subsequent measure."[56]

The same criteria apply in determining whether the provisions of a decision of an Association Council can have direct effect.[57]

Accordingly, one of the most important tools of Community law which gives individuals rights against the State, direct effect, has a consistent content and application in the third country agreements. However, as regards the

---

53 87/75 *Bresciani* [1976] ECR 129.
54 181/73 *Haegeman* [1974] ECR 449.
55 R. Gutmann, *Die Assoziationsfreizügigkeit türkisher Staatsangehöriger, Ihre Entdeckung und ihr Inhalt*, 2. Auflage, Nomos Verlag, Baden-Baden, 1999.
56 12/86 *Demirel* [1987] ECR 3719.
57 C-192/89 *Sevince* [1990] ECR I-3461.

agreements there is one important difference: the spirit, scheme and wording of the agreement may preclude such an effect. This proviso changed form somewhat when applied to provisions relating to persons in third country agreements:

"A provision of an Agreement concluded by the Community with non-member countries must be regarded as being directly applicable when, regard being had to its wording and the purpose and nature of the Agreement itself, the provision contains a clear and precise obligation which is not subject, in its implementation or effects, to the adoption of any subsequent measure."[58]

However, the change in wording is not significant and is possibly the result of translation variations. The three issues then are the nature, purpose and wording of the agreement. The "nature" of the agreement is important as it is reflected in the wording. What is important is the intent of the agreement reached with the third country. As regards "wording", this follows the Community law concern: what actual words were used in the various language versions, and what was intended by them? In one recent judgment, the Court has not only looked at different Community language versions to determine what the legislator meant but also the wording in the language of the third country.[59] In respect of the purposes of third country agreements the Court has indicated:

The Turkey Agreement: its purpose is to promote the continuous and balanced strengthening of trade and economic relations between the parties.[60] It is capable of having direct effect and provisions of its subsidiary legislation have been so held.

The Maghreb Agreements: the object of the agreements is to promote overall co-operation between the contracting parties, in particular in the field of labour. The fact that the agreements are intended essentially to promote the economic development of the Maghreb states and that they confine themselves to instituting co-operation between the parties without referring to the Maghreb countries' association with or future accession to the Community is not such as to prevent certain of their provisions from being directly applicable.[61]

The Court was invited to consider the purpose of the Morocco Agreement by analogy with the purpose of the Turkey Agreement. It declined to do so and made the following observations regarding the difference of purpose between the two:

---

58 C-18/90 *Kziber* [1991] ECR 199.
59 C-1/97 *Akman* [1998] ECR I-7519.
60 C-192/89 *Sevince* [1990] ECR I-3461.
61 C-18/90 *Kziber* [1991] ECR I-199; C-416/96 *El Yassini* [1999] ECR I-1209.

(a) The Morocco Agreement does not provide for any examination by the contracting parties, in due course, of the possibility for the third country concerned to accede to the Community. This is provided for in the Turkey Agreement;

(b) The Morocco Agreement, unlike the Turkey Agreement, is not intended progressively to secure freedom of movement for workers;

(c) The Co-operation Council established under the Morocco Agreement has not adopted any provision analogous to Article 6(1) of Decision 1/80 of the Turkey Agreement which, with a view to securing freedom of movement in the future, grants Turkish migrant workers, according to the length of time they have been in authorised gainful employment, specific rights intended to integrate them progressively into the labour market of the host Member State;

(d) For reasons of the substantial differences not only in the wording but also in the object and purpose of the rules governing the Turkey Agreement and the Morocco Agreement, the Court declined to apply the rules of the former by analogy to the latter.[62]

The agreements generally provide a framework for activities to be undertaken. Specificity is normally provided for through the establishment and measures adopted by an Association (or Co-operation) Council which is set up under the terms of the agreement. Therefore is it natural that the provisions of Decisions of Association Councils are more likely to be sufficiently clear, precise and unconditional as regards their effects to have direct effect than those of the agreements themselves. It is always the minority of provisions in an agreement itself which are likely to have these characteristics.

Direct Effect: Subsidiary Legislation under the EEC Turkey Association Agreement

In respect of the Turkey Agreement the Court has held that the following provisions of its subsidiary legislation on workers have direct effect:[63]

---

62 C-416/96 *El Yassini* [1999] ECR I-1209.
63 The preceding Decision 2/76 was generally superseded by Decision 1/80 though some provisions of the former remain important, particularly the standstill clause. The Court has held provisions of Decision 2/76 also to have direct effect.

Association Council Decision 1/80: Article 6(1) & (2)[64]

(1)   [Subject to Article 7 on free access to employment for members of his family,] a Turkish worker duly registered as belonging to the labour force of a Member State:

- shall be entitled in that Member State, after one year's legal employment, to the renewal of his permit to work for the same employer, if a job is available;

- shall be entitled in that Member State, after three years of legal employment and subject to the priority to be given to workers of Member States of the Community, to respond to another offer of employment, with an employer of his choice, made under normal conditions and registered with the employment services of that State, for the same occupation;

- shall enjoy free access in that Member State to any paid employment of his choice, after four years of legal employment.[65]

(2)   Annual holidays and absences for reasons of maternity or an accident at work or short periods of sickness shall be treated as periods of legal employment. Periods of involuntary unemployment duly certified by the relevant authorities and long absences on account of sickness shall not be treated as periods of legal employment, but shall not affect the rights acquired as the result of the preceding period of employment.[66]

Although Article 6(3) provides that the procedures for applying paragraphs 1 & 2 shall be those established under national rules, the Court held that the provision merely clarifies the obligation incumbent on the Member States to take such administrative measures as may be necessary for the implementation of Article 6, without empowering them to make conditional or restrict the application of the precise and unconditional right which the provision grants.

Article 7

The members of the family of a Turkish worker duly registered as belonging to the labour force of a Member State, who have been authorised to join him:

- shall be entitled – subject to the priority to be given to workers of Member States of the Community – to respond to any offer of employment after they have been legally residence for at least three years in that Member State;

---

64   C-192/89 *Sevince* [1990] ECR I-3461.
65   C-192/89 *Sevince* [1990] ECR I-3461.
66   C-434/93 *Bozkurt* [1996] ECR I-1475. The Court found that Article 6(2) is intended only to regulate the consequences, for the application of Article 6(1), of certain breaks in employment. While it did not need to go on to interpret the meaning of Article 6(2) it is apparent that its effects are the same as Article 6(1).

- shall enjoy free access to any paid employment of their choice provided they have been legally resident there for at least five years.[67]

Children of Turkish workers who have completed a course of vocational training in the host country may respond to any offer of employment there, irrespective of the length of time they have been resident in that Member State, provided one of their parents has been legally employed in the Member State concerned for at least three years.[68]

Article 13

The Member States of the Community and Turkey may not introduce new restrictions on the conditions of access to employment applicable to workers and members of their families legally resident and employed in their respective territories.[69]

A case is currently pending before the Court on whether Article 14 regarding the grounds of expulsion of a Turkish worker has direct effect or not.[70]
Association Council Decision 3/80:

Article 3(1)

Subject to the special provisions of this Decision, persons resident in the territory of one of the Member States to whom this Decision applies shall be subject to the same obligations and enjoy the same benefits under the legislation of any Member State as the nationals of that State.[71]

In contrast it has held that the following provisions on workers contained in the agreement and its additional protocol do **not** have direct effect:

No Direct Effect: The EEC Turkey Association Agreement and Additional Protocol

Article 12

The Contracting Parties agree to be guided by Articles 48, 49 and 50 of the Treaty establishing the Community for the purpose of progressively securing freedom of movement for workers between them.

Article 36

Freedom of movement for workers between Member States of the Community and Turkey shall be secured by progressive stages in accordance with the

---

67 C-351/95 *Kadiman* [1997] ECR I-2133.
68 C-355/93 *Eroglu* [1994] ECR I-5113.
69 C-192/89 *Sevince* [1990] ECR I-3461.
70 C-340/97 *Nazli* [2000] ECR I-4903.
71 C-262/96 *Sürül* [1999] ECR I-2685.

principles set out in Article 12 of the Agreement of Association between the end of the twelfth and twenty-second year after the entry into force of that Agreement.

The Council of Association shall decide on the rules necessary to that end.[72]

In respect of the Maghreb Agreements, the identical provisions on workers appear in all three. The Court held the following provisions of the Morocco Agreement (and mirrored in the Algeria and Tunisia Agreements) to have direct effect:

Direct Effect: The Morocco Agreement[73]

Article 40

The treatment accorded by each Member State to workers of Moroccan nationality employed in its territory shall be free from any discrimination based on nationality, as regards working conditions or remuneration, in relation to its own nationals.

Article 41

Subject to the provisions of the following paragraphs, workers of Moroccan nationality and any members of their families living with them shall enjoy, in the field of social security, treatment free from any discrimination based on nationality in relation to nationals of the Member States in which they are employed.[74]

The interpretation of these provisions in comparison with corresponding rights to Community nationals under the EC Treaty is the subject of a later chapter. At this point I am only looking at the structural framework and its coherence. What general observations then, can be made about coherence on the basis of the Court's judgments on direct effect? First, both in respect of Article 6 of Decision 1/80 and Article 41 Morocco Agreement, the inclusion in the provision of reference to implementation through national rules, or subsequent provisions is not a bar to direct effect. This is consistent with the interpretation of the EC Treaty.[75]

In the *Demirel* case the Court had to consider whether Article 12 of the Turkey Agreement which requires the parties to be guided by Articles 39, 40

---

72 12/86 *Demirel* [1987] ECR 3719.
73 This wording is that interpreted by the Court of Justice and as appears in the 1976 Agreements. In the 1995 and 1996 Agreements identical provisions appear at Articles 96 *et seq.*
74 C-18/90 *Kziber* [1991] ECR I-199; C-416/96 *El Yassini* [1999] ECR I-1209.
75 See Chapter I on Direct Effect.

and 41 EC for the purpose of progressively securing freedom of movement of workers, whether alone or together with Article 36 of the Additional Protocol could be relied upon by individuals. The Court found as regards these provisions that they essentially serve to set out a programme and are not sufficiently precise and unconditional to be capable of governing directly the movement of workers.[76] The Advocate General added as regards Article 12 "that in itself indicates that the rules governing the free movement of workers will not necessarily be identical to those laid down by Articles [39, 40 and 41] EC." Of course at the time of the reference, the transitional period referred to had not been completed. In respect of a provision of the EC Treaty which contained a similar type of transitional period, Article 43 on the right of establishment of Community nationals, after the end of the transitional period the Court found the provision to have direct effect. In so deciding, the Court first noted that it is founded in the obligation to prohibit discrimination on nationality contained in Article 12 EC (the counterpart in the Turkey Agreement is Article 9) and therefore the meaning of the framework had to be interpreted in that context:

> "As a reference to a set of legislative provisions effectively applied by the country of establishment to its own nationals, this rule is, by its essence, capable of being directly invoked by nationals of all other Member States. In laying down that freedom of establishment shall be attained at the end of the transitional period Article 52[43] thus imposes an obligation to attain a precise result, the fulfilment of which had to be made easier but not dependent on, the implementation of a programme of progressive measures. The fact that this progression has not been adhered to leaves the obligation itself intact beyond the end of the period provided for its fulfilment."[77]

A consistent framework of interpretation may require that Article 36 of the Additional Protocol to the Turkey Agreement acquire a mandatory character at the end of the transitional period (which has been over since 1986). This may be the corollary of a coherent framework.[78]

---

76 12/86 *Demirel* [1987] ECR 3719.
77 2/74 *Reyners* [1974] ECR 631.
78 This is the view of the Advocate General in C-37/98 *Savas* (25 November 1999) considering the effect of the standstill provision prohibiting disadvantageous new rules making the self employment of Turkish nationals in the Member States more difficult after the entry into force of the Additional Protocol: "C'est par conséquent, en se référant à l'application, par les États membres, d'autres dispositions normatives à des situations prévues et réglementées par des conventions que l'article 9 précité leur impose l'obligation de ne pas traiter différemment, en l'absence d'une justification logique et adéquate, leurs propres ressortissants et les ressortissants turcs résident sur le territoire de l'État en cause."

Good Faith

Next, can the duty of good faith fill in a missing element and provide in respect of the agreements the same enforcement mechanisms as apply in respect of Community law? Article 7 of the Turkey Agreement mirrors the good faith article in the EC Treaty.[79]

In Demirel[80] the Court found that Article 36:

"... does no more than impose on the Contracting Parties a general obligation to co-operate in order to achieve the aims of the Agreement and it cannot directly confer on individuals rights which are not already vested in them by other provisions of the Agreement."

The Advocate General, though, applied the jurisprudence of the Court on Article 10 EC[81] to Article 7 of the agreement to reach the same conclusion:

"In view of the similarity of Article 7 of the Agreement to Article 10 of the EC Treaty it is appropriate to refer to the rules defined by this Court for the application of the latter Article. The Court has held that specific effects may be ascribed to Article 10 only where there are concrete elements elsewhere serving to define the measures, provided that they represent 'the point of departure for concerted Community action' (*Commission v United Kingdom* [1981] ECR 1045). In a case such as the present one, no such finding may be made because no rules governing the free movement of workers under the Ankara Agreement have yet been laid down."[82]

Therefore what happens to those obligations which do not have direct effect? How can they be enforced? If there is a single and coherent structure to Community law then the same tools for enforcement should be available in respect of the third country agreements where obligations are created which are not directly effective as are available in respect of the Treaty and its subsidiary legislation.

---

79 "The Contracting Parties shall take all appropriate measures, whether general or particular, to ensure the fulfilment of the obligations arising from this Agreement. They shall refrain from any measure liable to jeopardise the attainment of the objectives of this Agreement".

80 12/86 *Demirel* [1987] ECR 3719.

81 "Member States shall take all appropriate measures, whether general or particular, to ensure fulfilment of the obligations arising out of this Treaty or resulting from action taken by the institutions of the Community. They shall facilitate the achievement of the Community's tasks.

They shall abstain from any measure which could jeopardise the attainment of the objectives of the Treaty."

82 12/86 *Demirel* [1987] ECR 631.

3.5.   THE PRINCIPLES OF IMPLEMENTATION: WHERE DIRECT EFFECT IS LACKING

Whether the Community has adopted internal measures to give effect to obligations under the agreement is not decisive to the duties of the Community and the Member States. Under all the agreements, provision is made for the establishment of an Association or Cooperation Council comprised of representatives of the parties and charged with the preparation and adoption of implementing measures under the agreements. A question arose as to the effect of the Decisions of such Councils. Again, the Court not only found that it had jurisdiction to interpret such Decisions, but also that the provisions of such Decisions are capable of having direct effect "in order to be recognised as having direct effect, the provisions of a decision of the Council of Association must satisfy the same conditions as those applicable to the provisions of the agreement itself".[83] This means that the acts of the Councils in addition to the acts of the Community (i.e. the agreements themselves) have the effect of limiting national discretionary power over third country nationals enjoying rights thereunder. Such a conclusion naturally follows from the Court's reasoning on its interpretative powers in respect of the agreements themselves.

The Court was subsequently asked to determine the status of a Decision of an Association Council which failed to include any provision on its entry into force.[84] In fact, disagreement in the European Council had resulted in a Community measure to give effect to the Association Council Decision not being adopted. The Advocate General took the view that such a Decision which has not entered into force does not form part of the Community legal order. It cannot therefore have legal effects.[85]

The Court disagreed. It considered that the lack of a provision on entry into force did not affect the binding character of the Decision:

"It follows from all those provisions that decisions of the EC-Turkey Association Council are measures adopted by a body provided for by the Agreement and empowered by the Contracting Parties to adopt such measures. In so far as they implement the objectives set by the Agreement, such decisions are directly connected with the Agreement and, as a result of the second sentence of Article 22(1) thereof, have the effect of binding the Contracting Parties. By virtue of the Agreement, the Contracting Parties agreed to be bound by such decisions and if those parties were to withdraw from that commitment, that would constitute a breach of the Agreement. Consequently, contrary to the

---

83   C-192/89 *Sevince* [1990] ECR I-3461.
84   C-277/94 *Taflan-Met* [1996] ECR I-4085.
85   C-277/94 *Taflan-Met* [1996] ECR I-4085.

contention of the defendants in the main proceedings and the Governments of the Member States which have submitted observations to the Court,[86] the binding effect of decisions of the Association Council cannot depend on whether implementing measures have in fact been adopted by the Contracting Parties."[87]

What then happens where implementing measures have not been adopted? If the measures of the Association Council have legal effects, how do they manifest and what is the position of the individual who seeks to rely on them?

One possible comparison with Community law is between an act of the Community, such as a directive or a regulation, which has been adopted by the institutions but which has failed to be implemented by a Member State. The act is binding on the Member States notwithstanding the failure of one Member State to take appropriate measures to implement it. The same principle is at play as regards acts of the Association Councils – here the act is adopted by the Association Council and it is the Community institutions as well as the Member States which are bound by it.

However, just because an act is binding does not mean that it necessarily has direct effect and can be relied upon by an individual directly to enforce a right. The solution found by the Court as regards failure by a Member State to implement an act of the Community which is binding and is intended to give rights to individuals but lacks the necessary qualities to have direct effect is a remedy in damages for loss to the individual occasioned by the Member State's failure.[88] Perhaps this is also the legal solution for failure by the Community institutions to give effect to the Association Council decisions.

At the moment, for the purposes of individual workers from third states living in a Member State, the key to accessing the benefits of the agreements (which inevitably means defeating a national administrative decision or legislative provision) is a finding of direct effect. In other words, if the potential prize under the agreement, for instance aggregation of social security contributions made in more than one Member State for the purpose of calculating a benefit, is subject as regards its execution or effects to the adoption of a subsequent act, the worker will not be able directly to enforce a remedy[89] even if that subsequent act is the responsibility of the Community alone, and must look to other remedies. But if it is not subject to such a qualification, for instance equal treatment as regards social security generally, the remedy will be awarded directly through Community law.[90] It is always

---

86 These were the Dutch, German, Greek and French Governments.
87 C-277/94 *Taflan-Met* [1996] ECR I-4085.
88 C-6, 9/90 *Francovich* [1991] ECR I-5357.
89 C-277/94 *Taflan-Met* [1996] ECR I-4085.
90 C-18/90 *Kziber* [1991] ECR I-199, C-262/96 *Sürül* [1999] ECR I-2685.

possible too, for an individual who has been unable to get a remedy from a national court to seek either directly or through his or her lawyers that the Commission use its powers of enforcement to bring an action against the Member State which is refusing the right. The individual can also, even where a third country national, seek that the European Parliament through its Committee on Petitions raise the question with the Commission and the Council.

3.6. CONCLUSIONS

I asked three questions at the beginning of this chapter, it may now be useful to distil the answers which derive from this discussion, how are the agreements part of Community law and what does this mean: while the agreements in their entirety are part of Community law, the responsibility for implementation of the undertakings contained depends on the division of competence between the Community and the Member States for the subject matter. Where the Community has exercised its competence in a field covered by an agreement then it will have exclusive external competence. Where it has not done so the competence will at best be mixed. Where the competence is reserved to the Member States then they are responsible for implementation.

Secondly, I asked, does the Court of Justice have competence to interpret these agreements: here the answer is emphatically yes. It is the Court's duty to determine where the dividing lines of competence lie for the purpose of question 1 and to interpret the content of the obligations undertaken. The Court has willingly accepted its competence in respect of third country agreements. The third question was: do the same principles of interpretation applicable to the EC Treaty and its subsidiary legislation apply to these agreements: according to the case law of the Court the answer depends on the wording, nature and purpose of the agreement which must be determined in respect of each agreement and each provision therein. However, this finding in itself indicates a similarity of approach. Where the provisions of an agreement reveal the characteristics necessary then the same principles of interpretation apply.

CHAPTER FOUR

THE EARLY AGREEMENTS, THEIR DEVELOPMENTS AND BENEFICIARIES

4.1. INTRODUCTION

In the last chapter I looked at the legal value of third country agreements in Community law. The importance of these agreements for the development of Community immigration law arises from the inclusion in them of provisions relating to economic activities and residence for nationals of the Contracting Parties. The impact of these agreements on policy only manifested in the 1990s but the seeds were sown in particular through the 1970s. In this chapter I will look at the migrant workers who acquire rights through the agreements specifically by reference to the early agreements. The questions which I will examine are as follows:

1. Is there a coherent pattern to the choice of countries with which agreements were settled and which contain provisions relating to labour?

2. Are the agreements coherent between themselves and what relationship do they have to one another?

3. How were the provisions on labour perceived at the time of entry into force and how do they fit into the development of an immigration policy of the Union?

Of the initial third country agreements settled by the Community only those with Greece[1] in 1961 and Turkey[2] in 1963 included provisions on movement of workers, the self employed and service provision. Both these agreements were intended to lead to accession. Both suffered from substantial delay in implementation on account of political turbulence in those countries. The Greece Agreement was delayed on account of the military takeover in that country in the mid 1960s and it was not until the return of democratic rule in 1974 that the way was open again to proceed towards accession. The accession agreement was finally signed in 1979. The Turkey Agreement acquired an additional protocol of particular importance to the position of workers in 1970. The Association Council established under the agreement was active promulgating Decisions to give effect to the gradual achievement of free movement from

---

1   63/106/EEC OJ 1963 293.
2   Confirmed by Council Decision 64/732 OJ 1973 C 113/1.

1976 (Decision 2/76) to 1980 (Decisions 1/80 and 3/80) when co-operation became strained as a result of the military coup in Turkey. By the time of the return to civilian rule in Turkey the political climate in Western Europe had moved on. The continuing concerns about human rights abuses in Turkey voiced most strenuously by the European Parliament have slowed progress towards accession though following the Helsinki European Council meeting in December 1999 it is now a candidate.[3]

The Yaounde Agreement concluded in 1963[4] with 18 countries in Africa, the Caribbean and Pacific included no provision on labour in its initial form but acquired bits as it went along. Rather than an accession agreement, this was more of a succession agreement: providing a close relationship with the Community for countries which had been colonies or otherwise ruled by Member States. On each re-negotiation it acquired more parties and changed its name to Lomé. It remains an unusual agreement in that it is multilateral, a form generally avoided by the Community. It is time limited requiring re-negotiation or extension at fixed points. By the end of the second re-negotiation in 1975, Lomé had acquired at Article 62 a provision on non-discrimination on nationality grounds in the exercise of self employment and services for nationals of the parties which was subsequently suppressed in the fourth re-negotiation. When Lomé III was settled in 1979 a declaration was annexed to the agreement including provisions on labour which corresponded to those provisions in the Maghreb Agreements (see below).

The Maghreb Agreements, foreseen in the declaration to the original Treaty, were settled in 1969 (with the exception of the Algeria Agreement) but it was not until their re-negotiation in 1976 that provisions on labour were included. They are individual agreements with each Maghreb state though the texts are identical. New agreements were signed with Tunisia in 1995 and Morocco in 1996, of which the Tunisia Agreement came into force on 1 March 1998. A new agreement with Algeria has been delayed on account of the political situation in that country. As regards the provisions of importance to the protection of migrant workers no diminution of rights occurred as a result of the re-negotiation.[5] The agreements with the Maghreb and Yugoslavia were never intended to lead to accession of those states to the Community. The agreements with Israel and Jordan are referred to in the same context as the Maghreb Agreements because of the similarity of the context.

---

3   Commission backs inviting all applicants to start talks, European Voice, 7-13 October 1999, p. 1. See also Conclusions from the Helsinki European Council Meeting 10-11 December 1999.

4   OJ 1964 1431.

5   There was a clarification that the rights accrued only to lawful workers. It is arguable whether this is in fact a diminution of rights or merely a clarification.

Also in 1976, the Yugoslavia Agreement was re-negotiated and identical provisions to those contained in the Maghreb Agreements on labour were included there. It has subsequently been denounced as a result of the civil war and new agreements with the successor states either have been negotiated or are contemplated.

A gap then occurs as regards the settling of agreements containing provisions relating either to the movement or protection of persons until the negotiation of the agreements with the Central and Eastern European countries (CEEC) post 1990. During that time no provisions on labour were included in agreements. However, this also coincides with a fairly slow period for the Community in the settling of third country agreements.[6] The contents of the CEEC Agreements will be dealt with in a separate chapter, as to some extent the treatment of persons in those agreements may be seen as the lesson learned by the Community from these initial experiments in dealing with immigration-related issues through third country agreements.

Some Initial Observations on Third Country Agreements

Third country agreements, like the EC Treaty itself, cover a wide range of issues primarily relating to commercial affairs such as the treatment of products originating from the parties in the territory of the other. The engine of such agreements is commercial necessity or facility, just as was the case for the EC Treaty. Very few agreements contain provisions relating to workers or persons. To the extent that they do contain such provisions, these are secondary to the overall purpose of the agreements, which is trade driven.

Such a view is not only apparent from the text of the agreements but also from the treatment they receive at the hands of academics and lawyers. For example, in 1974 for any lawyer even marginally interested in workers, the Greece and Turkey Agreements with the EC would have stood out as differentiated from other third country agreements of the time by the inclusion of provisions on labour. However in a detailed analysis albeit focussing on customs tariffs, these agreements are lumped as a single category with the agreements with Tunisia, Morocco, Spain, Israel, Malta, Cyprus, Lebanon, Egypt and Yugoslavia.[7] Further, for such lawyers, the most interesting aspect of the 1976 Maghreb Agreements is that they inserted provisions on workers which had not been included in the earlier 1969 Agreements (notwithstanding

---

6   D. Phinnemore, *Association: Stepping-Stone or Alternative to EU Membership*, Sheffield Academic Press, Sheffield 1999.
7   D. Touret, Le Tarif Douanier Commun de la CEE et les problèmes posés par son application, Cahiers de droit européen (1974), p. 323.

pressure from Morocco and Tunisia for their inclusion[8]). However, the description of these new agreements at the time in the leading French European law journal makes no mention of this feature.[9]

Just as was the case in respect of the EC Treaty, the cocktail of areas covered by the third country agreements was such that interest in and emphasis on the treatment of workers was considered marginal if of interest at all. Even in an in-depth analysis of foreigners in Community law in 1975, out of almost 30 pages, two-and-a-half are devoted to a consideration of rights of persons under third country agreements.[10] This, however may be an indication of the weight which was given to such provisions in third country agreements before the decisions of the Court of Justice on their potential and actual direct effect in the 1990s. Indeed, even a group of eminent experts concerned with the legal status of third country nationals within the Community meeting in the mid 1980s did not consider the third country agreements of particular importance.[11]

4.2. THE AGREEMENTS AND PROVISIONS ON LABOUR

In 1974 the European Commission published an Action Programme for Migrant Workers and their Family Members.[12] It specifically included migrant workers from third countries in its proposals. It noted first, that while in 1959 three-quarters of migrant workers in the Community of Six were Italian nationals and less than one-third came from third countries, by 1973 these percentages were reversed in a Community of Nine. This was of course the result of very substantial inward labour migration to the Community but particularly to Germany and the Benelux countries from Turkey and to France from the Maghreb. In the Commission's opinion expressed in the Work Programme, non-discrimination in working and living conditions for all migrant workers was a primary goal.[13]

---

8   A. Dubois, L'association de la Tunisie et du Maroc à la Communauté, Revue du Marché Commun (1969), p. 355.
9   Cahiers de droit européen (1976), p. 465.
10 W. Much and J.Cl. Séché, Les droits de l'étranger dans les communautes européennes, Cahiers de droit européen, 1975, p. 267.
11 K. Groenendijk, Strategien zur Verbesserung des Rechtsstatus von Drittstaatsangehöriger, K. Barwig, G. Brinkmann, L. Huber, K. Lorcher and C. Schumacher, *Vom Ausländer zum Bürger: Problemanzeigen in Ausländer-, Asyl- und Staatsangehörigkeitsrecht*, Nomos Verlagsgesellschaft, Baden-Baden, 1994, p. 413.
12 21 January 1974.
13 Commissie van de Europese Gemeenschappen, Actieprogramma ten behoeve van de migrerende werknemers en hun gezinnen, Bulletin 3/76.

Further, the Commission recommended the inclusion of third country nationals in the Community provisions relating to social security by progressive steps.[14] The Work Programme was followed two years later by a Council Resolution on 9 February 1976 approving the Programme which included at Article 2(c) approval of non-discrimination in working conditions for third country national workers legally resident in the Community.[15]

The wider political context also provided impetus for the inclusion of provisions on labour in the Community's third country agreements. It was after 1975 that labour and social security provisions began to appear in third country agreements and, in respect of the Turkey Agreement, its subsidiary legislation. This follows the publication of the Commission's Work Programme, and indicates a cross-fertilisation of approach: while the Commission's Work Programme was concerned with the position of third country national workers in general, the agreements provide specific protection for nationals of the Contracting Parties. The political decision to restrict labour migration into the main destination countries of North Western Europe in 1973/4 was to no small extent informed by rising unemployment. Castles and Kosack characterise this as part of the view of immigrant labour as expendable and short-term.[16] However, at the national and international level it was accompanied by the adoption of legal measures to protect immigrant labour already integrated into the European labour market from discrimination in working conditions.[17] It would not be entirely correct to see this as altruistic. The immigration stop was designed to protect domestic labour from foreign labour competition. The adoption of equal treatment rules on working conditions and wages of resident immigrant workers while protecting the position of immigrant workers also prevents them from competing with domestic labour by accepting lower wages and worse working conditions, and thereby exacerbating domestic unemployment, an argument consistently voiced by trade unions. However, the international framework on non-discrimination in working conditions did not also protect immigrant worker from expulsion on economic grounds such as unemployment. Therefore equal treatment rules coupled with either *de facto* or

---

14 "Ten einde dit doel te bereiken zou men in achtereenvolgende etappen:
 - de nationaliteit als criterium voor het toekennen van bepaalde prestaties moeten opheffen." Commissie van de Europese Gemeenschappen, Actieprogramma ten behoeve van de migrerende werknemers en hun gezinnen, Bulletin 3/76.

15 Resolutie van de Raad van 9 februari 1976 betreffende een actieprogramma ten behoeve van migrerende werknemers en hun gezinsleden. Bulletin 3/76.

16 S. Castles and G. Kosack, The Function of Labour Migration in the United Kingdom and the European Union in P. Braham, *Discrimination and Disadvantage in Employment; the experience of black workers*, Harper & Row, London, 1981.

17 See Chapter 2.

de jure preferences for nationals or EC labour in recruitment in fact placed migrant workers in a more precarious position as regards their residence rights in the Member States. The actual provisions prohibiting discrimination in working conditions were not sufficiently strong in themselves to protect the right to continue employment for workers and thus provide no protection from expulsion on the basis of unemployment.[18]

4.3. THE AGREEMENTS, THEIR COUNCILS AND SUBSIDIARY LEGISLATION

The third country agreements all contain provisions for the establishment of an Association or Cooperation Council to adopt measures to give effect to the general intention of the agreements. The role of these Councils as apparent from the text of the agreements is important. As these agreements tend to be less defined than the EC Treaty as regards rights, decisions of the Councils are critical to giving particularity to general competences.[19] The result is that fewer provisions of such third country agreements themselves are likely to be found to have the necessary clarity, precision and unconditionality to give rise to direct effect. Instead the Association and Cooperation Councils are instructed to draft the necessary measures to give such particularity to the agreements.

In respect of the agreements which are of interest here, the Association Council established under the Turkey Agreement is unique in having fulfilled to some extent at least its duties as regards measures on workers. It first adopted, in 1976, Decision 2/76 providing a framework for the protection of work and residence rights for Turkish workers within the territory of the Community (and Community workers in Turkey on a reciprocal basis). It is worth noting that this coincided with the year the Maghreb Agreements were renegotiated and which for the first time included provisions on labour. A certain parallelism may be discerned. This Decision of the Association Council established under the Turkey Agreement was followed by Decision 1/80 of 1980 (which to some extent replaced Decision 2/76[20]) and Decision 3/80 which finally gave

---

18 C-416/96 *El Yassini* [1999] ECR I-1209.
19 For a particularly clear example of this see below regarding the EC Macedonia Agree-ment where a very general competence is ceded to the Co-operation Council to regulate self-employment for legal and natural persons. No right accrues to an individual as a result of that provision but the Co-operation Council is empowered to promulgate decisions in respect of this.
20 This replacement was only partial as some provisions of Decision 2/76, most notably the standstill clause on the introduction of more restrictive national legislation, were held by the Court to have direct effect in a 1990 judgment (C-192/89 *Sevince* [1990] ECR I-3461).

particularity to the commitments under the agreement regarding social security rights.

As regards the other agreements, the Co-operation Councils have been silent on measures relating to workers. In respect of the Maghreb Agreements this is somewhat surprising as under the provisions relating to social security the Councils were specifically charged with adopting implementing legislation. Nonetheless, the failure of the Councils to do so did not inhibit the Court of Justice from finding the provision itself, without implementing measures as required, to have direct effect.[21]

Greece and Turkey

In 1961 the Community's external competence was exercised for the first time under Article 310 EC to enter into an association agreement with Greece[22] which foresaw the possibility of accession of Greece to the Community. That agreement included in Title II on Movement of Persons and Services, provisions for the achievement of free movement of workers.[23] However, the intervention of a military dictatorship meant that this did not occur for another two decades.[24] In 1963 a similar agreement[25] was concluded with Turkey however provisions relating to movement of persons were less definite than those in the Greece Agreement. Turkey had first applied for association with the Community on 31.7.1959. No date has been set for accession of that country to the Union and indeed it appears increasingly unlikely that this will take place within the first decade of the next century, as the Union will be absorbing the accession of the Central and Eastern European countries with which accession negotiations began in 1998 (to the express exclusion of Turkey). As Peers concluded in the EU's efforts to "bolster the pro-European forces in Turkey" the choice was for a Customs Union concluded as an

---

21 C-18/90 *Kziber* [1991] ECR I-199.

22 63/106/EC OJ 1963 293.

23 Articles 44 – 50 of the Greece Agreement.

24 "Depuis le coup d'état militaire survenu en Grèce le 21 avril 1967, chacun a mieux mesuré la signification politique de l'accord d'association. On sait que depuis cette date la Communauté applique la convention et les décisions du Conseil d'association dans la mesure où il s'agit uniquement d'obligations précises n'impliquant pas le développement de l'accord au-delà de sa gestion courante. C'est parce qu'elle a constaté que les dispositions de la constitution relative aux libertés individuelles et celles portant sur l'organisation des partis et des élections n'etaient pas appliquées que la Commission maintient la même attitude aujourd'hui encore." Droit et politique des relations extérieures des Communautés européennes, J.-V. Louis, Cahiers de droit européen (1971), p. 5.

25 Confirmed by Council Decision 64/732 OJ 1973 C 113/1.

alternative to membership in 1995. As a vehicle, it has serious flaws, not least the lack of tools of legal integration, for instance its deficient institutional structure.[26] Finally, on 6 December 1999 at the Helsinki European Council meeting, the EU offered to commence accession discussions with Turkey. The conditions, most notably, a substantial improvement in human rights standards and acceptance of the jurisdiction of the International Court of Justice as regards the territorial disputes between Greece and Turkey were accepted.

No provision of either the Greece or Turkey Agreements required the Community to change the associated status to full membership. Article 28 of the Turkey Agreement does, however, require the contracting parties to examine the possibility of the accession of Turkey to the Community.

In the Greece Agreement three provisions deal with the three freedoms for natural persons covered in the EC Treaty: workers, self-employed and service providers. These are contained in a Title "Movement of Persons and Services."[27]

Notwithstanding the title, it is unlikely that any of the provisions in themselves was likely to have direct effect. Indeed, the proviso in Article 47 that the time limit and procedures applicable to the right of establishment in the Treaty shall not apply to the Greece Agreement indicates that the Member States were already well aware of the potential direct effect of Article 43 EC.[28] However a clear intention to achieve freedom of movement for persons is evidenced. This

---

26 S. Peers, Living in Sin: Legal Integration Under the EC Treaty – Turkey Customs Union, 7 EJIL (1996), pp. 411-430.

27 Greece Agreement
    Article 44
    "Freedom of movement for workers under Articles 39 and 40 of the Treaty establishing the Community shall be secured between Member States and Greece at a date and in accordance with rules to be determined by the Council of Association, but not before the end of the transitional period laid down in Article 6 of this Agreement."
    Article 47
    "The Contracting Parties shall, in progressive and balanced stages, facilitate the establishment of nationals of Member States in the territory of Greece and of nationals of Greece within the Community, in accordance with the principles of Article 52 [43] to 56 [47] and Article 58 [49] of the Treaty establishing the Community, except for the provisions of those Articles which lay down time limits and the procedure for attaining freedom of establishment."
    Article 49
    "The Council of Association shall, during the transitional period laid down in Article 6 of this Agreement, decide on the appropriate measures to be adopted to facilitate the provision of services between the Community and Greece."

28 This makes their apparent surprise at this possible effect of Article 43 EC expressed in 2/74 Reyners [1974] ECR 631 somewhat disingenuous.

is not so apparent in the Turkey Agreement. In that Agreement, a reference to workers is only contained under the heading Other Economic Provisions at Article 12.[29]

Article 9 of the Turkey Agreement was also of substantial importance in that it mirrors Article 12 EC providing a right to non-discrimination within the scope of application of the agreement. This would be argued in some depth and with some success before the Court of Justice in 1999.[30]

The direct reference to the Community provision indicated an intention that there would be an assimilation of interpretation of the two.[31]

It was not until the adoption of an additional protocol under the agreement in 1970 that a title on Movement of Persons and Services was included. The provisions contained in the protocol are substantially more generous than those which appear in the Greece Agreement, giving greater specificity to the intentions of the parties. The most important in respect of workers are Articles 36 and 37.[32]

---

29 Turkey Agreement:
Article 12
"The Contracting Parties agree to be guided by Articles 48 [39], 49 [40] and 50 [41] of the Treaty establishing the Community for the purpose of progressively securing freedom of movement for workers between themselves."

30 Turkey Agreement:
Article 9
"The Contracting Parties recognise that within the scope of this Agreement and without prejudice to any special provisions which may be laid down pursuant to Article 8, any discrimination on the grounds on nationality shall be prohibited in accordance with the principle laid down in Article 7[12] of the Treaty establishing the Community." It has recently been referred to by the Advocate General in the case of C-37/98 *Savas* (25 November 1999) "C'est par conséquent, en se référant à l'application, par les États membres, d'autres dispositions normatives à des situations prévues et réglementées par des conventions que l'article 9 précité leur impose l'obligation de ne pas traiter différemment, en l'absence d'une justification logique et adéquate, leurs propres ressortissants et les ressortissants turcs résident sur le territoire de l'État en cause." It was also considered in the context of discrimination against Turkish nationals in social security benefits C-262 *Sürül*[1999] ECR I-2685.

31 EC Treaty:
Article 12
"Within the scope of application of this Treaty and without prejudice to any special provisions contained therein, any discrimination on grounds of nationality shall be prohibited."

32 Turkey Association Agreement: Additional Protocol
Article 36
"Freedom of movement for workers between Member States of the Community and Turkey shall be secured by progressive stages in accordance with the principles set out in Article 12 of the Agreement of Association between the end of the twelfth and the

The wording of Article 37 on non-discrimination in working conditions is close to that of Article 39(2) EC and matches very closely the wording used later in the Maghreb Agreements covering the same area and which have been held to have direct effect[33] which wording then travelled from the Maghreb Agreements to the declaration annexed to Lomé.[34] As regards self employment and services, the protocol contains a clear standstill clause which did not exist in the Greece Agreement.[35] This provision matches and indeed is even clearer than the equivalent standstill clause relating to self-employment in the Article 44 EC.[36]

The object of both the Greece and Turkey Agreements was accession to the Community. Article 6 of the Greece Agreement provided for a transitional period of 12 years. The Turkey Agreement contained a series of transitional periods: first a five-year period for a preparatory stage which could be extended to nine years. Secondly a transitional period of 12 years for the gradual abolition of customs barriers and the adaptation of the common customs tariff. The customs union was finally achieved after much delay on 31 December 1995.[37] According to reports of the time, the reason for the very long transitional periods and more limited scope of the Turkey Agreement was "the enormous economic and social differences between Turkey and the Com-

---

twenty-second year after the entry into force of that Agreement. The Council of Association shall decide on the rules necessary to that end."
Article 37
"As regards conditions of work and remuneration, the rules which each Member State applies to workers of Turkish nationality employed in the Community shall not discriminate on grounds of nationality between such workers and workers who are nationals of other Member States of the Community."
33 C-18/90 Kziber [1991] ECR I-199.
34 EC Treaty
Article 39(2)
"Such freedom of movement shall entail the abolition of any discrimination based on nationality between workers of the Member States as regards employment, remuneration and other conditions of work and employment."
35 Turkey Agreement: Additional Protocol
Article 41
"1. The Contracting Parties shall refrain from introducing between themselves any new restrictions on the freedom of establishment and the freedom to provide services."
36 EC Treaty:
Article 44
"Member States shall not introduce any new restrictions on the right of establishment in their territories of nationals of other Member States, save as otherwise provided in this Treaty."
37 Decision 1/95 OJ 1995 L 35/1.

munity".[38] Both the Greece and Turkey Agreements sparked off heated debate in the European Parliament.[39] A complaint which would occur continuously from the Parliament arose in respect of these agreements: it objected to the fact that the agreements were signed before it had been consulted.[40] It considered that the manner of conclusion of the agreements constituted a violation of Article 310 EC as the Parliament's advice would have little influence as the agreements had already been signed.[41] The achievement of the customs union in 1995 as foreseen by the Turkey Agreement raised bitter debate in the European Parliament where many MEPs were opposed to the move on the basis of reported widespread human rights abuses in Turkey.

Under the agreement, during the transitional stages, the Council of Association established under the agreement was charged with reviewing and making recommendations regarding "the geographical and occupational mobility of workers of Turkish nationality, in particular the extension of work and residence permits in order to facilitate the employment of those workers in each Member State".[42] The Association Council duly carried out its task of adopting decisions in respect of workers – first Decision 2/76, which was replaced by Decision 1/80 which came into force on 1 July 1980[43] and Decision 3/80, the date of entry into force of which has only recently been determined.[44] According to the agreement the end of the transitional period for workers was to have been in 1986. I will revisit these decisions later when considering the coherence of the contents of measures on Community nationals and third country nationals.

4.4.   YAOUNDE TO LOMÉ IV

In 1963, the same year as the Turkey Agreement, the Community concluded an agreement with 18 African states, the original Yaounde Agreement[45] which developed into the Lomé Agreements. These agreements succeeded one another – the Yaounde Agreement was replaced in 1969 by the Lomé I Agreement then Lomé II in 1975 which extended its scope to include countries

---

38 Legislation, CMLRev (1963-64) p. 372.
39 J. Costonis, The Treaty Making Power of the European Economic Community: the Perspectives of a Decade CMLRev 1966/67, p. 421.
40 Resolution European Parliament OG 2906/63.
41 Relationship with third countries, CMLRev (1963/64), p. 471.
42 Article 38, Additional Protocol.
43 Article 30, Decision 1/80.
44 C-277/94 *Taflan-Met* [1996] ECR I-4085.
45 OJ 1964 1431.

with historical links with one of the new, at that time, Member States, the UK. At the moment, the Lomé IV Agreement covers: Angola, Antigua and Barbuda, Bahamas, Barbados, Belize, Benin, Botswana, Burkina Faso, Burundi, Cameroon, Cape Verde, Central African Republic, Chad, Comores, Congo, Djibouti, Dominica, Dominican Republic, Eritrea, Ethiopia, Fiji, Gabon, Gambia, Ghana, Grenada, Guinea, Guinea-Bissau, Equatorial Guinea, Guyana, Haiti, Ivory Coast, Jamaica, Kenya, Kiribati, Lesotho, Liberia, Madagascar, Malawi, Mali, Mauritius, Mozambique, Namibia, Niger, Nigeria, Papua New Guinea, Rwanda, Saint Christopher Nevis, Saint Lucia, Saint Vincent and Grenadines, Sao Tome and Principe, Solomon Islands, Senegal, Seychelles, Sierra Leone, Somalia, Sudan, Surinam, Swaziland, Tanzania, Togo, Tonga, Trinidad and Tobago, Tuvalu, Uganda, Vanuatu, Western Samoa, [Zaire], Zambia and Zimbabwe. It is beyond the scope of this book to explain why those former colonies which are not on the list are absent or why those which are so appear. A search for coherence here would require substantial effort.

The objective of the agreement is to promote and expedite the economic, cultural and social development of the ACP States and to consolidate and diversify their relations in a spirit of solidarity and mutual interest. As revised in 1979, Lomé III includes Annex VI which contains a common declaration on workers nationals of the parties lawfully resident on the territory of one of the contracting states.[46]

The development of this article appears to be from a wording very close to Article 39(2) EC in the additional protocol to the Turkey Agreement to a slightly different wording but apparently the same intended content in the Maghreb Agreements and from there to the Lomé II Agreement. Its formulation in Lomé II was informed by the similar provisions which had been

---

46 *Lomé II Agreement*
Annex VI
"1. Each Member State shall accord to workers who are nationals of an ACP State legally employed in its territory treatment free from any discrimination based on nationality, as regards working conditions and pay, in relation to its own nationals.
Each ACP State shall accord the same treatment to workers who are nationals of the Member States legally employed on its territory.
Workers who are nationals of an ACP State legally employed in the territory of a Member State and members of their families living with them shall, as regards social security benefits linked to employment in that Member State, enjoy treatment free from any discrimination based on nationality in relation to nationals of that Member State.
Each ACP State shall accord to workers who are nationals of Member States and legally employed in its territory, and to members of their families, treatment similar to that laid down in paragraph 1."

included in the Maghreb Agreements three years earlier.[47] These provisions continued to appear in the subsequent Lomé Agreements.

Two aspects are of interest here, first the Community draftsman and legislator approved of consistency as regards the wording and content of the rights to persons between agreements with different states. This intention was expressed in a Council Resolution of 21 January 1974 among measures intended to co-ordinate provisions on migration.[48] Secondly, once such a provision is included in an agreement, even one of limited duration such as the Lomé agreements, on re-negotiation backtracking is unusual.

The question, however, arises: can a commitment made in an Annex have legal effects equivalent to those of a provision of a third country agreement itself? The Court of Justice had to consider a protocol to Lomé IV in the context of the "bananas" disputes.[49] Writing just after the Court's decision, Peers was not convinced that an Annex to the Lomé IV Agreement could enjoy the same interpretation as a Protocol. He only went so far as to confirm the Court's existing jurisprudence[50] that a declaration can confirm the intentions of the parties as indicated in the main text of the agreement.[51] He argues that as there is no provision in the main agreement to which the Annex's declaration can attach it is unlikely to have direct effect.

Relying on the analysis of declarations in Community law of A. Toth,[52] Van Raepenbusch considered that the existence of a provision of the Lomé IV Agreement itself was necessary before the Annex could be considered to have sufficient strength to be directly effective. Further he notes that Article 368 of the agreement only provides that protocols form an integral part of the agreement. It is silent as regards the Annexes containing the declarations.[53]

---

47 J.Cl. Gautron, De Lomé I à Lomé II: La Convention ACP-EEC du 31 octobre 1979, Cahiers de droit européen, 1980, p. 431.

48 W. Much and J.Cl. Séché, Les droits de l'étranger dans les communautes européennes, Cahiers de droit européen, 1975, p. 267.

49 C-469/93 *Chiquita Italia SpA* [1995] ECR I-4533.

50 C-280/93 *Germany v Commission* [1994] ECR I-4973.

51 S. Peers, Towards Equality: Actual and Potential Rights of Third Country Nationals in the European Union, CMLRev 33: 7-50 [1996].

52 A. G. Toth, The Legal Status of the Declarations annexed to the Single European Act, CMLRev, 1986, p. 806.

53 S. van Raepenbusch, La Jurisprudence de la Cour de justice des Communautés euro-péennes vis-à-vis des ressortissants des pays tiers, in M. Den Boer, The Implementation of Schengen: First the Widening, Now the Deepening, European Institute of Public Administration, Maastricht, 1997.

Elsewhere, Martin and I have argued[54] that the Annex may be capable of direct effect even though it is the only provision of the agreement which in practice covers the position of migrant workers. Our argument is based on the wording itself of the provision which is much stronger than that used in other declarations and mirrors the wording in the Maghreb Agreements. We concluded that the wording contains a sufficiently unconditional and precise obligation as to fulfil the direct effect requirements of Community law. As regards the effect of an Annex, we referred to the Court's finding in two cases that there is no hierarchy between the provisions of the text, in that case a Regulation and an Annex,[55] though in those cases the Court specifically referred to the fact that the Regulation or Annex were adopted pursuant to the same article of the Treaty, i.e. they implemented a Treaty provision. I am less convinced now than I was then that in fact the Lomé IV Annex can have direct effect. Nonetheless, it seems to me wrong in principle that workers of the ACP states should be promised equal treatment in exactly the same wording as that which protects workers from Maghreb countries in the agreement which their states settled with the Community, but then on purely technical grounds be told that the promise is of no real value to them. But their neighbours from Tunisia or Morocco are allowed to rely on the exact same wording to sustain a claim, for instance, to equal treatment in young persons' allowances.[56]

A more uncertain fate befell another provision of the Lomé II Agreement, which on its wording might have been thought to have at least a similar claim to direct effect as the bananas protocol. The timing of the two cases may explain to some extent the difference in treatment – the bananas decision came in 1995, while the dispute on non-discrimination in establishment and services arose in 1977, at a much earlier stage in the development of the jurisprudence on third country agreements. This early dispute revolved around the non-discrimination provision regarding services and establishment found at Article 62 of Lomé II. It is one of the very few examples of a reversal of rights of workers in re-negotiation of agreements.

Article 62 Lomé II[57] is perhaps not that far from the wording of Article 43 EC on establishment, though the second sentence has no equivalent in the EC

---

54 D. Martin and E. Guild, *Free Movement of Persons in the European Union*, Butterworths, London, 1996, p. 290.
55 C-12/93 *Drake* [1994] ECR I-4337; C-227/94 *Olivieri-Coenen* [1995] ECR I-301.
56 C-18/90 *Kziber* [1991] ECR I-199.
57 *Lomé II*
    Article 62
    "As regards the arrangements that may be applied in matters of establishment and provision of services, the ACP States on the one hand and the Member States on the other shall treat nationals and companies or firms of Member States and nationals and

Treaty. Another and potentially important difference was the use of the word "may" in Article 62 which inserted a substantial degree of state discretion. This was not, however, the basis of the decision which deprived the provision of its value for ACP nationals. A national of Madagascar, Mr Razanatsimba, had completed all his legal training in France and obtained all the certificates necessary to qualify as an advocate. However, France applied a nationality requirement to the profession of advocate which excluded him as he did not hold French citizenship. He argued that, on the basis of Article 62, as he wished no more than to provide legal services in France the discriminatory treatment accorded to him was unlawful. The Court did not agree. Its reasoning was that the wording of Article 62 refers to two groups of states, the Member States and the ACP states and does no more than require non-discrimination between the two groups. Therefore for example, Madagascar could not treat differently a German national in comparison with a Dutch national, and vice-versa.

On the basis of a bilateral agreement between France and Malagasy, advocates were permitted to provide services in each other's state on a non-discriminatory basis. The argument of Mr Razanatsimba continued that as a Malagasy national could provide legal services in France on the basis of that bilateral agreement, the same treatment must be afforded to him on the basis of Article 62. Not so according to the Court of Justice:

> "It suffices to find that it is not contrary to the rule as to non-discrimination laid down in Article 62 for a Member State to reserve more favourable treatment to the nationals of one ACP State, provided that such treatment results from the provisions of an international agreement comprising reciprocal rights and advantages".[58]

This decision contrasts with the interpretation of non-discrimination in Community law where the benefit of a bilateral agreement covering matters even outside the scope of the Treaty must be made available to a migrant worker's child in the Member State on a non-discriminatory basis with own nationals.[59]

Almost as surprising as the decision itself is the complete lack of interest which it aroused in the legal press. The *Razanatsimba* decision was handed down on 24 November 1977. In the same year (1977), a number of decisions were reached by the Court regarding freedom of establishment in the liberal profes-

---

companies or firms of the ACP States respectively on a non-discriminatory basis. However, if, for a given activity, an ACP State or a Member State is unable to provide such treatment, the Member States or the ACP States, as the case may be, shall not be bound to accord such treatment for this activity to the nationals and companies or firms of the State concerned."

58 65/77 *Razanatsimba* [1977] ECR 2229.
59 235/87 *Matteucci* [1988] ECR 5589.

sions. The foremost French Community law journal, *Cahiers de droit européen*, included in its commentary the following year, 1978, a number of articles on the topic not one of which made reference to the case. In one,[60] the author specifically considers the question of lawyers from non-Member States but makes no mention of the Lomé Agreement or the case. Further, in a detailed note on the right of establishment and equivalence of diplomas, published slightly later in the same year and same journal, on the question of provision of legal services the author specifically mentions French bilateral arrangements with African countries (self-evidently including those under consideration in the *Razanatsimba* case) but makes no mention of the Lomé Agreement or the Court's decision.[61] The provision on establishment survived from the 1976 Agreement[62] to Lomé II[63] to Lomé III[64] but is not to be found in this form in Lomé III,[65] which refers to service provision but not establishment.

Around the same time as the Yaounde Agreement in 1963, agreements were settled with a variety of countries such as Iran[66] and Israel[67] and a multilateral agreement which eventually lead to the World Trade Agreement.[68] There is no apparent pattern to the countries with which the EC chose to enter into agreements of one kind or the other. However, in none of these agreements were provisions on labour included.[69]

4.5. THE MAGHREB AGREEMENTS

Again on the basis of Article 310 EC agreements were entered into with Tunisia and Morocco in 1969[70] however these agreements made no reference to

---

60 P. J. W. de Brauw, La Libéralisation de la profession d'avocat en Europe après la directive émise par le Conseil des Ministres des Communautés européennes du 22 mars 1977, Cahiers de droit européen, 1978, vol. 1, p. 33.

61 G. A. Dal, Observations: droit de libre éstablissement et equivalence des diplomes, Cahiers de droit européen, 1978, vol. 2-3, p. 242.

62 OJ 1976 L 25 Article 62.

63 OJ 1980 L 347 Article 160.

64 OJ L 1986 L 86 Article 252.

65 OJ 1991 L 292.

66 OJ 1963 2555.

67 OJ 1964 1518.

68 Dillon (GATT) 1962 (1962) 3 UST & OIA 2877-99, TIAS No. 5253.

69 In the new agreement with Israel (signed on 19 March 1997) enabling provisions have been included at Articles 29 and 30 for the Association Council to adopt provisions relating to establishment (self-employment) and service provision. Similar provisions are included in the Jordan Agreement signed on 22 June 1999.

70 Tunisia: OJ 1969 L 198/1; Morocco OJ 1969 L 197/1.

workers or natural persons. These two states had only gained independence in 1956 a year before the EC Treaty. While Algeria and a number of other now independent countries were still dependants of France in 1957 when the Treaty was signed and therefore were subsumed into the provisions relating to overseas territories, these two countries had already gained independence and therefore fell outside those provisions. Declarations were attached to the EC Treaty confirming the intention to enter into agreements with these countries[71] though ten years elapsed before this was accomplished not least on account of the Algerian war of independence which made negotiations politically uncomfortable.[72]

According to an observer (and indeed participant as director of the Council of Ministers of the Community at the time) these two agreements were intended to put Morocco and Tunisia on the same footing as the overseas territories of France.[73]

Morocco and Tunisia did not achieve, in the first agreement, any reference to labour although this was an objective. At the Paris Summit of 1972 it was agreed that the Community should deal with the Mediterranean region globally though not on a multilateral basis as had been adopted for the ACP states. Negotiations for new agreements began in 1973 but were not concluded until 1976. The interim agreements were extended in 1974 for a year and then again pending the completion of negotiations for the second agreements, this time including Algeria, in 1976. On this occasion the Maghreb countries did achieve provisions on equal treatment for their workers in the territory of the Member States as regards working conditions and social security.

In 1975 when reviewing the position of foreigners in Community law, two participants, a Director General of the Commission's Legal Service and a Legal Counsellor of the Commission wrote that the Commission had proposed the extension of some social security rights to Maghreb nationals under the agreements: specifically, the transfer of pensions and invalidity benefits to the country of origin and the payment of family benefits for members of the family within the territory of the Community.[74] Reference is also made to the

---

71 The declaration stated that the Community was willing to conclude economic association Agreements with the independent countries in the franc zone "with a view to maintaining and intensifying the traditional patterns of trade and contributing to the economic development of these countries."

72 A. Dubois, L'association de la Tunisie et du Maroc à la Communauté, Revue du marché commun, (1969) No. 125, p. 355.

73 A. Dubois, L'association de la Tunisie et du Maroc à la Communauté, Revue du marché commun (1969) No. 125, p. 355.

74 W. Much and J. Cl. Séché, Les droits de l'étranger dans les communautes européennes, Cahiers de droit européen, 1975, p. 267.

possibility of an exchange of letters regarding working conditions. In fact, the Maghreb countries secured both provisions in the agreements themselves.

These agreements were never intended to lead to accession. Instead their purpose was and continues to be "to promote overall cooperation between the Contracting Parties with a view to contributing to the economic and social development of [Algeria/Morocco/Tunisia] and helping to strengthen relations between the Parties. To this end provisions and measures will be adopted and implemented in the field of economic, technical and financial co-operation, and in the trade and social fields."[75] On these grounds the Court declined to apply by analogy its jurisprudence on the protection of Turkish workers' employment and residence rights to Maghreb workers.[76]

However, the fact that they confine themselves to a form of co-operation between the parties which is not aimed at securing association or accession of the Maghreb countries to the Community does not preclude the direct effect of certain provisions.[77] On an analysis of the purpose, intent and wording of the articles on non-discrimination in working conditions and social security the Court was satisfied that they fulfilled the requirements of direct effect:

> "That conclusion applies in particular to Article 40 of the EEC Morocco Agreement, which forms part of Title III relating to co-operation in the field of labour, which, far from being purely programmatic in nature, establishes, in the field of working conditions and remuneration, a clear and unconditional principle the nature of which is sufficiently practical that it can be applied by national courts and is therefore capable of directly governing the legal situation of individuals."[78]

It was argued before the Court that a Moroccan worker who had been lawfully admitted to a Member State and had worked there for a number of years on a continuing employment contract was entitled to an extension of his work and residence permits on the basis of Article 40 of the Morocco Agreement. The Court disagreed, first pointing out that even Community nationals may be expelled from a host Member State on the grounds of public policy, security and health, therefore there could be no blanket limitation on expulsion. Secondly the Court differentiated the position of Turkish workers who are better protected under the subsidiary legislation of their agreement, noting the difference of the objectives of the agreements. Thirdly the Court addressed the question of what the prohibition on discrimination in the field of working conditions does mean as regards residence permits. It held:

---

75 Article 1 Morocco Agreement.
76 C-416/96 *El Yassini* [1999] ECR I-1209. Also see C-179/98 *Mesbah* [1999] ECR I-7955.
77 C-18/90 *Kziber* [1991] ECR I-199.
78 C-416/96 *El Yassini* [1999] ECR I-1209.

"The fact that the adoption of such a measure by the competent national authorities will oblige the person concerned to terminate his employment relationship in the host Member State before the contractual term agreed with his employer comes to an end will not, as a general rule, affect that conclusion [that the Member State is not in principle prohibited from refusing to extend the residence permit]. However, the situation would be different if the national court were to find that the host Member State had granted the Moroccan migrant worker specific rights in relation to employment which were more extensive than the rights of residence conferred on him by that State. That would be so if the host Member State had granted the person concerned a residence permit for a period shorter than the duration of his work permit and if, before the work permit expired, it then refused to extend the residence permit without justifying its refusal on grounds relating to the protection of a legitimate national interest, such as public policy, public security or public health."[79]

The consequences of this ruling are exceedingly different in the Member States depending on the underlying system of national law. In Germany there are very important consequences as spouses of German nationals get unlimited work permits but their residence permit may be curtailed on failure of the marriage. Rittsteig has outlined the judgment's consequences there which he considers to be very substantial on account of the interplay between national and Community law.[80] In the Netherlands, according to Groenendijk the consequences are more limited because of the structure of the underlying law where the circumstances where a person may be given a work permit of longer than the residence permit are less frequent.[81] In the UK and in France the consequences at first sight are even more limited as it is very rare for a work permit to have longer duration than a residence permit because of the very wide use of a single document which encompasses both.[82]

These variations which have very substantial consequences for Maghreb workers in different Member States are manifestations of the piecemeal development of Community immigration law. With the new Title IV EC which grants a competence to the Community to take measures on immigration policy on conditions of entry and residence of third country nationals,[83] a more comprehensive approach will need to be adopted. However, to be consistent with the existing interpretation of Community immigration law, particularly as developed in these agreements, the implementing measures will have to adopt the

---

79 C-416/96 *El Yassini* [1999] ECR I-1209.
80 H. Rittstieg, Anmerkung *El Yassini*, InfAuslR 5/99, p. 221.
81 K. Groenendijk, Jurisprudentie Vreemdelingrecht 1999.
82 N. Rogers, Case Note *El Yassini* EJML Vol. 1, Issue 3, p. 355, H. Gacon, Dictionnaire Permanent du Droit des étrangers no. 60. étude Accords CE/Etats tiers, June 1999.
83 Article 63(3)(a) EC.

highest standard of protection of third country nationals if there is to be uniformity at all.

As regards Article 41, on non-discrimination in social security, a long line of cases from the Court of Justice have confirmed its direct effect starting with *Kziber*.[84] It reiterated the same point in 1994,[85] in 1995,[86] in 1996,[87] and again in 1998.[88] In each case a national administration was having difficulty applying the right to non-discrimination on the basis of nationality to Maghreb workers and their family members in respect of specific national benefits. In each case the Court confirmed the direct effect of the provision.

The Maghreb Agreements have now been replaced by new agreements signed in 1995 and 1996 (with the exception of Algeria). The new 1996 Agreement with Tunisia[89] is the first to have come into force,. on 1 March 1998. In addition to the provisions on non-discrimination which appeared in the previous agreement, there is a widening to include non-discrimination in dismissal, a provision which had been included in the CEEC Agreements. Further, it expressly limits the benefit of the agreement to workers lawfully on the territory of the parties. Weber considers this to be no more than a reflection of the Court's case law[90] which position has some justification from the decision in *Krid*[91] upon which he relies but begs the question what is lawful residence, a question to which I will return when I consider the subsidiary legislation of the Turkey Agreement in the next chapter.

In the new agreement another provision appears at Chapter II regarding Dialogue in Social Matters. At Article 69(3)(c) among the matters for such dialogue is "illegal immigration and the conditions governing the return of individuals who are in breach of the legislation dealing with the right to stay and the right of establishment in their host countries". At the time that the agreement entered into force the contents of this provision were within the competence of the Third Pillar of the Treaty on European Union (TEU) and fundamentally intergovernmental. There was no restriction on the Member States as regards this aspect of dialogue. However, after 1 May 1999, the position changes, at least potentially. Article 63(3)(b) EC provides a Community competence regarding "illegal immigration and illegal residence, including

---

84 C-18/90 *Kziber* [1991] ECR I-199.
85 C-58/93 *Yousfi* [1994] ECR I-1353.
86 C-103/94 *Krid* [1995] ECR I-719.
87 C-126/95 *Hallouzi-Choho* [1996] ECR I-4807.
88 C-113/97 *Babahenini* [1998] ECR I-183.
89 OJ 1998 L 97.
90 C. Weber, Die Rechtsstellung tunisischer Staatsangehöriger nach dem neuen Assozi-
    erungsabkomen mit der Europäischer Gemeinschaft, InfAuslR 6/98.
91 C-103/94 *Krid* [1995] ECR I-719.

repatriation of illegal residents". Once this competence has been exercised, at least as far as the adoption by the Commission of a proposal for its exercise, then in accordance with the Community's rules on the relationship between external and internal competence the Member States may no longer exercise powers in this field.[92] The EC Treaty does provide at Article 63 that "Measures adopted by the Council pursuant to points 3 and 4 shall not prevent any Member State from maintaining or introducing in the areas concerned national provisions which are compatible with this Treaty and with international agreements." Exactly how wide a margin this will give the Member States to take unilateral action is unclear. On a strict interpretation, virtually any measure adopted by a Member State which deviates from a Community measure even when the Community measure is silent on a point could be held to be incompatible. Whether such a strict interpretation will be adopted depends to a substantial extent on what the Community and its Court consider to be the importance of the objective of Article 63 EC: the creation of an area of freedom, justice and security. I will return to this issue in the last chapter of this book.

One further important development is the inclusion of a new Title II on the right of establishment and services.[93] This is perhaps one of the more inter-

---

92 For an excellent analysis in general terms of the consequences of Treaty amendments on the external competence of the Community see C. Flaesch-Mougin, Le Traité Maastricht et les compétence externes de la communauté européenne: à la recherche d'une politique externe de l'union, Cahiers de droit européen, 1993 No. 1-2, p. 351.

93 *Tunisia Agreement*
Article 31
1. The Parties agree to widen the scope of this Agreement to cover the right of establishment of one Party's firms on the territory of the other and liberalisation of the provision of services by one Party's firms to consumers of services of the other.
2. The Association Council will make recommendations for achieving the objective described in paragraph 2.
In making such recommendations, the Association Council will take account of part experience of implementation of reciprocal most-favoured-nation treatment and of the respective obligations of each Party under the General Agreement on Trade in Services annexed to the Agreement establishing the WTO, hereinafter referred to as the 'GATS', particularly those in Article V of the latter.
3. The Association Council will make a first assessment of the achievement of this objective no later than five years after the Agreement enters into force.
Article 32
1. At the outset, each of the Parties shall reaffirm its obligations under GATS, particularly the obligation to grant reciprocal most-favoured-nation treatment in the service sectors covered by that obligation.
2. In accordance with the GATS, such treatment shall not apply to:

esting developments of the agreement. In his analysis of the new agreement, Weber does not analyse it, confirming, correctly, that until the Association Council adopts measures to give effect to the right of establishment there is no possibility of it having direct effect. In my view this is nonetheless an important innovation to the agreement: first because the extension of the material scope is vital; secondly because in the reference to GATS the parties bring into play in this context their obligations to one another multilaterally. As I have discussed elsewhere,[94] the concept of service provision in GATS covers four modes, two of which may or must involve the movement of persons: establishment by a company based in one of the General Agreement on Trade in Services (GATS) states of a commercial presence in another GATS state, and the detachment of personnel from a business based in one GATS state to another GATS state to provide services. By affirming their obligations under GATS in this agreement the parties also confirm its application to the implementation of the new powers here. Unfortunately Weber does not consider these issues in his commentary on the new agreement. This provision to adopt measures on establishment and service provision has been included now in the Israel and Jordan Agreements and is proposed for the Egypt and Lebanon Agreements.

Former Yugoslavia

An agreement similar to the 1969 Maghreb Agreements was settled with the former Yugoslavia in 1970[95] then revised along with the Maghreb Agreements to include provisions on labour identical to those in the 1976 Agreements. Indeed, the Yugoslavia Agreement can be classed very easily with the Maghreb Agreements as regards treatment of persons. It was subsequently denounced on the outbreak of civil war in that country.[96]

New agreements have since been concluded with Slovenia[97] and Macedonia.[98] These agreements are decidedly different from the earlier agreement with Yugoslavia and no longer bear any relation to the Maghreb Agreements.

(a) advantages granted by wither Party under the terms of an agreement of the type defined in Article III of the GATS or to measures taken on the basis of such an agreement;

(b) other advantages granted in accordance with the list of exemptions from most-favoured-nation treatment annexed by either Party to the GATS.

94 E. Guild and P. Barth, The Movement of Natural Persons at the GATS: A UK Perspective and European Dilemmas, European Foreign Affairs Review, Autumn 1999, p. 395.

95 OJ 1970 L 58 & L 67.

96 Council Decision 91/602 OJ 1991 L 325/23.

97 Signed on 10 June 1996.

98 OJ 1997 L 348/1.

The agreement with Slovenia follows the formula of the agreements with the Baltic States and is designed to lead to accession of Slovenia to the Union. Indeed, it is one of the states which has been included in the next wave for accession. A consideration of the provisions of this agreement will be included in the chapter on the Central and Eastern European countries as the form and rights contained in it are equivalent to those agreements. Macedonia, however, does not enjoy such privileged treatment – it has lost the equal treatment right for its workers in social security and working conditions and yet gained nothing except a power for the Association Council to regulate establishment.

4.6.   CONCLUSIONS

Notwithstanding the differences, The Maghreb, Machrek, Lomé and Yugoslavia agreements may be treated together insofar as they constitute agreements which regularise the economic relationship of the Community with states either on its physical or historical borders. Their provisions relating to labour have constituted an important step in the development of the Community's migration law on third country nationals though this was only formally acknowledged by the Commission in its Communication of 1991.[99]

Can a coherent pattern be discerned of the states with which the Community began to negotiate agreements which included provisions on labour? Three different elements combine in the pattern: first the inclusion of provisions on labour in agreements where the intention is to lead to accession by the third country to the Community. Such is the case of the Greece and Turkey Agreements. Secondly, a selective geographical approach towards the Mediterranean basin emerges. Thirdly, a very diverse group of countries in Africa, the Caribbean and Pacific enjoy provisions on labour in their multilateral agreement. This is the historical border of the Community: countries which had colonial links in the past with the Member States and which for various reasons retain strong ties.

Is there coherence between the EC Treaty and the agreements' provisions on labour? The relationship between the EC Treaty and the provisions on

---

99   "Looking more closely at the expert's report on policies on immigration and the social integration of migrants in the European Community", two specific proposals may be developed without delay:
- ensuring the observance of commitments already undertaken in Agreements concluded by the Community with non-EC countries providing for non-discrimination of their nationals in matters of remuneration, working conditions and social security" Commission Communication to the Council and the European Parliament on Immigration, SEC(91) 1855 final 23.10.91.

labour in the third country agreements appears close and is consistent with the Commission's Work Programme objectives of 1974 and the Council Resolution of 1976. Specifically, the wording of the provisions relating to labour in these agreements mirrors the corresponding provisions of the EC Treaty with appropriate adaptations to limit their scope to that intended by each agreement. Both sets of agreements (i.e. on the one hand the Greece and Turkey Agreements and on the other the Lomé, Maghreb and Yugoslavia Agreements) include a prohibition, within the scope of the agreements, on discrimination against workers (in their capacity as such) of the contracting parties.

The same framework of approach is utilised in all the agreements: workers, self-employed and service providers. The principal tools for considering labour are similar. The goal in the agreements leading to accession is free movement of workers, establishment and services. This similarity of intent is by no means self-evident. National legislation of the Member States based on discretion and selection does not have this objective. It is designed around labour market needs not a principle of initiative to the individual which is gradually achieved (or not as the case may be for the Turkey Agreement).

In the 1976 Maghreb, Yugoslavia and Lomé Agreements, the tool used is another Community law defining principle: non-discrimination. The framework of all the provisions is Article 39(2) EC. The objective of free movement is not present but the abolition of discrimination remains as a foundation and the areas covered are equivalent. The question of admission to the territory is left in the discretion of the Member States but once admitted, a Community law right to non-discrimination in working conditions and certain social security rights applies. In a sense, workers from these third states get half the Community loaf: no right of movement but a Community equivalent right to non-discrimination. The value of that right, as in respect of any right based on non-discrimination is circumscribed by national law and the advantages and obstacles which a state chooses for its own nationals.

In respect of both sets of agreements, the interpretation given to specific provisions extending protection to workers of those third states has resulted in the diminution of national discretion as regards their treatment and an approximation of their position, again within their limited scope, to that of own nationals. However, a consideration of that interpretation is the subject of a later chapter.

Another striking feature of these agreements as they pass through various stages of re-negotiation is that as regards workers, in only one case (Macedonia) has there been a diminution of rights. The stage of co-operation which is reached in each agreement is the basis for building rather than reconsidering which might result in diminution of protection. This feature is reminiscent of the operation of the EC Treaty itself which, according to its opening words, is "Determined to lay the foundations of an ever-closer union among the peoples of Europe". When the Member States began negotiations with the Central and

Eastern European countries in 1991 no provisions capable of direct effect or indeed guaranteeing non-discrimination in social security rights were included.[100] This decision was the direct result of the jurisprudence, unwelcome for some Member States, of the Court of Justice on the direct effect of the social security provision in the EC Morocco Co-operation Agreement.[101] Notwithstanding this reluctance to let any other country into the privileged group whose nationals get non-discrimination rights in this field, when the Maghreb Agreements were re-negotiated in 1995-6 there was no question of seeking to exclude the provisions from the new agreements.

Finally, how were these agreements perceived at the time they were negotiated? In the great spurt of conclusion of agreements which followed the entry into force of the EC Treaty substantial academic interest was expressed in the powers of the Community to enter into agreements and the meaning of those powers for the Member States.[102] Little or no attention was paid to provisions relating to workers. This situation would not change until the first references to the Court of Justice on the rights of workers under these agreements began to appear. The turning point then was 1987 with the *Demirel* case.[103]

---

100 D. Martin and E. Guild, *Free Movement of Persons in the European Union*, Butterworths, London, 1996.

101 C-18/90 *Kziber* [1991] ECR I-199.

102 For example, G. Testa, L'intervention des états membres dans la procédure de conclusion des accords d'association de la communauté économique européenne, Cahiers de droit européen 1966 p 492; J. V. Louis, Droit et politique des relations extérieures des communautés européennes, Cahiers de droit européen, 1971, p. 1.

103 12/86 *Demirel* [1987] ECR 3719.

CHAPTER 5

INTERPRETATION OF THE TURKEY AGREEMENT: NATIONAL DISCRETION AND COMMUNITY LAW COHERENCE

5.1. INTRODUCTION

In this chapter I will now turn to the content of the emerging immigration law of the Community as manifested through one third country agreement to see whether the application of the principles of Community law regarding nationals of the Member States have been applied. That agreement is the one with Turkey, which I have chosen for three reasons: first the detail which has been given to the agreement in subsidiary legislation is much more extensive in the field of workers than that of any other agreement; secondly the Court of Justice has been called upon on a number of occasions to interpret the agreement and its subsidiary legislation; thirdly, as a percentage of the total number of third country nationals resident on a long term basis in the Union, Turkish nationals are by far the most numerous.

Here I will investigate the development of a pyramid structure: as in the triangle there is the relationship of the Member State to the Community (in accordance with which the Community is ultimately responsible for the obligations assumed to third countries under agreements); third country to Community (here there are duties and obligations on both sides some of which from the Community's side may only be capable of fulfilment by the Member States so there is also the relationship through Community law between the third country and the Member States); individual to the Community (through the creation of rights upon which an individual may rely directly if necessary against a Member State) and to the host Member State (where through national law the third country national has acquired rights under Community law) and to his or her state of origin (which under the terms of the agreements will have a residual power to protect rights of its nationals through the dispute resolution mechanism built into the agreement).

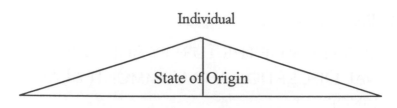

Community   Member States

In the preceding chapter the wording of the provisions of the third country agreements themselves in comparison with the EC Treaty's comparable provisions on workers was set out and compared. A clear picture emerged of similarity of wording and concepts. The approach adopted by the legislator in the primary legislation in both instances is clearly parallel: the division of movement of persons into the same categories of workers, self-employed and service providers; the utilisation of comparable wording on the material scope. However, the chief difference is in exactly that material scope of the third country agreements. In none of the third country agreements is there the comparable principle of the abolition of obstacles to free movement of persons contained in Article 3 EC. In the Turkey Agreement, Articles 12-14 provide for the progressive securing of freedom of movement for workers, abolition of restrictions on establishment and service provision. However, these provisions lack the clarity of intention of Article 3 EC. Is the lack of this objective decisive in the construction and interpretation of the relationship of the individual to the Member State and Community?

In order to investigate this I shall look first at the subsidiary legislation under the Turkey Agreement in comparison with its counterpart under the EC Treaty in order to determine the approach of the legislator.[1] Then I will consider specific issues relating to migration which have been the subject of interpretation by the Court both in the context of third country agreements and the EC Treaty to determine how similar provisions and concepts in the two are interpreted. Then it will be possible to draw some conclusions as to whether Community law on migration is uniform and, in so far as within the competence of the Community, a similar or identical interpretation of provisions relating to workers and persons whether they be nationals of other Member States or third country nationals obtains.

Once I have analysed the provisions and their interpretation then it will be possible to draw some conclusions regarding the consequences of this strand of the Community's immigration policy for national discretion.

The questions therefore for this chapter are as follows: `

---

[1]   Only under the Turkey Agreement has relevant secondary legislation been adopted.

1. Drafting subsidiary legislation: in the development of Community subsidiary legislation to achieve free movement of workers, and that to
   achieve the same objective under the Turkey Agreement does the legislator seek to apply the same or similar principles? Is there a parallel
   between the progressive implementation of Article 39 EC and Article 12
   Turkey Agreement?

2. Interpreting the provisions: does the Court of Justice interpret concepts
   contained in the agreements and their subsidiary legislation in the same
   way as it does those in respect of Community nationals contained in the
   EC Treaty and its subsidiary legislation?

3. In this first strand of the Community's immigration policy *vis-à-vis* third
   country nationals, albeit a policy which was not entirely consciously developed, is the balance between the individual and the State consistent
   with that in respect of Community nationals?

There are four major themes which I have chosen to consider the treatment of
third country nationals under an agreement with that of EU nationals under
the EC Treaty. Each part breaks down further, and each part engages different
combinations of the actors within the Community system: the legislator and
the Court.

(A) The approach of the legislator: a comparison of Decisions 2/76 and
    1/80 of the Turkey Agreement and Regulations 15/61 and 38/64 EEC
    (the predecessors of Regulation 1612/68 before the end of the trans-
    itional period for free movement of workers). This I will further break
    down into seven constituent parts so that a clear picture of comparison
    will emerge.

(B) The concept of a worker: does the interpretation of this concept vary
    depending on whether the individual concerned is a national of a
    Member State or a third country national benefiting under an agreement
    with his or her state of nationality?

(C) The treatment of family members: is there a consistent approach to the
    interpretation of family life under the subsidiary legislation of the EC
    Treaty and that of a third country agreement?

(D) The meaning of public policy and loss of status: to what extent is there
    a parallel between the ways in which an end can be put by the Member
    States to acquired rights?

5.2. THE APPROACH OF THE LEGISLATOR

The transitional period for the fulfilment of free movement of Community workers did not end until 1968. In accordance with Article 40 EC, however, the Council was under a duty from the entry into force of the Treaty to take progressive steps to achieve such free movement. In particular the Council was required systematically and progressively to abolish administrative procedures, practices and waiting periods for access to employment which formed an obstacle to liberalisation of the movement of workers between 1957, the date of the Treaty, and the end of the transitional period in 1968. Liberalisation of labour migration in Europe had been regulated through bilateral and multi-lateral agreements on a number of different levels since before WW II.[2] Labour migration was very much perceived as a benefit, collectively organised by many Member States, to meet the needs of their industry.[3] The framework of the Community for these activities was the new element, not the activities themselves.

The Turkey Agreement was signed during this same period of expansion of labour migration: 1963. The supply of East German workers in West Germany had begun to dry up as the Cold War intensified and the Berlin Wall was built. Turkish workers began to be recruited into Germany to fill vacancies on a collective basis.[4] The inclusion of a provision on labour migration in the Turkey Agreement fits naturally into the historical moment in which the agreement was signed. The duty in the EC Treaty on labour is not dissimilar to, though more fully spelled out than, that contained in Article 12 of the Turkey Agreement requiring the progressive securing of freedom of movement of workers. Indeed, Article 12 specifically refers to Article 49, now Article 40, EC by which it is to be guided. The period saw the collective recruitment of Southern European workers, most importantly, Italians who were Community nationals and Turks into Germany and other countries of North Western Europe. The legal regulation of their movement is similar. At the time a qualitative difference

---

2   See Chapter 2 and K. Lewin, The Free Movement of Workers, CMLRev (64/65), pp. 300-324; H. ter Heide, The Free Movement of Workers in the Final Phase, CMLRev (68/69), pp. 466-477 and W. van Gerven, The Right of Establishment and Free Supply of Services within the Common Market, CMLRev (66/67), pp. 344-362.

3   Indeed, in 1966, the Committee of Ministers of the Council of Europe included in its work programme the intention to draw up a convention which would set out the basic requirements of collective labour recruitment as well as the conditions of residence for workers so recruited. See E. Guild, *The European Convention on the Legal Status of Migrant Workers (1977): an analysis of its scope and benefits*, Council of Europe, Strasbourg, 1999.

4   S. Castles, The Guestworker in Western Europe, International Migration Review, 1986, Vol. 20. No. 3, pp. 761-778.

between these two groups of migrant workers was less clear than would become the case after the 1973 "recruitment stop".

The Community legislator adopted two implementing Regulations in respect of Community workers under Article 40 EC, first in 1961[5] then in 1964[6] before the adoption of Regulation 1612/68 at the end of the transitional period which gave effect to free movement of workers. Under the Turkey Agreement a similar process is followed. First, the Association Council, the equivalent of the Community legislator for the purposes of the agreement, adopted Decision 2/76 in 1976 on workers which was then replaced[7] by Decision 1/80 in 1980. A third (and final measure, if there were to be equivalence with the EC Treaty programme) has not been adopted for reasons set out previously regarding the political stalling of Turkey's accession to the Union. I will compare then, the provisions of the first Community Regulation with those of the first Decision of the Association Council as regards similarity of wording and intent. I will then look at the second Community Regulation and the second Association Council Decision to see what progress was made on the question of workers and their families and what comparability exists.

However, before embarking on this exercise, which enjoys the benefit of juridical parallelism, some remarks and about a lack of chronological parallelism are needed. In his work on the Turkey Agreement, Gutmann adopted the more chronological approach. comparing the Community Regulations and Association Council Decisions which most closely follow one another in time.[8] This is a valuable comparison and I agree with Gutmann's approach as a useful tool to examine the intention of the legislator comparatively at the time of adoption of the measures. But, here I wish to do something different: examine the stepping stones to liberalisation of labour migration. It is the juridical steps towards free movement of workers which are important to this study: what choices were made by the legislator in the progressive liberalisation of movement of workers. Were those choices comparable between the Community law regime and the association agreement regime? O'Leary's approach to the legislation in her analysis of the jurisprudence of the Turkey Agreement is less attractive. She compares primary EC provisions with secondary association

---

[5] OJ 1961 1073/61.
[6] OJ 1964 965/64.
[7] Though with continuing effect of some provisions, most importantly, the standstill provision, see C-192/89 *Sevince* [1990] ECR I-3461.
[8] R. Gutmann, *Die Assoziationsfreizügigkeit türkischer Staatsangehöriger, Ihre Entdeckung und Ihr Inhalt*, 2. Auflage, Nomos Verlagsgesellschaft, Baden-Baden, 1999.

agreement articles. In my view this does not assist greatly in gaining a clear view of the legislator's intention.[9]

In his book on association agreements and third country nationals in the European Union, Weber takes a different approach. As he is primarily concerned with the agreements, he first considers the primary legislation then the secondary legislation of the agreements themselves but in order of the degree of liberalisation.[10]

This Chapter must be read bearing in mind the importance, numerically, of Turkish workers. If one looks only at one Member State, Germany, the largest importer of labour, the number of foreigners living in Germany went from 686,200 in 1960 to 1,924,200 in 1968. By 1974 that figure had jumped to 4,127,400. In terms of percentage of the population the move had been from 1.2% foreigners to nationals to 6.7%. By 1980, the date of the last Association Council Decision under the Turkey Agreement on labour, the foreign population in Germany had risen to 4,453,300, 7.2% of the population, the overwhelming majority of whom were Turkish.[11] The big break came in 1973/74 when, as a result of the slowdown in the economies of Western Europe, the rise in unemployment and the oil crisis, the large labour importing countries announced a major change of policy: withdrawal from the collective recruitment of foreign labour.[12]

Therefore in terms of public policy in Europe on labour migration, the Community measures were all adopted before the dramatic change of 1973/74. The measures adopted under the Turkey Agreement both came *after* that critical date. It is, accordingly, not surprising that the implementing legislation under the Turkey Agreement never progressed to dealing with first access to the territory and labour market of the Member States. Its domain was limited to the acquisition of rights after admission.

---

[9] S. O'Leary, Employment and Residence for Turkish Workers and their Families: Analogies with the Case-law of the Court of Justice on Article 48 [39] EC, in *Scritti in onore di Giuseppi Federico Mancini*, Vol. II, Guiffre editore, 1998, p. 731.

[10] C. Weber, *Der assoziationsrechtliche Status Drittstaatsangehöriger in der Europäischen Union*, Peter Lang, Frankfurt am Main, 1996.

[11] The Federal Government Commissioner for Foreigners Affairs, Facts and Figures on the Situation of Foreigners in the Federal Republic of Germany, Bonn, March 1997, p. 19.

[12] J. Salt, *Temporary migration for employment and training purposes, Report and Guidelines*, Council of Europe, Strasbourg, 1996, p. 40.

Dates: Community and Turkey Legislation on Workers

Date	Community Law	Turkey Agreement
First Measure	1961 (Regulation 15/61)	1976 (Decision 2/76)
Second Measure	1964 (Regulation 38/64)	1980 (Decision 1/80)
Third Measure	1968 (Regulation 1612/68)	

As regards the missing next step in the progression of the Turkey Agreement on liberalisation of movement of workers, the Commission prepared a Communication to the Council in March 1986 on Implementation of Article 12 of the Ankara Agreement relating to the free movement of workers.[13] This was followed by a draft decision in July 1986.[14] This activity was spurred by the fact that Article 12 of the agreement provided that full free movement of workers was to be achieved by the 22nd year after entry into force of the agreement – in other words by 30 November 1986. In the opening paragraph of the Commission Communication as regards the socio-economic context it states: "No account of Turkish labour in the Community can ignore the employment situation in the Community, which is very different now from what it was in the 1960's and 1970's; at the end of the January 1996, the number of those out of work was high at 16.75 million, or 12.4% of the labour force of the Community of Twelve" (para. 2.1). As part of the picture the Commission also highlighted that "the socio-professional integration and even more the cultural integration of Turkish workers" was meeting with major difficulties and that the new acceding Member States of Greece, Spain and Portugal needed to have their workers protected against discrimination in comparison with Turkey.

It proposed as a solution three measures falling far short of free movement of workers:

(A) Consolidation and improvement of the status of Turkish workers and members of their families legally resident in the Community. This would include removal of the time limits for Turkish workers lawfully working in a Member State, for family members, admitted as such, the removal of qualifying residence periods before access to employment and free access

---

[13] European Commission SEC(86) 331 final.
[14] European Commission, Avant Project de Decision du Conseil d'Association relative à la mise en oeuvre de l'article 12 de l'Accord d'Association CEE-Turquie, SEC (86) 1020 final.

to employment of choice, the abolition of discrimination on grounds of nationality wider than that already available in Decision 1/80;

(B) Access to the labour market, the right for Turkish workers lawfully in one Member State to accept an offer of employment in another Member State subject to Community priority;

(C) Family reunion: a Turkish worker with legal employment for more than one year would have the possibility to be joined by his or her spouse and children who are not yet old enough to be economically active or who are dependant because of a permanent incapacity on condition that the parents reside in the same host country and are actually responsible for those children.

The Communication was never published and the draft Decision remained on the shelf.

Returning then to the measures which were adopted, to present a clear picture I will look at the treatment of seven elements covered in the legislation:

1. The recitals which set out the objectives;

2. Access to the labour market;

3. Extension of permission to work;

4. Calculation of time periods;

5. The presence and scope of equal treatment provisions;

6. The treatment of family members;

7. Standstill clauses.

Regulation 15/61 and Decision 2/76

1. The Recitals

The Community legislator adopted, in 1961, the first measures towards free movement of workers, Regulation 15/61.[15] According to the recitals, the first consideration is the abolition of all discrimination based on nationality between workers of the Member States as regards work, pay and other conditions of work. This objective requires the elimination of waiting periods and other restrictions which constitute an obstacle to free movement of workers by the end of the transitional period. The first stage was to last two years. No mention

---

15   OJ 1961 1073/61.

is made in the preamble to family reunion nor to the right to exercise free movement in freedom and dignity, both elements of importance in the final Regulation 1612/68 at the end of the transitional period.

The Association Council in Decision 2/76 limited itself to fewer recitals than did the Community legislator. However, this may have been to some extent because it was clearly drafted by reference to Community measures. The first recital highlights this, specifically referring to the fact that the Contracting Parties agreed to be guided by Articles 39, 40 and 41 EC "in gradually introducing freedom of movement for workers between their countries". The following recital states that priority is given to according access to respective employment markets:

> "Whereas this principle must be given effect under conditions that exclude any serious danger to the standard of living and the level of employment in the various regions and branches of activity in the Member States of the Community and Turkey."

Such a consideration of disruption to the national labour market does not appear in the Community Regulation, which is not surprising as there is no basis for such a consideration in the EC Treaty. The issue is not relevant to the Community measure in light of the obligation to secure free movement of workers.[16] In fact, provisions permitting a suspension of the Decision on the grounds of danger to the labour market have never been invoked.

2. Access to the labour market

Regulation 15/61 consists of three parts, admission and employment of workers and their families, the co-ordination of job offers and workers, the bodies responsible for implementation. Of these three parts only the first is of interest to this study.

In the first part, Articles 1-5 (Regulation 15/61) deal with access to the labour market. The principle in Article 1 of the Regulation is that if no national worker is available for a job within three weeks of its notification then a Community national worker must be authorised to take that job. Certain exceptions are made in respect of workers nominated by employers for jobs (i.e. the three week waiting period does not apply). In the Decision a very substantially lower level of state commitment is included. Article 5 (Decision 2/76) in much more general terms specifies that should it not be possible in the Community to meet an offer of employment by calling on the employment

---

[16] It is also a result of the different time period of the measures. In 1968 the Member States were not concerned about too much labour but rather too little. In 1976 the situation was the opposite.

market of the Member States and in the event that the Member States decide to authorise a call on workers who are not nationals of the Member States then they "shall endeavour" to give priority to Turkish workers. In other words, while Community nationals have an entitlement to take jobs which have been vacant for three weeks, Turkish workers may only gain access to the labour market of a Member State where no Community worker is available and the Member State authorises a call on third country national workers. Even there a discretion is reserved to the Member State in that it is only under a duty to endeavour to give privileged treatment to Turkish workers.

Therefore as regards the geometric model, for Community nationals the direct relationship granting rights between the Community and the individual is created as regards first access to employment. For Turkish nationals no such direct relationship is created on this point. The Member States retain a wide discretion over access to the labour market for Turkish workers in respect of which Community law does not provide a right to the individual to challenge. The geometric model here, for Turkish workers, is linear: individual – Member State – Community.

3. Extensions of permission to work

Chapter 2 of the Regulation relates to extension of work covering the same territory as Decision 2/76. Article 6 of Regulation 15/61 provides:

(A) After one year of regular employment on the territory of a Member State a national of another Member State is entitled to an extension of his or her work permit for the same job;[17]

(B) After three years of regular employment the national is entitled to authorisation to take other employment for which he or she is qualified;[18]

(C) After four years of regular employment he or she is entitled to free access in that Member State to any paid employment of his or her choice under the same conditions as own nationals;

(D) After five consecutive years of employment for which the worker has work permission for between eight and twelve months per year the worker is equally entitled to free access in that Member State to any paid employment of his or her choice.

---

[17]   The Regulation was never translated into English as it was no longer in force by the time the UK joined the Community. The French text is unofficially translated here by the author.

[18]   The wording in French is "Après trois ans d'emploi régulier, ce ressortissant reçoit l'authorisation d'exercer une autre profession salariée pour laquelle il est qualifié".

(E) Periods of employment completed before the entry into force of the Regulation count towards the calculation.

Article 2 of Decision 2/76, which covers the same subject for Turkish workers, follows a similar scheme though the provision is less generous:

(A) After three years of legal employment in a Member State a Turkish worker is entitled to respond to any offer of employment under normal conditions for the same occupation, branch of activity and region;

(B) After five years legal employment a Turkish worker is entitled to free access in that Member State to employment of his or her choice.

A number of characteristics are worth noting. First, structurally the two measures are consistent. The legislator clearly had in mind the same type of gradual access to the labour market both in respect of the work programme towards implementation of Article 39 EC and Article 12 of the Turkey Agreement. This programme is based on the acquisition of increasing rights depending on the number of years worked. In respect of both measures, the worker was confined to the same employer for three years. There is a difference of course in the speed at which rights are acquired, Community national workers gained free access to paid employment a year earlier under the first Community measure than Turkish workers under the first implementing measure of that agreement as regards workers. Implicit in this schema is an underlying assumption that the longer a worker is economically active and resident in a Member State the greater his or her claim to continue to reside and work. This must in turn find its justification in the assumption of integration achieved by the workers with the passage of time.

The concept of legal employment is used in both cases. It's interpretation did not come before the Court of Justice as regards Regulation 15/61 or indeed its successor 38/64 but as will be seen below, this is an issue which is arising with increasing frequency before the Court as regards Turkish workers.[19] Limitation of the exercise of the right of employment first to one employer is consistent in both measures. A second gradual step is access to employment in the same field, which is finally followed by free access to any paid employment. In both there is no inherent limitation that the employment must take place after entry into force of the measure. There is no cross fertilisation with self employment which is not regulated at all in these two measures.

---

[19] Regulation 38/64 has been referred to either by Advocates General or in the judgments of the Court in five cases: C-64/96 and C-65/96 *Uecker & Jacquet* [1997] ECR I-3171; 281, 283, 284, 285, and 287/85 *Germany & Others v Commission* [1987] ECR 3203; 267/83 *Diatta* [1985] ECR 567; 207/78 *Even* [1979] ECR 2019; 15/69 *Ugliola* [1969] ECR 363 but in no case was the question of legal employment defined.

In both these measures, however, for the first time we find directly applicable rights granted to the individual, whether Community national or Turkish national by the operation of Community law. The Member States' role is implementation of these rights but they are excluded from defining the content of the rights. As regards both types of workers, a triangular relationship has been created.

4. Calculation of the time periods

The next consideration is: what counts for the purpose of the acquisition of rights?

As regards the calculation, Regulation 15/61 is more specific than Decision 2/76 on the effects of acquired rights of workers. In Article 7 of the Regulation it states that absences of 40 days or less as well as annual holidays, absences on account of illness, maternity, accident at work or industrial injury form part of the period of regular employment. Involuntary unemployment, long absences on account of illness and the completion of military service do not affect acquired rights so long as the worker returns to work and in respect of unemployment as soon as an appropriate job offer is made to him or her, and in other cases within a specified period after the end of the illness or completion of military service.

In the Decision, less particularity is given to this issue of absence from work. Article 6(2)(c) of Decision 2/76 provides that annual holidays and short absences for sickness, maternity or accidents at work count as periods of work. Involuntary unemployment duly certified by the authorities and long absences on account of sickness do not affect acquired rights. Therefore again, the parallel is clear but with diminished rights for Turkish workers. Absences for military service did not protect the position of Turkish workers though they did for Community national workers.

In parallel, the protection of acquired rights in the event of specific risks features in both measures. In both cases this protection is direct, again in the triangular relationship between individual and Member State, Member State and Community, Community and individual. By specifying the circumstances under which acquired rights cannot be lost, the Community limits again the discretionary power of the Member States as regards the relation of work and residence on the territory of workers under Community protection.

5. Equal treatment

At this point there is a divergence between the Regulation and the Decision. Article 8 of Regulation 15/61 provides for equal treatment of Community national workers and own nationals as regards conditions of work, and employment, remuneration and dismissal. They are also entitled to equal treatment in participation in trade unions and protection under collective agreements. No similar provision is included in the Decision.

As I have discussed in Chapter 2, the right to non-discrimination has been vital to the development of movement rights of Community national workers. The Turkey Agreement at Article 9 provides for non-discrimination on the basis of nationality within the scope of the agreement generally. At Article 37 of the additional protocol this general right is given specificity as regards workers prohibiting discrimination on the basis of nationality as regards conditions of work and remuneration. The lack of a non-discrimination provision then in the implementing measure, Decision 2/76, is anomalous though perhaps legally superfluous in light of the provision in the additional protocol.

The Commission's Action Programme for migrant workers and their family members of 1976[20] specifically indicated that equal treatment in working conditions was an important aim as regards third country national workers in the Community.[21] Further in the Commission's Communication regarding the implementation of Article 12 of the Turkey Agreement in 1976, it stressed the equal treatment provision to be found at Article 37 of the Turkey Agreement.[22] It went further and recommended that greater specificity be given to the non-discrimination provision of the Decision with inclusion of a reference to trade union membership and the right to participate in elections for work councils. This proposal was not approved by the Association Council and the Decision was adopted with no reference to the non-discrimination provision.

6. Family members

In both the Regulation and the Decision, the next area covered relates to family members. Articles 11-14 of Regulation 15/61 regulate this issue. Here there is

---

20 Bulletin of the European Communities Supplement 3/76.
21 In dit verband is het bijzonder van belang:
    c) bevordering van de verwezenlijking van gelijke behandeling op het stuk van levens-omstandigheden en arbeidsvoorwaarden, lonen en economische rechten ten behoeve van werknemers die onderdaan zijn van derde Staten en hun gezinsleden die legaal in de Lid-Staten wonen.
    (In this regard it is particularly important: (c) ensuring the benefit of equal treatment in the fields of standard of living and working conditions, pay and economic rights for all workers whether from third countries or otherwise and their family members legally resident with them in a Member State.") (unofficial translation.).
22 European Commission, Tenuitvoerlegging van artikel 12 van de associatie-overeenkomst EEG-Turkije betreffende het vrije verkeer van werknemers, COM (76) 180 def. Brussels, 28 April 1976. (Interpretation of Article 12 of the EEC Turkey Association Agreement as regards free movement of workers).

substantial divergence with the Decision. From the beginning the Community allowed spouses and children under 21 of workers to enjoy family reunification in the host State. The only limitation (other than that the worker must have regular employment) is adequate housing, a requirement which continues to exist in the Regulation currently in force, 1612/68. These family members always were entitled to work subject to the same conditions applicable to the principal. The children of Community national workers were entitled to equal treatment in access to vocational training and apprenticeships.

Decision 2/76 refers only to children. In Article 3 of Decision 2/76, Member States were required to accord access to general education to the children of Turkish workers provided the children were lawfully residing with their parents in a Member State. This is a curious variation from the Regulation. While Community workers' children were expressly entitled to equal treatment only in higher education, the children of Turkish workers are only specifically entitled to access to general education. It is not until the next stage of the Community's implementation of free movement of workers that Community workers' children get access to all forms of education (see below). Here the time period involved is important to understanding the development. The Member States, in the 1950s and 1960s, viewed labour migration as short term. As Böhning has made clear in his study of migration in Western Europe, the receiving states of migrant workers at that time intended and believed that these workers would return to their countries of origin.[23] Therefore the insertion of provisions regarding children were not particularly relevant. By the 1970s it was clear that migrant workers had become immigrants and the education of their children was necessary.

Perhaps in recognition of this, the Commission had proposed in its Communication of 1976 that all forms of education be included for Turkish workers.[24]

Therefore as regards the structure of the two measures, Community workers are entitled to a direct family reunion right through Community law subject to very limited qualifying criteria – the creation of the triangular relationship is apparent. Turkish workers do not benefit from such a relationship as regards family reunion. Just as access to the labour market of Turkish workers is left in the discretionary power of the Member States, so too is family reunion. Only after family reunion has been effected, and permitted through

---

[23]   R. Böhning, *The Migration of Workers in the United Kingdom and the European Community*, OUP, Oxford, 1972.

[24]   European Commission, Tenuitvoerlegging van artikel 12 van de associatie-overeenkomst EEG-Turkije betreffende het vrije verkeer van werknemers COM (76) 180 def. Brussels, 28 April 1976. (Interpretation of Article 12 of the EEC Turkey Association Agreement as regards free movement of workers).

national law does a Community right accrue to a Turkish worker's family members: residence, employment and access to general education for his or her children.

7. Standstill clauses

Finally, as regards the introduction of new restrictions in areas covered by the two measures, the Regulation prohibits such restrictions in all areas covered by it and requires the withdrawal of any such measure introduced after its entry into force (Article 39).[25] The Decision gives more limited protection. Article 7 of Decision 2/76 only prohibits the introduction of restrictions on the conditions of access to employment applicable to workers legally resident and employed within the territory.

These standstill provisions have a curious effect: they freeze the situation in national law by the application of Community law but in no way affect the validity of that national law. If, in a Member State, no measures are in place covering the area subject of the standstill then there is either nothing or everything on which it can bite. Although the introduction of new restrictive measures within the applicable field is prohibited, the effect, in the absence of any measures already in existence, is to require the Member State to retain complete discretionary power over the area. The introduction of any measure would constitute a restriction contrary to the standstill. Further, the rationale of the standstill clause is to prevent any erosion of the existing rights of individuals in national law and to avoid any increase in divergence in the law of the Member States. Such a measure therefore anticipates that Member States will or are likely to wish to introduce more restrictive measures contrary to the intentions of the agreements. Therefore by its very existence a standstill clause presupposes the possibility of bad habits on the part of the Member States.

What conclusions can be drawn as regards the legislator's intentions from the first measures adopted under the two agreements? There is a clear parallel between the two measures adopted to give effect to rights in the Treaty and agreement. The same categorisations and fields are covered. However, as would be expected, while the Regulation provides a wider set of rights reflecting the aim of the Community to abolish obstacles to free movement, the Decision is more limited, covering only those areas considered necessary to protect the position of Turkish workers already admitted to the labour market of a Member State. The difference therefore is not so much in the quality of the

---

[25] The lack of a standstill provision in the EC Treaty to protect Community migrant workers is noteworthy. Such a provision is to be found in Article 43 EC on establishment and Article 49 EC on services but not Article 39 EC on workers.

rights conferred or the way in which they are conferred but in the extent of the field over which they are conferred.

In both cases the rights based approach applies with particular force the longer the workers are employed in the host State. As regards these workers, the wording of the Regulation and the Decision clearly devolve to the worker the choice to continue to participate in the host State's labour force or to leave. The discretion of the Member State to authorise or not continued participation by the worker is excluded (except on grounds of public policy, health and security common to both regimes). The threshold of years of work at which the worker acquires the right varies between the two measures but the process is parallel.

In both cases a triangular relationship is established: individual to Member State, Member State to Community, Community to individual. However, the contents of that relationship are more restricted as regards Turkish workers than Community national workers. The indeterminate nature of the intention to achieve free movement of workers under the Turkey Agreement in comparison with the express purpose in Article 3 EC of the abolition of obstacles to free movement does not appear to have had a determining role in the nature of the subsidiary legislation. While the difference of objective is important as regards the material scope of the two measures, it does not result in a qualitative difference as regards those areas that do come within the material scope.

Regulation 38/64 and Decision 1/80

1. Recitals

Moving then to the second measures adopted by the Council and the Associ-ation Council respectively, what comparisons can usefully be made about the legislator's intention by reference to the same seven areas? Regulation 38/64 followed the first Regulation by a period of three years and constituted a second step towards the fulfilment of the gradual abolition of obstacles to free movement of workers as required by Article 40 EC. The preamble of the Regulation commences with the same purpose and reasoning as set out in Regulation 15/61. However, an innovation is the inclusion of a differentiation between types of workers: permanent, seasonal and frontier. Further, specific reference is made to workers who are agents of service providers. In contrast, the Association Council on adopting Decision 1/80 four years after the first measure acknowledges the decision to revitalise the development of the Association and specifies that in the social field this makes it "necessary to improve the treatment accorded to workers and members of their families in relation to the arrangements introduced by Decision 2/76". No further clarification is provided by the preamble. However, the measures are part of a wider programme and consistent with the legislator's approach in respect of Article 40 EC. In both cases there is a development towards an extension of rights. There is no question of a reversal of the process.

2. Access to the labour market

Regulation 38/64 is divided into four sections of which only the first is of concern here. This covers the employment of workers, equal treatment, recruitment criteria, family members and work permits. As regards access to employment, the waiting period of three weeks has disappeared. Subject to certain possible reservations, the limitation on changing employment also disappears in Regulation 38/64. Once admitted as a worker the individual is entitled to change employment. However, here provision is made that workers who are sent by their employer to another Member State to carry out services remain covered by the Regulation. The exceptions permitted to the right to take any employment (which require a positive act by the Member State notified to the Council and not to exceed three months) cannot be applied to workers who:

(A) Have been regularly employed for one year on the territory of the Member State and wish to continue employment in the same field;

(B) Have been regularly employed for two years or 27 months over the preceding three years as a seasonal worker or 20 months over the preceding three years whatever the occupation or region on the territory of the Member State.

Article 8 of Decision 1/80 sets out the conditions of access to employment for Turkish workers. This remains subject to the Member State decision as regards a call on workers and is limited by the wording "shall endeavour" which clearly makes it non-binding. Further, it is subject to a priority to Community national workers. However, an additional provision has been inserted: the right to Turkish workers who are registered as unemployed and legally resident in the territory of the Member State to the services of the national employment agency (subject again to the Community national priority). The other side of this right means an obligation on national employment agencies to find employment (or at least to try to do so) for Turkish workers.

Further, at Article 7 of Decision 1/80 provision is made for access to employment for the children of Turkish workers who have already formed part of the labour market for three years. Once such children have completed a course of vocational training in the host State they are entitled to take an offer of employment. The effect of this provision was the object of two important decisions of the Court of Justice.[26] What is apparent is that the area of access to employment is, by gradual steps, becoming part of the triangular relationship between: individual and Member State, Member State and Community and Community and individual through which the discretion of the Member State is limited by the application of rules which constitute part of Community law and are enforceable by the individual. The two provisions which form the subject matter of this relationship as regards Turkish workers both presuppose the lawful residence of the Turkish national on the territory of the Member State. So again, the question of first admission to the territory remains the preserve of national discretion. However, access to employment following admission is now in specific circumstances regulated by Community law.

3. Extensions of permission to work

Under the Community Regulation, Community national workers no longer need to seek extensions of their permission to work. As regards continuation of employment, Decision 1/80 provides at Article 6 that Turkish workers:

(A) Are entitled to renewal of the permit to work for the same employer if a job is available after one years' legal employment;

(B) Are entitled to change employment within the same occupation after three years' legal employment;

(C) Enjoy free access to paid employment of his or her choice after four years' legal employment (limited to that Member State but without regional limitation within that Member State).

Two ways of looking at what has happened in respect of Community national workers are: (1) the relationship between the State and the individual has been reversed – the worker has the right to take any employment subject to restrictions which can be placed only on certain categories of workers; the discretion of the Member State is excluded unless it can be brought within the exceptions; (2) free access to employment has been cut loose from the progressive acquisition of rights and is no longer the prize of economic integration, itself measured by numbers of years of economic activity on the territory of the Member State. For Turkish workers, the framework remains fundamentally the same, but the number of years' employment before acquisition of free access to employment has been reduced and brought into line with the first Community Regulation on Community national workers. Although the workers' rights are no greater than spelled out (in other words, there is no reversal of the

---

[26]   C-355/93 *Eroglu* [1994] ECR I-5113; C-210/97 *Akman* [1998] ECR I-7519.

relationship with the host Member State), the period of time which gives rise to a presumption of integration sufficient to acquire free access to employment is diminishing. In both cases, then, the development may be seen as conceptually consistent: an increase in the power of choice of the individual worker at the expense of Member State discretion.

4. Calculation of the time periods

How are the time periods calculated? According to Regulation 38/64 there is little change from the preceding one, other than that special provisions are included relating to seasonal workers and a limitation to a period of 30 days after recovery from an illness and completion of military service.[27] Over these periods acquired rights are retained and the periods themselves are to be counted as periods of employment. In Decision 1/80 the calculation of time periods has not changed. However for the children of Turkish workers, it is irrelevant whether, by the time the child has completed the course of vocational training, his or her parent(s) are still on the territory of the Member State (or indeed alive).[28]

5. Equal treatment

The right to equal treatment remains a central feature of Regulation 38/64, first as regards access to employment (in contrast to Turkish workers who remain subject to a Community national priority). This now extends to equal treatment not only in working conditions, remuneration and dismissal but also to access to housing (Article 10) and of course the services of employment agencies. The critical right to equal treatment in tax and social advantages does not appear in Regulation 38/64 and will not arise until the next Regulation, 1612/68.[29]

---

[27] Article 7, Regulation 38/64:
"1. Pour l'application de l'article 6 paragraphe 1, les absences ne dépassant pas au total 40 jours par ans, ainsi que les congés annuels et les congés pour cause de maladie, maternité, accident du travail ou maladie professionelle sont assimilé à des périodes d'emploi régulier.
2(b) Dans un délai de 30 jour au plus après la cessation de la maladie ou des obligations militaire."

[28] C-210/97 *Akman* [1998] ECR I-7519.

[29] Article 7(2) of Regulation 1612/68 provided "[a worker] shall enjoy the same social and tax advantages as national workers". This provision has been the subject of extensive jurisprudence by the Court of Justice, see D. Martin and E. Guild, *Free Movement of Persons in the European Union*, Butterworths, London, 1996.

In Decision 1/80, the right to non-discrimination which appears at Article 37 of the Additional Protocol of the Turkey Agreement finds a place for the first time at Article 10. This is limited to equal treatment for Turkish workers duly registered as belonging to the labour force in respect of remuneration and other conditions of work.[30] Dismissal is not expressly included. Equal treatment with Community workers in assistance from the employment services in looking for work for both workers and their family members is also guaranteed.[31]

6. Family members

As regards family members, Regulation 38/64 provides for the admission of spouses, children under 21 and all dependent relatives in the ascending or descending line of the worker or his/her spouse. Further, the admission of other family members who are either dependent or lived under the same roof as the worker is to be facilitated. Here it is specifically stated that the nationality of the family member is irrelevant to the exercise of the right. This list of family members is consistent with the subsequent Regulation 1612/68. The exercise of the right is subject to a housing requirement and only available to a worker who is regularly employed on the territory of the host State (Article 17). The family members are entitled to work and may only be placed under limitations if these are applicable to the principal upon whom they are dependent (Article 18). Children of workers and those who have worked on the territory of the host State are entitled to equal treatment not only as regards vocational training and apprenticeships as was permitted under the preceding Regulation but also to courses of general education.

Decision 1/80 does not regulate the access of family members to the territory of the Member States. However, once family members have been authorised to join a Turkish worker they may acquire rights under the Decision. There is no definition of which family members may benefit from these rights. Two possibilities therefore arise:

---

[30] Conditions of work (which in some other Agreements is phrased as working conditions) can encompass a substantial number of different aspects of working life, including, for instance, work related social security benefits 41/84 *Pinna* [1986] ECR 1; see E. Guild, The Europe Agreements: Natural Persons and Social Security, in Y. Jorens and B. Schulte, *European Social Security Laws and Third Country Nationals*, die kleure/La Charte, Brussels, 1998, p. 333.

[31] The Court of Justice has clarified that once a Turkish worker has free access to paid employment, the priority reserved for Community nationals falls away and the Turkish worker is entitled to equal treatment C-171/95 *Tetik* [1997] ECR I-341.

(A) In light of the general intention of the agreement to be guided, *inter alia*, by Article 40 EC it must apply to the same category of family members as appear in the Regulation. This would have the result of uniformity of rights for the same category of workers across the Union;

(B) It applies to family members who are admitted under national law (or at the discretion of Member State). This inserts a national law definition of the family. This would mean that national law takes priority in admission of these family members though arguable not in their treatment after admission.

As will appear later when considering the jurisprudence of the Court, the general trend of the judgments is that while the Member States retain discretion over admission to the territory and labour force of Turkish workers, once so admitted (and once rights have accrued under the agreement's subsidiary legislation) Member State discretion is excluded as regards the conditions of residence and continued access to the labour market. If there is a parallel here between the two areas, then it would seem more probable that the first option is intended. This would mean that once a family member is admitted to the territory of the Member State so long as he or she comes within the definition of family members in Article 10 of Regulation 1612/68 then he or she would be entitled to the rights contained in Article 7 of Decision 1/80. This could be a wider class of persons than those who might be entitled to such rights under national family reunion law, but of course, national law applies there. This latter solution is certainly the indication from the Advocate General in the matter of *Eyup* where he considered that protection under the Decision continues where the form of relationship between the spouses is no longer covered by marriage but nonetheless is strong.[32]

A further problem arises as regards the meaning of the phrase "authorised to join". This only applies to the first indent of Article 7 of Decision 1/80. Children who rely on the second indent i.e., have completed a course of

---

[32] C-65/98 *Eyup* "La notion de 'membre de la famille' visée à l'article 7, premier alinéa de la décision n° 1/80 du Conseil d'association CEE-Turquie du 19 septembre 1980, relative au développement de l'association entre la Communauté économique euro-péenne et la Turquie s'étend au concubin d'un travailleur turc vivant en union libre, à condition qu'il y ait, entre les intéressés, un lien familial sérieux et stable comme celui qui s'instaure lorsque ceux-ci ont vécu ensemble, sans interruption, après le divorce et contracté par la suite un nouveau mariage. La condition de cohabitation pour une durée minimale de cinq ans prévue par l'article 7, premier alinéa, second tiret, de la décision n° 1/80 précitée, est remplie dès lors qu'un travailleur turc a contracté mariage, a divorcé et s'est remarié avec la même personne, si les conjoints ont effectivement continué à vivre ensemble entre les deux mariages et que les périodes de vie conjugale commune, prises dans leur totalité ont été d'au moins cinq ans." 18 November 1999.

vocational study are not required to have been authorised to join a parent in the host State. It is sufficient that they were admitted albeit, for instance, as a student, completed the studies and had a parent who filled the length of employment requirement.[33] Gutmann and Rittstieg separately have considered some of the consequences of this provision in the practical situation of families. For instance, what happens when the child finishes his or her studies and is in the process of seeking work. They argue that there is a right of continued residence at least for a reasonable period of time.[34] But the question is whether this means authorised to join for the purpose of family reunification on a long-term basis or whether it includes authorisations for a shorter period of time. In view of the different national regimes in the Member States this issue is of some interest. Some Member States place probationary periods on admission of family members who are third country nationals; others make residence subject to the continuing fulfilment of various criteria, most often in respect of financial matters and housing. This is a problem which is most likely to find its solution in the interpretation of the Court of Justice rather than the adoption of legislation.

There is no clear limitation of the family members to those holding Turkish nationality under Article 7 of Decision 1/80. Under Article 9, children of Turkish workers residing legally with their parents who are or have been legally employed in a Member State are entitled to admission to courses of general education, apprenticeships and vocational training under the same educational entry qualifications as children of nationals of the Member States. Further they are eligible to benefit from advantages provided under national legislation "in this area". Here an equivalence has been reached with the children of Community national migrants. The equal treatment right as regards education is critical to recognition that migrant workers are in fact immigrants, in the Member States. As such they are entitled to equal access for their children to all forms of education. Family members of Turkish workers are entitled to benefit from the provisions of the Decision relating to acquisition of an independent right of employment (Article 11 of Decision 1/80).

The right to integrate for children is exemplified by their treatment after their parents have definitively left the territory of the host State. For a Community national's child the right to continue vocational training after the parents' departure was clearly established in *Echternach*.[35] There the family

---

[33] C-355/93 *Eroglu* [1994] ECR I-5113; C-210/97 *Akman* [1998] ECR I-7519.

[34] R. Gutmann, *Die Assoziationsfreizügigkeit türkischer Staatsangehöriger, Ihre Entdeckung und Ihr Inhalt*, 2 Auflage, Nomos Verlagsgesellschaft Baden-Baden, 1999, p. 143; H. Rittsteig, Anmerkung zum Beschluss des Bundesverwaltungsgerichts vom 23.12.1993 – 1 B 63.93, InfAuslR 170.

[35] 389 & 390/87 [1989] ECR 723.

returned to the country of origin after a period of employment and residence in the Netherlands. A child shortly thereafter sought to return to the host State on his own to finish his education there. The Court held that Article 12 of Regulation 1612/68 gave him a right to do so as it was not dependent on his parent's continued exercise of an employed activity there or indeed residence there. A similar question arose as regards a Turkish child whose father had lived and worked in Germany for more than three years but had then returned to Turkey before his son had finished his vocational training. The Court did not refer to its judgment in *Echternach*. Instead, after a detailed comparative analysis of the wording in different language versions of Article 7 second indent of Decision 1/80 from which it concluded that an unequivocal answer could not be gleaned, it considered the context, spirit and purpose of the provision. It concluded that children are entitled to equal treatment in education irrespective of whether their parents are working on the territory of the host State. According to the Court, it would undermine the coherence of the Decision to imply such a requirement to Article 7 second indent. It accepted the Commission's reasoning that such a child will in any event be materially independent. The Court found that the purpose of Article 7 second indent was not to provide the conditions for family unity, therefore it would be unreasonable to require the parents to still be resident on the territory for the child to continue to enjoy the independent right.[36] This decision reflects Community law on children of Community national migrant workers.

7. Standstill clauses

Finally, as regards the introduction of new restrictive measures, both Regulation 38/64 and Decision 1/80 prohibit these within the field of their application (Article 55 Regulation 38/64 and Article 13 Decision 1/80). While the wording of the standstill provision of the Regulation follows in a simplified form that of its preceding measure, that in the Decision is slightly wider as it now encompasses family members of Turkish workers as well.

Conclusions on the Legislator

What structural observations arise from this comparison? First, there has been no substantial change in the division between Decision 1/80 and Regulation 38/64 as regards the areas covered: the intention of Decision 1/80 to implement Article 12 of the agreement, free movement of workers, guided by Articles 39 and 40 EC has still not developed as regards access to the territory and

---

[36]   C-210/97 *Akman* [1998] I-7519.

labour market for Turkish workers. This question remains within the discretion of the Member States. As regards the Regulation, substantial progress has been made towards reducing obstacles to access to the territory for workers, the relationship of the individual and the State has been reversed in that the State must now raise and justify objections to free movement within the limits of the exceptions permitted. As regards continued employment, both measures provide greater security to individuals covered by them than the preceding measures and the structure of that protection continues to be by reference to a sliding scale of increasing rights depending on the length of time spent in the Member State. Equal treatment, one of the most powerful tools of the EC Treaty is now included in both measures though with slight differences in its material scope. Family members are now included to a much more substantial degree in the Decision and in the Regulation their rights are developed.

Both measures are drafted in terms of the rights of workers with little or no margin of discretion left to the State to vary their content. They are, accordingly, both measures which give specificity to the creation of the direct link between the individual and the supra-national legislator without clear evidence of the need for an intermediary in the form of the Member State. In the Decision, the rights of workers to extensions of work permits are to be subject to procedures established under national rules.[37] However, the Court of Justice has treated this provision as equivalent to the Community Directive on provision of residence permits:[38]

"Article 6(3) of Decision 1/80 merely clarifies the obligation of the Member States to take such administrative measures as may be necessary for the implementation of those provisions without empowering the Member State to make conditional or restrict the application of the precise and unconditional right which it grants to Turkish workers."[39]

Therefore in terms of the geometric structure, we have an equivalence of a triangular relationship both for workers, nationals of the Member States and Turkish workers.

Having considered the subsidiary legislation of the EC Treaty and the Turkey Agreement, it is now time to consider the consistency and coherence of the content of the concepts which are used in the EC Treaty and subsidiary legislation and that in the third country agreements. There is a high degree of parallelism between the agreements and the Treaty as regards the structure and form through which the legislator has dealt with workers, but does that

---

[37] Article 6(3) Decision 1/80.
[38] Now Directive 68/360.
[39] C-237/91 *Kus* [1992] ECR I-6781.

parallelism transform itself into consistency of interpretation of content? How has the Court considered the concepts?

5.3.   THE CONCEPT OF A WORKER[40]

In order to make the comparison between Community national workers and Turkish workers, I will consider nine characteristics of a worker which the Court has identified in respect of Community nationals:

1. The essential features of an employment relationship: for a certain period of time a person performs services; for and under the direction of another; in return for which he or she receives remuneration;[41]

2. Intentionality: the intention of the individual in moving and taking employment is not decisive as to whether he or she is a worker;[42]

3. Genuine and effective nature of work: a worker may retain this status even if the remuneration he or she receives for the work is so low that he or she qualifies for (and claims) public benefits for the poor provided that the work is genuine and effective;[43]

4. Low productivity and wages: persons employed under a scheme set up for their social rehabilitation or integration into the community whereby they perform work under the direction of another person in return for which they receive remuneration are employees, the essential features of an employment relationship being present. This is not altered by the fact that their productivity is low, that the work scheme is not economic in market economy terms and that consequently their remuneration is largely paid out of public funds;[44]

5. Trainees and apprentices: trainees and apprentices are workers if they provide work for an "employer" and are paid for their work, even though they are under supervision and the work is preparatory for a qualifying examination. The main point is that the activity should have

---

[40]   For the purposes of this study I will only consider the concept of worker for the purposes of work and residence. A different meaning applies in other spheres of Community law, most specifically social security.

[41]   66/85 *Lawrie-Blum* [1986] ECR 2121.

[42]   53/81 *Levin* [1982] ECR 1035.

[43]   139/85 *Kempf* [1986] ECR 1741.

[44]   344/87 *Bettray* [1989] ECR 1621.

the character of work performed for remuneration and be subject to supervision;[45]

6. Part-time work: this also qualifies a person as a worker: even as little as 10 hours of work a week does not exclude a Community national from being a worker under Article 39 of the Treaty;[46]

7. The purpose of the work: whether it be of a non-economic nature, such as teaching in the state sector or as part of the public service is irrelevant;[47]

8. Public or private employer: it is also irrelevant that the worker's employment status is governed by public law. Indeed, it would appear that almost any quasi-economic paid activity will qualify so long as there is a relationship of subordination and it is genuine and effective;[48]

9. Loss of work: a worker does not automatically lose that status by virtue of loss of employment.[49] However, once the employment relationship has ended, the person concerned as a rule loses his or her status as a worker, although that status may produce continuing effects after the relationship has ended, and a person who is genuinely seeking work must be classified as a worker.[50]

I will consider these nine elements below as regards Turkish workers. O'Leary has adopted a different categorisation in her comparison of employment and residence for Turkish workers *vis-à-vis* Article 39 EC rights of Community nationals. She has proceeded thematically looking at what she terms consolidation of the position of Turkish workers – the Article 39 EC rights which are transposable to Turkish workers such as the right to remain, search for work and the benefits which derive therefrom. This is a useful division which follows more closely the jurisprudence of the Court of Justice than the one I have

---

[45]   C-27/91 *Le Manoir* [1991] ECR I-5531.
[46]   171/88 *Rinner-Kühn* [1989] ECR 2743.
[47]   66/85 *Lawrie-Blum* [1986] ECR 2121.
[48]   389 & 390/87 *Echternach* [1989] ECR 723.
[49]   This is implicit from Article 7(1) and (3) Regulation 1612/68 "A worker who is a national of a Member State may not, in the territory of another Member State, be treated differently from national workers by reason of his nationality in respect of any conditions of employment and work, in particular as regards remuneration, dismissal and should he become unemployed, reinstatement or re-employment." And "He shall also, by virtue of the same rights and under the same conditions as national workers have access to training in vocational schools and retraining centres."
[50]   C-85/96 *Martinez Sala* [1998] ECR I-2691. Not all rights of a worker continue but as yet the Court has not clarified which rights are forfeit.

chosen. I have worked from a more detailed dissection of the constituent elements of the status of Community workers and then looked to the jurisprudence on Turkish workers to make the comparison. I have also had the benefit of publishing after the watershed decision of the Court of Justice in Birden,[51] which has provided much needed clarity on the comparison we have both undertaken.[52]

I will now turn to the nine features of a worker as defined for the purposes of Community nationals (Article 39 EC) which I identified above to see whether there is in fact one definition of a worker for Article 39 EC and Article 12 Turkey Agreement or whether there has only been only a partial assimilation of some aspects of two different definitions.

1. The essential features of the employment relationship as identified are the performance of services for and under the direction of another in return for remuneration. In considering the essential elements of the employment relationship as regards Turkish workers the Court stated "the [Turkish] worker is bound by an employment relationship pursued for the benefit and under the direction of another person for remuneration".[53] This is the same test as for Community workers. As regards the source of remuneration, the Court stated that it makes no difference whether:

   "The remuneration of a [Turkish worker] is provided using public funds since, by analogy with the case-law relating to Article 49 [39] of the Treaty, neither the origin of the funds from which the remuneration is paid nor the 'sui generis' nature of the employment relationship under national law ... can have any consequence in regard to whether or not the person is to be regarded as a worker."[54]

   The definition of remuneration itself must be consistent for both Community nationals and Turkish workers as Article 10 of Decision 1/80 requires non-discrimination between the two categories of workers as regards "remuneration and other conditions of work". For this equal treatment provision to have effect a consistent content must exist.

2. Intentionality: the question arose as regards the intention of a Turkish worker who had entered a Member State as the spouse of a national of

---

51 C-1/97 [1998] ECR I-7747.
52 As an author I would like to believe that the courageous and well-argued position which O'Leary took in her article was well received by judges of the Court when deliberating on the case. Indeed, the Court was her employer.
53 C-36/96 Günaydin [1997] ECR I-5143.
54 C-1/97 Birden [1998] ECR I-7747.

that State and then sought to rely on the fact of his continuous employment for a period of more than one year to establish a right of continued work and residence after his marriage had broken down. The Member State argued that he could not enjoy the protection of the Article 6(1) of Decision 1/80 because his intention (but more importantly its on admitting him) had been other than to come to the Member State *qua* worker. The Court followed its approach as regards Community national workers:

"Consequently, even if the legality of employment for the purpose of these provisions presupposes a stable and secure situation as a member of the labour force and thereby implies the existence of an undisputed right of residence and even possession of a legal residence permit, if necessary, the reasons why such right is recognised or such permit granted are not decisive for the purpose of their application. It follows that, if a Turkish worker has been employed for more than one year on the basis of a valid work permit, he must be regarded as fulfilling the conditions laid down by the first indent of Article 6(1) of Decision 1/80, even if his residence permit was originally issued for purposes other than that of paid employment."[55]

The test, therefore, is consistent as between Community workers and Turkish workers. Their intentions on arrival and the intentions of the Member State on admission are not decisive. It is the factual circumstance of having completed the relevant period of time in the labour market which is determinant of the acquisition of the quality of worker.

3. Genuine and effective nature of work: the same test appears to apply to Turkish workers for the purpose of determining their status as such. In the case of *Birden*[56] the Court considered the question of a genuine and effective activity as regards the definition of a worker for the purposes of Decision 1/80 and Article 12 of the Turkey Agreement. In its clearest statement of a single concept, the Court applied all the elements of the definition of a worker in respect of Article 39 EC to Article 12 of the Turkey Agreement. On the question of genuine and effective nature of the work it stated "Reference should consequently be made to the interpretation of the concept of a worker under Community law for the purposes of determining the scope of the same concept employed in Article 6(1) of Decisions No. 1/80".[57] It went on to assess the genuine and effective nature of the activity – to the situation of the Turkish worker, by reference to the hours of work and pay. The respondent

---

55   C-237/91 *Kus* [1992] ECR I-6781.
56   C-1/97 *Birden* [1998] ECR I-7747.
57   C-1/97 *Birden* [1998] ECR 1-7747.

government argued that a job could not be genuine and effective even as regards Community workers where it "constitutes merely a means of rehabilitation or reintegration for the persons concerned" relying on the Court's decision in *Bettray*.[58] Not only did the Court distinguish its earlier decision, but even the respondent government moved to the position of accepting an equivalence of definition. On the question of the consistency of the jurisprudence on genuine and effective nature of work, O'Leary's[59] dissatisfaction with the *Bettray* approach as sitting uneasily with the previous case-law of the Court on the point, in particular its decision in *Steymann*[60] is redressed in this judgment.

4. Low productivity and wages: As regards wages the Court has held that a Turkish worker is bound by a normal employment relationship where:

"He is entitled to the same conditions of work and pay as those which may be claimed by workers who pursue within the undertaking in question identical or similar activities, so that his situation is not objectively different from that of those other workers."[61]

The inclusion of a reference specifically to *paid* employment in the Decision has been mooted as a possible reason for differentiation between Community workers and Turkish workers.[62] This is not self evident in the light of the Community definition of a worker for Community nationals which includes a requirement for remuneration of some sort. Although the test has been set at a very low level, such as to include members of religious communities who receive remuneration in kind in return for their participation in the community, this is a test of remuneration not an abolition of the requirement altogether.[63] On this point the Court has stated that the finding that a Turkish worker holds such quality under the Turkey Agreement:

"is not altered by the fact that the remuneration of the person concerned is provided using public funds since, by analogy with the case law relating to Article 48 [39] of the Treaty, neither the origin of the funds from which the remuneration is paid nor the "sui generis" nature of the employment can

---

[58] 334/87 [1989] ECR 1621.
[59] S. O'Leary *supra*.
[60] 196/87 [1988] ECR 6159.
[61] C-36/96 *Günaydin* [1997] ECR I-5143.
[62] S. Peers, Towards Equality: Actual and Potential Rights of Third-Country Nationals in the European Union, CMLRev 33: 7-50, 1996, see footnote 47.
[63] 196/87 *Steymann* [1988] ECR 6159.

have any consequence in regard to whether or not the person is to be regarded as a worker."[64]

5. Trainees and apprentices: after an uncertain start on this issue[65] the Court found that the fact that the initial work and residence permits of a Turkish national had been for the purpose of training could not deprive him or her of the right to rely on Article 6 of the Decision.

"In the circumstances, the worker cannot be prevented from relying on rights acquired under Decision 1/80 on the ground that he allegedly stated that he wished to pursue his professional career in his country of origin after being employed for several years in the host Member State with a view to perfecting his vocational skills and that he initially accepted the restriction placed upon his permit to reside in that State."[66]

Clearly trainees and apprentices enjoy the same status as workers whether they are Community or Turkish nationals.

6. Part-time work: The Court has yet to be faced with the question of part-time work. According to the premise here of coherence, the same application of the Community worker's right to that status notwithstanding the limited nature of his or her economic activity should obtain. Arguments to the contrary require a differentiation between the meaning of a worker under the agreement and a worker in Article 39 EC. This is of course possible, but so far such a differentiation has been avoided by the Court.

7. The purpose of the work: The fact that the purpose of the work is one which under national law is time limited and cannot lead to an extension of a work and residence permit is irrelevant for the acquisition of rights under the Decision:

"The fact that a Member State imposes on all Turkish nationals whose occupation is that of specialist chef a restriction as to the duration of their residence in the Member State concerned and prohibits them from changing employers cannot affect [the] interpretation" [that the legal situation of a

---

64 C-1/97 *Birden* [1998] ECR I-7747.

65 "It is sufficiently clear from the foregoing that the answer to the first question must be that the first indent of Article 6(1) of Decision No 1/80 is to be construed as not giving the right to the renewal of his permit to work for his first employer to a Turkish national who is a university graduate and who worked for more than one year for his first employer and for some ten months for another employer, having been issued with a two-year conditional residence authorisation and corresponding work permits in order to allow him to deepen his knowledge by pursuing an occupational activity or specialised practical training." C-355/93 *Eroglu* [1994] ECR I-5113.

66 C-36/96 *Günaydin* [1997] ECR I-5143.

specialist chef is in no way different to that of Turkish workers as a whole employed in the host Member State].[67]

As has already been considered, the fact that the work and residence permits issued to a Turkish national were limited to vocational training also does not affect the quality of his or her capacity as a worker.[68] The Court took this occasion to clarify its jurisprudence on the purpose of work as regards Community nationals as well as stating that the same interpretation applies to Turkish workers. The Court distanced itself from its decision in *Bettray*:

"It is thus apparent from the reasoning of that judgment that the case concerned a person who, by reason of his addiction to drugs had been recruited on the basis of a national law intended to provide work for persons who, for an indefinite period, are unable, by reason of the circumstances related to their situation, to work under normal conditions; furthermore, the person concerned had not been selected on the basis of his ability to perform a certain activity, but, to the contrary, had performed activities adapted to his physical and mental possibilities in the framework of undertakings or work associations created specifically in order to achieve a social objective. Under those circumstances, the conclusion reached by the Court in *Bettray*, according to which a person employed under a scheme such as that at issue in that case could not, on that basis alone, be regarded as a worker and the fact that the conclusion does not follow the general trend of the case law concerning the interpretation of that concept in Community law ... can be explained only by the particular characteristics of that case and it cannot therefore be applied to a situation such as that of the applicant in the main proceedings [a Turkish worker], the features of which are not comparable."[69]

8. Public or private employer: Whether the funds from which the Turkish worker is paid are public or private makes no difference to his or her characterisation as a worker:

"Neither the origin of the funds from which the remuneration is paid nor the 'sui generis' nature of the employment relationship under national law and the level of productivity of the person concerned can have any consequences in regard to whether or not a person is to be regarded as a worker."[70]

9. Loss of work: the status of worker in Community law may be ongoing so long as the person is continuing to look for employment after having

67 C-98/96 *Ertanir* [1997] ECR I-5179.
68 C-36/96 *Günaydin* [1997] ECR I-5143.
69 C-1/97 *Birden* [1998] ECR I-7747.
70 C-1/97 *Birden* [1998] ECR I-7747.

been employed in the host State.[71] However, a person who has not yet worked in a host State but is looking for employment is categorised as a work-seeker.[72] By analogy with the position of a Community national who is a work-seeker in a host Member State the Court considered the situation of a Turkish worker, who after working lawfully in a Member State for over eight years, left his employment voluntarily in search of a new job. His residence permit expired and after an interval of 11 days he applied for a further permit to continue his search for employment and residence in the host State. This was refused.

The Court found that the right to free access to any paid employment would be deprived of any content if a Turkish worker lost his or her residence right on leaving employment in search of another job. How long the worker must be allowed to remain while looking for a new job rests with the Member States (subject to Article 6(3) of Decision 1/80). "That period, must, however, be sufficient not to deprive of substance the right accorded by the third indent of Article 6(1) by jeopardising in fact the Turkish worker's prospects of finding new employment."[73] In contrast, however, where a Turkish worker has definitely left the labour force of a Member State because he or she has for example reached retirement age or become permanently incapacitated for work he or she falls outside the scope of Article 6 of Decision 1/80.[74]

What is not entirely clear is whether this means that the Turkish worker continues to be a worker for the purposes of Community law but loses the protection of the provision of the Decision or whether the individual ceases to be a worker full stop. The later interpretation seems more likely according to the Court's jurisprudence as the defining characteristic of employment is fundamental to the quality of "worker". A worker who is not and never again will be in employment loses that basic characteristic. On the other hand, the child of a Turkish worker who enjoys free access to the labour market after completion of vocational training and in accordance with Article 7 second indent of Decision 1/80 has greater protection, his or her right to free access to the labour market appears to be indefinite, whether or not she or he is in fact using the right.

---

[71] 66/85 *Lawrie-Blum* [1986] ECR 2121; 39/86 *Lair* [1988] ECR 3161; C-85/96 *Martinez Sala* [1998] ECR I-2691.
[72] C-292/89 *Antonissen* [1991] ECR I-745.
[73] C-171/95 *Tetik* [1997] ECR I-341.
[74] C-434/93 *Bozkurt* [1995] ECR I-1475.

This must be differentiated from the meaning of "worker" for other purposes in Community law, specifically for social security purposes. There a worker may retain that status after leaving the labour force for retirement. This also applies to third country national workers protected by agreements between their state and the Community as regards equal treatment in social security. The question arose regarding the status of a retired Moroccan worker whose daughter sought to rely on the equal treatment provision relating to social security in the Morocco Agreement. The Court held:

"As regards the concept of 'worker' in Article 41(1) of the Agreement, it encompasses both active workers and those who have left the labour market after reaching the age required for receipt of an old age pension or after becoming victims of the materialisation of one of the risks creating entitlement to allowances falling under other branches of social security."[75]

The differentiation of the concept of worker in Community law is not helpful to its comprehensibility. Nor does it seem particularly necessary to exclude retired and permanently disabled workers from the concept of worker for the purposes of coherence. However, the division and differing meaning of worker for one or another purpose in Community law does not appear to depend on the nationality of the worker.[76] Nor does it depend on whether an individual is seeking to rely on that quality through a third country agreement or through the EC Treaty.

At the start of this section, I asked the question whether there is a consistent interpretation by the Court of Justice of the concept of worker in Community law as regards third country nationals protected as such under agreements between their state of nationality and the Community and nationals of the Member States. The answer, which appears from an analysis of the Turkey case-law, is that there is. While the concept of worker is not uniform under different provisions of the EC Treaty itself, the variations which occur are not dependent on the nationality of the worker. The width of the concept varies from one third country agreement to another and of course is in all cases more limited than that found in the EC Treaty. Nonetheless, the content of the concept remains constant.

---

[75] C-18/90 *Kziber* [1991] ECR I-199.

[76] Leaving aside, of course the question of the rights of workers living in their state of nationality, who, because they have never exercised a free movement right to take employment in another Member State find themselves outside the scope of Community rights attaching to free movement of that kind.

5.4. THE TREATMENT OF FAMILY MEMBERS

So far I have looked at two areas in respect of a third country agreement where there has been a substantial assimilation of the design and concept to that used in the EC Treaty. By creating a framework which is governed by the same principles of law and an interpretation which seeks coherence of concepts, the relationship of the individual third country national to the Member State and Community is fundamentally the same as for Community nationals. The difference then rests in the material scope.

I will now turn to an area where there is less consistency, not least because of the more limited material scope. The purpose in looking, then, at the rights of family members under the EC Treaty and third country agreements is to see what happens when a derived right attaches to an individual right of a worker exercising economic activities in a host Member State. For Community national workers, the right to family reunion is governed by Article 10 of Regulation 1612/68. The right contained there accrues to family members of any nationality, and is to install themselves with the worker employed in the host Member State. A direct (though adjectival) right is extended to spouses and descendants under 21 years or who are dependants, and to any dependent relatives in the ascending line of the worker and his or her spouse. The admission of other family members who are dependent on the worker or living under his or her roof must be facilitated by the host State. The only limitation on the right is the existence, at the time of the right's exercise, of "normal housing" for the family.[77] By Article 11 most of these family members are entitled to take up economic activities in the host Member State. Article 12 guarantees equal treatment for the children of Community national workers in the State's general, educational, apprenticeship and vocational training courses (and a duty to encourage the best possible conditions for such education).

The purpose of family reunion provisions for Community nationals according to the Regulation's preamble is:

> "that obstacles to the mobility of workers shall be eliminated, in particular as regards the worker's right to be joined by his family and the conditions for the integration of that family in the host country."

Although the right accrues to the family members, as far as spouses are concerned it is dependent on the worker and cannot survive once the worker has finally left the territory of the host Member State.[78] As far as children are concerned however, the situation is different. The only third country agreement which deals with the issue of residence of family members of third country

---

[77]   249/86 *Commission v Germany* [1989] ECR 1263.
[78]   36/82 *Morson* [1982] ECR 3723; C-297/88 *Dzodzi* [1990] ECR I-3763.

national workers is the Turkey Agreement by virtue of Decision 1/80. At Article 7, the Decision does not identify which family members come within its ambit (see discussion above) but once they have been authorised to join a Turkish worker they are entitled, subject to the priority to Community national workers, to respond to any offer of employment after three years legal residence in the State and free access to paid employment after at least five years' legal residence.

A separate regime applies to children who have completed a course of vocational training. Irrespective of the length of time they have been resident in the Member State they are entitled to respond to an offer of employment provided one of their parents has been legally employed in the State for at least three years. Such children residing legally in the host State are entitled to equal treatment as regards entry qualifications for courses of general education, apprenticeship and vocational training and "to benefit from the advantages provided for under national legislation in this area" (Article 9 Decision 1/80).

Within this differing material and personal scope, what comparisons can be made which may be useful to the question under consideration? I will look at the following:

(1) Cohabitation *versus* employment in determining the residence rights of spouses;

(2) Education as a tool of integration.

1. Cohabitation

Do spouses need to cohabit to enjoy the right to family reunion under Community law? This question arose both in respect of Article 10 of Regulation 1612/68 and Article 7 of Decision 1/80. The judgments of the Court differ very substantially in the two cases: for the spouse seeking to rely on Regulation 1612/68 it held that cohabitation was not required; as regards the Turkish spouse, three years cohabitation was required to establish a residence right. The two cases and *Diatta* [79] *Kadiman* [80] appear, at first reading, to conflict. Before accepting a fundamental difference in the concept of family reunion for the two categories of workers, it is worth investigating the reasoning of the Court. It is my view that the logic of the Court employed in the two cases is the same, it is the underlying difference of the subsidiary legislation in respect of employment rights which results in the variation between the answers.

---

[79]   267/83 [1985] ECR 567.
[80]   C-351/95 [1997] ECR I-2133.

In both cases, the Member State against whom the actions were brought and the intervenors argued that cohabitation is a requirement. In the first case,[81] relating to the spouse of a Community worker the arguments were as follows:

For the plaintiff, Mrs Diatta: there is no express requirement of cohabitation in Article 10 of Regulation 1612/68; further the "normal housing" requirement does not by implication impose such a condition as housing may be provided separately by the couple; it is not appropriate for the immigration authorities to seek to determine whether a couple in dispute is likely to be reconciled; if cohabitation were a requirement this would give the Community national worker an unacceptable degree of power over the spouse as by refusing to cohabit he or she could at any moment cause the spouse's expulsion; finally, Article 11 giving the right to engage in economic activities provides in itself a separate right of residence for a spouse who is working (irrespective of his or her nationality).

For the respondent, Land Berlin: the purpose of the family reunion provisions is to protect migrant workers and to guarantee their mobility by enabling them to maintain family ties. Therefore there are no grounds for granting a right of residence to family members where that right is not based on cohabitation. The German, UK and Dutch governments supported the Land Berlin, arguing that the purpose of the provision is to enable cohabitation and once that ceases no residence right can be sustained. Further there can be no independent right of residence resulting from the right to work.[82]

The Commission argued that the right of free movement is fundamental and cannot be made dependent on how spouses wish to conduct their married life. Attitudes towards marital relations vary according to the Member States and individuals, which is exactly why there is no cohabitation requirement in Article 10. The only requirement which could be placed on a couple was evidence of the marriage. Further the Commission argued that the right of residence of a family member would not be extinguished by the dissolution of the marriage.

The Court accepted most of the Commission's arguments, with the notable exception of a right of residence enduring after the dissolution of the marriage. Its reasoning was that the purpose of the Regulation is to enable workers to move freely within the territory of other Member States. To achieve this, a right must be accorded to family members to follow the worker should they so wish. No requirement of cohabitation can be placed on this right. This interpretation is supported, according to the Court, by the right contained in Article 11 for the spouse to take up economic activities which may well be either in other

---

[81] 267/83 *Diatta* [1985] ECR 567.
[82] This is interesting in comparison with Articles 6 and 7 of Decision 1/80 which presuppose exactly this situation.

parts of the host State or could require the spouse to live apart from the Community worker.

What is noteworthy here is the interrelated nature of the right not to cohabit with the right to take employment. This arises in two ways, first, the right of the Community national to move from the home State to a host State is the underlying rationale for a right of family reunion. Secondly, the right to engage in economic activities for the spouse underpins the right of the spouse not to cohabit with the Community worker. Therefore, arguing *a contrario*, if there is no right of free movement then a right to family reunion does not accrue; secondly until or unless the spouse has the right to engage in economic activities a requirement to cohabit may be justified but once such a right is acquired such a limitation cannot be applied.

The same question of cohabitation arose 12 years later as regards a Turkish worker and his spouse.[83] The husband had worked and been resident in Germany since 1977. The couple were married in 1985 but as the husband did not obtain an unlimited residence permit until 1988, family reunion was delayed. The wife was authorised to join her husband in Germany in 1990, which she did. Then the trouble started. Amidst confusing and disputed facts, the Court came to the conclusion that the couple cohabited until, at the latest, February 1992. The wife had been working in Germany, and at the relevant time had a job. So the question was whether she could rely on having resided as the spouse of a Turkish worker under Article 7(1) of Decision 1/80 for three years in order to found a right to continue in employment and therefore to continue to live in Germany.

The plaintiff, Mrs Kadiman, argued that, as she had been resident in Germany for more than three years, and was still married to her husband she was entitled to an extension of her residence permit under Article 7(1) of Decision 1/80. The respondent government, Germany, supported by the Dutch and French governments argued (in essence) that the right to continued residence under Article 7(1) is predicated on cohabitation. Only after the couple have cohabited for three years can the spouse claim a right to accept employment and therefore (as accepted by all and established in the *Kus* judgment[84]) a right of residence. The Commission accepted that within the first three years of the spouse's residence in the host State it is open to the Member State to place a requirement of cohabitation on the family. However, it argued that within that period, should there be objective justification, such as the places of employment or vocational training of the spouses, the requirement must not be applied.

---

83   C-351/95 *Kadiman* [1997] ECR I-2133.
84   C-237/91 *Kus* [1992] ECR I-6781.

The Court commenced by holding that Article 7 of Decision 1/80 has direct effect. It pointed out that Turkish workers do not enjoy a right of free movement within the Community. Under the provisions of Decision 1/80 they benefit only from certain rights "in the host Member State whose territory they have lawfully entered and where they have been in legal employment for a specified period of time". It added:

> "Decision 1/80 does not encroach upon the competence of the Member States to regulate both the entry into their territories of Turkish nationals and the conditions under which they take up their first employment, but merely regulates, in Article 6, the situation of Turkish workers already legally integrated into the labour force of the Member State."

As Turkish workers are not entitled to free movement and their initial access to the territory and labour market are subject to national legislation, so their spouses' access to the territory may be subject to an authorisation requirement. The purpose of Article 7, according to the Court, is "to favour employment and residence of Turkish workers duly registered as belonging to the labour force of a Member State by ensuring that their family links are maintained there". In other words, the provision is not designed to create the links but only to maintain them once created: enabling family members to be with a migrant worker and then consolidating their position by granting them the right to obtain employment.

Therefore on this point, the Court held:

> "Decision 1/80 does not in principle prevent the authorities of a Member State from making extension of the residence permit of a family member authorised to join a Turkish worker in that Member State in order to enable the family to be together subject to the condition that the person concerned actually lives with that worker for the period of three years."

The national discretion of the Member State applies throughout the first three years. However, it is a fettered discretion as the family member is now within the scope of Decision 1/80. That discretion is limited by the continuing right of the family member not to be expelled except as authorised by Article 14 of Decision 1/80 (see below, page 162). As the purpose of the provision is to maintain family links but is not accompanied by a right of free movement of the principal, there is no right of family reunion arising from the Decision and the spouse remains subject to national discretionary requirements until, but only until, he or she is eligible to take employment. On the other hand as the

Advocate General correctly stated in *Eyüp*, cohabitation can in fact overcome irregularities in the marriage relationship under the provisions of Article 7.[85]

Once the spouse is entitled to take employment then the restriction on cohabitation appears to cease. To this extent then, there is an assimilation of the position of the spouse of a Turkish worker to that of a Community national worker, in that their right to live separately from their spouse but still on the territory of the host State arises in conjunction with the right to take employment. In respect of both categories, an independent right to work and reside only accrues if the spouse can bring him or herself within other provisions relating to that category: for Community nationals, the spouse must be a national of a Member State in order for his or her residence right to survive dissolution of the marriage. For the spouse of a Turkish national, provided he or she is also a Turkish national, once he or she has worked for one year for an employer which wishes to continue the employment he or she may be able to rely directly on the rights contained in Article 6 of Decision 1/80.

2. Education and Children

Both the children of Community workers and those of Turkish workers have a right to equal treatment as regards education.[86]

---

[85] "La notion de 'membre de la famille' visée à l'article 7, premier alinéa de la décision n° 1/80 du Conseil d'association CEE-Turquie du 19 septembre 1980, relative au développement de l'association entre la Communauté économique européenne et la Turquie s'étend au concubin d'un travailleur turc vivant en union libre, à condition qu'il y ait, entre les intéressés, un lien familial sérieux et stable comme celui qui s'instaure lorsque ceux-ci ont vécu ensemble, sans interruption, après le divorce et contracté par la suite un nouveau mariage. La condition de cohabitation pour une durée minimale de cinq ans prévue par l'article 7, premier alinéa, second tiret, de la décision n° 1/80 précitée, est remplie dès lors qu'un travailleur turc a contracté mariage, a divorcé et s'est remarié avec la même personne, si les conjoints ont effectivement continué à vivre ensemble entre les deux mariages et que les périodes de vie conjugale commune, prises dans leur totalité ont été d'au moins cinq ans." C-65/98 *Eyüp* Opinion: 18 November 1999. Similarly from the decision in C-179/98 *Mesbah* [1999] ECR I-7955 it appears that family members protected under the third country agreements include wider family members such as mothers-in-law, in accordance with Article 10 of Regulation 1612/68.

[86] Article 9 of Decision 1/80 provides that Turkish children residing legally in a Member State of the Community with their parents who are or have been legally employed in that Member State shall be admitted to a course of general education, apprenticeship and vocational training under the same educational entry qualifications as the children of nationals of that Member State. They may, in that Member State, be eligible to benefit from the advantages provided for under the national legislation of this area.

But when does a child cease to be a child? A child over 21 of a Community national worker sought to rely on his right to equal treatment in respect of education, contained in Article 12 of Regulation 1612/68, to defeat a national rule which excluded him (but not nationals of the Member State) from the personal scope of an education grant because he was over 21 and no longer dependent on his parents, and therefore outside the scope of Article 10 of the Regulation on family reunion. The Member State argued that the age limit of 21 years must apply equally to both the family reunion provision and the education provision. The Court disagreed, emphasising that the purpose of the provision is to make it possible for such children to achieve integration in the society of the host State.[87] The Advocate General stated that the rationale underlying the Article is to ensure the fullest possible integration of the migrant worker's family into the society of the host State. For this reason the age limit to be found in Article 10 could not apply to equal treatment in education. In the light of the Court's finding in *Akman* it is clear that the same rule applies in respect of the children of Turkish workers under Article 9 of Decision 1/80.

For the children of Turkish workers not only the question of age arises but also their categorisation under national law. The children of Turkish workers are entitled to take employment on completion of any course of vocational training irrespective of the length of time they have spent there provided one of their parents has worked for at least three years in the host State. But who is a child? The child of a Turkish worker had been admitted to Germany exclusively for the purpose of vocational training and related employment. Her parents had been resident and working in Germany for many years. At the end of her training she sought an extension of her permit, which was refused under national law. As she had not completed one year's employment with an employer who was seeking an extension of her employment, she could not rely on Article 6(1) of Decision 1/80. So the question arose: could she rely on the second paragraph of Article 7 of the Decision even though she had not been admitted to the State for the purpose of family reunion?

The issue which underlay the case was, of course, the fact that the child was over the age limit under national law for family reunion purposes. If an age limit could be implied into the provision in question, she would not have been able to remain in the Member State where her parents were resident. The Member State argued that national law on admission must also regulate access to the benefits of Article 7, in other words, unless the child had been admitted for the purpose of family reunion then he or she could not rely on Article 7. The Court limited its reasoning to the wording of the provision which it found

---

[87]   C-7/94 *Gaal* [1995] ECR I-1031.

to be free-standing. It followed its earlier jurisprudence regarding the irrelevance of the ground of first admission of the Turkish national so long as the requirements of the provision relied upon had been fulfilled[88] and held that the child of a Turkish worker, in order to enjoy the right to respond to an offer of employment after completing his or her vocational education in the Member State, does not need to have been admitted to the host State for the purpose of family reunion.[89] The Advocate General, emphasised that:

> "a requirement that the child should enter the Member State with a view to family reunification would in effect render the provision inapplicable to children over the age of 18 who, at least in certain Member States, no longer have the right to enter for that purpose."

The Court has insisted that the right of children of Turkish workers to seek employment in the host Member State is not limited to his or her parent's presence:

> "A Turkish national ... is entitled to respond to any offer of employment in the host Member State after having completed a course of vocational training there, and is consequently to be issued with a residence permit, when one of his parents has in the past been legally employed in that State for three years, however, it is not required that the parent in question should still work or be resident in the Member State in question at the time when his child wishes to gain access to the employment market there."[90]

The comparison then, between the treatment of children of Community national workers and of third country national workers protected by the agreement, reveals a tendency towards assimilation of concepts: implied limitations on the basis of age are not accepted where the result would be to exclude the child from a benefit. Only an express limitation can have this effect. The purpose of the restrictive interpretation appears, in both cases, though not clearly stated as regards the third country agreement, to be based in the principle of integration of children into the host community's labour market.

5.5.   THE MEANING OF PUBLIC POLICY AND LOSS OF STATUS

Before leaving the subsidiary legislation of the Turkey Agreement, I will look at the question of public policy and loss of status. This covers two primary areas: (1) the uniformity of the concept of public policy as regards expulsion; and (2) under what circumstances can a right to work and reside be lost.

---

[88]   C-237/91 *Kus* [1992] ECR I-6781.
[89]   C-355/93 *Eroglu* [1994] ECR I-5113.
[90]   C-210/97 *Akman* [1998] ECR I-7519.

1. Public Policy, Public Security and Public Health

The EC Treaty states that the right of free movement for workers is subject to limitations justified on grounds of public policy, public security or public health.[91] These limitations are the subject of the Directive which has been longest in force as regards Article 39 EC – Directive 64/221. The Directive states that these grounds may not be used to serve economic ends; shall be based exclusively on the personal conduct of the individual concerned; cannot justify expulsion on the ground exclusively of criminal convictions and cannot be used to justify expulsion for expiry of an identity card or passport.

There is no provision of the Turkey Agreement itself which corresponds to Article 39(2) EC. If such a limitation is to be found in the agreement, it would have to be implied from Article 12, the intention of the parties to be guided by Articles 39 et seq of the EC Treaty for the implementation of free movement of workers. Article 14 of Decision 1/80, however, does provide that the whole of the Decision and the rights contained therein are subject to limitations justified on grounds of public policy, public security or public health, in other words the same grounds as for Community nationals.

As regards Community workers, the Court has given a very restrictive interpretation to the provisos. The worker's presence must constitute a sufficiently serious threat to public policy (security or health) to justify the measure. In general, as has been discussed in some depth in Chapter 2, in interpreting the provisos the Court has consistently stressed the fact that their purpose is to limit the discretionary power of Member States as regards the expulsion of foreign nationals.[92] The interpretation of the provisos by the Court has been framed in the context of a restriction on the free movement of persons. That element is missing as regards the Turkey Agreement, where free movement has not been achieved. The test for Community nationals in respect of criminal activity is that it must involve "a genuine and sufficiently serious threat affecting one of the fundamental interests of society".[93]

Can the same wording in a third country agreement's secondary legislation carry the same interpretation? The question has been asked of the Court in the case of C-340/97 Nazli. In that case a Turkish worker had acquired rights under Article 6 of Decision 1/80. He was subsequently convicted of a criminal offence for which the sentence was suspended and a decision to expel him was made on general preventative grounds, which cannot be applied to Community

---

[91] Article 39(3) EC.
[92] 41/74 Van Duyn [1974] ECR 1337.
[93] 30/77 Bouchereau [1977] ECR 1999; 115-116/81 Adoui & Cornaille [1982] ECR 1665. A serious threat does not exist where the activity is one against which the State does not take measures in respect of its own nationals.

workers. The Advocate General, while considering that a difference in interpretation between the wording of the EC Treaty and the Turkey Agreement's subsidiary legislation is possible, nonetheless rejected that possibility in respect of the Article 14 protection from expulsion in respect of a Turkish worker who has completed more than four years work and residence within a Member State.

The premise which I have developed here is that once the issue of the purpose and intent of an agreement has been resolved, then in the absence of very strong countervailing factors, a consistent interpretation of concept of a worker and his or her family members contained in the EC Treaty and third country agreement is appropriate. It is apparent that in the development of the jurisprudence of the Court regarding the third country agreements the structural approach to the issue of workers follows the same form as in respect of the EC Treaty – the creation of a direct relationship between the worker, be he or she Community national or third country national and the Community, in addition to the relationship which exists as between the worker and the Member State and of course the Member State to the Community. Therefore, where such a relationship is created which enables the worker to rely on rights of work and residence acquired by virtue of and enforceable in Community law, the interference with those rights should not be subject to a lower level of protection than in respect of Community nationals in the absence of a clear indication by the legislator that that is the intention. What is missing from the equation is of course Turkey, the third state. The Community's relationship with the worker excludes, in this regard, the role of the state of origin.

In theory at least, the triangle has become a pyramid as there is another party, the third country which is a party to the agreement. However, so far the role of the third country has been limited to the participation in the promulgation of legislation. It has not involved itself directly in the protection of rights before the Court of Justice. The Turkish government has however, provided financial and other support for Turkish individuals to pursue claims before the Court.

2. Loss of Acquired Rights: Fraud and Documentation

The second aspect of this question is that of loss of rights once acquired. This divides into three branches – first, where the acquisition is apparent but challenged: the presence of fraud; secondly, where the acquisition has taken place but has not been documented according to national law; thirdly where rights have been acquired by an individual who is no longer working.

Fraud

The consistent approach of the Court in respect of the risk of fraud within the context of the EC Treaty may be found in the *Singh* decision:[94]

> "As regards the risk of fraud the Court has consistently held that the facilities created by the Treaty cannot have the effect of allowing the persons who benefit from them to evade the application of national legislation and of prohibiting Member States from taking the measures necessary to prevent such abuse."

In other words, fraud cannot result in a person acquiring a right in Community law which but for the fraud he or she would not enjoy. The question then is, how is fraud to be determined and upon whom does the burden of proof or disproof rest. In free movement of persons cases, this issue has arisen more than once in respect of social security matters.

Mr Paletta and his family are Italian nationals working in Germany. They not only took their annual holidays on a regular basis in Italy, but the family, as a whole, became ill while on holiday and submitted medical certificates to their German health insurance fund on the basis of which their employer continued to pay their wages until they recovered, returned to Germany and continued work. After a number of such occasions, the employer refused to pay their wages, on the basis that it was not satisfied that the medical certificates properly attested to an illness which prevented the family from returning to work on time. In a series of references to the Court of Justice relating to the validity of Mr Paletta's medical certificates, the Court finally held that the national court may query the genuineness of a medical certificate and:

> "Take account – on the basis of objective evidence – of abuse or fraudulent conduct on the part of the worker concerned, in order, where appropriate, to deny him the benefit of the provisions of Community law on which he seeks to rely, they must nevertheless assess such conduct in the light of the objectives pursued by those provisions."[95]

Further, the Court found that even on the basis of adequate supporting evidence that there are serious grounds for doubting the existence of the alleged incapacity, the worker him or herself who claims to be incapacitated cannot be required to produce additional evidence that the medically certified incapacity for work is genuine.

In another case of alleged fraud, the plaintiff, Mrs Dafeki, produced a birth certificate amended by court order indicating her age as some years older than the host Member State had been led to believe by the original birth certificate

---

[94]   C-370/90 *Singh* [1992] ECR I-4265.
[95]   C-206/94 *Paletta* [1996] ECR I-2357.

which she had produced. The result of the order changing the certificate's date of her birth was that she was entitled to an old-age pension earlier than would otherwise have been the case.[96] The administration in the host Member State was reluctant to accept the amended birth certificate and the resulting challenge eventually arrived at the doors of the Court of Justice. The Court held that the competent authorities and the courts of a Member State must accept certificates and analogous documents relative to personal status issued by the competent authorities of the other Member States unless their accuracy is seriously undermined by concrete evidence relating to the individual case in question. This is indeed a high threshold for an allegation of fraud.

Both cases relate to the genuineness or otherwise of documents produced in one Member State whether by public or private authorities and presented for the purpose of accessing rights in another Member State. In both cases, the Court gave guidance to the national court to the effect that an allegation of fraud must be substantiated to a high degree by the authority making the allegation and the national courts cannot accept a displacement of that burden of proof onto the applicant unless the evidence produced by the authority is concrete and seriously undermines the accuracy of the document.

When examining the question of fraud in respect of rights acquired under Decision 1/80, is there a similar approach? Mr Kol was convicted of having made a false declaration in order to obtain a German residence permit. Only as a result of the aggregation of periods of time worked after the acquisition by fraud of the residence permit with periods worked before under a residence permit properly obtained did Mr Kol purport to acquire rights under Article 6 of Decision 1/80. The Court held that the requirement that a Turkish worker's position in the labour force be stable and secure in order to acquire rights under Article 6 could not be satisfied where such an aggregation was required. Therefore the worker could not rely on rights attached to completion of one year or more of employment. On the issue of fraud, the Court stressed twice that the interpretation which left Mr Kol without protection, was based on his conviction:

> "*a fortiori* that interpretation must apply in a situation such as that in the main proceedings where the Turkish migrant worker obtained a residence permit of unlimited duration in the host Member State only by means of inaccurate declarations in respect of which he was convicted of fraud ... Periods of employment after a residence permit has been obtained by means of fraudulent conduct which has led to a conviction cannot be regarded as legal for the purposes of application of Article 6(1) of Decision 1/80."[97]

---

[96] C-336/94 *Dafeki* [1997] ECR I-6761.
[97] C-285/95 *Kol* [1997] ECR I-3069.

The strict approach of the Court to an allegation of deception such as to vitiate the right of a Turkish worker is also evidenced in another decision regarding Mr Günaydin.[98] He was admitted to Germany for the purpose of training. At the time of his admission, both he and his employer confirmed that he would not stay beyond the limited period permitted by the German legislation. At the end of that period both Mr Günaydin and his employer wanted him to remain working for the company in Germany which was not permitted under national law. The question was then, could he rely on Article 6(1) of Decision 1/80 to establish a right to remain (he had already completed more than one year's employment in Germany with the company) for employment? The German government argued that as both Mr Günaydin and his employer had agreed at the outset that he would return to Turkey it was an abuse (not quite an allegation of fraud) for him to be able to rely on the rights contained in Article 6(1) of the Decision. The Court disagreed:

> "The fact that a Turkish worker wishes to extend his stay in the host Member State, although he expressly accepted its restriction, does not constitute an abuse of rights. The fact that he declared his intention of returning to Turkey after having been employed in the Member State for the purpose of perfecting his vocational skills is not such as to deprive him of the rights deriving from Article 6(1) of Decision No 1/80 unless it is established by the national court that that declaration was made with the sole intention of improperly obtaining work and residence permits for the host Member State."

The Court therefore makes it clear that an allegation amounting to fraud must be established by a court and cannot depend on an assessment by an administrative authority alone. Further, the test which the Court applies is that the sole purpose of the declaration was deceit.

Accordingly, fraud appears to be a consistent concept: it is subject to a very high substantiation requirement before an allegation of fraud can result in the loss of apparently acquired rights. In the *Kol* judgment, the Court did not go on to consider the burden of proof such as was at issue in the social security cases relating to Community migrant workers. However, from the approach it would seem appropriate and indeed likely that should this question arise under a third country agreement the result would be the same: i.e. the burden of proof rests heavily on the authority alleging the fraud and only exceptionally may be displaced.

---

[98]   C-36/96 *Günaydin* [1997] ECR I-5143.

The Consequence of Documentation and Lack Thereof

Moving then to the second branch of this section: apparent acquisition of rights but without the relevant documentation: this question strikes directly at the heart of the theme here – where a direct relationship between the individual and the Community has come into existence as a result of which the individual seeks to rely directly on a right arising from Community law to defeat an exercise of national discretion, can the claim be disallowed as a result of the failure of the national authorities to document the acquisition of the right?

As regards Community nationals, the answer is clear and was established as early as 1976. Mr Royer was a rather nasty character, with a string of convictions for armed robbery. But he was a French national running a discotheque in Belgium where he had failed to obtain a residence permit. So the Belgian police issued an order requiring him to leave the territory on account of his failure to obtain a residence permit. Among other things, the Court held that his right to move to another Member State is acquired independently of the issue of a residence permit; the permit does no more than evidence the right which Community law granted to Mr Royer.[99] Accordingly, the value of a residence permit is only declaratory of the right already acquired by Mr Royer by virtue of his exercise of the free movement right granted directly by virtue of the EC Treaty.

What then is the situation as regards, for instance, a Turkish worker who has acquired a right of continued residence and employment after one year on the territory of a Member State in accordance with Article 6 of Decision 1/80? It took a number of steps to get to a full answer to this question. The first step was in the case of Mr Kus, a Turkish national, who had acquired a right of residence and work on the basis of marriage to a German national, which marriage was subsequently dissolved. He was refused an extension of his permits. The Court considered the wording of Article 6(1) of Decision 1/80 and concluded that provided the requirement of one year's legal employment had been fulfilled under the conditions set out, then the reasons why the right to work was granted are not decisive for the acquisition of protection under Decision 1/80.[100] The Court had, however, already read into the rights contained in Article 6 of Decision 1/80 another requirement not self-evidently present on the wording of the provision: a requirement that the legality of the employment presupposes a stable and secure situation as a member of the labour force.[101] Therefore the exclusion of regard for the Member State's

---

[99]   48/75 *Royer* [1974] ECR 497.
[100] C-237/91 *Kus* [1992] ECR I-6781.
[101] C-192/89 *Sevince* [1990] ECR I-3461.

ground for initial admission to the territory and labour force of a Turkish worker already had a compensating counterbalance: a Community requirement (and definition) of stability and security.

The purpose of the requirement that the worker's position be stable and secure arises from the concern that persons in unstable positions, such as working lawfully pending the outcome of an appeal against refusal of an extension of a work permit or asylum seekers (though persons in this position have not been specifically referred to by the Court) could otherwise acquire rights of work and residence by the passage of time while the subject matter of the right is under dispute. A stable and secure situation implies the existence of an undisputed right of residence[102] even if this is time limited or ceases to exist on the occurrence of an event (such as divorce) so long as the event occurs after the completion of the minimum period of time to accrue protection.

The Court justified this interpretation on the grounds that the reserve to Member States to implement through national rules the rights contained in Decision 1/80:

> "cannot be construed as reserving to the Member States the power to adapt as they please rules governing Turkish workers already integrated in their labour force, permitting them to adopt unilaterally measures preventing certain categories of workers who already satisfy the conditions of Article 6(1) from benefiting from the progressively more extensive rights enshrined in the three indents of that paragraph."[103]

The sensitivity of the Court to potential abuse by the Member States is an attribute of the direct relationship between the Community and the individual: the individual is entitled to protection on account of his or her relationship with the Community. Any interference with that relationship of rights by the Member States constitutes abuse because in effect it strikes at the heart of the relationship. Therefore the Community must be arbiter of the decision when a worker has acquired a right: national discretion is thereby excluded.

The next step in the development of this jurisprudence then, should not have come as any surprise. Mr Bozkurt, a Turkish national who had worked for many years as an international lorry driver for a Dutch company, sought to rely on Article 6 of Decision 1/80 to reside in the Netherlands. When in the Netherlands working and residing, Mr Bozkurt did not, under national law, require a work or residence permit as the legality of his stays was regulated by his visa. The question before the Court was twofold: was he integrated into the Dutch labour force? This was a matter of fact for the national court which was directed to take into account the same principles as applicable in respect of

---

102 C-98/96 *Ertanir* [1997] ECR I-5179.
103 C-192/89 *Sevince* [1990] ECR I-3461

determining the issue of Community nationals: whether the employment relationship retains sufficiently close links with the territory of the Member State considering in particular the place where the person was hired, the territory on which the paid employment was based and the applicable national legislation in the field of employment and social security law.[104] If the first part of the question was answered in the affirmative and the worker was so integrated, could the Member State retain discretionary control over the determination of such integration by making it subject to a requirement to hold a particular form of evidence, i.e. residence or work permit?[105]

The Court followed the same line of reasoning as in respect of Community nationals:

> "It follows that the rights conferred under Article 6(1) on Turkish nationals who are already duly integrated into the labour force of a Member State are accorded to such nationals irrespective of whether or not the competent authorities have issued administrative documents which, in this context, can only be declaratory of the existence of those rights and cannot constitute a condition for their existence."[106]

Therefore once a Turkish worker has acquired rights of work and residence, it appears that the administrative formalities documenting those rights become declaratory rather than constitutive. This places, then, the Turkish worker in the same position as regards renewing work and residence permits as a Community national obtaining and renewing residence permits.

5.6. CONCLUSIONS

What conclusions then can be drawn from the legislator and court? First the legislator drafted the subsidiary legislation under the Turkey Agreement with a high degree of consistency with Community legislation covering the same area. This consistency is manifested by the similarity of concepts used, the form of the development of rights and the progressive nature of the process.

The consistency of the approach of the legislator in turn permits and indeed requires a consistency of interpretation by the Court of Justice. This becomes apparent in the judgments which, just as for Community nationals, demonstrate a concern to protect the individual worker whose rights are based on the agreement from the vagaries of Member State discretion. Therefore the triangular relationship in evidence as regards Community nationals and the

---

104 9/88 *Lopes da Veiga* [1989] ECR 2989.
105 C-434/93 *Bozkurt* [1995] ECR I-1475.
106 C-434/93 *Bozkurt* [1995] ECR I-1475.

Member State, the Member State and the Community and the Community and its nationals which involves the creation and assumption of direct rights and obligations along all three sides is equally applicable to third country nationals on the basis of agreements between their state and the Community. The additional point of reference is of course the third state which entered into the agreement. The existence of rights and obligations between that state and all three other parties in the Community triangle changes the form to one of a pyramid. However, so far, the involvement of the third state in the development of rights of third country nationals has been limited to one type: participation in the drafting of legislation (primary in the agreements themselves and secondary through participation on the Association Councils). As regards the rights of nationals, no specific use of the dispute resolution mechanisms of the agreement has been invoked.[107]

Before the creation of citizenship of the Union by the Maastricht Treaty, Community nationals exercising economic activities in a host Member State were, without exception, aliens. The regime established by the EC Treaty to regulate their migratory movements entailed the abolition of obstacles to free movement resulting in the creation of a direct relationship between the individual and the supra-national authority, the Community. The sphere of discretion of the Member States was accordingly diminished. The choice of movement, residence and economic activity was transferred from the Member State to the individual, guaranteed by the Community. When the Community came to enter into agreements with third countries the subject matter of which included natural persons, the same structure was adopted. These aliens were not, in law, treated fundamentally differently from Community national aliens. The difference was, instead in the extent of rights granted to them, not the nature of the rights or the form of their grant and enforcement. Under the Turkey Agreement and within its more limited scope, personal rights accrue to the individual as prescribed under the terms of the agreement and subsidiary legislation which within their material scope have the effect of excluding Member State discretion to the benefit of the choice of the individual.

For example, the Turkish seaman who had worked for almost eight years in a Member State and voluntarily chose to leave his job to look for work on land was entitled to rely on rights accruing under the agreement to make this choice contrary to the wish of the Member State.[108] On the same basis the daughter of a Turkish worker who had completed her vocational training in a Member State had a right to look for and accept work in that Member State irrespective of the

---

[107] Nor has the Commission exercised its powers under Article 226 EC in respect of the Agreements.
[108] C-171/95 *Tetik* [1997] ECR I-329.

wish of the Member State to force her to return to her country of nationality.[109] This strand of immigration law of the Community, based on a reciprocal agreement with a third state mirrors in style and content the law which the Community developed for nationals of the Member States. The difference between the two systems is one of material scope rather than basic design.[110]

---

[109] C-355/93 *Eroglu* [1994] ECR I-5113.

[110] For this reason the Court's jurisprudence on the Turkey Agreement may well have implications for the interpretation of rights for Community nationals.

CHAPTER 6

IMMIGRATION LESSONS:
THE CENTRAL AND EASTERN EUROPE AGREEMENTS

6.1. INTRODUCTION

In this chapter I will consider the reactions of the Member States to the first experiments in immigration legislation relating to third country nationals as carried out through the inclusion within the scope of some third country agreements of provisions on natural persons. After the experiments with Turkey, the Maghreb and Lomé countries, the tool of regulating work and residence of third country nationals through the Community's third country agreements was next used in the agreements[1] with the Central and Eastern European countries (CEECs)[2] from 1990 onwards.[3] In this chapter I will look at the use of third country agreements to provide a mechanism for legal economic migration from countries with substantial pressure to emigrate to the European Union.

The history of these agreements begins properly in June 1988 with the Declaration of Luxembourg. According to Toledano Laredo who was a participant for the Commission in the discussions, the Declaration led to putting ideological concerns on one side and allowing the Community and Comecon to establish economic discussions.[4]

---

1 These agreements are collectively known as the Europe Agreements.
2 These are comprised of Bulgaria, the Czech Republic, Estonia, Hungary, Latvia, Lithuania, Poland, Romania, Slovakia and Slovenia.
3 This tool was subsequently used in the Economic Free Trade Agreement with the EFTA states (excluding Switzerland) in accordance with the provisions of which nationals of those states got immediate free movement rights within the territory of the Union. The EEA Agreement was signed on 2.5.92, amended by protocol to exclude Switzerland as a result of the rejection of the Agreement by referendum in that State on 19.3.93. The EEA Agreement entered into force on 1.1.94 for all states except Liechtenstein for whom it entered into force on 1.5.95. As Austria, Finland and Sweden became Member States of the Union on 1.1.95 its value now is mainly for Norwegian, Liechtenstein and Icelandic nationals.
4 "conduisent à la mise à l'écart des questions idéologiques entre la Communauté et les pays du Comecon, qui peuvent établir avec elle des relations diplomatiques et engager ou poursuivre des négotiations ouvertes et formelles appélées à traiter les problèmes économiques et tarifaires, les restrictions quantitatives, le respect des droits de l'homme, le dialogue entre entités souveraines." A. Toledano Laredo, L'Union Européenne, l'ex-

Between 1991 and 1996 the European Community concluded agreements with ten CEECs formerly within the sphere of influence of the former USSR. These agreements are noteworthy not least because they provide for: safeguarding rights of workers from CEEC countries, though these rights do not extend as far as those of Turkish workers under the subsidiary legislation of the Turkey Agreement; a right of access to the territory and economic activity for nationals of the CEECs engaging in self-employment and for service provision.[5]

While it may well be the case that the Member States were not entirely aware, at the time of the conclusion of the pre-1990 agreements of their impact on domestic immigration law and policy, the same cannot be said of this generation of agreements (i.e. the Europe Agreements). By the time of the signing of the first of these agreements in December 1991, the Court of Justice had already handed down judgment in the most important immigration cases on the first and second generation agreements: spelling out the consequences of the secondary legislation of the Turkey Agreement[6] and the direct effect of the non-discrimination provisions in the Maghreb Agreements[7] and what they meant for national immigration and social security laws. The Member States were well aware of the impact of these two cases[8] and indeed, in the drafting of provisions in the Europe Agreements relating to social security, no reference to non-discrimination is made as a result of the intention of the Member States to avoid the possibility of direct effect as found by the Court of Justice in respect of the Morocco Agreement.[9]

On 16 July 1997 the Commission presented its Communication "Agenda 2000" to the European Parliament which set out in a single framework the outline for the development of the European Union and its policies beyond the turn of the century, the impact of enlargement of the Union as a whole and the future financial framework beyond 2000, taking into account the prospect of an enlarged Union.[10] On the same day the President of the Commission speaking to the Parliament confirmed the Commission's proposal to open

---

Union Soviétique et les pays de l'Europe centrale et orientale: un aperçu de leurs accords, Cahiers de droit européen, No 1-2 1994 p. 543.

5   I will not treat this issue here in view of the complexity of the interchange with the GATS which would require a much wider exploration.

6   C-192/89 *Sevince* [1990] ECR I-3461.

7   C-18/90 *Kziber* [1991] ECR I-199.

8   S. van Raepenbusch, La jurisprudence de la Cour de justice des Communautés européenes vis-à-vis des ressortissants de pays tiers, in M. den Boer, *The Implementation of Schengen: First the Widening, Now the Deepening*, Maastricht, 1997, p. 41.

9   D. Martin & E. Guild, *Free Movement of Persons in the European Union*, Butterworths, London, 1996, p. 295 *et seq.*

10 European Commission, Agenda 2000 Press Release IP/97/660 16.7.97.

negotiations on accession to the Union with five CEECs as well as Cyprus, specifically, Hungary, Poland, Estonia, the Czech Republic and Slovenia.[11] The announcement of the choice of the first five for accession negotiations was carefully couched in terms not to offend the others, reaffirming that as they achieve the requirements of the Copenhagen criteria of June 1993[12] for membership so their applications will be reviewed. In 1999 the Commission proposed commencement of negotiations towards accession with all the CEEC, Baltic and related applicants including Cyprus and Malta. Following the Helsinki European Council meeting in December 1999, negotiations have been commenced with all the remaining CEECs, Baltic States, Malta and Cyprus and Turkey has been accepted as a candidate for accession. Russia has not applied for membership. Separate partnership and association agreements have been settled with it and the successor states of the former USSR.

The certainty regarding accession of the CEECs has not always been so stable.[13] Nonetheless, from the fall of the Berlin Wall the pressure to include in the European Union these former Eastern block states had been growing.

The agreements settled with the CEECs are similar and were drafted and negotiated by the European Community with this intention. The agreements are mixed in that they include provisions, which are exclusively within the competence of the Community, such as free movement of goods, and provisions in respect of which primary competence rests with the Member States, such as political dialogue.[14]

Maresceau and Montaguti date the adaptation of the agreements to the objective of accession from the Copenhagen Council meeting on 21 and 22 June 1993 "where it was accepted that the associated states of Central and Eastern Europe could apply for membership".[15] According to their analysis of

---

11 Address to the European Parliament by Mr J. Santer, President of the European Commission, Speech 97/161 16.7.97.

12 The European Council of June 1993 adopted three main criteria for membership to be applied to the CEECs: (1) stable institutions guaranteeing democracy, the rule of law, human rights and the protection of minorities; (2) the existence of a functioning market economy as well as the capacity to cope with competitive pressure and market forces within the Union; (3) the ability to take on the obligations of membership, including adherence to the aims of political, Economic and Monetary Union.

13 See for instance EU complaints about Poland, BBC Summary of World Broadcasts, May 2 1997, source: TV Polonia, Warsaw.

14 See for instance Title III: Free Movement of Goods and Title I: Political Dialogue of the EC Poland Agreement. For the purpose of analysing the agreements, I will make reference to the Poland Agreement in particular. It was used in the political negotiations as the blueprint for the other agreements.

15 M. Maresceau and E. Montaguti, The Relations Between the European Union and Central and Eastern Europe: A Legal Appraisal, CMLRev 32:1327-1367, [1995].

the available documents, they conclude that the Community was at first very reluctant to make any reference to possible membership of the associated countries. However, the flexibility of the agreements is such that a change of direction by the Community could easily be incorporated into its structure.[16]

The Europe Agreements: Central and Eastern European Countries, Baltic States and Slovenia (* for individuals a right of establishment is delayed in these Agreements)

Country	Date of Signature	Entry into Force
Bulgaria[17]	08.03.1993	01.02.1995
Czech Republic[18]	04.10.1993	01.02.1995
*Estonia[19]	12.06.1995	01.02.1998
Hungary[20]	16.12.1991	01.02.1994
*Latvia[21]	12.06.1995	01.02.1998
*Lithuania[22]	12.06.1995	01.02.1998
Poland[23]	16.12.1991	01.02.1994
Romania[24]	08.03.1993	01.02.1995
Slovakia[25]	04.10.1993	01.02.1995
*Slovenia[26]	10.06.1996	01.03.1999

---

16 O'Leary suggests that the drafting of the objectives of these agreements, which intentionally focuses on the ambition of the CEEC to accede to the Union, could have consequences for the interpretation of the agreements (see S. O'Leary, Employment and Residence for Turkish Workers and their Families: Analogies with the Case-Law of the Court of Justice on Article 48[39] EC in *Scritti in onore di Giuseppe Federico Mancini* Vol. II, Diritto dell Europea Guiffrè Editore 1998, p.731). In my view, it would not be correct for the Court to interpret the intention of the agreements from the preamble alone. In view of the developments as discussed by Maresceau and Montaguti, and most importantly the Agenda 2000 Commission White Paper, it would be most peculiar to limit the interpretation of the purpose of the agreements in such a way.
17 OJ 1994 L 358.
18 OJ 1994 L 360.
19 OJ 1999 L 0000.
20 OJ 1993 L 347.
21 OJ 1998 L 26.
22 OJ 1998 L 51.
23 OJ 1993 L 348.
24 OJ 1994 L 357.
25 OJ 1994 L 359.
26 OJ 1999 L 5I/I.

6.2.   FORMAT OF THE AGREEMENTS

The agreements cover a very wide range of areas and subject matters as diverse as agriculture, capital and movement of workers.[27] It would be difficult to draw the balance of the positive versus negative effects of the agreements for any particular Member State or CEEC individually. As I have discussed in Chapter 1 this approach to an agreement where everyone is simultaneously a winner and loser in such a complicated fashion and with a huge number of disparate factors affecting different ministries and national interests that a balance sheet approach is useless makes it nigh on impossible to un-pick the fabric.

However, at the initial stage of determining the contents of the negotiating mandates, it was clearly possible to exclude (and indeed, if the immigration ministries have been in charge, likely) movement of natural persons. This area was included, though, not least in recognition of the desire of natural persons from the Member States to gain access to the markets of the CEECs and their need for a framework within which to do so. When looking at migration from the Community perspective, too often we focus on the pressure from persons outside the Union to enter it and engage in economic activities. The other side of the coin, the wish of nationals of the Member States to gain preferential access to third countries, is overlooked. The inclusion in the negotiating mandates of movement of persons for economic activities was fuelled by the Union's desire to access those markets. The principle of reciprocity in the Community's commitments within third country agreements meant that equal rights of access to economic activity were guaranteed to nationals of the CEECs in the Member States as were granted to nationals of the Member States in the CEECs.

Peers has suggested that if the objective of the Union is to achieve integration through law of the CEECs then the framework of the European Economic Area Agreement (EEA) is a more appropriate vehicle. The failure to use this mechanism he concludes demonstrates a reluctance on the part of the European Union to move towards integration.[28] His observation is confirmed by the work of Marescceau and Monteguti who recount the dynamic nature of the intentions behind the agreements, particularly on the side of the European

---

27 For the purpose of analysing the agreements, I will make reference to the Poland Agreement in particular. It was used in the political negotiations as the blueprint for the other agreements.

28 S. Peers, An Ever Closer Waiting Room? The Case for Eastern European Accession to the European Economic Area, CMLRev 32: 187-213 [1995].

Union.[29] However, time has now moved on giving the impression of immutability to the CEEC/Baltic and island accession.

6.3. PEOPLE AND PRESSURE TO EMIGRATE

The inclusion in the agreements of provisions presupposing access by natural persons nationals of the CEECs to economic activity and accordingly residence on the territory of the Member States may be viewed in the light of the numbers of nationals from those states who were seeking to enter and remain in the Member States at that time.[30] For these purposes, it is interesting to look at the statistics on asylum applications from CEEC nationals in the main receiving countries of the Union as these figures give some indication of the numbers of persons who do not come within other traditional immigration "gates" such as family reunion or labour migration. The duty to grant asylum as contained in the UN Convention relating to the Status of Refugees 1951 and Protocol 1967 (the Geneva Convention) is one of last recourse: the duty not to send someone back to a country where he or she is likely to suffer persecution.[31] If an individual can found a right of residence (and economic activity) on some other ground, in principle such right should be determined before the asylum application as protection under this heading is fundamentally against expulsion. Therefore consideration of asylum statistics as an indicator of pressure to move to a state is not unwarranted. In practice, the enormous delays in determining asylum applications in a number of Member States means that asylum applicants in fact apply, during the consideration of their asylum applications, for residence on other grounds, such as marriage to a national, or the establishment of a successful business etc.

The inter-relationship between asylum and economic migration was also evident in political and academic discussion about movement of persons from Central and Eastern Europe at the time.[32] It forms the background, appearing

---

29 M. Maresceau and E. Montaguti, The Relations Between the European Union and Central and Eastern Europe: A Legal Appraisal, CMLRev 32: 1327-1367 [1995].

30 It is also noteworthy that Germany at the time chose to regulate labour migration on the basis of bilateral agreements with some of the CEECs rather than through these Agreements. See K. Groenendijk and R. Hampsink, *Temporary Employment of Migrants in Europe*, Reeks Recht & Samenleving No. 10, Nijmegen, 1995.

31 Article 33 UN Convention relating to the Status of Refugees 1951 and Protocol 1967.

32 "Fragen des Asylrechts und der Aufname von Flüchtlingen aus Ländern der Dritten Welt und aus Staaten Mittel- und Osteuropas werden immer mehr zu einem gemeinsamen Problem der westeuropäischen Staaten. Das wachsende Gefälle zwischen den Wohlstandsländern und den Schwellenländern oder den Armutsländern der Dritten Welt hat zu einem immer stärker werdenden Wanderungsdruck geführt. Hinzu kommen

again and again in the contributions to a conference organised in Trier in March 1992 on comparative law of asylum and immigration in Europe published later that year and to which numerous Government officials from Member States contributed.[33] What is interesting in that debate is the silence regarding the agreements. Even experts who at the time were calling for a widening of temporary labour programmes did not refer to this in the context of the agreements: "Similarly, the temporary labour programmes in the West for citizens of Eastern European Countries, presently some 150,000-200,000 places, could well be expanded. This is a cheap price indeed for the West for the hard-won liberty of the East."[34] The linking of the asylum debate[35] with the need to find new means of dealing with migration pressures was consistently tied instead to activities which the Member States were undertaking inter-governmentally and the prospect of action under the new Third Pillar of the TEU.[36] These developments are the subject matter of the next chapter.

I have chosen three main asylum receiving countries in the Union: France, Germany, and the Netherlands for which there is substantial statistical data and

---

die tiefgreifenden politischen Veränderungen in den Staaten Mittel- und Osteuropas, der Wegfall früher bestenhender Grenzssicherungssysteme und damit einhergehend die Liberalisierung des Reiseverkehrs." O. Reermann, Ministerialdirigent, Bundes-ministerium des Innern, Bonn, Grundzüge des geltenden Asyl- und Einwanderungs-rechts, in K. Hailbronner, Band 1 *Schriftenreihe der Europäischen Rechtsakademie Trier, Asyl- und Einwanderungsrecht im euroäischen Vergleich*, Bundesanzeiger Verlagsges. GmbH, Cologne, 1992, p. 16.

33 K. Hailbronner, Band 1 *Schriftenreihe der Europäischen Rechtsakademie Trier, Asyl- und Einwanderungsrecht im europäischen Vergleich*, Bundesanzeiger Verlagsges. GmbH, Cologne, 1992.

34 J. Widgren, The Need to Improve Co-operation of European Asylum and Migration Policies in K. Hailbronner, Band 1 *Schriftenreihe der Europäischen Rechtsakademie Trier, Asyl- und Einwanderungsrecht im europäischen Vergleich*, Bundesanzeiger Verlagsges. GmbH, Cologne, 1992, p. 101.

35 This was particularly so in Germany where the overall numbers had risen so dramatically as to persuade the Government that an amendment of the constitution to remove the right to asylum (old Article 16 of the Grundgesetz) was necessary. The amendment of the German constitution was also necessary so that Germany could ratify the Schengen Implementing Convention 1990 as the principle of returning an asylum seeker to the first host country without a substantive determination of his or her claim which was basic to the Schengen Convention was inimical to Article 16 of the German Con-stitution, R. Marx, The German Constitutional Court's Decision of 14th May 1996 on the concept of Safe Third Countries – A Basis for Burden-Sharing in Europe?, IJRL 8 (1996) p. 419.

36 See for instance the Podiumsdiskussion published in K. Hailbronner, Band 1 *Schriften-reihe der Europäischen Rechtsakademie Trier, Asyl- und Einwanderungsrecht im euopäischen Vergleich*, Bundesanzeiger Verlagsges. GmbH, Cologne, 1992.

three CEECs, Bulgaria, Poland and Romania from which states there has been not insignificant movement between the period 1988 and 1994.[37] In Germany asylum applications from Polish nationals peaked in 1988 with 29,000 applications, in France in 1989 at 1,200 and in the Netherlands in 1990 with 1,185. Applications from Romanians do not peak until 1992 in Germany (103,787) and 1994 in France (4,009) and the Netherlands (2,762). Bulgarian applications reach their heights in the Netherlands and Germany in 1991 and 1992. The numbers of such applications in France are negligible.

The agreement with Poland was signed in December 1991, six months after the lifting of mandatory visa requirements for Poles by the Schengen States (which included France and Germany). There is clearly no explosion of asylum applications but rather a constant drop in numbers.[38] In Germany and France

---

37 All data in the table comes from: Eurostat, Migration Statistics 1994, 1995 and 1996, Luxembourg 1995, 1996 and 1997 respectively; Eurostat, Asylum Seekers and Refugees a Statistical report, Volume 1: EC Member States, Luxembourg 1993 and Home Office, Control of Immigration Statistics United Kingdom 1996, Cm 3737, London, 1997

38   *France: Asylum Applications from CEEC Nationals: 1988 – 1994*

To France from:	Bulgaria	Poland	Romania
1988	n/a	1,000	700
1989	n/a	1,200	1,200
1990	n/a	700	3,300
1991	n/a	406	2,486
1992	116	129	2,207
1993	122	159	2,709
1994	140	347	4,009

Germany: Asylum Applications from CEEC Nationals: 1988 – 1994

To Germany from:	Bulgaria	Poland	Romania
1988	200	29,000	2,600
1989	400	26,100	3,100
1990	8,300	9,200	35,300
1991	12,100	3,400	40,500
1992	31,540	4,212	103,787
1993	22,547	1,670	73,717
1994	3,367	n/a	9,581

Netherlands: Asylum Applications from CEEC Nationals: 1988 – 1994

To the Netherlands from:	Bulgaria	Poland	Romania
1988	n/a	461	155
1989	n/a	892	444
1990	512	1,185	2,202
1991	440	548	1,662

the numbers had been tapering off over the preceding three years and were dropping dramatically by 1991.

The Bulgaria and Romania Agreements were signed in March 1993 at a time when numbers of applications for asylum from nationals of those two countries had gone right off the scale in Germany over the preceding three years and in respect of Romanian nationals seeking asylum in France and the Netherlands had remained high since 1989/90. Indeed in France the number of applications from Romanians was still rising to an all-time high in 1994 (4009).

In the light of this level of pressure to enter and remain in the Member States (especially Germany) the inclusion of chapters in the agreements relating to Movement of Workers and Establishment, specifically designed to regulate movement of persons bears some further reflection. Although free movement of workers is not achieved or even aimed for in the agreements certain protection is extended to workers nationals of the Parties to the agreements. As regards establishment, a right is created which accrues to individuals and is framed in the same terms as the right of establishment in the EC Treaty. This means that notwithstanding the migration pressures, the Community followed its traditional approach towards movement of persons, creating a direct link between the individual, albeit a third country national, and the Community which entitled the individual to chose whether to move or not for the purpose of exercising economic activities to the exclusion of Member State discretion.

What is the consequence then, of creating a right for individuals to move from a country from which there is substantial pressure to emigrate to the Union to engage in economic activities? It provides the possibility for such persons to eschew the asylum procedure, the only avenue of migration which at the time permitted access to the territory at the election of the individual,[39] and to have the decision to move for the purpose of economic activity respected by the host State irrespective of any fear of persecution. The mechanism used is

To the Netherlands from:	Bulgaria	Poland	Romania
1992	19	338	960
1993	343	164	1,085
1994	465	139	2,762

39 I am intentionally leaving aside the question of choice of marriage partner as a voluntary act which may lead to access to the labour market and residence in a state other than that of the nationality of one of the parties to the marriage. The fear of immigration possibilities as a motivating force in the choice of a spouse has resulted in increasingly draconian legislation in various Member States relating to residence of foreign spouses, see I. Macdonald, *Immigration Law and Practice*, 2nd Edition, Butterworths, London, 1987, chapter 8.

one that had already been deployed by the Community to regulate economic activities of third country nationals within the territory of the Union, the agreements. It is arguable how conscious the choices of the Community and Member States were from this perspective.[40] I have already mentioned the interest of the Member States to get access for their nationals to the CEECs. Similarly, regard should be had to a number of temporary labour programmes in Germany directed at the CEEC pressure in the early 1990s. But leaving aside the Member States' intentions, the consequences of the experiment deserve attention. Now it is time to look at the provisions of the agreements relating to persons and the extent of rights that are contained in them.

6.4.   MOVEMENT AND RIGHTS OF WORKERS

Each of the agreements contains a title "movement of workers, establishment and supply of services". As regards movement of workers, this is something of a misnomer as there is no right for workers to move either between the CEECs and the Member States or within the Community.

In view of the sensitivities of the Member States in respect of protection of the labour market, it is not surprising that no right of free movement of workers was included in any of the agreements with CEECs. Between 1991 and 1994 when the majority of the Europe Agreements were signed, unemployment rates in the Union were moving inexorably upward, from 8.2% in 1991 to 11.2% in 1994.[41] The rate in Germany, by far the main country of destination for nationals of CEECs, had moved from 5.6% to 8.4% over that period of time and with the increased stress of reunification with the former East Germany had become a pressing political issue. However, in the period preceding and during the commencement of negotiations towards the agreements, from 1987 to 1991 the unemployment rate of persons aged 25 and over moved from 8.0% down to 6.8%.[42] Perhaps the Member States anticipated, at the time of negotiation, the impending rise, however, it is more likely that in view of the sensitivities surrounding unemployment, the German approach of regulating access to the labour market through bilateral agreements was preferred.

What is perhaps more surprising is that these agreements do not expressly include protection of residence and continuing access to the labour market for CEEC workers already present and working in the Member States (and vice-

---

40 The interest of the Member States are by no means monolithic.
41 *Eurostatistics: Data for Short-Term Economic Analysis*, 01/1996 Eurostat, Luxembourg 1996.
42 Eurostat, *Labour Force Survey 1983-1991*, Luxembourg 1993.

versa). Such a right of continuing access to the labour market and residence would have been appropriate bearing in mind the objective of accession. As regards security of continued employment and residence, until parallel secondary legislation is adopted under the Europe Agreements the position of their nationals is less secure than that of Turkish workers under the secondary legislation of the Turkey Agreement which has been discussed at some length in the preceding two chapters.

As regards workers, provision is made for non-discrimination in working conditions, remuneration or dismissal, access for legally resident family members to the labour market for the duration of the principal's employment, some co-ordination of social security and examination of the possibility of improving bilateral agreements on employment. This reference, coupled with the shortage of provisions on workers confirms the impression that labour migration was intended to be regulated bilaterally, as Germany was in the process of doing. The Association Council is given competence to consider other improvements including access for professional training. The main provision on workers' rights is contained in Article 37 of the Poland Agreement which is followed by a reciprocal provision placing similar obligations on Poland.[43] The comparable provision of the EC Treaty is Article 39(2).[44] I will consider the question of a uniform definition of non-discrimination later on as it applies both to this question of working conditions and also to the right of establishment. Here I will embark directly on a consideration of the concept of working conditions, first does the provision confer rights on individuals, if so what sort of rights and what limitations may there be.

Conferring Rights on Individuals

Is Article 37(1) of the Poland Agreement (and as mirrored in the other agreements) capable of conferring directly on individuals rights enforceable in

---

43 "Subject to the conditions and modalities applicable in each Member State:
- The treatment accorded to workers of Polish nationality, legally employed in the territory of a Member State shall be free from any discrimination based on nationality, as regards working conditions, remuneration or dismissal, as compared to its own nationals;
- The legally resident spouse and children of a worker legally employed in the territory of a Member State, with the exception of seasonal workers and of workers coming under bilateral agreements within the meaning of Article 41, unless otherwise provided by such agreements, shall have access to the labour market of that Member State, during the period of that worker's authorised stay of employment."

44 "Such freedom of movement shall entail the abolition of any discrimination based on nationality between workers of the Member States as regards employment, remuneration and other conditions of work and employment."

the Member States? Article 39(2) EC, which is similarly worded, has been held by the Court of Justice to confer rights directly on individuals, nationals of the Member States.[45] In addition, the text of the first indent of Article 37(1) mirrors the content of Article 40 of the Morocco Agreement[46] that the Court of Justice has held to have direct effect.[47] The Morocco Agreement similarly does not contain an objective of abolition of obstacles to free movement of persons, which was not an objection to the direct effect of the non-discrimination provision contained in Article 40 thereof.[48] In comparison with the Community law provision and taking into account the interpretation of the Court of Justice of another agreement which creates less strong links with the Community than the Europe Agreements it would seem likely that the content of that indent is sufficiently clear, precise and unconditional as regards its implementation to have the quality of direct effect. The Europe Agreements are intended to lead to accession thus the likelihood that the provision here has direct effect increases as regards the criterion of the aim of the agreement. Therefore on the criteria of wording, nature and purpose which the Court has held relevant to determining direct effect, the Europe Agreements have a strong claim. But for contrary indications, which I will discuss below, this would then mean that Polish workers within the Member States could rely directly on the provisions against any decision by a national authority, which contravenes their right to equal treatment with own nationals as regards working conditions.

Working Conditions and Conditions of Work

What is the scope of the concept of "working conditions" for the purposes of the agreement; is it a national or Community concept? The differentiation in the English language text between "conditions of work" in Article 39(2) EC and "working conditions" in Article 37 of the Poland Agreement is not significant. It is unlikely that they are in fact two concepts but rather two formulations of one concept. For instance, the term "conditions of work" is found in the Additional Protocol to the Turkey Agreement,[49] while in the Maghreb Agreements the term "working conditions" is used.[50] There does not appear to be any difference in substance between the two concepts. Indeed, in

---

45 48/75 *Royer* [1976] ECR 497.
46 "The treatment accorded by each Member State to workers of Moroccan nationality employed in its territory shall be free from any discrimination based on nationality, as regards working conditions or remuneration, in relation to its own nationals."
47 C-18/90 *Kziber* [1991] ECR I-199.
48 C-416/96 *El Yassini* [1999] ECR I-1209.
49 Article 37 Additional Protocol, Turkey Agreement.
50 Article 40 Morocco Agreement.

other language versions of the texts, the difference of terminology is not apparent.[51]

In its early case law, the Court takes a fairly broad approach to the concept of "conditions of work". Laws of a Member State which determine that a period spent in the armed forces shall count towards calculating the period of service with an employer[52] fall within "conditions of work and employment". Similarly, laws granting special protection against dismissal for severely handicapped persons are also conditions of work.[53] A separation allowance, in so far as it constitutes compensation for the inconveniences suffered by a worker who is separated from his or her home also falls within conditions of work.[54] In another early case the Court held that social security could be included in the concept of working conditions.[55] However the objective of free movement of workers and its status as one of the fundamental freedoms of the Community was emphasised by the Court in giving a broad interpretation to "conditions of work and employment" both in Regulation 1612/68 and Article 39(2) EC.[56]

From the mid-1980s onwards, a number of judgments categorise job security, a proper career structure and chances of promotion as "conditions of work" within the meaning of Article 39(2) EC.[57] In these cases, the Court's reasoning is based on eliminating discrimination against migrant Community nationals in comparison with own nationals. This development of the case law would support a consistent interpretation of "working conditions" in the EC Treaty and the Europe Agreements as the rationale, following the teleological approach towards interpretation of Community law, is the same: achieving equality of rights.

Of particular interest here may be the interpretation which has been given to this concept in the context of Directive 76/207 on equal treatment between men and women. This Directive is unrelated to Article 39 EC therefore considerations relating to free movement and the interpretation of rights by reference to a right of free movement are irrelevant. Instead this Directive is aimed at eliminating gender discrimination, a more limited aim than that contained in Article 39 EC but an aim closer to the wording of Article 37 of the Poland

---

51 See for instance the Dutch text where the word used in the EC Treaty and Poland Agreement is the same "arbeidsvoorwaarden"; and the German text which uses the word "Arbeitsbedingungen". The expressions "working conditions", "conditions of work", or, "conditions of employment or work" appear not only in Article 39(2) EC, but also in Article 7 of Regulation 1612/68 and in Article 5 of Directive 76/207.
52 15/69 *Ugliola* [1969] ECR 363.
53 44/72 *Marsman* [1972] ECR 1243.
54 152/73 *Sotgiu* [1974] ECR 153.
55 41/84 *Pinna* [1986] ECR 1.
56 See in particular 152/73 *Sotgui* [1974] ECR 153.
57 225/85 *Commission v Italy* [1987] ECR 2625 and C-272/92 *Spotti* [1993] ECR I-5185.

Agreement. In considering the scope of the concept of "working conditions" within that Directive the Court found that it included all benefits which are related to the status of employment.[58] On this basis the Court held that the concept of "working conditions" included family benefits related to a contract of employment.[59]

In a variety of different circumstances and in relation to different provisions of the Treaty and subsidiary legislation, the Court has taken an approach to the concept of "working conditions" which is not limited to any definition that may appear in national law. It has considered the subject matter of each claim and determined, according to the rationale of the Treaty, whether a situation is directly covered by an employment relationship or not. This would indicate that the concept has a Community law content. From the way in which the Court has considered the different situations that have come within the concept of working conditions in different Community law provisions, it appears to have a uniform content.

If the concept of non-discrimination in "working conditions" is uniform in Community law then the interpretation given in the context of Article 39(2) EC and Directive 76/207 should apply to Article 37 Poland Agreement. This would then mean that benefits such as a separation allowance for inconvenience to a migrant worker or family benefits related to employment must be accorded to Polish workers legally employed on the territory of a Member State on a non-discriminatory basis with own nationals. This right of non-discrimination would not of course deal with the issues of aggregation and export of social security contributions and benefits.

A difficulty here with a uniform interpretation of the concept of working conditions is the fact that the Europe Agreements specifically avoid any provision giving a right to non-discrimination in social security. The refusal on the Community's part to include such a provision was because the Member States were unwilling to extend the Court's jurisprudence in *Kziber*[60] to nationals of the CEECs.[61] The intertwining of the concepts of equal treatment and social security as regards Community nationals makes it very difficult to separate out the strands as regards other agreements.

---

58 The Court held that "to confine [this] concept solely to those working conditions which are set out in the contact of employment or applied by the employer in respect of a worker's employment would remove situations directly covered by an employment relationship from the scope of the Directive". C-116/94 *Meyers* [1995] ECR I-2131.

59 C-116/94 *Meyers* [1995] ECR I-2131.

60 C-18/90 [1991] ECR I-199.

61 D. Martin & E. Guild, Free Movement of Persons in the European Union, Butterworths, London, 1996, p. 295 *et seq.*

Before leaving the question of the meaning of working conditions for third country nationals, again reference to the similar non-discrimination right in the Morocco Agreement is relevant. The Court rejected the argument that working conditions equality prevented a State from refusing to renew the residence and work permit of a Moroccan worker. It did however indicate that the right to non-discrimination in working conditions could require a State to extend a residence permit if the third country national had a valid work permit.[62]

The piecemeal approach by the Court towards working conditions makes it difficult to reach any definitive conclusion as to what the concept means. However, what is apparent from the jurisprudence in respect of the EC Treaty and its subsidiary legislation is that national law definitions are not decisive. The Community has reserved for itself the right to determine what is and what is not a working condition. Further that concept is not limited by the contents of a contract of employment but extends to those situations which the Court holds to be covered by an employment relationship.

Contrary Indicators

It is now time to return to the opening words of Article 37(1): "subject to the conditions and modalities applicable in each Member State". It is by no means clear what this proviso means. Two opposite interpretations[63] are:

1. The proviso applies only to the administrative procedures for the application of the non-discrimination provision;

2. The proviso applies to every concept which is contained in the provision: in other words not only is the concept of working conditions governed exclusively by national law but also that of non-discrimination.

A more extreme position, that the provision in fact only refers to the provisions which may or may not exist in national law, is possible but would deprive the provision of any *effet utile*, a position which is not easily accepted by the Court.

On the first interpretation the proviso does no more than safeguard national procedures in the areas of working conditions, remuneration or dismissal but does not affect the content of the non-discrimination right. In other words, the application of national conditions and modalities would suggest procedural content rather than a content of rights. Such an interpretation would not constitute a bar, *per se*, on the direct effect of the provision. The content of the right would not cease to be sufficiently clear, precise and unconditional so as to

---

62 C-416/96 *El Yassini* [1999] ECR I-1209.

63 In between these two poles there are of course a wide variety of variations, but the legal arguments found themselves on these two extremes.

fail the test. This then would mean that as regards this provision of non-discrimination, the personal relationship between the individual and the Community is created upon which the individual may rely to require the application of national law procedures to give effect to the content.

A comparison can be made with Article 6(1) & (3) of Decision 1/80 adopted under the Turkey Agreement. The first provision relates to the right to extension of work permits for Turkish workers within the territory of the Member States.[64] Article 6(3) provides that: "The procedures for applying paragraphs 1 and 2 shall be those established under national rules." The Court of Justice held that the rights contained in Article 6(1) of the Decision were capable of having direct effect.[65] It further found that the purpose of Article 6(3) was merely to require the Member States to take administrative measures to give effect to the rights contained in Article 6(1). It did not constitute a provision giving a discretion to the Member States to vary the content of the rights contained in Article 6(1).

I would draw a parallel with Article 37 of the Poland Agreement. If an article stating that procedures for implementation of a Decision's provisions are by way of national law cannot act as a bar to the direct effect of the provision's contents, it may be that the application of "conditions and modalities applicable in each Member State" cannot deprive a non-discrimination provision of its direct effect if those conditions and modalities are in fact procedural. However, account must be taken also of the possibility that the difference in wording between the two is intended to avoid this conclusion.

The second possible interpretation is that the proviso strikes at the heart of the provision and makes all of its contents subject to the national laws of the Member States. This covers both the concept of non-discrimination and the content of working conditions. If national law only applies to both concepts: of non-discrimination and working conditions then a question mark is raised not only over the provision's direct effect but whether it has any effect at all. The provision would not necessarily be sufficiently clear and precise to give rise to rights as its material scope would be so completely regulated by national legislation and interpretation that there would no longer be any Community wide consistency. For example, a national law interpretation of non-discrimination is not necessarily consistent with its Community law counterpart. This differentiation is particularly in evidence as regards gender discrimination where, notwithstanding national provisions prohibiting gender discrimination in working conditions in the Member States, the decisions of the Court of Justice

---

64 To that extent it is not directly equivalent to Article 37 of the Poland Agreement.
65 C-192/89 *Sevince* [1990] ECR I-3461.

still come as a surprise.[66] Wiess supports this position in his analysis of direct effect in third country agreements. He takes the position that in the Europe Agreements the inclusion of reference to national conditions and modalities is fatal to direct effect. His argument is that for a provision to have direct effect it must not only be unconditional but it also must not be dependent on measures being subsequently taken by the Member States with a discretionary power in the matter. The introduction of the intermediary of national law means that this requirement is not meet.[67] But what can a "conditions and modalities" requirement add to a non-discrimination provision? In any event non-discrimination will apply to national law. Its clarity derives from that regime. The problem with this position is that if it were adopted then any non-discrimination provision could be challenged as regards direct effect.

Further the concepts of work and working conditions may well vary under the national laws of the Member States. In Chapter 1, I have outlined the arguments put to the Court by the Member States as regards Community national workers for a national definition of the concept of "worker" to define who is entitled to rights under Article 39 EC. The Court, in favour of a Community definition, rejected those arguments.[68] The Court's reason for doing so was clearly stated to be to exclude the possibility that the Member States control, through their national legislation, who is and who is not a worker for the purposes of Article 39 EC and thereby exclude persons seeking to exercise free movement rights at national discretion.[69] The inclusion of the proviso in Article 37 reopens this discussion.

While both interpretations are possible, I prefer the first interpretation as this is closer to what I think the general intention of the agreements to be – to consolidate the position of Polish (and other CEEC national) workers and assimilate their position to that of Community national migrant workers in the Member States. The answer to this question also determines whether the provision is capable of direct effect. In my view, taking into account the wording purpose and intention of the agreement, and the need for coherence and consistency in the application of Community law, both the concept of discrimina-

---

66 C. Barnard, The Principle of Equality in the Community Context: P, Grant, Kalanke and Marshall: Four Uneasy Bedfellows, Cambridge Law Journal, July 1998, Vol. 57, pp. 352.

67 W. Weiss, Zur Wirkung des arbeitsrechtlichen Gleichbehandlungsgebot in den Assoziations-abkommen der EG mit Drittstaaten insbesondere auf Auslanderklauseln, InfAuslR 7/8/98, p. 313.

68 The Community definition of a worker as applicable to Article 39 EC is not necessarily consistent with the definition for other provisions of the Treaty. Nor is it necessarily a uniform definition for other purposes such as Article 42 EC, see C-85/96 *Martinez Sala* [1998] ECR I-2691.

69 53/81 *Levin* [1982] ECR 1035.

tion and that of working conditions are within the exclusive domain of the Community to the exclusion of national law definitions.[70]

A tension has been created in the drafting of the provision, which must be ascribed to a compromise between competing policy aims of the drafters of the agreement. On the one hand, the wording used for the non-discrimination provision mirrors other provisions of Community law in the Treaty and third country agreements that have been held to be capable of conferring rights directly on individuals. However, this wording is then prefaced by an unaccustomed phrase the meaning and purpose of which throws doubt on the direct effect of the remainder of the provision.

6.5. The Right of Establishment

All of the Europe Agreements include provisions in virtually identical terms to the Poland Agreement relating to the right to exercise self-employment. In the Poland Agreement Article 44 states:

"Each Member State shall grant from entry into force of this Agreement, a treatment no less favourable than that accorded to its own companies and nationals as defined in Article 48[71] and shall grant in the operation of Polish

---

70 S. van Raepenbusch "Est-ce de nature à priver l'article de tout effet direct? Nous ne le pensons pas: l'égalité de traitement est par essence inconditionelle. On ne peut à la fois octroyer cette égalité et la soumettre à une réserve et ce dans la même disposition, de telle sorte que si un contenu doit être donné à la règle de l'égalité de traitement, le renvoi aux 'conditions et modalités applicables dans chaque Etat membre' devient superflu". La jurisprudence de la Cour de justice des Communautés européennes vis-à-vis des ressortissants des pays tiers, in M. den Boer, *The Implementation of Schengen: First the Widening, Now the Deepening,* Maastricht, 1997, p. 41.

71 Article 48 states: 1. A 'Community company' and a 'Polish company' respectively shall for the purposes of this Agreement mean a company or a firm set up in accordance with the laws of a Member State or of Poland respectively and having its registered office, central administration, or principal place of business in the territory of the Community or Poland respectively. However, should the company or firm, set up in accordance with the laws of a Member State or of Poland respectively, have only its registered office in the territory of the Community or Poland respectively, its operations must possess a real and continuous link with the economy of one of the Member States or Poland respectively.

With regard to international maritime transport, shall also be beneficiaries of the provisions of this Chapter and Chapter III of this Title, a national or a shipping company of the Member States or of Poland respectively established outside the Community or Poland respectively and controlled by nationals of a Member State, or Polish nationals respectively, if their vessels are registered in that Member State or in Poland respectively in accordance with their respective legislations.

companies and nationals established in the territory a treatment no less favourable than that accorded to its own companies and nationals.

"For the purposes of this Agreement, "establishment" shall mean as regards nationals, the right to take up and pursue economic activities as self-employed persons and to set up and manage undertakings, in particular, companies, which they effectively control."

The equivalent provision in the EC Treaty is Article 43, which states:

"Within the framework of the provisions set out below, restrictions on the freedom of establishment of nationals of a Member State in the territory of another Member State shall be abolished by progressive stages in the course of the transitional period. Such progressive abolition shall also apply to restrictions on the setting up of agencies, branches or subsidiaries by nationals of any Member State established in the territory of any Member State.

Freedom of establishment shall include the right to take up and pursue activities as self-employed persons and to set up and manage undertakings, in particular, companies or firms under the conditions laid down for its own nationals, by the law of the country where such establishment is effected ... ".

The right of establishment as interpreted in Community law[72] includes a right of access to the territory of the Member States in order to carry out the economic activity in addition to a right to remain on the territory for that purpose. In the change of wording from the EC Treaty to the Europe Agreements, what is most noticeable is the move from a provision that is designed around the natural person to one designed around the legal person. In Article 43 EC only by a forced interpretation and some assistance elsewhere is the legal person encompassed. In the Europe Agreements, the whole thrust is in favour of the legal person behind which the natural person trailing along, subject to special limitations.

A Community and a Polish national respectively shall, for the purpose of this Agreement, mean a natural person who is a national of one of the Member States or Poland respectively.

The provisions of this Agreement shall not prejudice the application by each Party of any measure necessary to prevent the circumvention of its measures concerning third country access to its markets through the provisions of this Agreement.

72 2/74 *Reyners* [1974] ECR 631.

Defining Establishment: the Europe Agreements and the EC Treaty

The right of establishment (i.e. self-employment) covers two types of activity: first the right of individuals,[73] nationals of the Europe Agreement states to establish themselves personally in self-employment in the Member States. This is the right to take up employment and pursue economic activities as self-employed persons and to set up and manage undertakings, in particular companies, which they effectively control.[74] Secondly, as regards companies, the right to take up and pursue economic activities by means of setting up and managing subsidiaries, branches and agencies and in order to do this to send key personnel, as defined in the agreements.[75] The right is subject to a limitation on grounds of public policy, public security or public health.[76]

The concept of establishment is a broad one within the EC Treaty, allowing a national to participate, on a stable and continuous basis, in the economic life of a Member State other than that of his or her origin.[77] The activity must be economic in nature but this has been held to include activities performed by members of a community based on religion or another form of philosophy as part of the commercial activities of that community in so far as the services which the community provides to its members may be regarded as the indirect *quid pro quo* for genuine and effective work.[78] Where there is a question about the duration of the activities, before Article 43 EC can be excluded, the temporary nature of the activities in question has to be determine in the light, not only of the duration of the provision of the service but also of its regularity, periodicity or continuity.[79] In other words, the concept of establishment involves the actual pursuit of an economic activity through a fixed establishment in another Member State for an indefinite period of time.[80]

As regards the definition of establishment, Community law relating to free movement of Community nationals does not appear to permit the Member States to insert their own national definitions.[81] As with employment, establish-

---

73 Their rights were delayed for some countries such as Hungary, the Baltic States and Slovenia.
74 For instance, Article 44(4)(a)(i) of the Poland Agreement.
75 For instance, Article 52 Poland Agreement.
76 There are also sectoral limitations which are to be lifted in accordance with a timetable and the possibility of temporary suspension of the provisions under specified circumstances: see for example Articles 49 & 50 Poland Agreement.
77 C-55/94 *Gebhard* [1995] ECR I-4165.
78 196/87 *Steymann* [1988] ECR 6159.
79 C-55/94 *Gebhard* [1995] ECR I-4165.
80 C-221/89 *Factortame* [1991] ECR I-3905.
81 An exception to the Community definition of employment and self-employment exists as regards these concepts for the purposes of Article 51 EC and its implementing

ment as regards natural persons is a Community concept the defining feature of which is whether or not the individual carries out work within a relationship of subordination.[82] So long as a person is not subordinated to another person or an organisation but is performing services for remuneration then he or she is self-employed for the purposes of Community law. There are of course factual problems related to self-employment that do not arise in respect of employment. For instance, establishing the date on which the right is exercised is more difficult in respect of self-employment where there may be a lapse of time between the decision to become self-employed and the point at which the self-employed activity becomes economically viable. There is no clear guidance from the European Court of Justice on this issue. Guidance may however be taken from the Court's pronouncements as regards employment in that so long as the activity is genuine and effective, and irrespective of the intention of the individual, it comes within the Community concept of employment.[83] Indeed, in considering the economic activities of a religious community the Court applied this test.[84]

Legal persons and Establishment

As regards the exercise of the right of establishment by businesses within the Community, the Court has acknowledged that for the purposes of exercising the Article 43 EC right companies are creatures of the law and, in the present state of Community law, creatures of national law. They exist only by virtue of the varying national legislation that determines their incorporation and functioning.[85] The Article 43 right, however extends equally to legal persons as to natural persons. Legal persons are likely to exercise the right by the setting up of agencies, branches or subsidiaries[86] but all that is required is the maintenance of a permanent presence in the host Member State even if that presence does not take the form of a branch or agency but consists merely of an office managed by the undertaking's own staff or by a person who is independent but

---

Regulation 1408/71, co-ordination of social security systems. Because Article 51 EC and Regulation 1408/71 do no more than co-ordinate between national social security systems, national definitions of these terms apply. To find otherwise would throw into disarray the Member States social security systems, which are outside Community law except for the purposes of co-ordination.

82 C-107/95 *Asscher* [1996] ECR I-3089.
83 53/81 *Levin* [1982] ECR 1035.
84 196/87 *Steymann* [1988] ECR 6159
85 181/87 *Daily Mail* [1988] ECR 5483
86 181/87 *Daily Mail* [1988] ECR 5483.

authorised to act on a permanent basis for the undertaking, as would be the case with an agency.[87]

The dividing line between when an individual or a business is exercising a right to provide services under Article 49 EC in a host Member State and when it is establishing itself under Article 43 EC is one of intention and the degree of stability.[88] The right of establishment and that of service provision are mutually exclusive, with the services right being subordinate to the establishment right. This means the provisions relating to services only apply if those relating to establishment do not.[89] The use of the same terminology: "establishment" in the Europe Agreements as is used in the EC Treaty indicates a common content. The definition of establishment provided in the two treaties is virtually identical which strongly suggests that the Court's jurisprudence on the interpretation of the concept should be consistently applied to the relevant provisions of the Europe Agreements as well.

When the Europe Agreements were settled, clearly the Member States and the Community envisaged the situation where a business in one of the CEECs would seek to rely on its right of establishment by sending members of its staff to the Member States to carry out the activity and vice versa. The agreements provide for a limitation to the exercise of the right for businesses in two forms. First, the business must be in the form of a company, which must be established in accordance with the laws of the respective party; have its registered office, central administration or principal place of business in the place of formation; and where it only has its registered office on the territory of the country of formation its operations must possess a real and continuous link with the economy of that country.[90]

These requirements as to the nature of the company do not differ substantially in comparison with Community rules relating to companies in the Member States exercising a right of establishment. However, it does appear to exclude the exercise of the right of establishment by any entity that does not come within the definition of a company or natural person. Such a limitation does not apply to Community businesses.[91]

Under the Europe Agreements, companies exercise their right of establishment by sending natural persons who are their employees to the territory of a Member State only where these natural persons come within the definition of the key personnel. The key personnel provision in the Europe Agreements does

---

87 205/84 *Commission v Germany* [1986] ECR 3793.
88 C-53/95 *Kemmler* [1996] ECR I-703.
89 C-55/94 *Gebhard* [1995] ECR I-4165.
90 This is in fact codification of the jurisprudence of the Court of the Justice.
91 Some Member States' legislation permits other forms of economic activity such as legal status for partnerships, clubs and others which are neither companies nor persons.

not have any counterpart in the EC Treaty. According to its wording,[92] first the employee must be a national of the same country as the company, secondly he or she must come within one of two categories: senior personnel or persons possessing high or uncommon qualifications, skills or knowledge. Further the individual must have been employed by the organisation for one year before the deployment.

These limitations fetter companies seeking to exercise a right of establishment in a way in which natural persons are not. For instance, a Polish self-employed cleaner may exercise the right of establishment in any Member State. However, if he or she is an employee of a Polish company being detached to a Member State as a cleaner then he or she must come within one of the categories of senior employees[93] and have been employed by the business for at least one year. The limitations then encourage individual entrepreneurs to the detriment of companies.

Three justifications for the limitations on companies, from the perspective of the Member States, are: first generally they do not present a problem from the perspective of Community based companies seeking to send personnel to CEECs; secondly, the nationality requirement prevents nationals of other countries using CEEC based companies to facilitate immigration; and thirdly the introduction of criteria to be assessed by the national administration increases the discretionary control that it retains over the admission of persons. On the other hand, in general, the introduction of these limitations on the concept of establishment in comparison with the comparable concept in the EC Treaty confuses the question of non-discrimination.

Direct Effect in the Europe Agreements: National Courts

The first national court to hand down a final decision on the question of the Europe Agreements and the right of establishment was the Belgian Raad van State.[94] It was faced with the question of whether a self-employed Pole was entitled to rely directly on the agreement to support a claim to a right of residence. The court found that Article 44(4) had direct effect, having considered the Court of Justice's decision in *Demirel*[95] that the provisions of third country agreements are capable of direct effect. It noted from the Court's judgment in *Eroglu*[96] that a right to economic activity gives rise to a right to residence. It

---

92 Article 52(1).
93 For instance a specialist cleaner of medieval manuscripts supervising a team.
94 3 April 1995 Nr 52.631-10 Kamer, Tijdschrift voor Vreemdelingenrecht 1995 No 2, p. 150.
95 12/86 [1987] ECR 3719.
96 C-355/93 [1994] ECR I-5113.

considered the scope of the non-discrimination right and found that the Pole had the right to register on the same conditions as Belgians as a self-employed person and did not need to obtain a special permit designed for third country nationals intending to exercise a self-employed activity. The Belgian court considered the answer sufficiently clear as not to require a preliminary question to be put to the Court of Justice.

Oddly, the Belgian court limited itself to looking at the provision from the perspective of third country agreements. It did not refer to the Community law provision. In my view the key to the direct effect of Article 44 of the Poland Agreement is the Court's reasoning on direct effect of Article 43 EC. The two provisions cover the same material scope in a similarly worded manner. Therefore the comparison between the two is most natural. I will first look at this reasoning and then return to the question of its application to the Poland Agreement.

Mr Reyners, a Community national, wished to establish himself as a lawyer in Belgium against the wishes of the Belgian authorities who limited access to the profession to own nationals. Mr Reyner relied on the fact that the transitional period for establishment had already ended (in 1968) and therefore he was entitled to non-discrimination on the basis of nationality in setting up in Belgium as a lawyer. He argued that his right of establishment under Article 43 EC gave him a direct entitlement that could not be prejudiced by the fact that the Community institutions had not yet adopted implementing measures for Article 43 EC. Was Article 43 EC capable of direct effect? This requires the answer to two sets of questions, first, was it sufficiently clear and precise? The answer here was yes based on the wording of the provision, a Member State was able clearly to determine the extent and meaning of the obligation upon it. Was the obligation unconditional? Here again the answer was yes, the obligation had to be attained by the end of the transitional period. Was there a complete and legally perfect obligation? The non-discrimination provision fulfils this requirement as its scope is complete.

> "As a reference to a set of legislative provisions effectively applied by the country of establishment to its own national, this rule is by its essence capable of being directly invoked by nationals of other Member States."

Secondly, were the provisions' implementation dependent on measures being subsequently taken by the Community institutions or Member States with discretionary power in the matter? This last point was critical to the case as the Member State argued that the fact of the passing of the transitional period was only half the story. Article 43 EC needed implementing measures to be adopted to give it effect, which measures had been proposed by the Commission but had not been adopted by the Council. The Court held that:

> "The fact that [the] progression has not been adhered to leaves the obligation itself intact beyond the end of the period provided for its fulfilment. This

interpretation is in accordance with ... the Treaty according to which the expiry of the transitional period shall constitute the latest date by which all rules laid down must enter into force and all measures required for establishing the Common Market must be implemented. It is not possible to invoke against such an effect the fact that the Council has failed to issue Directives provided for by [the Treaty] or the fact that certain of the Directives actually issued have not fully attained the objective of non-discrimination."[97]

Can the Court's reasoning on Article 43 EC be transposed to Article 44 Poland Agreement? In favour of such a transposition are the direct effect criteria, the obligation is the same in the two provisions: non-discrimination on the basis of nationality in the field of establishment. In so far as it is sufficiently clear and precise to have direct effect when contained in Article 43 EC I would argue it is similarly sufficiently clear and precise for the purpose of Article 44 Poland Agreement. Similarly, as regards unconditionality, both provisions contain the same unconditional obligation. I do not think there is a reason on grounds of unconditionality to differentiate between the two. Finally, does the provision's implementation require subsequent measures that permit the exercise of discretionary power? I would take the view that the same criteria apply to Article 43 EC as to Article 44 Poland Agreement – there is provision to take subsequent implementing measures but those measures do not permit an exercise of discretionary power either by the Community or by the Member States such as to affect the substance of the right.

Next, two Dutch first instance courts came to consider the question of the effect of the establishment provision in the agreements in 1997 and 1998 respectively. They also considered that they had sufficient clarity on the issue so as not to need to put a preliminary question to the Luxembourg Court. However, their findings were the opposite of those of the Belgian court. In 1997 a Dutch court concluded that the establishment provision of the Czech Agreement lacked sufficient unconditionality to have direct effect.[98] The Court's reason was that as Article 43 EC had required implementing measures to give effect to the right, so the same must be required of the establishment provision of the Czech Agreement. This indicates a flawed understanding of the Court of Justice's decision in *Reyners*, which in fact held the contrary.[99] A second Dutch court considered the question in 1998 again deciding that a reference to the Luxembourg Court was unnecessary. In this case the court was subtler in its

---

97 2/74 *Reyners* [1974] ECR 631.
98 Rechtbank 's-Gravenhage, zp Amsterdam, 1 July 1997 Rechtspraak Vreemdelingenrecht 1997, p. 94.
99 2/74 [1974] ECR 631.

reasoning but again concluded that the provisions of national law applied,[100] this time making reference to Article 58 of the Poland Agreement to which I shall return in depth below. It is a valid consideration whether the intentions of a third country agreement permit direct effect or whether the agreement creates duties for states to implement through national provisions only. Less clear is the issue of the purpose and aim.[101] The Court has recently compared the purposes of two third country agreements, that with Morocco and that with Turkey. It was important to its reasoning in favour of an interpretation closer to that of the EC Treaty that the latter agreement was intended to lead to accession. The lack of such an intention in the Morocco Agreement was significant to its interpretation.[102] In respect of the Europe Agreements, the CEECs have now all commenced negotiations towards accession to the Union. This must be a strong indicator, as it was in the Court's reasoning on the Turkey Agreement, for uniformity of interpretation. For these reasons I would argue that the Court's jurisprudence on Article 43 EC is transposable to Article 44 Poland Agreement and that the result of such an interpretation is that the right of establishment for nationals of the Europe Agreement countries is directly effective.

At the same time in 1998, the English High Court was considering two cases of Poles seeking to rely on the establishment right of the agreement to found a right to remain on the territory. In these cases, the court felt less certain that the question was *acte claire*, and in December 1998 decided to refer the question of the direct effect of the establishment provision in the Poland Agreement to the Court of Justice. A number of important flanking questions were requested as well. A reference has now also been made by a Dutch court on the right of establishment in the Czech Agreement.[103]

Direct Effect in the Europe Agreements: Commentary

As yet there has not been a wealth of commentary on the question of direct effect. The position which Martin and I have taken on direct effect we have

---

100 Rechtbank 's-Gravenhage, zp Haarlem, 6 Feburary 1998, Jurisprudentie Vreemdelingenrecht 1999, p. 51.

101 270/80 *Polydor* [1982] ECR 329. The Polydor principle requires a consideration of provisions in the light of the objectives and activities: "the instruments which the Community has at its disposal in order to achieve the uniform application of Community law and the progressive abolition of legislative disparities within the common market have no equivalent in the context of relations between the Community and Portugal.

102 C-218/97 *El Yassini* [1999] ECR I-1209.

103 C-63/99 *Gloszczuk* OJ 1999 C 121/9; C-239/99 *Kondova* OJ 1999 C 246/15; C-257/99 *Barkoci & Malik* OJ 1999 C 265/2; and a reference from a Dutch court C-268/99 *Jany & Ors* OJ 1999 C 265/4.

both repeated in other work.[104] A recent book makes reference to the Poland
Agreement in the chapter on establishment but does not consider the issue of
direct effect nor indeed directly the provision on establishment.[105] An
interesting article on the Europe Agreements refers to the right of
establishment but only raises the perennial problem in Community law of
regulated sectors. The issue of direct effect is not considered.[106] In their review
of the Europe Agreements, Maresceau and Montaguti do not deal with the

---

104 See D. Martin and E. Guild, *Free Movement of Persons in the European Union*, Butterworths,
London, 1996, p. 295 *et seq.* E. Guild, A Guide to the Right of Establishment in the
Europe Agreements, ILPA/BS&G, London, 1996; E. Guild, Waltzing towards
Accession: the Case of the Central and Eastern European Countries, European Business
Law, 1998, p. 34. D. Martin, Association Agreements with Mediterranean and with
Eastern Countries: Similarities and Differences, in A. Antalovsky, R. Konig, B.
Perchinig, H. Vana (eds.) *Assoziierungsabkommen der EU mit Drittstaaten*, 1998, p. 23.

105 A. Evans, *A Textbook on European Union Law*, Hart, Oxford, 1998 p. 320. "Limited
requirements regarding freedom of establishment may be made in association agreements. For example, Article 113 of the Europe Agreement with Poland provides that, in
the fields covered by this Agreement and without prejudice to any special provisions
contained therein, Poland must not discriminate between Member States, their
companies, or firms. Conversely, the arrangements applied by the Union in respect of
Poland shall not give rise to discrimination between Polish nationals or companies or
firms." It is odd that Evans should mention this provision which only prohibits discrimination between nationals and does not deal at all with the actual right of establishment
provision at Article 44.

106 *Right of Establishment*. "The Association Agreements provide that the EC is required to
grant the right of establishment to nationals of Hungary, Poland and the CSFR
immediately, while those countries are required to phase in the right over a 5-10 year
period with respect to EC nationals. In fact, of course the EC right of establishment,
particularly in regulated sectors like banking and insurance, is the subject of detailed EC
legislation (part of the *acquis communautaire*), which is not applicable under the Association Agreements." D. Kennedy and D. Webb, The Limits of Integration: Eastern
Europe and the European Communities, CMLRev 30: 1095-1117, 1993. In their
consideration of workers they compare the position of CEEC workers with that of
Turkish workers under the Turkey Agreement and conclude that there would be no
remedy for failure to provide equal treatment basing their argument on the Court's
decision in *Demirel* (12/86 [1987] ECR 3719) that the programmatic effect of Article 36
of the Additional Protocol Turkey deprives that provision of the quality. They refer to
the Court's finding that further action is required by the Association Council and
conclude that in respect of Association Council Decisions "the Court of Justice would
not be prepared to fashion a remedy". Of course this position is no longer sustainable
after the Court of Justice's decision in *Sevince* (C-192/89 [1990] ECR I-3461) where the
Court held directly effective a number of provisions of the Association Council's
Decisions. Accordingly, the comparison which D. Kennedy and D. Webb make
between the Europe Agreements and the Turkey Agreement must be taken with some
caution.

question of direct effect though brief reference is made to the right of establishment.[107]

Of those commentators in favour of direct effect, Peers has twice considered the question and concluded that the establishment provision does have direct effect though the reasoning is not as full as might be hoped.[108]

Peers considers together the test of direct effect in Community law for provisions of the EC Treaty and the question of the conditions necessary for the application of that test to third country agreements: "The test for direct effect of international agreements in twofold: is there 'a clear and precise obligation which is not subject, in its implementation or effects, to the adoption of any subsequent measure' and what is the 'purpose and nature of the agreement'?" I do not find this particularly useful as an approach as it blurs the two issues: direct effect as regards the provisions of the EC Treaty, which is more complex, and the application of those principles to provisions of third country agreements. It is clearly not the intention of the Community or the Court that the test for direct effect is lower as regards the provisions of third country agreements than in respect of the EC Treaty provisions. The Court's shorthand on this in some judgments[109] is perhaps confusing.

On the second occasion, Peers sets out the less than satisfactory, in his opinion, position of the Court on the purpose and intention of third country agreements, highlighting different approaches in different areas of law. While he reaches some conclusions as regards provisions on workers in the agreements, he does not touch on the establishment provision except as regards key personnel. Here he only goes so far as to conclude that in the context of the mixed agreements these "would fall under EU competence". This is rather ambiguous.[110]

---

107 M. Maresceau and E. Montaguti, The Relations Between the European Union and the Central and Eastern Europe: A Legal Appraisal, CMLRev 32: 1327-1367 (1995).

108 On the specific issue of the right of establishment: "The Europe Agreements grant the most extension rights. Companies *or nationals* of the EA States may establish themselves in the EU under the same conditions as nationals of the Member States, either to 'take up and pursue economic activities as self-employed persons or to 'set up and manage undertakings. However, Baltic nationals get this right only from the end of 1999 and the Slovenians after six years (probably 2003): Subject to any jitters about the 'nature and purpose' of the agreement, the EA clauses are not framework provisions or subject to further negotiation or a general safeguard, so should have direct effect". S. Peers, Towards Equality: Actual and Potential Rights of Third Country Nationals in the European Union, CMLRev 33:7-50 [1996].

109 For example in 12/86 *Demirel* [1987] ECR 3719 or C-18/90 *Kziber* [1991] ECR I-199.

110 S. Peers, An Ever Closer Waiting Room? The Case for Eastern European Accession to the European Economic Area, CMLRev 32: 187-213 (1995).

Van Ooik considering the establishment provision of the Poland Agreement concluded that it was sufficient clear, precise and unconditional to have direct effect, again applying the approach of the Court to EC Treaty provisions.[111] In a case note on the first Dutch decision, Groenendijk reviews very carefully the arguments on the comparison of the establishment provision in the Czech Agreement and Article 43 EC. He notes the adoption of national implementing legislation in the Netherlands, UK and Germany (Nordrhein-Westfalen) on the right, as evidence of the intention of some Member States at least that the right must be implemented. Groenendijk concludes that the application of the provision and national legislation adopted under it must be consistent with the Court's jurisprudence on establishment.[112]

6.6.   DISCRIMINATION, OBSTACLES AND COHERENCE

Non-discrimination

Is the content of the non-discrimination provision the same and should it be interpreted in the same way for the Poland Agreement as for the EC Treaty? Article 39(2) EC on workers attaches the right to non-discrimination securely to the freedom of movement that requires the abolition of obstacles. Article 43 EC on establishment is worded exclusively in terms of non-discrimination. In the Poland Agreement no right to free movement accrues for workers. As their rights are limited to non-discrimination, the Court's jurisprudence on abolition of obstacles is unlikely to be applicable. A right of movement is implied for the self-employed which raises the question of the application of the obstacles jurisprudence to their situation, a question I will return to below. As I have discussed at some length in Chapter 2, the two concepts, abolition of obstacles and non-discrimination, are not hermetically sealed.

Is there a consistent interpretation in Community law of non-discrimination for persons exercising economic activities which interpretation is independent of whether they are nationals of a Member State or third country nationals? In the context of Article 39(2) EC the Court has consistently held that the concept prohibits not only overt discrimination by reason of nationality but

---

111 R.H. van Ooik, Het verkeer van personen volgens de Europa akkoorden, Migrantenrecht, 98/10.

112 His comment is particularly interesting on the comparison of the treatment of prosti-
tutes in Community law. This is relevant as the Dutch case revolves around the right of
a Czech prostitute as a self-employed person in the Netherlands. C. Groenendijk, case
note Rechtspraak Vreemdelingenrecht 1997, Nr. 94, Ars Aequi Libri, Nijmegen, 1998,
p. 344.

also all covert forms of discrimination which, by the application of other distinguishing criteria, lead in fact to the same result. Unless it is objectively justified and proportionate to its aim, a provision of national law must be regarded as indirectly discriminatory if it is intrinsically liable to affect a migrant more than a national worker and if there is a consequent risk that it will place the former at a particular disadvantage.[113]

In respect of the establishment right, there is no Court jurisprudence on third country agreements. However, the Morocco Agreement contains a prohibition on discrimination in working conditions and social security for Moroccan workers in the Member states. In 1991 the Court held it to have direct effect.[114] On the facts, the discrimination complained of was direct discrimination on the basis of nationality: the child of a Moroccan worker was excluded from a social security benefit on the basis of her nationality. However, the Court did not make any differentiation as regards the scope of the concept of discrimination in considering that situation. It confined itself to considering the scope of underlying subject matter:

> "In order to determine the scope of the principle of non-discrimination laid down in Article 41(1) of the Agreement, it is necessary to define in the first place the scope of social security as it appears in that provision and then to analyse the concept of "worker" in the meaning of that provision before specifying the conditions under which the members of the family of a Moroccan worker may claim entitlement to social security benefits."[115]

The Court appears to have taken as self-evident that the principle of non-discrimination is consistent. I would suggest that it is consistent as regards all provisions, whether in the EC Treaty or a third country agreement relating to movement of persons.

Obstacles

In the EC Treaty where a right of movement for the purpose of economic activity is created, obstacles to the exercise of the right are prohibited.[116] This means that measures which are likely to hinder or inhibit the exercise of the right by an individual entitled to take advantage of it may be contrary to the right itself even where indistinctly applicable to own nationals.[117] However, it finds its basis in the objects of the EC Treaty itself: Article 3 (c) EC requires

---

113 C-237/94 *O'Flynn* [1996] ECR I-2617.
114 C-18/90 *Kziber* [1991] ECR I-199.
115 C-18/90 *Kziber* [1991] ECR I-199.
116 C-415/93 *Bosman* [1996] ECR I-4921.
117 C-4 & 5/95 *Stöber* [1997] ECR I-511.

"an internal market characterised by the abolition, as between Member States, of obstacles to the free movement of goods, persons, services and capital".

The jurisprudence of the Court of Justice as regards obstacles to free movement extends more widely than the concept of non-discrimination. Its purpose is to give effect to the exercise of the rights. For example, the right to family reunion in Community law derives not from a non-discrimination right which would result in the application of national family reunion provisions to Community nationals exercising their free movement rights. Instead it comes from the right to the abolition of obstacles which could hinder the exercise of the right.[118] On this basis then Community rules on family reunification are unaffected by national rules unless the latter are more generous than the former in which case on the basis of the right to non-discrimination, the superior rights must be accorded to the Community national migrant worker.

The dividing line between obstacles and discrimination is evolving in the case-law of the Court.[119] As I have argued, discrimination may be an obstacle to free movement though the inverse is less likely. I would argue that on the basis of the creation of a right to move for CEEC nationals to exercise their right of establishment, for that right of access to the territory to be effective, obstacles to its exercise are only lawful to the extent permitted expressly by the agreements (Europe and EC). Even in the absence of an object comparable to Article 3(c) EC, the Europe Agreements contain a prohibition on obstacles in the form of the nullify and impair provision in Article 58(1) Poland Agreement. In my view two aspects must be considered together: first the closeness of the concept of discrimination and obstacles and secondly the nullify and impair provision should be interpreted as prohibiting obstacles to the exercise of the establishment right contained in the Europe Agreements.

What does this mean then, what are the limitations of the obstacles jurisprudence and in what circumstances can obstacles be justified? An obstacle or measure liable to hinder or make less attractive the exercise of an EC Treaty right must fulfil four conditions before it can be valid: it must be applied in a non-discriminatory manner; it must be justified by imperative requirements in the general interest; it must be suitable for securing the attainment of the objective pursued; and it must not go beyond what is necessary to obtain it.[120]

If this jurisprudence is transposable to the Europe Agreements, then the rights of CEEC nationals are enhanced. For example, a Polish national who seeks to take up self-employment in the UK may have overstayed or been

---

118 Preamble, Regulation 1612/68.
119 See in particular the recent decisions in C-4 &5/95 *Stöber* [1997] ECR I-511; C-266/95 *Marino Garcia* [1997] ECR I-3279.
120 C-55/94 *Gebhard* [1995] ECR I-4165.

classified as an illegal entrant.[121] If the *Gebhard* principles apply to his or her situation, then any measure by a national authority to penalise the individual on the basis of his or her unlawfulness must meet the criteria not least that the measures must be suitable to secure the attainment of the objective pursued and must not go beyond what is necessary to attain it. The object is the maintenance of firm immigration controls. However, the Court of Justice has consistently held that a measure amounting to expulsion is not proportional to the offence of failure to comply with immigration requirements as regards the exercise of free movement rights by Community nationals.[122] An extension of this reasoning would mean that any measure by the national authority designed to require the individual to return to Warsaw to obtain a visa in order to return to resume self-employment would be disproportionate.

Limitations: "Nullify and Impair" and Visas

A number of provisions of the agreements undermine either the conclusion of direct effect or the potential uniformity of the interpretation of Community law. I will consider a number of these that are applicable to all the provisions in the agreements.

Article 58(1) Poland Agreement raises question marks over the direct effect of the provisions on natural persons:

> "For the purpose of Title IV of this Agreement, nothing in the Agreement shall prevent the parties from applying their laws and regulations regarding entry and stay, work, labour conditions and establishment of natural persons, and a supply of services, provided that, in so doing, they do not apply them in a manner as to nullify or impair the benefits accruing to any parties under the terms of a specific provision of this Agreement."

What are the benefits to the parties? According to the International Court of Justice (PCIJ), a State when asserting the right of one of its nationals, is "in reality" asserting its own right to secure, in the person of its nationals, respect for the rules established by international law.[123] The benefit to Poland as regards Article 37(1) of the agreement is that accruing to its nationals on the territory of the Member States. This includes the benefit of its nationals to the rights

---

121 I have considered above the arguments about the direct effect of the establishment provision and so I will not repeat them here. Suffice it to say that if my position that the establishment provision does have direct effect is accepted, then from the moment that the CEEC national commences a genuine and effective self-employed activity he or she is exercising the right.

122 48/75 *Royer* [1976] ECR 497; 118/75 *Watson* [1976] ECR 1185.

123 *Mavrommatis Palestine Concessions Case* PCIJ Series A No 2 (1924); *Panevezys-Saldutiskis Railway Company Case* PCIJ Series A No 76 (1939).

contained in the agreement and access on an equal basis to national courts and tribunals to enforce these rights.[124] I would therefore argue that where an individual national asserts a right the government has achieved for him or her, he or she is exercising a benefit to a party: the country of origin.

Next, there is the question of the meaning of nullifying and impairing a benefit. This is not a term that has been used elsewhere in Community law. It is both a definitional element and a key to invoking the GATT (now the expanded WTO) dispute-settlement mechanism and has been described as "an unfortunately ambiguous phrase".[125] Jackson notes that in the GATT setting, the term meant that it was neither sufficient nor necessary to find a breach of obligation. From an early stage "nullify and impair" began to be defined to include actions by a contracting party which harmed the trade of another and that could not reasonably have been anticipated by the other at the time a concession was negotiated. This interpretation introduced a reasonable expectations concept. Jackson notes the development of a practice of the contracting parties and their panels to find *prima facie* nullification and impairment in three situations: breach of obligation; use of domestic subsidies to inhibit imports in certain cases; use of quantitative restrictions (even where they would have been otherwise lawful in GATT):

> "In such a case the burden of proof of showing that no N or I [nullification or impairment] occurred as a result of the breach, subsidy or quantitative restriction shifted to the country that breached or used those actions. Lacking a clear showing that no N or I occurred, the GATT practice assumed that the panel was obligated to make a *prima facie* N or I ruling, usually calling for the offending nation to make its actions conform to the GATT obligation."[126]

The introduction of a prohibition on measures which have the effect of nullifying and impairing the right may be interpreted as a prohibition on obstacles. If the jurisprudence of the GATT is used as a guide, two of the three situations in which *prima facie* nullification and impairment occurs are obstacles-related when translated into Community law: domestic subsidies[127] and quantitative restrictions.[128] Such an approach to the provision would assist consistency

---

124 Article 111 Poland Agreement.

125 J. Jackson, The *World Trading System, Law and Policy of International Economic Relations*, 2nd edn, The MIT Press, Cambridge Massachusetts, 1997, p. 115.

126 J. Jackson, *The World Trading System, Law and Policy of International Economic Relations*, 2nd edn, The MIT Press, Cambridge Massachusetts, 1997, p. 115.

127 The Community law concept is state aids. It is based entirely on preventing distortion of competition and is not tied to the concept of discrimination, see A. Evans, *A Textbook on European Union Law*, Hart, Oxford, 1997, p. 406 *et seq*.

128 On quantitative restrictions the Court has held on numerous occasions that "all trading rules enacted by a Member State which are capable of hindering directly or indirectly,

in Community law on obstacles and would provide a framework for what is otherwise a rather heterogeneous provision.

Taken literally, virtually any restriction will impair the exercise of a right. Any administrative requirement to document the exercise of the right which exceeds that required of Community nationals who are self employed on the territory of a host State would be difficult to justify. It could be argued that any measure which does not satisfy the *Gebhard* criteria (above) would have the effect of impairing the exercise of the right. This approach is in essence equivalent to maintaining that the nullify and impair provision does no more than reinforce the proportionality requirement which is implicit in Community law already. If this approach is correct, then the provision may lack a necessary characteristic of Community law: *effet utile*.

Another approach would be to argue that the nullify and impair test represents a higher threshold within which Member State action is permissible than would otherwise be the case. But what could that threshold be? If indeed the provision does import another test, then it is likely that it must be one balanced on the factual situation of the individual concerned. This then brings the concept back close to, if not the same as, the proportionality test.

The only assistance to be found in the agreements themselves as to the meaning of "nullify or impair" is to be found in the Joint Declaration on visas to which I will return below. This Declaration, interestingly, states that a visa requirement for natural persons *per se* does not have the consequence of nullifying or impairing the right of establishment. If this is the test against which the "nullify or impair" provision is to be examined, then the threshold before discriminatory national measures on entry can apply is high. Further, it makes it clear that the prohibition of measures which may nullify or impair the right apply equally to measures of the Member States' representatives abroad as activities relating to obtaining a visa will take place normally in the country of origin.

In my view, the provision on the application of national laws and the addition of a nullify and impair proviso in fact does not add to the tools of control available to the Member States. What it means is that the Member States are entitled to apply their national laws on entry etc but only in so far as this application does not result in disadvantage to the CEEC national seeking to exercise his or her right of establishment in comparison with own nationals. Therefore if own nationals are required to present their passports on entry into a State then so too such a provision is applicable to CEEC nationals exercising a right under the agreement. National rules on access to regulated forms of

---

actually or potentially, intra-Community trade" are prohibited; see 8/74 *Dassonville* [1974] ECR 837. Under the formulation a measure may be prohibited, irrespective of whether it is discriminatory. If it is not discriminatory then it is an obstacle only.

self-employment must be respected, though subject always to the *Gebhard* principles. Or, for instance, a Member State may be entitled to require a CEEC self employed person to obtain a residence permit but limits the penalties which the Member State can impose for failure to do so.

Another provision in the agreements may also indicate a concern of the Member States to control by national means the exercise of individual rights under the agreements. Article 48(4) Poland Agreement states:

> "The provisions of this Agreement shall not prejudice the application by each Party of any measure necessary to prevent the circumvention of its measures concerning third country access to its markets through the provisions of this Agreement."

Again, this is a very oblique clause: it is by no means clear that it could be considered to regulate immigration which does not naturally present itself as a measure on access to markets. It has been suggested that this provision was drafted in the light of GATT 1994[129] provisions particularly in Article VI relating to preventing evasion of measures restricting market access.[130] It would require a very forced interpretation of this provision to make it applicable to natural persons. What becomes apparent from the discussion is that the Member States were keen to have access to the CEECs for their nationals and companies but less delighted at relinquishing discretionary control over admission of persons to their territory. One finds a tension between the use of the Community form of migration law: the right to move for the purpose of self employment and the introduction of ambiguities which render its exercise more susceptible to discretionary control by the national authorities.

A Joint Declaration attached to the agreements provides that:

> "The sole fact of requiring a visa for natural persons of certain Parties and not for those of others shall not be regarded as nullifying or impairing benefits under a specific commitment."

The force of declarations in Community law remains unclear territory. Assuming, that the declaration may be referred to as an aid to interpretation,[131] what does this declaration mean? The first problem is that there is no clarification as to whether the declaration refers to short stay visas or long stay visas or both. In chapter 8 I will consider in depth the conundrum of visas in the Union.

---

129 In view of the over 14-year negotiating history of the Uruguay Round, these provisions were well in circulation before the commencement of the EC negotiations with the CEECs.

130 R. Plender QC, The Europe Agreements and the UK Immigration Rules: Opinion for JCWI/ILPA 20 May 1998 (unpublished).

131 The question of declarations arises a number of times in this book, notably in chapters 4 and 8. A fuller discussion of their effect may be found there.

Suffice it here to make a few observations. As the Member States have increasingly externalised immigration control by requiring persons who seek to come to and reside on their territory for an extended period to obtain authorisation for that purpose in their country of origin before arrival the concept of a visa has become increasing unclear. In respect of some countries such as the UK the same document, called a visa,[132] fulfils two purposes: permission to cross the border and authorisation to seek to reside and to engage in economic activities. In my opinion, considering the structure of the declarations, only the first aspect of a visa is properly encompassed by the provision.

This would mean that the application of national law on entry is limited only to an examination of whether the CEEC national is required to have a visa as defined in the Regulation or not. Whether the individual is planning to exercise a right of self-employment is not an issue for determination at the border nor is it acceptable as a ground for rejection of the individual at the border.

Member States have reacted differently to the possibility of loss of discretion over CEEC nationals who are self-employed. Some, like the Netherlands, have introduced a mandatory visa requirement for all CEEC nationals seeking to exercise an establishment right on the territory. Even where they are present in the Member State in some other capacity they must return to their country of origin to obtain a visa in order to come back to enjoy the right of establishment. Such an obligation is not sanctioned overtly by the declaration, which does no more than permit discrimination between nationals of CEECs as regards visa requirements. Such provisions are questionable as potentially contrary to the nullify and impair prohibition. Other Member States like the UK have been more cautious on this point and do not require CEEC nationals lawfully on the territory to return to their country of origin to obtain visas only so that they can return to the Member State to continue their self-employment.

What is noteworthy about all the contrary indicators is their vagueness. On the one hand the Member States and the Community extend a right of self employment to CEEC nationals on the territory of the Union and on the other hand they insert into the agreements a series of what appear to be paper tigers in the form of obstacles and hindrance under national law to the right granted. So while the classic relationship between the individual, host State and Community is one of a triangle with rights and obligations in each direction, these indicators of a power to the Member States to interfere with the right apparently guaranteed by the Community to CEEC nationals sends conflicting signals. Measures which are vague always create problems for coherence, comprehension and application.

---

132 Or in the case of the UK entry clearance.

6.7. CONCLUSIONS

When these agreements were settled the Member States and the Community needed to make some political choices about whether to open up access to the territory and economic activities for nationals of the CEECs. The choice they made was to use the agreements to provide a means for those nationals to move to and exercise economic activities lawfully within the Member States. This decision was fuelled by the wish to secure reciprocal rights for Community nationals within the territory of the CEECs. However, it is not beyond the realm of international negotiations for such a provision not to be reciprocal – that is to say, for nationals of the Member States to have been permitted to exercise economic activities in the CEECs to the exclusion of an equal right for CEEC nationals to do the same in the Member States. This option was not chosen.

Notwithstanding the substantial numbers of nationals from the CEECs who were, at the time of negotiation of the agreements, seeking to move to and reside in the Member States, the Community chose to extend a right for such persons to live and engage in economic activities in the Union. The result is the achievement of a balance between the desire to come to the Union to exercise economic activities on the part of nationals of countries closely associated with the Union and directly on its borders and the concern of the Member States to protect their labour markets. Self-employment is permitted, employment prohibited. As regards the latter it was for the Member States individually to determine whether they wished to make facilities available and under what conditions. The exclusion of the possibility of employment for CEEC nationals also has the effect, in many Member States, of excluding those nationals from the most costly forms of social security and assistance benefits which are available to workers or potential workers only.[133]

This balance is a fundamental characteristic of immigration law: determining the basis on which aliens may have access to the territory and economic activities in the light of the pressures which are being manifested. Further, the form used to achieve this balance is consistent with the Community's traditional approach to migration: the creation of a right to move, reside and exercise economic activities for aliens which has the effect of depriving the Member States of the right to apply national discretionary criteria to the exercise of the right. The choice, whether to exercise the right or not, is then devolved from the Community to the individual subject to a minimum of criteria which involve an exercise of discretion.

---

133 For instance, eligibility for the main social assistance benefit in the UK, job-seeker's allowance is tied to the applicant's availability to take work.

Just as in respect of Community nationals, the Member States' interpretation has been half-hearted including an effort to retain some form of control through the use of visa requirements, which in practice prevent the operation of direct effect as the individual is kept away from the territory of the Member State as regards the purpose of the right. He or she has no chance of lawfully setting up his or her business until the Member State has authorised this through the issue of a visa.

The legal framework within which this immigration policy has taken place is uniform. Just as in the first experiments with immigration by the Community, the process was one of the exclusion of national discretion through the creation, first of a direct link between the individual and the supra-national authority, the Community, and secondly the investing of rights to move and engage in economic activities in the individual, so this experiment follows the same pattern. The main difference is the legal timidity of the Member States and the Community, which is manifested through the inclusion of a series of provisions, which could act as checks on the right itself.

These fetters of the establishment right in particular, could be interpreted in three ways: first they deprive the provision of direct effect because it is for the Member State to determine the content of implementation in national law. Here the result risks depriving the provision of *effet utile*. Secondly, there is a limited discretion to the Member States to qualify the content of the right. The difficulty with this approach is that it is not supported by the text of the agreements. Finally, there is no discretion left to the Member States as regards admission and exercise of the right of establishment beyond the limitation on grounds of public policy, health and security expressly included. Such a position, which in my view is correct, does not however, relieve the individual from the same requirements as regards residence permits etc. as are applicable to migrant Community nationals.

The benefits of the rights-based approach may be threefold at least: first the clarity of a rights based law reduces administrative delay and cost as the rules are clear and simple and do not require senior officials to weigh up discretionary elements in order to reach a decision; secondly, the individual alien can regulate his or her life in accordance with clear rules with a degree of security as to the consequences of any particular choice or action; thirdly, the alien and the society benefit from security as to who is and who is not entitled to reside, leave, return and exercise economic activities. The suspicions of the host society that the alien is "abusing" immigration laws should be diminished by the application of transparent rules agreed by 15 Member States in common.

PART III

THE TREATY AND THIRD COUNTRY NATIONALS: THE
IMPETUS TOWARDS COMPETENCE AND COHERENCE

CHAPTER SEVEN

THE DRIVE TOWARDS COMPLETING THE INTERNAL MARKET: DIVIDED LOYALTIES

7.1. INTRODUCTION

Depending on who is counting, there are probably between 13 and 15 million third country nationals living in the Union.[1] Many are nationals of countries with agreements with the Community which protect them. Others do not benefit from any work or residence right based in Community law. In this Chapter I will look at how the Union became interested in these third country nationals. At work here is a different approach to immigration regulation than that which I have examined so far. Up to this point, Community immigration regulation was informed by a clear objective,[2] consistency[3] and enforceability.[4] The mechanism for achieving this was the creation of a direct link between the individual migrant and the supra-national body in which the supra-national body devolved power to the individual to make choices and protected the choice made by the individual from Member State interference. In order to consider what happens to these objectives when faced with the question of treatment of third country nationals who are not otherwise encompassed by Community law (i.e. as family members of Community migrant workers or protected under third country agreements) I will consider the following questions:

1. In the development of immigration regulation of third country nationals at supra-national level, what is the objective sought by the Member States and the Community (as an entity separate from the Member States, the voice of which is the Commission)?

---

1 P. Stangos, Les ressortissants des états tiers au sein de l'ordre juridique communautaire, Cahiers de droit européen, 1992, p. 305. According to Eurostat, Statistics in Focus, Population and Social Conditions 1998 No. 3, p. 6 in 1995 there were approximately 12 million third country nationals resident in the Union.
2 Free movement of economic actors within the Union: Articles 39-49 EC.
3 Through the application of the Treaty provisions and subsidiary legislation uniformly within the territory of the Member States.
4 Through the powers of the Court of Justice to give binding interpretation to the rights contained in the Treaty.

2. What are the steps along the way, what compromises and choices as to how to regulate immigration are made by the Member States and the Community?

The chronology of events becomes as complicated as the differing policy initiatives, Member State responses and Court judgments. I will not always follow the discussion chronologically. Therefore I will start with a chart of the critical dates to which I will refer for this consideration and which may assist the reader.

Immigration in the European Union: 1984 – 1993

Date	Event	Significance
25/26 June 1984	European Council at Fontainebleau creates an Ad Hoc Committee for Citizens Europe.	Among the tasks of this Committee was to consider measures to abolish police and customs checks at internal borders.
13 July 1984	Signature by French President Mitterrand and German Chancellor Kohl, at Saarbrücken, of an agreement to abolish border controls.	The creation of a bilateral agreement between two of the largest Member States to reduce border obstacles to trade gives a strong political push to the discussion of border controls including in particular those Member States concerned about being left out.
June 1985	Commission publishes its White Paper on the internal market which envisages measures on immigration, asylum and national visa policy.	The completion of the internal market will become the venue for revitalising the European integration project and some Member States' *bête noire* on the question of competence over third country nationals.
June 1985	Opening of the Inter-Governmental Conference leading to the Single European Act.	The impetus for amending the Treaties is the need for strengthening the legal power to complete the internal market. Border controls will be an issue.
12 June 1985	Accession Agreements with Spain and Portugal signed.	On entry into force an immediate right of freedom of movement for establishment for Spanish and Portuguese nationals in the Member States (and vice versa) arose. The right of free movement for workers was delayed (originally) until 1 January 1993.

Date	Event	Significance
15 June 1985	Five Member States sign the Schengen Agreement.[5]	The regulation of the abolition of border checks is started by an intergovernmental agreement of five Member States: Belgium, France, Germany, Luxembourg and the Netherlands.
July 1985	The Commission issues a Decision on prior consultation on immigration law and policy.	This Decision triggers a strong reaction from the Member States against the Commission over the question of competence.
September 1985	Five Member States commence an action before the Court of Justice against the Commission's Decision.	Such a strong reaction from the Member States against the Commission in the field of migration was unprecedented.
February 1986	The Single European Act is signed.	This included at Article 14 EC the requirement to abolish intra Member State border controls, *inter alia* on persons, by 31.12.92.
October 1986	UK Presidency proposes the formalisation of the inter-governmental group within the Council to consider immigration and asylum: the Ad Hoc Group Immigration.	The intergovernmental venues will become the main forum for discussion of immigration and asylum matters in the forth coming years. The inter-governmental venue of the 12 Member States is contrasted against the inter-governmental venue of the Five Schengen states. The overlap is substantial.
1 July 1987	The Single European Act enters into force.	The removal of physical, technical and fiscal barriers to trade kicks off in earnest.

---

5   The Schengen Agreement of 1985 between Belgium, France, Germany, Luxembourg and the Netherlands, provided a framework for relaxation of border controls between the participating states and in the longer term their abolition with a deadline of 1 January 1990. Among the compensatory measures to be taken were those on checks at external borders, police and judicial co-operation, harmonisation of visa and immigration policies, control of drugs and firearms and transfer of checks on goods away from the border. The original 1990 deadline turned out not to be realistic and instead the participating states sought by that date to achieve a second implementing agreement which would provide the needed detail to give effect to the objective.

Date	Event	Significance
9 July 1987	The Court of Justice hands down judgment in *Germany & Ors v Commission* [1987] ECR 3203.	The Court showed itself less than sympathetic to the Member States arguments in favour of complete national control over immigration.
1 January 1988	End of transitional period of free movement of workers from Greece.	The removal of restrictions does not result in a sustained surge of movement of workers from Greece to other Member States.
December 1988	The Rhodes Council meeting establishes the coordinators group on immigration.	The co-ordinators group is asked to prepare a report and work programme on immigration and asylum.
9 November 1989	The Berlin Wall falls.	This is the beginning of the end of the regulation of East/West migration by means of the Iron Curtain. Western European states are about to have to take responsibility for movement of persons across these borders.
15 June 1990	Signature of the Dublin Convention on responsibility for determining asylum applications.	This is the first intergovernmental agreement in the field involving all 12 Member States. It covers the same ground as the asylum part of the Schengen Implementing Agreement which will be signed 4 days later.
19 June 1990	Signing of the Schengen Implementing Agreement.	This agreement put flesh on the bones of the original agreement in particular as regards immigration and asylum and provides the legal basis of the creation of the Schengen Information System.
12 September 1990	German re-unification takes place.	The reunification of Germany has the *de facto* effect on enlarging the Community.
20 September 1990	Court of Justice's ruling in *Sevince* [1990] ECR I-3461.	For the first time the Court finds that subsidiary legislation of a third country agreement can give real residence and work rights to third country national migrant workers.

Date	Event	Significance
14-15 December 1990	Opening of the Inter-governmental conference which will lead to the Maastricht Treaty.	The institutional structure is created for discussing the creation of monetary union. As a minor side issue the reshaping of competences over immigration and asylum will be considered.
1991: 11 October (asylum) and 23 October (immigration)	The Commission produces two Communications one each on immigration and asylum.	The Commission's Communications propose a restrictive regime for immigration and asylum but within a Community law framework.
3 December 1991	The Co-ordinators Group produces its report to the European Council on immigration and asylum.	The thrust of the report is that immigration and asylum should remain in essence intergovernmental.
10 December 1991	The Maastricht Treaty is agreed (signature followed on 7 February 1992).	No amendment is made to the Treaty regarding border controls but a whole new structure is created for intergovernmental agreement on immigration and asylum.
16 December 1991	EC Poland Association Agreement signed.	The Community extends the right of economic activity as self employed to nationals of Poland with the intention of extending this right to all the CEECs.
1 January 1992	Transitional delay on free movement for Spanish and Portuguese workers is lifted.	The Accession Agreements provided that the transitional provisions would continue for a further year. The Council decided that the delay was not necessary.

Date	Event	Significance
2 May 1992	The European Economic Area Agreement is signed.	The Community is expanding again to accommodate a very close relationship with the Scandinavian countries (Finland, Norway and Sweden), Austria and potentially Switzerland. Full Community free movement rights are granted to third country nationals for the first time.
11-12 December 1992	Under the UK Presidency three intergovernmental resolutions on asylum are adopted.	These are the first resolutions on asylum adopted by the Member States inter-governmentally. The format will be used many times again.
1 January 1993	End of the transitional period for Article 14 EC.	The debate on the legality of border controls reaches its zenith.
1 November 1993	The Maastricht Treaty comes into force.	There is a split of competence between the Community and the new Third Pillar (an intergovernmental venue within the structures of the new Union) on third country nationals.

In this schedule I have included only those events which I consider to be vital to the development of European immigration law: the competing interests of the internal market drive for the abolition of border restraints on the movement of goods and the perceived need of a number of Member States to maintain a discretion over the control of the movement of persons to their territory: the Commission White Paper on completion of the internal market in 1985 matched with the Member States' legal challenge to the Commission's proposal for a consultation procedure on immigration. These two aspects become mixed with the Schengen Agreement which intended the abolition of border controls between five Member States, but as a multilateral agreement in international law had not the strong effect of a Community law provision on the subject. Of course it also left out those Member States who were yet to be convinced that the benefit of the abolition of border controls on persons outweighed the disadvantages. The position of the "doubters" became formalised in the meetings of the immigration ministers. The consequences of three events: two of which the Community had control over – enlargement: the end of transitional provisions on workers from Greece and the accession of Spain and Portugal – and one which was a surprise – the fall of the Berlin Wall after which the unification of Germany and the further enlargement of the Community eastwards very soon seemed inevitable and changed the perspective on the Community's role in migration policy. The shock of rising numbers of asylum seekers from the East also contributed substantially to the sense in a number of Member States of both the need for action at national level and co-ordination with other Member States. The resolution of the competing interests and concerns is the subject of this chapter.

7.2.   THE ECONOMIC INCENTIVE: CREATING THE INTERNAL MARKET[6]

The European Union is based in economic policy. The driving force for the three initial treaties was to bind Europe together through the integration of national economies. The strategy set specific economic objectives which would act as steps towards the long-term political objectives. However, by the 1970s all was not moving smoothly.

As Keohane and Hoffmann argue, a series of circumstances both external and internal had begun to squeeze the European Community. Externally the transformation of the world political economy and the competitive pressures arising from that required a response. According to Keohane and Hoffmann, capital movements rather than trade balances were becoming the dominant force on exchange rates. The development of competition from East Asian economies, particularly Japan, had to be contended with. This, together with the adoption of assertive economic policies, created friction with the US. Internally, by the mid-1960s institutional transformation was slowing dramatic-ally. French President De Gaulle's opposition to supra-nationality combined with enlargement brings Keohane and Hoffmann to conclude that "the inter-secting struggles meant that throughout the period from 1966 to 1985, Europe was often viewed as politically and economically stagnant ... ".[7]

The Commission's White Paper on completing the internal market was pub-lished in June 1985 and endorsed by the Summit of that year.[8] The objective of the internal market was to remove barriers, physical, technical or fiscal to trade

---

6   This chapter builds on and develops some ideas which appear in my chapter: The impetus to harmonise: asylum policy in the European Union, in F. Nicholson & P. Twomey, *Refugee Rights and Realities, Evolving International Concepts and Regimes*, CUP, Cambridge, 1999, pp. 313-335.

7   R. Keohane & S. Hoffmann, Institutional Change in Europe in the 1980s, in R. Keohane & S. Hoffmann, *The New European Community Decision-Making and Institutional Change*, Westview Press, Boulder, 1991, p. 6.

8   European Commission *White Paper on Completing the Internal Market*, Brussels, 1985.

among the Member States.[9] In this context, extensive research was undertaken on the cost to business of barriers:

> "The most obstructive barriers to cross-border trade, in the view of business itself, are administrative formalities and the border controls to which they are so often linked. This emerges clearly from the business survey[10] in which company executives pinpoint paperwork, red tape and frontier checks as high on the list of obstacles hampering the dispatch of goods to other Community markets."[11]

The package was a whole: barriers of all kinds had to be abolished and where those barriers included obstacles to the movement of persons then these too had to be abolished. The transition taking place in Europe from an economy dominated by production of goods[12] to one where the provision of services plays an increasingly important role is evident.[13] Because the individual had been defined as an economic actor as regards his or her right to move in the Union, the push to abolish obstacles to economic integration swept persons along with its logic. The difficulty of excluding persons from the benefit is almost impossible – a problem the UK would encounter shortly. Whether the Member States wanted it or not, the determination to succeed in economic integration symbolised by the abolition of border controls meant a sudden and for some Member States disconcerting loss of control over the entry of non-nationals be they third country nationals or nationals of other Member States.

This issue was raised in the Commission's White Paper, which envisaged the need for measures on immigration and asylum. However, it is important here to note that at the time of negotiating the Single European Act, the issue of movement of people was not a priority in the negotiations. Looking at those negotiations from a variety of theoretical and practical perspectives, focussing

---

9   P. Cecchini, *The European Challenge, 1992, The Benefits of the Single Market*, Gower, London, 1988.

10 European Commission Research on the 'Cost of Non-Europe' – the Completion of the Internal Market: A Survey of European Industries' perception of the likely effects, Brussels, 1988.

11 P. Cecchini, *The European Challenge, 1992, the Benefits of the Single Market*, Gower, London, 1988.

12 Including agricultural goods.

13 In the Europe of the 12, in 1986 37,492,000 people were working in industry and 60,144,000 in services. By 1991 those figures had risen to 38,956,000 for industry and 68,010,000 for services. The difference not only in overall figures but in the rate of growth of the different sectors is indicative of the shift which was taking place at the time of the negotiations towards the Single European Act and would continue to take place. *Labour Force Survey 1983-1991*, Eurostat, Luxembourg, 1993.

on the issues of concern to the participants, Moravcsik does not identify movement of persons as vital or indeed noteworthy to any of them.[14]

The preparatory work towards the new push for the Community led to the first major intergovernmental conference on re-negotiation of the Treaties between June 1985 and February 1986. The result was the Single European Act (SEA). Article 14 inserted into the Treaty by the SEA which determined the internal market as "an area without internal frontiers in which the free movement of goods, persons, services and capital is ensured" became the flash point for the issue of Member States versus Community control of persons and in particular third country nationals.[15]

Commission officials emphasised that the objective of free movement of persons only found a new formulation in the article and was no more than the same principle which had always existed in the EC Treaty in Article 3 as an object.[16]

Article 14 was complemented by two declarations adopted by the Intergovernmental Conference[17] to which I will return in due course. The abolition

---

14 A. Moravcsik, Negotiating the Single European Act, in R. Keohane & S. Hoffmann, *The New European Community, Decision-Making and Institutional Change*, Westview Press, Boulder 1991, pp. 41-84.

15 Article 14 was not the only provision dealing with third country nationals inserted by the SEA. It also inserted a second paragraph into Article 49 EC which states "The Council may, acting by a qualified majority on a proposal from the Commission, extend the provisions of the Chapter to nationals of a third country who provide services and who are established within the Community." Only in 1999 was an implementing measure proposed. The Member States here agreed to a specific competence to the Community over third country nationals in respect of one of the three economic free movement rights applicable to natural persons. Of course the exercise of the competence would require an implementing measure proposed by the Commission and subject to adoption by the Member States in the form of the Council. More important though is the principle. What is operating here is a tension between the benefit perceived by the Community and the Member States' trade and foreign ministries of reducing and eliminating barriers to trade and the concern of the Member States ministries responsible for immigration and control of movement of persons. Article 14 EC no longer observes the Community principle of free movement only for the economically active (and in due course self sufficient). It brings into play a wider group of people: everyone within the Union – it proved, for some Member States, a step too far too fast.

16 W. de Lobkowicz, Quelle libre circulation des personnes en 1993? Revue du marché commun, No 334 Février, 1990, pp. 93-102.

17 "The Conference wishes by means of the provisions in Article 8A [14] to express its firm political will to take before 1 January 1993 the decisions necessary to complete the internal market defined in those provisions, and more particularly the decisions necessary to implement the Commission's programme described in the White Paper on the Internal Market. Setting the date of 31 December 1992 does not create an automatic legal effect."

of intra-Community border controls had already been presented by the Commission in the White Paper on the internal market as entailing a series of common measures regarding the position of third country nationals, in particular, within the Union. Once intra-Union borders are abolished, then there is no frontier check on persons travelling within the territory of the Member States. The logic therefore is that common measures are needed on immigration, asylum and visa requirements. Five of the then twelve Member States already had experience of formally abolishing (or failing to introduce) border controls with their neighbours. The Benelux Union[18] consisted of just such an area, as did the Common Travel Area.[19] In the first case these border control free areas were achieved with overt harmonisation of external immigration rules, in the second less so. A different group of five Member States had already signed the Schengen Agreement and were committed to the abolition of border controls among themselves here accompanied by extensive external border co-ordination provisions. However, the extension of these areas to the twelve would prove more difficult: the problem was fundamentally one of confidence among the Member States complicated by the fact that the question was elevated into a test of sovereignty.[20]

The lack of confidence was translated into a series of legal arguments as to the meaning of Article 14 within its context:

1. Is the article capable of direct effect at the end of the transitional period?

And:
"Nothing in these provisions shall affect the right of Member States to take such measures as they consider necessary for the purpose of controlling immigration from third countries, and to combat terrorism, crime, the traffic in drugs and illicit trading in works of art and antiques."

18 Consisting of Belgium, Luxembourg and the Netherlands.
19 Consisting of the UK and Ireland.
20 "In his memoirs, former British Home Secretary Kenneth Baker wrote that a collision with the European Community over the central justice and home affairs issue of maintaining of national frontier controls will be the ultimate test of who governs? The national or the supranational state [Kenneth Baker: *The Turbulent Years*, London, Faber & Faber 1993, pp 442-443]. One may not agree with the dramatic tone of Baker's phrase (the tense relations between London and Brussels can certainly do without it), but it points to a fundamental aspect of justice and home affairs as areas of Union policy-making which at the same time is one of its major problems: more or less all aspects falling within these areas concern the internal security of Member States, and traditionally the enormous concentration of political, administrative and financial power of the modern state has found one of its main reasons of legitimacy in the guarantee of the internal security of its citizens." J. Monar, Cooperation in the Fields of Justice and Home Affairs: Progress, Deficits and the Need for Reform, TEPSA Seminar 7-8 November 1996.

2. Does the article require the abolition of all controls on persons crossing internal EU borders even if it is not of direct effect?

3. What is the status of the declarations?

The judicial answer to these questions was handed down in mid-1999, and I will finish this section with a discussion of that case. But the history of the legal argument is critical to the political developments. The first legal question which arises is whether Article 14 is capable of having direct effect at the end of the transitional period. Here the argument was whether the provision is sufficiently clear, precise and unconditional to apply directly within the legal order of the Member States without the need for intervening measures such as proposals for directives introduced by the Commission in 1995[21] which I will consider under the second question. The argument in favour of direct effect of the provision was not without support. The broadly comparable provisions on establishment did acquire direct effect, according to the Court, at the end of the original transitional period.[22] Not least because of the sensitivities, though, question sparked substantial academic[23] and political interest.[24]

Timmermans[25] considered that the provision required at the least a re-interpretation of all other provisions in the Treaty:

"The argument that border controls will be automatically rendered incompatible with the EEC Treaty from 1 January 1993 by virtue of Article 8A [14] [is] open to question. If the objective of removing all internal border controls is to be derived from Article 8A [14], this objective must be taken into account, according to the most orthodox interpretation methods developed in the Court's case law, when interpreting other Articles of the Treaty."[26]

---

21 A proposal was also put forward by the Commission in 1993 when it proposed a version of an external frontiers convention to be adopted within the new structure created by the Treaty on European Union. However, only the 1995 proposals dealt fully with the position of third country nationals moving within the territory of the Union.

22 2/74 *Reyners* [1974] ECR 631.

23 See for instance: H.G. Schermers, *Free Movement of Persons in Europe, Legal Problems and Experiences*, The Hague, Martinus Nijhoff, 1993. In this section I wish to acknowledge my debt to Peter Duffy QC (deceased) with whom I worked closely on this question and who was so generous with his knowledge, experience and research.

24 The UK's House of Lords Select Committee on the European Communities undertook an inquiry into the question which resulted in the Report of the House of Lords Select Committee of the European Communities 1992: *Border Control of Persons*, Session 1988-9 22nd Report (HL Paper 90).

25 Timmermans was at the time Adjunct Director General of the Commission's Legal Service.

26 A. Timmermans, Free Movement of Persons and the Division of Power between the Community and its Member States, in H. G. Schermers, *Free Movement of Persons in Europe, Legal Problems and Experiences*, The Hague, Martinus Nijhoff, 1993, pp. 352-368.

It is less than clear what the added value for persons would be of this approach. For example, when considering the correct interpretation of Article 39 EC the Court has already held that those benefiting from the right may not be subject to a purposive examination at the border.[27] Therefore there is no added value here for the Community national of Article 14. However, as no provision of the Treaty other than Article 14 could give a third country national the right to cross an intra-Member State border, there would be nothing on which the "interpretative" function of Article 14 could bite. In effect, such an interpretation of Article 14 EC for persons does no more than justify the maintenance of border controls on persons without providing any *effect utile* to the Article.

Another observer, Toth, was straightforward in acknowledging a conundrum on which he was not willing to take a view.[28] From the perspective of a Court which is subject to criticism for judicial activism this approach would be unwelcome. It invites the Court to take the decisive role in a highly political dispute, indeed in one where even respected academic observers are unwilling to state a view. Dollat analyses the concept of direct effect as an emanation of the Court and therefore a tool which is available to the Court to achieve the objectives of the Union. He concludes however, that Article 14 is not substantially different from Article 3 EC which as an objective of the Community is not directly effective. In his view further measures are therefore required to be taken for Article 14 to take effect.[29]

A challenge before the UK courts ventilated the issue in the context of a British national who refused to show his passport on returning to the UK from France after the end of the transitional period. He was delayed for some time and eventually allowed to go on his way in the UK. He brought an action against the UK authorities for the delay which he suffered as a result. He argued that the UK's failure to implement Article 14 EC properly and within the deadline had resulted in his inconvenience. The case eventually came before the English Court of Appeal which considered the question *act claire* (after many days of oral argument) against direct effect at the end of the transitional period. The UK's court of final instance declined to give leave to appeal to the applicant.[30] The English Court of Appeal reasoned that Article 14 lacked the necessary attributes of direct effect as it was insufficiently clear, precise and unconditional to apply without implementing measures.

---

27 C-68/89 *Commission v Netherlands* [1991] ECR I-2637.
28 A. Toth, The Legal Status of the Declarations Annexed to the Single European Act (1986) CMLRev 803.
29 P. Dollat, *Libre circulation des personnes et citoyenneté: enjeux et perspectives*, Bruylant, Brussels, 1998, pp. 360-364.
30 *R v Secretary of State for the Home Department ex p Flynn* [1995] Imm AR 594, CA.

On the second question: who is covered by Article 14, the odd Member State out was the UK. It maintained that the article only applied to nationals of the Member States as only such nationals have a right of free movement. In order to determine whether a person crossing an internal border has the right of free movement a check on his or her passport is required. Therefore Article 14 could not be read to mean that controls at the frontier had to be abolished. The UK remained without overt support from other Member States on this question, though in the end it would receive support from the Court.

"For the Commission and eleven Member States, Article 8A [14] of the Treaty relates to the abolition of controls at internal frontiers for all persons, regardless of nationality. For the United Kingdom, the move to dismantle controls applies only to Community nationals."[31]

The European Parliament took a strong position on the universal application of Article 14[32] and demand implementation by the Council and Commission.

Notwithstanding the Parliament's agitation the Commission did not introduce legislation to give effect to Article 14 as regards movement of persons by the end of the transitional period. It did, however, issue a Communication to the Council and Parliament on 10 December 1993 proposing the adoption a convention under the new powers inserted by the Maastricht Treaty in Article K.3 TEU on the crossing of the external frontiers of the Member States, accompanied by a proposal for a Regulation on nationals of which countries must be in possession of a visa when crossing those frontiers.[33] This was a move designed to revive the proposal for a convention which had been introduced in the intergovernmental forum but has run adrift on a jurisdictional dispute between the UK and Spain over the status of Gibraltar.[34] Earlier intergovernmental drafts of the convention were very similar to that proposed by the Commission, the most notable change was, though, the introduction of jurisdiction to the Court of Justice over disputes arising form the convention.[35]

---

31 Answer to written question E-2692/92 of D. Rogalla (PSE) MEP given by V. d'Archirafi (Commissioner) on behalf of the Commission (9 December 1993) OJ 1994 C 349/2.

32 Report of the Committee on Civil Liberties and Internal Affairs on the abolition of controls at internal borders and free movement of persons within the European Community, K. Tsimas, 2 October 1992; A3-0284/92.

33 COM(93) 684 final.

34 H. U. J. D'Oliveira, Expanding External and Shrinking Internal Borders: Europe's Defence Mechanisms in the areas of Free Movement, Immigration and Asylum, in D. O'Keeffe & P. Twomey, *Legal Issues of the Maastricht Treaty*, Chancery Law Publishing, Chichester, 1994, pp. 261-278.

35 This introduction of the Court of Justice brought the measure into direct fire as regards the differing opinions among the Member States on the correct role of the Court of

The question which was increasingly considered fundamental to the abolition of intra-Member State border controls: the common policy on the crossing of external borders was thus incorporated into a proposal from the Commission very early after the introduction of a right of initiative to the Commission in the field. However, the dispute between the UK and Spain over the status of Gibraltar remained inexorably, and indeed, it would seem that some Member States were happy to have the issue block progress on a binding instrument which would have introduced judicial supervision to an inter-governmental reserve.[36]

The problem though with the external frontiers convention was that it was seen as a preliminary step to the achievement of the abolition of intra-Member State frontier controls. It did not in fact require the abolition of the internal controls and therefore did not satisfy, in the view of some, the obligation contained in Article 14. Accordingly, the Parliament instituted proceedings against the Commission on 18 November 1993 before the Court of Justice seeking a declaration that the Commission had failed, in contravention of the Treaty and in particular Articles 14 and 211, to put forward the necessary proposals to facilitate achieving freedom of movement for persons.[37] Still the Commission did nothing. Finally, on 12 July 1995, when the Parliament's action against it was moving up in the Court's lists, the Commission presented three proposals for measures to abolish border controls within the Union:[38]

1. Proposal for a Council Directive on the elimination of controls on persons crossing internal frontiers.[39] The objective of this proposal was to eliminate controls and formalities on persons, whether Community nationals or third country nationals, at the internal frontiers of the Com-

---

Justice in the whole field of justice and home affairs – see W. Robinson, The Court of Justice after Maastricht, in D. O'Keeffe & P. Twomey, *Legal Issues of the Maastricht Treaty*, Chancery Law Publishing, Chichester, 1994, pp. 179-192.

36 D. O'Keeffe, The Convention on the Crossing of the External Frontiers of the Member States, in A. Pauly, *De Schengen à Maastricht, vois royale et course d'obstacles*, EIPA, 1996, pp. 33-44.

37 C-445/93 *Parliament v Commission* "Achieving freedom of movement for persons in the internal market requires the adoption of legal measures as provided for in the Commission's White Paper, essentially consisting in the abolition of border controls. For the Commission, which is the only institution with the power to initiate the procedure for creating Community law, the right to initiate accordingly becomes an obligation. It is no longer open to the Commission to put forward no proposals; at most, it has a certain degree of latitude in drawing up draft laws." OJ 1994 C 13/1.

38 See also E. Guild, The Right to Travel: three new directives from the European Commission, I&NL&P (1996) Vol. 10/2, p. 5.

39 OJ 1995 C 139.

munity. It defines "internal frontiers"[40] and "frontier controls or formalities" broadly in such a way as to prevent systematic border checks on persons. However, in the explanatory memorandum the Commission was careful to point out that "In the same connection, it should be stressed that the elimination of controls on persons crossing internal frontiers does not mean that any obligation imposed by Member States' national laws to carry identity papers or travel documents while on the public highway has to be done away with."[41]

2. Proposal for a Council Directive on the right of third country nationals to travel in the Community.[42] Its objective was to provide a legal basis in Community law for third country nationals on whom there would no longer be an internal border check on travel among the Member States to move lawfully within the territory of the Union. The right is limited to third country nationals lawfully on the territory.[43] In the explanatory memorandum to this proposal the Commission emphasised: "It should be stressed that this proposal for a Directive concerns only entry into and movement in the territory of the Member States by *persons who are already lawfully in the territory of a Member State*. It concerns neither the first entry into the Community by a third country national nor the decision of a Member State to authorise such a person to remain in its territory for a short or long stay, nor *a fortiori* national decisions on access to the labour market or to self-employed activities."[44]

3. Proposal for a European Parliament and Council Directive amending Directive 68/360 on the abolition of restrictions on movement and residence within the Community for workers of the Member States and their families and Directive 73/148 on the abolition of restrictions on movement and residence within the Community for nationals of Member States with regard to establishment and the provision of services.[45] This proposal was designed to bring existing Community legislation into

---

40 The issue of the definition of external frontiers is the ostensible reason for the delay in finalising the External Frontiers Convention OJ 1994 C 11.

41 COM(95) 347 final.

42 OJ 1995 C 306.

43 To be determined on the basis of a list provided by the Member States of documents which they issue which are treated as the equivalent to residence permits for the purpose of the article, and to include a visa which is valid throughout the Community and is mutually recognised for the purpose of crossing the external frontiers of the Member States. This was drafted with a view to Regulation 1683/95 on a uniform format for visas adopted on 29 May 1995 (OJ 1995 L 164).

44 COM(95) 346 final.

45 OJ 1995 C 307.

line with the abolition of internal border checks. Here the Commission considered it appropriate again to reassure the more nervous Member States: "The bringing-about of an area without internal frontiers has no impact on the arrangements applicable to the right of residence proper (cases in which a residence permit must be applied for, procedure for the delivery of such permits), nor does it prevent Member States from carrying out checks on individuals other than in connection with the crossing of internal frontiers."[46]

In my view there is an obvious connection between the Parliament's challenge on the border control issue and the appearance of the three proposals for directives.[47] The UK immediately confirmed that if put to a vote in the Council it would block the adoption of the measures.[48] As a result of the Commission's proposal, the European Parliament withdrew its action before the Court of Justice, though, in the Court's order, the Parliament was required to pay the attendant costs. With the introduction of the three proposals for directives the question of who is covered by Article 14 was not resolved but at least clarified. The Commission, as guardian of the Treaties, introduced a legislative proposal inclusive of all persons crossing internal borders (to the exclusion only of those unlawfully present in one Member State and moving to another).

The final legal question which arises in this context is the status of the Declarations. The issue of Declarations arises periodically in Community law. The frequency, however, is increasing as with each amendment to the Treaty the Member States feel obliged to attach more and more such Declarations, a practice which has been criticised.[49] The first Declaration on Article 14 EC

---

46 COM(95) 348 final.
47 This view is shared by P. Dollat, *Libre circulation des personnes et citoyenneté: enjeux et perspectives*, Bruylant, Brussels, 1998 pp. 363. However other do not draw this connection. M. Hedemann-Robinson, Third-Country Nationals, European Union Citizenship, and Free Movement of Persons: a Time for Bridges rather than Divisions, 16 YEL (1996), p. 321.
48 See also A. Cruz, Visa Policy under the First Pillar: A Meaningless Compromise in M. den Boer, *Schengen, Judicial Cooperation and Policy Coordination*, EIPA, Maastricht, 1997, pp. 213-239.
49 "The practice of adopting declarations at the time of signing the Final Act of Intergovernmental Conferences comes from the origins of the Communities. Their number, however, has tended to increase substantially: 9 at the time of signing the Treaty of Rome, 20 on the signing of the Single European Act, and 33 at the time of the Maastricht Treaty. The same tendency may be found as regards the signing of agreements concluded by the Community with third states. This is a most regrettable tendency as it clouds legal transparency and certainty, particularly when it takes the form of unilateral declarations by certain Member States. Further these declarations may be legally challengeable where their purpose appears to be to complement or interpret provisions

indicates that the objective is a political one rather than a legal one. The second Declaration has been less contentious as it does not necessarily apply to the question of internal border controls. The second Declaration preserves the Member States' right to take measures for the purpose of controlling immigration from third countries. This can easily be consistent with even the most expansive interpretation of Article 14 which, in any event, only concerns internal EU borders not external borders.

Differing views have been expressed on the effect of these Declarations. Schermers took the view that as declarations are not part of a treaty their status must be inferior to that of the treaty itself. However, in his opinion the Declarations to the SEA were intended to have legal effect and, unless in conflict with the Act itself, must be considered as authentic additions. On this basis he concluded that while the Declaration on automatic legal effect is binding, in the event of conflict with the Treaty itself the Treaty prevails.[50] This does not take us much further as the Declaration, by designating a political rather than a legal effect to Article 14 appears to seek to change the nature of the provision itself. Again, a respected observer seems to be ducking the fundamental question and leaving it to the Court to form a view without the support of academic positions one way or the other.

According to Waelbroek, the creation of clear obligations to be met within a time limit but qualified by the declaration may mean that the provision cannot have direct effect but the failure to fulfil the obligations by the deadline would create some legal effects, if only the right to commence legal proceedings against the Community institutions or Member States for failure to honour their duties under the Treaty.[51] This at least is clear as regards the legal position which might flow from the Declaration.

Toth, on considering all the Declarations to the SEA, comes up with five conclusions about them. They:

1. Are not susceptible of precise legal characterisation;

2. Possess binding force neither under public international law nor under European Community law;

3. Are not subject to the jurisdiction of the European Court of Justice;

4. Can in no way restrict, exclude or modify the legal effects of the SEA;

---

of a Treaty or Protocol." D. Martin & E. Guild, *Free Movement of Persons in the European Union*, Butterworths, London, 1996, p. 92.

50 H.G. Schermers, The Effect of the Date of 31 December 1992, CMLRev 28:275-289 1991.

51 M. Waelbroek, Le Role de la Cour de Justice dans la mise en oeuvre de l'Acte unique européen, Cahiers de droit européen, 1989, p. 41.

5. Cannot have an effect on the interpretation of the Act by the European Court.[52]

Here again is a clear and decisive approach to the question of Declarations. If correct, this would mean that the Declarations really do not do anything at all from the legal perspective but no doubt provide some political comfort for Member States' politicians when questioned back home about what they were doing at the inter-governmental conference. What is interesting in this discussion on the effect of the Declarations is the reluctance of most observers to express firm positions. The dates at which the various observers published their views may also be relevant. The clearest position is taken by Toth in 1986 when the SEA was yet to enter into force. The most nuanced position is taken by Schermers in 1991 when the debate at the political level had become intense.

Finally, in an article more generally on the question of the end of transitional periods in Community law, Schockweiler also queried whether the Court would find the Declarations useful in interpreting the meaning of Article 14.[53]

The Commission, in Annex I, Commission Position on the Interpretation of Article 8A [14] of the EEC Treaty, to its 1992 Communication[54] took a robust view of the general question of the second Declaration in particular:

"A declaration can never deprive an article of the Treaty of its practical effectiveness. In any case, the Declaration in question [on the right of the Member States to control immigration from third countries] does not give rise to a different interpretation from Article 8A [14]. It refers to the distribution of powers between the Community and the Member States, and that cannot affect the definition of the objective to be achieved."

The Commission did not venture a view in the Communication on the legal effect or otherwise of the first Declaration. The purpose of the Communication was to set out a position on the need to achieve the objective. The question of direct effect was not primary to its position.

---

52 A. Toth, The Legal Status of the Declarations Annexed to the Single European Act, CMLRev 23:803-812, 1986.

53 "il est permis de s'interroger sur les effets que cette manifestation de volonté des Etats membres peut avoir sur l'évolution de la jurisprudence de la Cour qui, dans sa méthode d'interprétation s'est toujours référée davantage à l'économie générale du traité et à sa finalité qu'au texte et à l'intention de ses auteurs pour dégager des solutions allant au-delà, et parfois même à l'encontre, de la lettre du texte." F. Schockweiler, Les conséquences de l'expiration du délai imparti pour l'établissement du marché intérieur, Revue du Marché Commun de l'Union européenne, 1991, pp. 882-886.

54 European Commission, Abolition of Border Controls, Communication to the Council and to Parliament, SEC(92) 877 final.

The question of the direct effect of Article 14 after the end of the transitional period although now answered by the Court remains important.[55] Although the Amsterdam Treaty has changed the landscape of the EC Treaty on movement of persons, the issue has not become irrelevant. The implementing power for Article 14 is now in Article 61 which comes within Title IV, Visas, Asylum, Immigration and Other Policies Related to Free Movement of Persons. If Article 14 had direct effect then intra-Community border controls on persons were unlawful and had been unlawful since the end of the transitional period. As Article 14 applied to all Member States, all Member States were required to dismantle intra-Community border controls on 31.12.92 in that scenario. Article 1 of Protocol X of the Amsterdam Treaty permits the UK "notwithstanding Article 7A [14] of the Treaty" to exercise at its frontiers with other Member States such controls on persons seeking to enter the UK as it may consider necessary. If Article 14 had direct effect from the end of its transitional period then the UK would have been under a legal duty, which it did not observe, to abolish intra-Community border controls of persons between 1.1.93 and the entry into force of the Amsterdam Treaty. Thereafter, the legality of the continued application by the UK of border checks on person travelling within the Union would have depended on the legal force to be accorded to the X Protocol.

Needless to say, from 1986 to 1999 this was an extremely messy situation which lacked the clarity and transparency for which a lawyer would wish. However, it was the natural result of the inability of the Member States to reach agreement on the relinquishing of discretionary control over the intra-Union movement of third country nationals. While the UK was most outspoken in its refusal to accept the results, the commencement of the Schengen experiment – discretionary abolition of border controls – indicates a wider acceptance of its position. For the Schengen Member States the issue was not so much whether to abolish border controls among themselves at all, although this was a sufficiently difficult issue, but rather whether to create a legal right enforceable by the individual to cross a border without a check. This would be the practical result of the direct effect of Article 14 EC or its implementation by a Community measure. On this question, the use by the Schengen five of an intergovernmental agreement which does not necessarily give rise to rights to individuals but creates *inter partes* relationships only was consistent with the British position.

The debate over the meaning of Article 14 gave both a public and academic face to what had been transformed into a sovereignty struggle: borders controls and third country nationals. A number of NGOs pressed for the implementa-

---

55   C-378/97 *Florus Ariël Wijsenbeek* [1999] ECR I-6207.

tion of Article 14 by the abolition of intra-Member States, perhaps the most highly publicised was the action by ECAS[56] in setting up in 1993 a hot line for all persons suffering difficulties or indignities when crossing internal borders.

The academic discussion which I have outlined above also indicates how widely the issue was canvassed over the period from 1986 to 1999. The subsequent amendments first by the Maastricht Treaty and then by the Amsterdam Treaty in the field of immigration and asylum were to a substantial extent fuelled by this debate. So, when the Court of Justice finally came to consider the question, it could not but be an anticlimax. First, the Court's judgment had been rendered otiose in practice by the development of the Schengen system whereby intra-participating state border controls were abolished or in the process of being so abolished.[57] By the time of the judgment in September 1999, 13 of the 15 Member States had signed up to the Schengen acquis and the two completely outside the system, Ireland and the UK had secured opt outs in the Amsterdam Treaty which would enable them to continue to apply intra-Member State border controls for as long as they wished notwithstanding the Court's judgment on the legal effect of Article 14 EC.

No dispute resolution mechanism accepts easily the overturn of its decisions by subsequent legislation. Courts like even less to have their judgments anticipated by apparently hostile legislative action designed to enable the parties to continue their disputed practices irrespective of the Court's view on legality. It would seem that the Court of Justice is no exception. The decision in *Wijsenbeek*[58] may be read as an expression of this phenomenon. The Court only answers the most fundamental of the questions on the application of Articles 14 and 18 EC put to it by the Rotterdam court:

> "[Article 14] cannot be interpreted as meaning that, in the absence of measures adopted by the Council before 31 December 1992 requiring the Member States to abolish controls on persons at the internal frontiers of the Community, that obligation automatically arises from expiry of that period."

As to the many subsidiary questions, for instance on the effect of the Declarations and the meaning of Article 18 EC on citizenship of the Union, the Court remained laconically silent. At great length it sets out the arguments of the applicant, the Netherlands government, the Commission and the intervenors

---

56 European Citizens Action Service, a Brussels based-umbrella NGO for many primarily consumer rights NGOs at national level in all the Member States.

57 This of course did not impede the introduction of random checks just within the territory of some states, which included a citizenship test. Such practices, at least in principle contrary to the spirit of the abolition of border controls among the Member States, have yet to be tested in the courts.

58 C-378/97 [1999] ECR I-6207.

which consisted of Spain, Ireland, Finland and the UK. Then in two paragraphs dismissed the whole business, as if not sufficiently interesting to engage the attention of such a Court. However, of all the positions spelled out, perhaps the greatest sympathy is to be found in the description of the applicant, Mr Wijsenbeek. He was a member of the European Parliament who, on a flight from France to his home in the Netherlands, refused to show his passport and was subject to delays and fines. It is apparent that his decision to challenge the passport check regime, within Schengen states no less, was intentional. It is a pity that the courage of such an individual to challenge the development of intergovernmentalism at the expense of individual and enforceable rights has meet with such a check. Politically, of course, the judgment makes great sense. What would be the point now of re-engaging with the issue of the direct effect (or otherwise) of Article 14 EC in autumn 1999? The political dilemma has been resolved after a fashion (see Chapter 9) and there is no longer a role for judicial balancing. The Court has been included in the new framework for immigration, asylum and border controls post-Amsterdam, there is no need for it to assert a right here which would only exacerbate some Member States and create a situation of major legal uncertainty about acts which had taken place before the entry into force of the Amsterdam Treaty.

Nonetheless, in a legal discussion about rights and powers of individuals, states and supra-national bodies, the winners on the issue of the legality of border controls on persons, notwithstanding the opinion of civil society as expressed by NGOs in many Member States, are the Member States in the exercise of their power within the Council to block legislation, such as that proposed by the Commission in 1995. In effect the Court's position is that if the question is liable to resolution by Treaty amendment then it is a political question in respect of which the Court's role is merely to acknowledge that political characteristic. And, so the one personal right of movement which those resident in the Member States would have obtained as a result of the SEA finally vanished in September 1999.

7.3.   PULLING IN DIFFERENT DIRECTIONS: THE COMPETENCE CHALLENGE

At the same time that the Member States were negotiating towards and developing the concept of the internal market which would include the abolition of border controls on persons, five Member States[59] were challenging

---

59 Germany, France, the Netherlands, Denmark and the UK.

the competence of the European Commission over any aspect of migration and third country nationals.[60] The leader of the pack, Germany, was also a front runner pushing for the Schengen Agreements and the abolition of border controls. The timing of the various activities is worth noting: the first Schengen Agreement was signed in 1985 and established the objective of abolition of intra-state border controls. The challenge to the Commission over competence was lodged before the Court of Justice the same year. The inter-governmental conference leading to the SEA was already underway. Two conflicting desires of the Member States had met head on: the creation of an internal market with sufficient strength and cohesion to challenge even the mightiest of its trading partners, and the desire to keep people, at least in so far as they were third country nationals within the discretionary control of the Member States. It would take over ten years to move to a position where a resolution of these aims would be possible. In the process, as becomes apparent, the positive goal, which is trade-oriented, consistently if slowly overcomes the inertia goal of maintaining the *status quo* on control of persons.

In 1985 the Commission made a foray into third country nationals and immigration policy: it adopted a Decision on a consultation procedure whereby the Member States would be required to notify it of proposals for amendments to their immigration laws.[61] This Decision was based on Article 137 EC which empowered the Commission "to promote co-operation between Member States in the field of social policy and to organise appropriate consultations to this end". The Decision contained three types of obligations for the Member States:

1. A duty to provide information (Article 1);

2. The achievement of the objectives of the consultation procedure in which the Member States must participate (Article 3);

3. Procedural rules which must be observed (Articles 2 and 4).

The Advocate General summarised the history of the Commission's relations with the Member States in the field commencing with the Code of Conduct adopted in 1963 on the Commission's involvement in the area of immigration up to the date of the action by the Member States attacking the Decision. He then asked the critical question:

> "Hence, there was dissension, but above all coldness, distrust and vigorous defence of national sovereignty, even in the face of exhortatory or fact-finding instruments. Why was this case brought? What brought before the Court a

---

60 281/85, 283-85/85 & 287/85 *Germany & Ors v Commission* [1987] ECR 3203.
61 OJ 1985 L 217/25.

number of Member States which is scarcely less than the number required to bring the Council itself into the field? Logically, it must be concluded that there was no reason. On six occasions the Council states that consultation is indispensable: twice it spurred the Commission on to implement it and, when the Commission decided to act, asked it on a further two occasions to inform the Council of its proposals. For their part, the Member States raised doubts, put forward suspicions, gave warnings; but they never said – either before 1985 or, even less, during the procedure – that they were unwilling to provide each other with information and take part in consultations."[62]

As the Advocate General points out, the Member States' intentions and actions appear to indicate an ambivalence which is difficult to reconcile. The Member States' arguments against the Community's competence in the field are revealing about the underlying concerns. The main argument was that migration policy in relation to third countries is not part of the social field envisaged by Article 137 EC or alternatively it falls only partly within that field.

All five Member States argued that Article 137 EC procedurally was not capable of founding a base for a binding instrument such as the Commission had adopted. They further argued that there could be no implied extension of the Commission's powers to enable it to undertake the task assigned to it. In support of this position, they argued that Article 137 is essentially programmatic in nature. Giving the argument more specificity, the French government contended that the whole area of policy on foreign nationals falls outside the social field inasmuch as it involves questions of public security for which the Member States alone are responsible. The German government argued that the duty of notification is liable to jeopardise the requirements of secrecy and confidentiality, particularly in negotiations with non-member countries. The UK government stressed that the immigration policies of the Member States are fashioned or determined by historical, cultural and social factors on which the Community has nothing to say.[63] The Dutch government took a technical approach, arguing that the Decision has too many lacunae, is too imprecise and contradictory to enable its addressees accurately to determine the extent of the obligations to which they are subject. The Danish government appears to have relied exclusively on technical arguments.[64]

The Commission defended its Decision on the basis that it was entrusted with an organisational power in respect of migration policy. Under this duty it was necessary to obtain information though there was no power to compel

---

62 Case 281/85, 283-285/85 & 287/85 *Germany & Ors v Commission* [1987] ECR 3203.

63 This argument is interesting as it reveals a not unusual approach of the UK Government that the Community is somehow different from and only tenuously connected with the Member States.

64 281/85, 283-285/85 & 287/85 *Germany & Ors v Commission* [1987] ECR 3203.

Member States to adopt jointly agreed measures. The Parliament was more clear-sighted about the fundamental issue at stake and argued that if the Decision was annulled for lack of competence this in fact would alter the division of powers between the Community and the Member States in the field to the detriment of the Community. In fact, the Parliament was correct. Even though in the event, the annulment of the Decision was on very limited grounds the consequence was a change in exactly that balance.

The Court found:

> "As regards the applicants' main argument it must be observed that the employment situation and, more generally, the improvement of living and working conditions within the Community are liable to be affected by the policy pursued by the Member States with regard to workers from non-member countries. In the preamble to Decision 85/381/EEC the Commission rightly considers that it is important to ensure that the migration policies of Member States in relation to non-member countries take into account both common policies and the actions taken at Community level, in particular within the framework of Community labour market policy, in order not to jeopardise the results."[65]

It noted that Article 137 gives the Commission the task of promoting close co-operation between the Member States in the social field and to that end to make studies, deliver opinions and arrange consultation. It then reviewed the activities of the Community in the field starting with the resolution of 21 January 1974 concerning a social action programme where the Council recognised that the migration policies of the Member States affected the Community's social policy and finishing with the resolution on guidelines for a Community policy on migration approved by the Council in July 1985. What the Court appears to be doing is focussing on the inconsistency of the Member States arguments in that they, in the form of the Council, had already approved and adopted over a substantial period of time resolutions confirming that their national migration policies affect Community social policy.

As regards the connection of migration policy with public security, again the Court was not convinced:

> "The French Republic's argument that the whole area of policy on foreign nationals falls outside the social field inasmuch as it involved questions of public security for which the Member States alone are responsible cannot be accepted. Whilst it is true that pursuant to their rules governing foreign nationals Member States may take measures with regard to workers who are nationals of non-member countries either by adopting national rules or by negotiating international instruments – which are based on considerations of public policy, public security and public health and which are, as such, their sole responsibility,

---

65 281/85, 283-285/85 & 287/85 *Germany & Ors v Commission* [1987] ECR 3203.

this does not mean that the whole field of migration policy in relation to non-member countries falls necessarily within the scope of public security."

On the question of the German government's concerns about confidentiality the Court stated:

"The effect that the duty of notification is liable to jeopardise the requirements of secrecy and confidentiality, particularly in negotiations with non-member countries, must likewise be rejected since there is no imperative requirement for the drafts to be notified until such time as they are published."

The Court went on to consider the secondary submission of the Member States that the decision covers matters falling outside the social field within the meaning of Article 137 EC. Here the Court was more sympathetic to the Member States' position:

"The promotion of the integration into the workforce of workers from non-member countries must be held to be within the social field within the meaning of Article 118 [137], in so far as it is closely linked to employment. This also applies to their integration into society, having regard to the objectives pursued by the contested decision, inasmuch as the draft measures in question are those connected with problems relating to employment and working conditions, and there is no reason to consider that the decision intended to give a different meaning to the concept. As regards the cultural integration of immigrant communities from non-member countries, whilst this may be linked, to an extent, with the effects of migration policy, it is aimed at immigrant communities in general without distinction between migrant workers and other foreigners, and its link with problems relating to employment and working conditions is therefore extremely tenuous. Moreover, migration policy is capable of falling within the social field within the meaning of Article 118 [137] only to the extent to which it concerns the situation of workers from non-member countries as regards their impact on the Community employment market and on working conditions."[66]

The judgment is important as a clarification of the extent of the powers of the Community institutions where they are charged with a task. That aspect of the judgment is not central to the discussion here. However, one further matter is important: the Court found that under the powers conferred by Article 137 on the Commission "cannot determine the result to be achieved in that consultation and cannot prevent the Member States from implementing drafts, agreements and measures which [the Commission] might consider not to be in conformity with Community policies and actions".[67]

---

66 281/85, 283-285/85 & 287/85 *Germany & Ors v Commission* [1987] ECR 3203.
67 281/85, 283-285/85 & 287/85 *Germany & Ors v Commission* [1987] ECR 3203.

Decaux, among the first to analyse the case, recalls the Advocate General's Opinion – the surprise of the Member States that the Commission had actually taken a step in this disputed field.[68] He usefully refers to the declarations attached to the SEA, in particular the second one. The SEA had been signed in February 1986, the judgment was delivered on 9 July 1987. In his opinion, by refusing to find in favour of the Commission on the wide interpretation of the social field in Article 137 (i.e. inclusive of culture) the Court was directly or indirectly noting the concerns of the Member States expressed in the SEA.[69] From the subsequent action of the Member States it does not seem that the Court's reassurance in their direction, assuming that Decaux is correct and this was the intention of the Court, was sufficient to head off a surge of inter-governmental activity in the field which by its nature ensured no further inter-ference from the Court.

A rather different perspective on the case is given by Hartley. In his analysis of the case:

"Two points immediately strike one. The first is that [Article 137] is not on its face concerned with immigration, especially not from non-member States; the second is that nowhere does it confer any legislative power on the Commission. These were the two grounds on which its validity was challenged by five Mem-ber States in the case which forms the subject of this comment. Both grounds were rejected by the European Court, though a few crumbs were thrown to the applicants."[70]

Although he is most concerned with the issue of the implied powers of the Commission, as regards the application of Article 137 one notes a certain sarcasm:

"On the question whether the decision fell within the scope of Article 118 [137], the European Court pointed out that immigration from non-member States can affect employment and working conditions within the Community. It is well known that the presence of large numbers of 'guest workers' from third countries can keep wages low and deprive Community immigrants, and even

---

68 E. Decaux, Jurisprudence, revue trimestrielle de droit européen 23 (4) oct-dec 1987, p. 707-716.
69 "Ainsi, tout en refusant de faire du 'domaine social' une véritable peau de chagrin, la Cour tient-elle compte directement ou indirectement des préoccupations essentielles des requérants en refusant l'interprétation généreuse que la Commission faisait de son champ de compétence. Bien plus, elle va rogner les moyens d'action de la Commission, en donnant de substantielles garanties procédurales aux Etats." E. Decaux, Juris-prudence, revue trimestrielle de droit européen 23 (4) oct-dec 1987, pp. 707-716.
70 T. Hartley, The Commission as Legislator under the EEC Treaty, European Law Review, 1988, pp. 122-125.

local workers of employment. The first ground of challenge to the validity of
the measure was therefore rejected ... ."[71]

This does not seem to me to be particularly fair to the Court. In view of the
resolutions of which there were numerous of the Council in the field of
activities under Article 137 which include issues relating to migrant workers
from third countries, it is not unreasonable for the Court to accept what in
essence had already been accepted by the Council: the treatment of third
country national workers within the Union at least for some purposes must be
considered within the scope of Article 137 EC.

Desolre picks up on this naturalness of the Court's judgment. He points
out, though, the somewhat arbitrary decision of the Court to draw the line at
cultural integration. While the Court was willing to go so far as to find
employment and working conditions within the scope of Article 137 it rejected
culture not with an argument which placed it is a different field but on a
tenuousness ground.[72]

There is much which the Court refrained from deciding in this case.[73]
Simmonds focuses on the non-compliance with procedural requirements part
of the judgment in this regard. However, in his view:

"It had appeared, to judge from the official pronouncements, that the social
advancement of migrants was accepted as necessary for social justice, economic
efficiency and to counter racial and ethnic tension. Against the background of
an increasingly uncertain social and economic climate, the promotion of
migrants' rights – whatever their country of origin – had come to be regarded
as one of the principal social objectives of the Community. The resident
migrant population within the territory of the Community is now over 13
million, of which some 5 million are nationals of the Member States. The
belated attention paid in recent years to the position of migrants from non-
member countries has received a major set-back with this judgment – and from
an unexpected source."[74]

As far as Simmonds suggests that the protection of migrant workers had come
to be regarded as one of the principle social objectives of the Community, he is

---

71 T. Hartley, The Commission as Legislator under the EEC Treaty, European Law
Review, 1988, pp. 122 – 125.
72 "La Cour a ainsi 'sauvé' la partie névralgique de la décision en acceptant qu'une portée
assez large soit donnée à l'expression *intégration sociale*. La compétence de la Commission
est dès lors reconnue étant donné que l'intégration professionnelle et sociale des travailleurs (à l'exception de la promotion de leur intégration culturelle) des Etats tiers présente
une étroite connexité avec le marché du travail interne." G. Desolre, Observations,
Cahiers de droit européen, 1990, 1-2, pp. 453-464.
73 K. Simmonds, CMLRev 52:177-200 [1988].
74 K. Simmonds, CMLRev 52:177-200 [1988].

perhaps not entirely supported. The activities of the Community in the field of equal treatment between men and women and the protection of workers' rights for instance on the transfer of undertakings certainly evidence other major social policy concerns of the Community which might have a better chance of finding themselves in first place of importance. Otherwise, this assessment most clearly accords with my own view of the importance of the judgment and echoes the concern which was voiced by the Parliament in its submissions to the Court.

Following the Court's judgment, the Commission reverted to a role of observing progress in the area taking place under the Schengen Agreement and within the Ad-hoc Group on Immigration. It is not possible to say whether the Court's judgment influenced the determination of the Member States to retain discretionary control remaining to them over all questions relating to admission, work and residence of third country nationals. Certainly the arguments put forward by the Member States to the Court in the case reveal their anxiety to keep the whole question of third country nationals within the realm of international affairs and national security. The lack of sympathy of the Court to these considerations at least in respect of the Commission's competence may indeed have caused officials in Bonn, Paris, London and elsewhere to worry about how the Court would interpret competence in the field next if there were to be a gradual leeching of control from the national level to the Community level in the field.

7.4. PERSONS, BORDERS AND DISCRETION

The challenge thrown down by the internal market push and the overt withdrawal of the Commission from introducing measures to regulate third country nationals was paralleled by the first moves of the immigration ministries to arrange matters intergovernmentally. Under the British Presidency in the second half of 1986, a first meeting of ministers responsible for immigration was held in London.[75] Doubts were already arising in the immigration ministries of some Member States regarding the compatibility of the abolition of internal frontier controls with control of movement of third country nationals. The potential unravelling of competence over third country nationals was already apparent.

---

75 This was the first formal meeting of Interior and Justice Ministers of the Member States in their new capacity as "Ministers responsible for immigration". Previous meetings had taken place informally. See D. Papademetriou, *Coming together or pulling apart? The European Union's struggle with immigration and asylum*, Carnegie Endowment for International Peace, New York, 1996.

In a review by the European Commission in 1992 on the implementation of Article 14 EC it stated:

"The situation is worrying at all political levels where free movement of individuals is concerned. While considerable progress has been made since the Rhodes European Council in 1988 on the back-up measures for the abolition of border controls, the lack of political consensus on the actual scope of Article 8A [14 EC] is still apparent. The second meeting of the European Council at Rome on the subject of free movement of persons noted with regret that a delay had occurred in relation to the programme. It considers it necessary to give full scope to the provisions of the Single Act on free movement of persons. It wants the necessary decisions, in particular, on the crossing of external borders, to be taken at an early date to ensure that the 1 January 1993 deadline is met. The two Conventions on the examination of applications for asylum and on the administration of the external frontier, the basic elements of which had been ready for more than a year, have not yet come into force for want of ratification in the case of the former and for want of signing in the case of the latter."[76]

The problem was one exclusively about persons. As the Commission pointed out in its Communication:

"The Commission's interpretation of Article 8A [14] would not appear to pose any political problem of principle as regards its application to goods. The determination to give full effect to that Article has been clearly asserted in all Member States; the establishment of new monitoring arrangements in the field of indirect taxation permitting the abolition of the single administrative document in intra-Community trade testified to that determination and is prompting a reorganisation of all the controls carried out by the customs or other authorities."[77]

As the trade and industry ministries across the Union adjusted to the abolition of border controls for the purposes of customs, immigration ministries were increasingly concerned about the consequences of the commitment to the abolition of border controls on persons travelling intra Community. As leader of the pro-frontier control group of Member States, the UK's Home Office was asked in 1992 by a Parliamentary Committee to account for the difference in approach between the relatively painless transition away from frontier customs checks and the adamant insistence on border controls. In reply the official stated:

---

76 European Commission, Abolition of Border Controls: Commission Communication to the Council and to the Parliament SEC [1992] 877 Final, Brussels 1992.
77 European Commission, Abolition of Border Controls, Commission Communication SEC (92) 877 Final, 1992, p. 4.

"I was explaining that immigration officers need to give leave to enter the United Kingdom individually to third country nationals and that is simply not a responsibility which is analogous to the Customs officer's responsibility. If I could just go on for a moment, I believe myself that that statutory structure reflects the basic reality of the situation, in that the immigration officer is looking at a very large number of individual cases; if I could use a metaphor, it is like a shoal of small fish and needs to be put through a fairly fine mesh if it is to be controlled at all, whereas the Customs officer is looking for the odd, very big fish."[78]

The attempt to differentiate the role of customs and immigration officers is less than satisfactory. What is apparent from the answer on the part of the UK's Home Office is that while the trade-oriented Customs and Excise Agency was willing and able to adjust to the political objective of the abolition of frontier controls, the UK government was unwilling to relinquish discretionary control over each individual third country national seeking entry to the UK irrespective of the Community goal of abolition of intra-Union frontiers.

As Nanz has analysed, ever since the late 1980s there was general agreement among the Member States that compensatory measures on external border controls, a common visa policy, asylum and judicial co-operation were needed to ease intra-Member State border controls. The provisions of the Schengen acquis provided this.[79] Elsen, a participant in the debate as a Director General of DG H – Justice and Home Affairs of the European Council at the time, has focussed on the role of Schengen as a laboratory for the Twelve, a highly debatable proposition when one remembers that Schengen is exactly inter-governmental and as such gives no rights to individuals rather than Community law which would be capable of creating rights.[80] What is not directly addressed is the fundamental point: is this to be Community law which creates a relationship between the individual and the Community in addition to that of the individual with the Member State or the Community with the Member

---

78 Mr A. Langdon, Immigration and Nationality Department, UK, Evidence to the House of Commons Home Affairs Committee Inquiry into Migration Control at External Borders of the European Community 5.2.92 Session 1991-92, p. 11.

79 K-P. Nanz, Free Movement of Persons According to the Schengen Convention and in the Framework of the European Union, in A Pauly, *De Schengen à Maastricht: voie royale et course d'obstacles*, EIPA, Maastricht, 1996, pp. 61-79.

80 "Schengen et Maastricht n'ont pas ete créés pour coexister ni pour se concurrencer, mais l'un doit préparer à l'autre. La meilleure formule pour caractériser Schengen a été et reste celle du laboratoire d'essai. Schengen doit préparer la libre circulation dans le cadre de l'Union européenne et la création d'un espace de liberté et de sécurité." C. Elsen, Schengen et la coopération dans les domaines de la justice et des affaires intérieures. Besoin actuels et options future, in M. den Boer, *The Implementation of Schengen: First the Widening, Now the Deepening*, EIPA, Maastricht, 1997, p. 5.

State, or something else where the relationship remains exclusively between the individual and the Member State with the Community's role limited to consultation. If Elsen is correct and Schengen is a laboratory entirely compatible with the Community framework does he mean that the intergovernmental nature of Schengen which leaves to the signatory States the relationship of the individual to the State and does not create either a body capable of entering into a relationship nor a basis of such a relationship is the model for transposition to the Community? This question will find its answer in the implementation and interpretation of the Schengen Protocol to the Amsterdam Treaty (see chapter 9).

In the second half of the 1980s two steps can be discerned: first an indication to the immigration ministries that the question of movement of persons would remain inter-governmental and outwith co-ordination by the Commission for the Community. Secondly, such co-ordination as was perceived to be necessary to the achievement of the trade related aspects of abolition of border controls within the internal market should take place intergovernmentally. The European Council of 1988 in Rhodes set up an inter-governmental co-ordinators group charged with responsibility to identify and make progress on the adoption of the necessary flanking measures.[81] Under this mandate the Co-ordinator's Group produced the Palma Programme.

The Palma Programme, a Report to the European Council by the Co-ordinators Group was adopted by the Council in June 1989. Its Note on the Free Movement of Persons deserves further attention. It sets the agenda for the dispute between national discretion over third country nationals and Community competence. It was produced at the request of the European Council to establish the measures which would be necessary for the creation of the internal market. It sets out the plan for the abolition of internal frontier controls outlining a dual strategy first of strengthening checks at the Community external frontiers and then abolishing internal border checks.

The discretion/competence conflict is summarised in the Programme as follows:

"in the course of the group's discussions it was recognised that different views were held on their legal and political framework in particular on the interpreta-

---

81 "The Co-ordinators' meetings are not an extra forum for discussions; the Co-ordinators are responsible for co-ordinating, giving an impetus to and unblocking the whole inter-governmental and Community work in the field of the free movement of persons and submitting to the Madrid European Council a report on the free movement of persons and the establishment of an area without frontiers, including the measures to be adopted by the responsible bodies and a timetable for their implementation." The Palma Document in E. Guild and J. Niessen, *The Developing Immigration and Asylum Policies of the European Union*, Kluwer Law International, The Hague, 1996, p. 443.

tion and scope of the relevant Treaty provisions *inter alia* 8A EC [14 EC] and the obligations flowing therefrom, to the extent to which political decisions in this field have already been taken and where the competence for taking decisions and action lay. It was agreed to set those differences on one side for the purposes of the co-ordinators' discussions and this is reflected in this report".[82]

It is worth noting that at this crucial initial point in time the dispute as regards the competence of the Member States and that of the Community in respect of free movement of persons was already recognised as fundamental within the group established by the Council to examine the field. The political decision not to address the issue but to seek to make progress on a practical level was decisive of future developments. The Palma Programme specifies that the achievement of an area without internal frontiers would involve the approximation of national laws and their rules of application and scope, collaboration between national administrations and the prior strengthening of checks at external frontiers. To this end a set of legal, administrative and technical instruments were needed to harmonise immigration and asylum policy .

In the Palma Programme, the areas which needed to be addressed were divided into the "ad intra" and the "ad extra" categories. In the ad intra group are the security-related issues of terrorism, drug trafficking, policing and judicial co-operation including "the control of articles accompanying travellers" such as weapons. The ad extra group deals with checks on persons at external frontiers, followed by a heterogeneous list of areas in respect of which legal measures would be required in two main categories: the conditions governing entry into the Community of third country nationals and the grant of asylum and refugee status.

As regards content, then, the flanking measures would be kept within the intergovernmental forum. Because of the starting point of border controls and the link which was made very early on between easing controls at internal border with strengthening them at external borders, three concepts were thrown together: crime, security and third country nationals. For some observers this has been the most important consequence: the grouping together of the three separate topics has led to a construction of migration as a security issue.[83]

---

82 The Palma Document, Free Movement of Persons. A Report to the European Council by the Co-ordinators Group in E. Guild and J. Niessen, *The Developing Immigration and Asylum Policies of the European Union*, Kluwer Law International, The Hague, 1996, pp. 444-448.

83 D. Bigo, Frontiers and Security in the European Union: The Illusion of Migration Control, in M. Anderson and E. Bort, *The Frontiers of Europe*, Pinter, London, 1998, pp. 148 -164.

The forum chosen for development in the field of immigration and asylum as flanking measures to the completion of the internal market was intergovernmental. This choice was the direct result of the conflict apparent in the Palma Programme as to the legal effect and scope of Article 14 EC. Between 1986 and the 1993 entry into force of the Treaty on European Union, the only venue for discussion the harmonisation of immigration asylum law in the European Union was intergovernmental. This arena lacked any clear relationship in law to the EC Treaty and structurally lacked an administration. By the end of that period a structure had been developed which consisted primarily of groupings of national officials which included the Trevi Group designed to co-ordinate efforts against terrorism and extended in 1980 to include illegal immigration and asylum flows.[84] This Group included four sub-groups (1) Terrorism; (2) Police co-operation; (3) Serious crimes and drug trafficking; (4) Policing and security implications of the Single European Act.

The Ad Hoc Group on Immigration which grew out of the Trevi Group in 1986 did not replace it and was charged with responsibility for developing Community policies on immigration and asylum. It had six sub-groups: (1) Aylum; (2) External frontiers; (3) False documents; (4) Admissions; (5) Deportation; and (6) Information exchange.

Two further groups were involved, the Horizontal Group on data processing, the primary function of this group was to produce the European Information System designed to combat serious forms of crime, strengthen external border controls and police co-operation in the fighting of illegal immigration networks through the exchange of information; and the Customs Mutual Assistance Group was charged with co-ordination of customs and other technical information exchange and maintenance issues in order to strengthen external border controls.[85]

Each of these groups was in one way or another involved in an immigration aspect of the 1992 internal market project.[86] However, a stable administrative structure for these groups did not exist. Back-up was provided primarily by

---

84 According to Den Boer, Trevi was created in 1975 against the background of numerous terrorist attacks in the Member States. See M. den Boer, *Taming the Third Pillar: Improving the Management of Justice and Home Affairs Co-operation in the EU*, EIPA, Maastricht, 1998, p. 7.

85 A. Cruz, *Schengen, Ad Hoc Immigration Group and other European Intergovernmental bodies in view of a Europe without internal borders*, Briefing Paper No 12, Churches Committee for Migrants in Europe, Brussels 1996.

86 In addition, more than a few of them found a counter part in the structures which were being established under Schengen, see A. Pauly, De Schengen à Maastricht: voie royale et course d'obstacles, EIPA, Maastricht, 1996, and M. den Boer, *Schengen's Last Days? The Incorporation of Schengen into the New TEU, External Borders and Information Systems*, EIPA, Maastricht, 1998.

Member State ministries and co-ordinated, in so far as possible, by the European Council. The Commission was less than sympathetic.[87]

In the field of immigration and asylum under the Palma Programme, priority was given in the initial years to asylum policy first determining which State would be responsible for processing asylum applications of persons inside the Community territory. The Dublin Convention determining the State responsible for examining applications for asylum lodged in one of the Member States of the European Community was signed in June 1990 and finally came into force in September 1997. It addressed the first issue identified as pressing for the Member States that asylum seekers would be equally able to take advantage of the abolition of internal border controls to make duplicate, multiple or successive applications in the Member States as no border officials would prevent them crossing from the territory of one Member State to that of another.

The Convention, although drafted in terms of the European Community is an international law convention, supervision of which is delegated to a committee established under the Convention. Its implementing measures were published in the Union's Official Journal.[88] Its provisions are addressed to the Member States and include technical measures to deal with the allocation of responsibilities. From the perspective of an asylum seeker it is by no means apparent whether rights accrue under the Convention other than a promise that at least one Member State will take responsibility for his or her case. The subject matter of the Dublin Convention: responsibility for considering asylum applications is now included in Article 63(1)(a) EC. The Community is under a duty to adopt implementing legislation within five years of the entry into force of the Amsterdam Treaty on 1 May 1999. So far the Dublin Convention approach – attempting to determine through which Member State an asylum applicant first arrived in the territory of the Union – has not proven outstandingly successful as the main criterion for determining which Member State should be responsible for determining the application. The difficulty appears to have two sources: a reluctance on the part of asylum applicants to go to a Member State other than the one where they have applied for asylum; a reluctance on the part of some Member States with substantial external borders to get serious about harmonising asylum policy.

---

87 "As the Member States have chosen to rely on intergovernmental instruments necessitating national ratification procedures, they alone are responsible for ensuring that those instruments enter into force by the end of the year." European Commission, *Abolition of Border Controls*, Commission Communication SEC (92) 877 Final, 1992, p. 6.
88 Decisions of the Committee established under the Dublin Convention 1/97 and 2/97 OJ 1997 L 281/26.

The reluctance on the part of asylum applicants to move to other Member States appears to be fuelled by a lack of confidence in the procedures and appeal rights which apply, though this may be no more than the legal expression which reluctance on other grounds takes. The reluctance of some Member States with substantial borders to catalogue asylum applicants may have other foundations: the more seriously an asylum system is put in place the easier it will be for other Member States, further from the external borders to manage to return asylum applicants to the border Member States and hence move back the cost of reception and processing.

In December 1990 an intergovernmental conference was opened which would lead to the Maastricht Treaty signed in December of the following year. When the Member States opened the intergovernmental conference many forces were at work pulling in different directions on the issue. The immigration ministries had been charged with preparing a report on immigration and asylum which they produced on 3 December 1991,[89] only a week before the agreement of the Maastricht Treaty. The Commission voluntarily produced two Communications one on immigration[90] and one on asylum[91] in October 1991. The same tension is apparent in these documents as in all the preceding ones: the ministers' Report promotes an intergovernmental framework for immigration and asylum; the Commission proposes that competence be transferred to it and the field be regulated within the Community framework. The Commission's approach was rejected in the intergovernmental conference. Although the ministers' Report itself is unlikely to have appeared soon enough to have had a substantial influence on the outcome of that conference, the concerns of the immigration ministries were accommodated in the Treaty.

The compromise was the inclusion of the field of immigration and asylum within a new structure known as the European Union which comprised three parts: the European Community (i.e. the three Treaties and their acquis which form the European Community), the Common Foreign and Security Policy and Justice and Home Affairs (Title VI of the TEU). This was the result of the Maastricht Treaty which amended the existing Treaties and established the new one: the Treaty on European Union. Among others, Laursen and Vanhoonacker, Dehousse and Baun have all produced excellent analyses of the competing interests which lead to the Maastricht Treaty.[92] According to Baun an

---

89 Report of the Ministers of Immigration to the Council 3 December 1991.
90 Communication on Asylum, COM (91) Final, European Commission, Brussels 1991.
91 Communication on Immigration, COM (91) Final, European Commission, Brussels 1991.
92 F. Laursen & S. Vanhoonacker, *The Intergovernmental Conference on Political Union: Institutional Reforms, New Policies and International Identity of the European Community*, EIPA, Maastricht, 1992; F. Dehousse, *Les résultats de la Conférence intergouvernementale*, CRISP,

analysis of the *travaux* confirms that the most important characteristic of the new Title IV (which became known as the Third Pillar following the analogy of the construction of the Union with a Greek temple) was its intergovernmental system which was kept separate from the Community's processes.[93] As Den Boer has described, although other commentators may disagree on the importance of positions taken by different governments at the intergovernmental conference, there is general accord on the importance of the intergovernmental mode in this field.[94] She usefully picks up one of the more durable descriptions of the meaning of intergovernmentalism for the European Union:

> "Under the intergovernmental mode, national governments have agreed to co-ordinate their policies, but these are implemented by national institutions, under national law, and continue to be determined to a large extent by national policy-makers. The paradigm of decision making in the supranational mode – though not always practised – is decision by (qualified) majority, while the paradigm of intergovernmentalism is unanimity ... the vision behind intergovernmentalism sees integration as a particularly close form of cooperation among nation states. The nation state is still regarded, however, as the highest conceivable forum of democratic political activity. Intergovernmentalism therefore aims to preserve nation states as independent entities as much as possible."[95]

By far the most important aspect of the Maastricht Treaty is the inclusion of a basis and schedule for the achievement of monetary union. However, in its wake a structure was designed for justice and home affairs which comprised the mixture of immigration, asylum, policing and security issues in Title VI Treaty on European Union – Co-operation in the field of justice and home affairs. This structure was in essence intergovernmental. The objective was co-ordination only.[96] The right of initiative on proposals for measures was in theory shared between the Member States and the Commission though in

---

Brussels 1997; M. Baun, *An Imperfect Union: The Maastricht Treaty and the New Politics of European Integration*, Westview Press, Oxford, 1996.

93 M. Baun, *An Imperfect Union. The Maastricht Treaty and the New Politics of European Integration*, Westview Press, Oxford, 1996, p. 58.

94 M. den Boer, *Taming the Third Pillar: Improving the Management of Justice and Home Affairs Co-operation in the EU*, EIPA, Maastricht, 1998, pp. 3-6.

95 Centre for Economic Policy Research, Flexible Integration. Towards a More Effective and Democratic Europe, Series: Monitoring European Integration as quoted in Den Boer, *Taming the Third Pillar: Improving the Management of Justice and Home Affairs Co-operation in the EU*, EIPA, Maastricht, 1998, p. 5.

96 Article K.1 TEU "For the purposes of achieving the objectives of the Union, in particular the free movement of persons, and without prejudice to the powers of the European Community, Member States shall regard the following areas as matters of common interest: (1) asylum policy; ... (3) immigration policy and policy regarding nationals of third countries;"

practice the Member States occupied the field.[97] The European Parliament was entitled to consultation on principal aspects of the co-operation but it would be a matter of dispute over the forthcoming eight years the extent of that consultation right.[98] The Court of Justice was excluded from interpretation of the measures adopted by the Council in the new Title VI.[99] However, the field was placed within a framework which included the Community. Aspects of the field were shared between the new framework and Community competence, most importantly responsibility for visas in Article 100 c EC (now repealed). In this area the tension between the objective sought and the means provided for its attainment became most clearly apparent. It is this aspect which I will focus on in the next chapter to exemplify how the relationship between the individual, a third country national not privileged under Community law, the Member States and the Community began to change.

7.5. CONCLUSIONS

The Single European Act by including Article 14 on abolition of internal borders in the Community sparked off a major revolt by immigration ministries against their perceived loss of control over movement of persons within the Union.[100] The symbol of the border had greater or lesser importance in different Member States, contributing to the positions adopted by different ministries. The tension created by the lack of agreement on the question of borders led to the creation of an alternative structure, fundamentally inter-governmental and outside the structures of the European Community within which to regulate the question of borders and movement of third country nationals in general. As a result of competing interests, difficulty in attaining an acceptable level of achievement and criticisms about the democratic legitimacy of this intergovernmental process, the Member States created a new structure attached to the Community but separate from it institutionally which by virtue of its intergovernmental nature limited the role of the European Parliament

---

97 Article K.4(2) TEU: "The Commission shall be fully associated with the work in the areas referred to in this Title."
98 Article K.6 TEU: "The Presidency shall consult the European Parliament on the principal aspects of activities in the areas referred to in this Title and shall ensure that the views of the European Parliament are duly taken into consideration."
99 Article L TEU and K.9 TEU (before amendment by the Treaty of Amsterdam).
100 "The difficulty as regards competence lies in the reluctance of the Member States to give up their prerogatives in the field of home affairs and internal security. Immigration policy including that relating to visa and asylum is politically sensitive, and is a jealously guarded national competence." D. O'Keeffe, The Free Movement of Persons and the Single Market, European Law Review 17 1992, pp. 3-19.

and excluded the Court. This response was not irrational. If, as the description of intergovernmentalism suggests, the main actor in the field is the nation state then all the emanations of the nation state should have equal importance in the process. The democratic deliberation should take place at national level, judicial control too should apply there. Den Boer analysing the effectiveness of the intergovernmental approach from a point further along in its history in the field of European justice and home affairs, after its institutionalisation in the Maastricht Treaty identifies six main weaknesses:

1. Lack of an institutional driving mechanism;

2. Integration is allowed to progress at multiple speeds;

3. Decision-making is overburdened by bureaucracy and time-consuming briefing and consultation procedures;

4. Decision-making is dominated by the unanimity requirement;

5. The application and implementation of the legal instruments that have been concluded under the Third Pillar are insufficiently evaluated and monitored;

6. Transparency and accountability continue to be minimal as the decision-making process is mainly executive driven and dealt with by relatively closed bodies like the European Council.[101]

The difficulty with all these criticisms is that they are only valid if the objective which is sought is harmonisation. The lack of an institutional driving mechanism is a problem only where there is a schedule and a timetable for action. If instead a group of countries wish only to react to problems which arise and appear to them to have an international character such an institutional driving mechanism may not be needed. Similarly, multiple speeds of application is not necessarily a problem if the agreements reached are designed to be of assistance only to the national policy maker if it wishes to make use of them. If the character of measures is truly intergovernmental, then time-consuming briefing and consultation is normal in democracies. One does not complain of these procedures in the settlement of international treaties, indeed, anything less would be inappropriate. Again in the case of unanimity, this is a prerequisite of an intergovernmental system, anything less would deprive the nation state of its prerogative as "the highest conceivable forum of democratic political activity".[102] Application and implementation are the responsibility of the nation state

---

101 M. den Boer, *Taming the Third Pillar, Improving the Management of Justice and Home Affairs Co-operation in the EU*, EIPA, Maastricht, 1998, p. 43.
102 See *supra*, definition of intergovernmentalism.

in the intergovernmental procedure, usually subject to some overview by a body established by the intergovernmental forum. Transparency and account-ability are the responsibilities of the national parliaments and courts. Whether they fulfil their functions properly or not is a matter of the national polity.

My criticisms of the intergovernmental approach in the field of immigra-tion and asylum in particular come from a different source. I do not think that it is sustainable to criticise the process on the basis of the classic grounds of intergovernmentalism. This is in effect an attack on the concept of inter-governmentalism which finds many legitimate uses, not least for example in regulating international trade.[103] The problem which I see with the intergovern-mental approach here is the mismatch of the field of activity and the method of its regulation. Immigration and asylum laws and policy in the Member States are highly sensitive and contested ground. In many Member States there are extremely vocal non-governmental organisations which enjoy a not insignificant degree of support in their communities and are highly critical of national government policy. Both issues arise frequently on the political agendas and political platforms of the larger Member States. Further, as a result of the conflict which exists at national level, increasing emphasis has been placed on international human rights instruments which regulate[104] or touch upon[105] the field, and pressure on their regulatory bodies to provide remedies for indi-viduals who are aggrieved by the application of national law.

Therefore in this field one is already in a legal and political space where a substantial struggle is taking place between the state and some people who are claiming a legitimacy which is contested. In the terms of my triangle analogy, in immigration and asylum third country nationals and their family members, who may be nationals of the nation state, are seeking to establish rights vis-à-vis the state which are not fully or indeed at all accepted. They are demanding a linear relationship of rights with the state. In this struggle not only is national law being used on both sides: by the individual through legal challenges and political action, by the state in changing it: making more tenuous or strengthening the position of third country nationals[106] but international law is

---

103 Though the popular protest at the opening of the new negotiating round of the World Trade Organisation in November 1999 in Seattle raises doubts even about this.
104 As in the case of refugees, the Geneva Convention.
105 As in the case of long-resident aliens, Article 8 EHCR.
106 In the Member States through the 1970s and 1980s both trends are apparent in Europe: on the one hand a codification of the right of asylum in some states, e.g. the UK, on the other the abolition of a right of asylum in others, e.g. Germany; at the same time in some Member States there was a strengthening of the right of the position of long-resident third country nationals. See J. van Selm-Thorburn, *Refugee Protection in Europe – Lessons from the Yugoslav Crisis*, Kluwer Academic Publishing, The Hague, 1997; and H. Lambert, *Seeking Asylum: Comparative law and practice in selected European countries*, Nijhoff,

also being called upon. The individual is seeking to establish a direct relationship of rights in respect of residence and economic activity with the nation state which the nation state is reluctant or unwilling or slowly coming to accept. Such a disputed territory is not *prima facie* an appropriate one for intergovernmental activity. The position of the nation is too fluid for intergovernmental activity, the establishment of international agreement on policy, to be helpful. The lack of a durable settlement at the national level[107] leaves too little space for genuine intergovernmental activity. The powers of the Community in the field will have to be exercised either by enforcing harmonisation or by withdrawing from the field and legitimating national practice.

For example, in 1993 the UK's immigration laws included a provision relating to the admission of foreign spouses which required the parties to a marriage to prove to the satisfaction of the authorities that the primary purpose of the marriage was not to obtain settlement in the UK.[108] This rule, commonly called the primary purpose rule, was unrelated to any question of the genuineness of a marriage which requirement was covered by another provision of the national rules. A provision reminiscent of the UK's primary purpose provision was inserted into the Member States' intergovernmental resolution in 1993 on the admission of family reunion policy. Its provenance while uncertain on account of a restriction on access to the *travaux préparatoires*,[109] is likely to be the UK as the only State at the time with such a national provision. On the basis of substantial social pressure in the UK the national rule was administered more and more generously towards family members and then abolished in June 1997. However, it has a shadow life which continues in the 1993 intergovernmental resolution. In the example then, no one, neither the individuals who are seeking to establish a right in respect of the nation nor indeed the nation itself ultimately would have wanted the intergovernmental agreement to have been binding or to have fulfilled any of the criteria which den Boer sets out as the subject of her criticism.

The mismatch of the mode of operation with the subject matter resulted, as such mismatches usually do, in a misuse of the mode. As in the example above, because of the fluidity at national level, the tendency was for the intergovern-

---

Dordrecht, 1995; and K. Groenendijk, E. Guild and H. Dogan, *Security of residence of long-term migrants: a comparative study of law and practice in European countries*, Council of Europe, Strasbourg, 1998.

107 The lack of durability is in particular evidenced by the number of immigration, asylum and indeed nationality laws which have been introduced by the larger Member States over the period under consideration.

108 The provision was introduced into UK domestic law in 1985.

109 S. Peers, Building Fortress Europe: The Development of EU Migration Law, 1999 CMLRev 35:1235-1272 (1999).

mental forum to be used to provide a political legitimacy for what might well be a transient position of a Member State.[110] In other words, the intergovernmental process was used by the Member State governments as a tool in their national debates on the rights of third country nationals, to legitimate the refusal to extend rights to third country nationals and thereby create a direct relationship with them. Therefore, it is not surprising that the creation of a direct right relationship between third country nationals and the Community through the intergovernmental process was not a priority and indeed was something which those Member States where these discussions were particularly vivid wished to avoid. On the other side, some non-governmental organisations were in favour of strengthen the Community component in immigration law exactly in order to achieve this result.

Therefore, there is a process: a conundrum is created in the Single European Act: the desire for economic reasons to abolish intra-Member State border controls notwithstanding the lack of consensus on the treatment of third country nationals. The Member States challenge the Commission's attempt to enter the field by way of providing direction, which could ultimately result in the creation of rights not only with the Community but via the Community with the Member States for third country nationals. A flurry of the intergovernmental agreements results, which attracts criticism as being inadequate for the purpose to be achieved: abolition of border controls between the Member States. However, in the light of the developments at national level, the Member States were not yet in a position to contemplate the introduction of yet another actor and level of governance into what was already a highly disputed territory of rights and discretion at the national level. The mixture of fields of responsibility; Community objectives and Member State concerns, the contested nature of the field at national level; the demand for the creation of rights which are disputed, and the attempt by different participants in the field to use the question of Community competence to achieve different aims all lead to the rejection of the possibility of the creation of a legal relationship between third country nationals and the Community. This was particularly so as the relationship proposed for the Community with the individual in the case of some Member States would exceed the relationship of rights which existed at national level. Although exactly this had occurred in respect of the development of free movement rights for Community nationals, the position of third country nationals was increasingly differentiated from that of Community migrants. The immigration ministries, at least, were reluctant to accept a parallelism which would diminish their control over third country nationals.

---

110 E. Guild, The Constitutional Consequences of Lawmaking in the Third Pillar of the European Union in P. Craig & C. Harlow, *Lawmaking in the European Union*, Kluwer Law International, London, 1998, pp. 65-88.

CHAPTER 8

PILLAR TALK: THE MAASTRICHT TREATY COMPROMISE

8.1. INTRODUCTION

After the entry into force of the Maastricht Treaty, the law and policy on third country nationals in general was divided between the First Pillar and the Third Pillar. The difficulties of the division between the two Pillars of an area as sensitive as immigration and asylum created new challenges for the Community and for the Member States. In this chapter I will look at Article 100c EC inserted into the EC Treaty by the Maastricht Treaty (and now repealed by the Amsterdam Treaty) creating a responsibility for visas in the First Pillar and the responsibility in the Third Pillar for "rules governing the crossing by persons of the external borders of the Member States and the exercise of controls thereon". The consequences of dividing responsibilities on this rather basic aspect of immigration illuminates the issues at stake in the treatment at Community level of the whole area.

The question I will look at is the effect of the Maastricht Settlement on the relationships between:

1. The Community and the Member States;

2. The Member State and third country nationals;

3. The Community and third country nationals.

I will start with an outline of the changes which came about on where the responsibility for law and policy on immigration and asylum lay, provide a short outline of the issues which visas entail and then look more closely at how the Community's new competence was exercised. I will then analyse what those changes meant as regards the relationship of the Community and Member States to individuals through two decisions of the Court of Justice which interpreted the scope of the new Community power and the relationship between the Community power and the new framework of the intergovernmental power.

In the preceding chapter I looked at the development of the field of immigration and asylum from undifferentiated third countries at the Union level. That development is characterised by very substantial differences of opinion among the Member States and the Community institutions on whether, how and to what extent the Community should have responsibility for law making in the field. The difference on substance between the Commission and the Member

States as represented by the immigration ministries was not so great, both categorised immigration and asylum in similar ways and perceived the control of immigration as of paramount importance. The structural position however, was different. Some of the Member States, or at least some of their ministries through the intergovernmental process, wished to retain discretionary control over as much of the field of immigration and asylum as was still within their power. This would mean that the relationship between the Community and the individual third country national would remain fundamentally unchanged: the Community had no direct relationship as regards entry, residence and economic activities with third country nationals and in the intergovernmental logic should not acquire such a relationship. The relationship between the Community and the Member States would change only in so far as the Community would be entitled to adopt measures in a limited field: visas. But the competence here should not be exclusive. The relationship between the individual third country national and the Member State would remain the territory of the struggle.

The Commission, as the guardian of the Treaties, took a different view. It would seek to establish a direct relationship with the individual third country national through the exercise of its competence under Article 100c EC (now repealed). In this effort it would find an ally in the European Parliament. The venue within which this interaction would take place was visa law and policy. All the main institutional participants of the Union would take part – the Member States, the Council, the Commission, the Parliament and the Court.

The history of the negotiations and descriptions of the Maastricht Treaty compromise have been well documented.[1] The result of the Maastricht Treaty in this field for the EC Treaty was to insert into the later competence for visas, limited to format and countries whose nationals must have them. It created a new forum in the Treaty on European Union Title VI, Co-operation in the fields of Justice and Home Affairs which gave an institutional framework to the intergovernmental work which was being carried out by the Member States in the field of immigration and asylum and which was the subject matter of the preceding chapter.

---

1   Amongst others see J-P. Jacque and J. Weiler, On the Road to European Union – A New Judicial Architecture: An Agenda for the Intergovernmental Conference, CML Rev 27:185-207 1990; H. Labayle, Coopération dans les domaines de la justice et des affaires intérieures, Rép communautaire Dalloz, Mai 1998, p. 1; K. Hailbronner, Die europäische Asylrechtsharmonisierung nach dem Vertrag von Maastricht, ZAR 1/1995, p. 3; A. Weber, Einwanderungs- und Asylpolitik nach Maastricht, ZAR 1/1993, p. 11; J. Haberland, Die Entschliessungen der Justiz- und Innenminister der Europäischen Union im Bericht der Aufname, ZAR 1/1996, p. 3; S. Peers, Building Fortress Europe: The Development of EU Migration Law, CMLRev 35:1235-1272, 1999.

O'Keeffe stresses that a differentiation needs to be made between a purely intergovernmental procedure and that under the Third Pillar. He takes the position that "although competence is not transferred to the Community, and although the Community *process* as such is generally excluded, nevertheless there are a number of connecting points to the Community."[2] For this purpose he points to the fact that the Commission was fully associated;[3] the European Parliament was entitled to be informed and consulted on principal aspects of the activities;[4] conventions adopted under it could be specified to be within the jurisdiction of the Court of Justice;[5] Article K.9 TEU (before amendment by the Amsterdam Treaty) permitted the communitarisation of Third Pillar competences (a matter to which I will return shortly below) and that the European Council was also the Council for the purposes of the Third Pillar. Weiler similarly questions whether the dividing line between the Community Pillar and the Third Pillar was in fact a "bright" one.[6] While he accepts that decisional procedures were different, the Commission's role was different (indeed excluded from some fields outside the scope of this study) and the forms of action were weaker, he contends that "the possibility of implementation by qualified majority (Article K.3(2)(b)[7])" in fact makes this open ended.[8] I find this somewhat Delphic. Yes, Article K.3(2)(b) does permit the Council to decide whether it wishes to decide measures implementing a joint action by qualified majority voting. But the initial decision on the joint action must be by unanimity, and the decision to apply qualified majority voting to any implementing measures must be by unanimity. For this reason it appears to me that

---

2   D. O'Keeffe, A Critical View of the Third Pillar, in A. Pauly, *De Schengen à Maastricht, voie royale et course d'obstacles*, EIPA, 1996, pp. 1-16.
3   Article K.4(2) TEU, before amendment by the Amsterdam Treaty.
4   Article K.6 TEU (before amendment by the Amsterdam Treaty). The Parliament consistently expressed its dissatisfaction with the information and consultation on the Third Pillar which it received from the Council and Commission. From the ratification of the Treaty to the entry into force of the Amsterdam Treaty it constituted a substantial source of friction between the Parliament and Council in particular.
5   Article L TEU, before amendment by the Amsterdam Treaty.
6   J. H. H. Weiler, Neither Unity nor Three Pillars – The Trinity Structure of the Treaty on European Union in J. Monar *et al.*, *The Maastricht Treaty on European Union: Legal Complexity and Political Dynamic*, European Interuniversity Press, Brussels, 1993.
7   "Adopt joint action in so far as the objectives of the Union can be attained better by joint action than by the Member States acting individually on account of the scale or effects of the action envisaged; [the Council] may decide that measures implementing joint action are to be adopted by a qualified majority."
8   J. H. H. Weiler, Neither Unity nor Three Pillars – The Trinity Structure of the Treaty on European Union in J. Monar *et al.*, *The Maastricht Treaty on European Union: Legal Complexity and Political Dynamic*, European Interuniversity Press, Brussels, 1993, pp. 49-65.

the reference to qualified majority voting is more along the lines of window dressing: an indication of the good faith of the Community towards achieving more flexible decision making which was a major issue at the intergovernmental conference. It seems to me that Weiler is too eager to find coherence in the face of too little evidence in support of it. If the proof of the pudding is in the eating, one must remember that the power was never used and has now been abolished.

Equally, as regards O'Keeffe's arguments, I am not so convinced that the First Pillar links are so fundamental as to change the nature of the Third Pillar. In my view he does not give enough weight to the intention of the Member States in creating the Third Pillar: to avoid in this field the consequences of communitarisation. The Third Pillar links with the Community were designed to provide some legitimacy to the Third Pillar and most importantly to justify financing. Article K.8(2) TEU (before amendment by the Amsterdam Treaty) states: "Administrative expenditure which the provisions relating to the areas referred to in this Title entail for the institutions shall be charged to the budget of the European Communities".

The Third Pillar had as its stated purpose achieving the objectives of the Union "in particular the free movement of persons". Therefore, in this sense, at least I agree with O'Keeffe, that it is intrinsically tied to Articles 3 and 14 EC. However, beyond this general purpose it had no objective to be achieved in the area of immigration and asylum, such as that of Article 39 EC: achieving free movement of workers. Its purpose was limited to "Member States shall regard the following areas as matters of common interest".[9] Thus I am not convinced that the wording of the first sentence is as meaningful as O'Keeffe suggests. Institutionally, it was to be driven by the Member States' administrations though it was serviced by the Council and co-ordinated by a new group of officials, the K4 Committee, named after the provision of the TEU which provided for its existence. The fact that the Commission was, in principle, fully associated did not in fact change the inter-governmental functioning.[10] As Den Boer points out, Dinan suggests that this was the result of the attitude of the Justice Ministers to the Commission.[11] Again, this indicates that the inclusion of a reference to the full association of the Commission was not as genuine an invitation to the Commission to participate as O'Keeffe suggests. Finally, the Court of Justice was in principle excluded from interpreting any matter relating

---

9   Article K.1 TEU, before amendment by the Amsterdam Treaty.
10 M. den Boer, *Taming the Third Pillar: Improving the Management of Justice and Home Affairs Co-operation in the EU*, EIPA, Maastricht, 1998, p. 18.
11 As quoted in Den Boer, *supra*, D. Dinan, The Commission and the Reform Process in G. Edwards & A. Pijpers (eds.), *The Politics of European Treaty Reform: the 1996 Inter-governmental Conference and Beyond*, London, 1998, pp. 326-339.

to the Third Pillar.[12] At the time of the signature of the Maastricht Treaty it was already clear that the Member States were looking for different forms of acts other than conventions within which to agree policy in the field of immigration and asylum. The Dublin Convention had been signed but it would be many years before it would be ratified. The external frontiers convention was under discussion but blocked on a political technicality which no Presidency would ever be able to budge.[13] Two alternative forms of acts had already been used in December 1992: under the UK Presidency two Resolutions and a Recommendation had been adopted on asylum intergovernmentally. The Member States would use the convention form again within the Third Pillar but not in the field of immigration and asylum.[14]

The Maastricht Treaty also attached to the EC Treaty the Social Protocol to which all Member States except the UK signed up which also gave a competence to the Community, as constructed for the purposes of that Protocol (11 out of the 12), with regard to third country nationals: "conditions of employment for third country nationals legally residing in Community territory".[15] This competence, which has not been exercised, at least in theory overlapped with the Third Pillar competence on access to employment and conditions of residence for third country nationals.[16]

The Maastricht compromise was less than satisfactory for many Member States, some of whom wished for greater integration, others less. This unease is reflected not least in Article K.9 TEU (before amendment by the Amsterdam Treaty), the so-called *passarelle*, which provided that by decision of the Council, Article 100c could be applied to action in areas encompassed by the Third Pillar. In other words, the Council could decide to move any subject matter out of the intergovernmental Pillar into the Community Pillar by unanimous

---

12 The permissive nature of the provision permitting its jurisdiction to be extended to conventions under the Third Pillar turned into a field of struggle. Some Member States were in principle in favour of a general extension of this competence to all conventions, for instance the Netherlands while others, such as the UK were adamantly opposed to its extension to almost all Third Pillar conventions.

13 A dispute between the UK and Spain about the status of Gibraltar.

14 The only quasi exception is the Eurodac Convention on the fingerprinting of asylum seekers and illegal immigrants which is in fact a flanking measure of the Dublin Convention and was agreed only under the German Presidency in 1999. It was destined never to be signed but will reappear in a Community form under Title IV EC.

15 Now Article 137(3) indent 4 EC.

16 The Court of Justice held that a provision prohibiting discrimination in working conditions could have consequences for continued residence "... if the national court were to find that the host Member State had granted the Moroccan migrant worker specific rights in relation to employment which were more extensive than the rights of residence conferred on him by that State" C-416/96 *El-Yassini* [1999] ECR I-1209, para 64.

decision. Declaration 31 to the Treaty provided that as a matter of priority the Council would consider applying Article K.9 to the field of asylum. At the time, 1991, Germany, was coming to terms with a substantial increase in the numbers of persons seeking asylum and to a certain degree, suffering from shock at those numbers when added to the numbers of *Aussiedler* (ethnic Germans from other countries mainly in Central and Eastern Europe) seeking to settle there. Solidarity from other Member States in the form of a strict European asylum policy was a priority for the German government. In the event, this was not forthcoming[17] and the German government took on the national debate on asylum with only the intergovernmental support of the 11 other Member States in 1992/3.[18] It won an amendment to the constitution which restricted the right of asylum, though at what political cost still remains uncertain.[19]

Noll has looked again at the subsequent developments in Germany after the completion of the German reform of asylum law in 1993. In a detailed analysis of the German legislation and court decisions on non-admission and return of protection seekers from Germany he concludes that the model adopted cannot work on a European level. Focussing on the concept of return of asylum seekers to safe third countries, i.e. countries through which they passed on route to Germany, he concludes "pre-procedure return to Safe Third Countries emerges as the most problematic feature. It is in some regards discriminatory, it impedes equitable burden sharing and it promotes fragmentation of European refugee law."[20]

The *passarelle* provision was in fact never used. Following a report by the Commission, the Council concluded in 1994 that it was too soon to consider the application of Article K.9 pointing to the delay in ratifying the Maastricht Treaty. [21] It suggested the matter be revisited in 1995, by which time prepara-

---

17 Even though the amendment to the German Constitution was required not least by the Schengen Implementing Convention which Germany could not ratify without removing the right of asylum contained in Article 16A.

18 I have elsewhere argued, on the basis of the use by one Member State's government of the intergovernmental asylum measures in Parliamentary debates, that this support can be significant for various reasons. See E. Guild, The Constitutional Consequences of Lawmaking in the Third Pillar of the European Union, in P. Craig & C. Harlow, *Lawmaking in the European Union*, Kluwer Law International, London 1998, pp. 65-88.

19 K. Groenendijk, Regulating ethnic immigration: the case of the *Aussiedler*, New Community, 23(4) 461-482.

20 G. Noll, The Non-Admission and Return of Protection Seekers in Germany, International Journal of Refugee Law, Vol. 9, 1997, pp. 415-452.

21 "[The Council] considers however, like the Commission, that the time is not yet right to propose such application so soon after the entry into force of the Treaty on European Union. Nevertheless, it believes that it might be advisable to reconsider this matter at a

tions were under way for a new intergovernmental conference. In considering Article K.9 TEU (before amendment by the Amsterdam Treaty) Lepoivre interestingly does not refer at all to the Declaration but speculates about the use of the *passarelle* to the consolidation of the Union's visa regime, the issue to which I shall return shortly.[22] Fernhout, writing in 1995, agrees with the Commission that as a result of the delay in entry into force of the Maastricht Treaty which resulted from the Danish rejection of it in its first referendum the application was not deemed expedient.[23]

Visas

The field where the division of responsibility for the treatment of third country nationals between the First and Third Pillars was to create the most substantial uncertainty between the institutions (the Commission and the Parliament were generally on one side and the Council and the Member States on the other) was visas. This is because from the beginning, the division of responsibility for countries whose nationals require visas, and the format of a visa on the one hand (Article 100c EC now repealed) to the Community and Article K.1(2) on the rules governing entry and movement of nationals of third countries to the Third Pillar, was less than logical. As Dollat notes, the Treaty denied to the Community a genuine legal basis for a common visa policy by limiting its role to formal issues. However, he does see the basis of a common visa policy here in so far as this cannot be detached from free movement of persons.[24] For the reasons which emerge from the judgments of the Court of Justice in this contested field I do not agree with him. As I will discuss later, the Court limited the field as regards action by the Community to such a degree as to allow visa policy and free movement of persons to remain separate. An analysis of this challenge is the foundation of this chapter.

A fundamental factor in the Union's engagement with visas was the creation of the Schengen system. In the preceding chapter I have given some back-

---

later date in the light of experience and by the end of 1995 at the latest." Council Conclusions of 20 June 1994 concerning the possible application of Article K.9 of the Treaty on European Union to asylum policy, OJ 1996 C 274 34.

22 M. Lepoivre, Le domaine de la justice et des affaires intérieures dans le perspective de la conférences intergouvernementale de 1996, Cahiers de droit européen, 1995, No. 1-2, pp. 323-349.

23 R. Fernhout, Justice and Home Affairs: Immigration and Asylum Policy From JHA cooperation to communitarisation in J. de Winter *et al.*, (eds.), Reforming the Treaty on European Union, *The Legal Debate*, Kluwer Law International, The Hague, 1995, pp. 377-398.

24 P. Dollat, *Libre Circulation des personnes et citoyenneté européenne: enjeux et perspectives*, Bruylant, Brussels, 1998, p. 352.

ground to this development whereby five of the original six Member States decided to move more quickly to abolition of intra-State border controls on goods and persons. By 1 May 1999, the date of entry into force of the Amsterdam Treaty which incorporated the Schengen acquis into the EC Treaty, 13 of the 15 Member States had signed up to the system (Ireland and the UK remaining outside) and the abolition of intra-State border controls had been abolished at least formally, in nine.[25] Three key elements of the Schengen system are: the common short stay visa; the common rules on the crossing of the external border and a common list of inadmissible persons (the Schengen Information System). The Schengen visa system, as applicable among an increasing number of Member States became, with each enlargement of that system, the definitive European norm.

What are Visas?

Before commencing a consideration of visa law and policy at the European Union level after the entry into force of the Maastricht Treaty, it may be useful briefly to look at some aspects of visas which will arise in this chapter.

The first question is *what is a visa?* In Community law this is by no means straightforward. For the purposes of Article 39 EC as interpreted by the Court of Justice it means: any formality for the purpose of granting leave to enter the territory of a Member State which is coupled with a passport or identity card check at the frontier, whatever may be the place or time at which that leave is granted and in whatever form it may be granted.[26] However, Article 100c EC which was repealed by the Amsterdam Treaty was the legal basis for the Visa Regulation which defined it in the following terms: For the purposes of this Regulation 'visa' shall mean an authorisation given or a decision taken by a Member State which is required for entry into its territory with a view to: an intended stay in that Member State of no more than three months in all; or transit through the territory of that Member State or several Member States, except for transit through international zones of airports and transfers between airports in a Member State.[27] *Transit visas* were defined differently and in a Justice and Home Affairs measure in the Third Pillar (more about which will follow shortly): documents affixed to passports or travel documents which permit a third country national to pass through an airport but not to enter a state.[28]

---

25 In many cases though, the border controls have been replaced by controls just inside the border. D. Bigo, *Polices en Reseaux*, Presses de Sciences – Po, Paris, 1996.

26 157/79 *Pieck* [1980] ECR 2171.

27 Article 5 Regulation 2317/95.

28 OJ 1996 L 63/11.

Next there is the problem of the purpose of the visa. This manifests in a number of ways, first *short stay visas* have been defined as: documents affixed to passports or travel documents which *prima facie* permit the holder to arrive at the border of the issuing state and subject to further checks to pass that border limited for a period of time, normally between three months (as provided for in the Schengen acquis) or six months (provided for in UK law); these visas usually prohibit employment but permit economic activities such as attending meetings with clients or customers and settling contracts;[29] Schengen visas are a form of short stay visa regulated, however, by the Schengen acquis which was incorporated into Community law by the Amsterdam Treaty. The Schengen visa does not require the issue of a visa to any person but obliged the refusal of a visa to persons with various characteristics – such as those whose details appears on the 'unwanted persons' list of the Schengen Information System. On the other hand, *long stay visas* are: documents affixed to passports or other travel documents which permit the holder to travel to a country with the intention of staying for a period in excess of that permitted by a short stay visa, or to engage in activities not permitted by short stay visas such as employment; these may or may not also constitute work permits depending on the national system of regulation.

One must then consider the rules applicable to visas: for instance, *place of issue of visas:* visas can be issued at consular posts abroad or at the border;[30] visas or their equivalent can be issued in the country after admission if the national system is so designed or waived if the national system provides for this. Similarly, the *format of visas* is a Community definition: normally a document affixed to a passport or other travel document. It was defined for some purposes by a Community Regulation;[31] but depending on national law it can take other forms or indeed be deemed where it is not physically present. *Who issues a visa*: normally it is issued by an official at a consular post abroad;

---

29 OJ 1999 L 72/2.
30 The Council's Recommendation made in the Third Pillar on local consular co-operation regarding visas promotes "local co-operation on visas, involving an exchange of information on the criteria for issuing visas and an exchange of information on risks to national security and public order or the risk of clandestine immigration" (Article 1 OJ 1996 C 80/1). Controls on the propriety of information exchange are not included even though the Recommendation continues "their consular services should exchange information to help determine the good faith of visa applicants and their reputation, it being understood that the fact that the applicant has obtained a visa for another Member State does not exempt the authorities from examining individually the visa application and performing the verification required for the purposes of security, public order and clandestine immigration control" (Article 6). The concepts of public order and clandestine immigration control are not defined.
31 OJ 1995 L 164/2.

however, it can be issued by a border guard or official or after entry into the state by an official in the state's administration. Most importantly in this discussion is the question *what are the criteria for the issue of a visa*: these depend on the type of visa requested and the legal regime applicable to the visa; for instance third country national family members of migrant citizens of the Union may be required to obtain a visa. A purposive reading of the Community Directive usually leads to the conclusion that the documents which an official may request before issuing a visa are limited (Directive 68/360). The criteria for the issue of other visas, for instance the commonly recognised Schengen visa are different, most importantly that the person seeking the visa has not been registered on the Schengen Information System, a computerised data base of information about people and objects which are not to be permitted to enter the Schengen territory.[32]

Finally, there is the fundamental question, what is *the purpose of visas*: according to a member of the European Parliament it is "traditionally ... an instrument of the foreign policy of States and has been used in certain circumstances as a protective measure or even as an unfriendly act".[33] However, increasingly in the European context it is the mechanism for deterring visitors from countries which the Member States consider to be sources of illegal immigration; a way of preventing access to the territory of unwanted asylum seekers and in general a way of controlling the movement of persons before they have moved. It is also used increasingly as a tool of prior certification as regards categories of entry for third country nationals: for instance the move towards mandatory

---

32   A very important difference of approach may be discerned here. In "classic" Community law, the issue of visas is subject to an investigation limited by a Directive setting out the documents which may be requested by a Member State official. The individual's right arises from Community law and must be applied by the Member State's employee. The Schengen intergovernmental approach is characterised by the opposite starting point. National discretion on the question of to whom to issue a visa is paramount. It is limited only by excluding factors relating to concerns of other Schengen States. In terms of the design I am looking at, in the Community law framework, the individual has a right guaranteed by Community law to a visa from national authorities on production of the specified documents; in the intergovernmental system, a participating State has the right to require refusal of a visa by another participating State; the individual's right to a visa, if such exists at all, applies only in respect of the State to which the application is made and is subordinate to the demand of the other participating States for exclusion.

33   C. Beazley, Report on the Communication of the Commission Containing a Proposal for a Decision based on Article K.3 of the Treaty on European Union establishing the Convention on the crossing of the external frontiers of the Member States (COM(93) 0684-C3-0011/94), Committee on Civil Liberties and Internal Affairs of the European Parliament, Doc A3-0190/94, 1994 as quoted in A. Cruz, Visa Policy under the First Pillar: A Meaningless Compromise in M. den Boer, *Schengen, Judicial Co-operation and Policy Co-ordination*, EIPA, 1997, pp. 213 – 239.

entry visas for long stay purposes such as family reunion irrespective of the individual's nationality. At the level of the Community, it was traditionally used as a means of verifying a claim to admission – as such it created a presumption of rights, though this aspect was about to change as a result of the Maastricht Treaty which I will discuss shortly.

Competence for visas: 1993 – 1999

QUESTIONS	TRANSIT VISAS	SHORT STAY VISAS	LONG STAY VISAS	SCHENGEN VISAS
Issue	abroad/border	abroad/border	abroad/border	abroad/border
Nationals of which countries?	Member States decide – to be harmonised in the Third Pillar (or possibly the Second Pillar).	Community decides – to be regulated by a Regulation, but is the list conclusive: this will be the subject of a Court case.	Member States decide – regulated loosely on the basis of Third Pillar resolutions on long stays.	The Schengen list of visa countries was the basis for the Community list but became conclusive in December 1998.
Validity	Member States decide on basis of Third Pillar measure.	Community regulates through Regulation which is defined in terms of three month stays.	Member States decide except in respect of third country national family members of migrant Community nationals and CEEC nationals seeking to exercise the right of establishment.	The Participating States issue a common visa valid for a stay of three months or less in the combined territory.

QUESTIONS	TRANSIT VISAS	SHORT STAY VISAS	LONG STAY VISAS	SCHENGEN VISAS
Discretion	Member States must refuse anyone likely to be a threat to the public order of any Member State.	Member States retain under the Regulation the right to refuse admission to visa holders.	Member States decide according to national law. The limitation is as regards persons entered on the SIS. Exception: third country national family member of migrant Community nationals and CEEC nationals seeking to exercise establishment rights.	The issue of the visa is always discretionary; its refusal however, is mandatory if the person's details are entered on the SIS. In law at least in such cases national visas may be issued.

The concept of a visa, then is clearly high flexible. At Community level mandatory visas were also being used as a foreign policy tool, most clearly in the context of the discussions with the CEECs regarding their relationship with the Union. As I have discussed in chapter 6, the inclusion of provisions on visas in the Europe Agreements has helped to create uncertainty about the position of those nationals in law. Nonetheless, the abolition of mandatory visas for CEEC nationals has been a high priority for their governments in discussions with the Community. The fairly rapid abolition of mandatory visa requirements for Poles by the Member States and the continuing application of visa requirements to Bulgarians corresponding to the approach taken by the Community to their respect applications for accession indicates the use by the Community of visas as a foreign policy tool. The proposal of one Member State that before Schengen mandatory visa requirements be lifted in respect of Estonia and the other Baltic states (ExCom (98) rev 9.12.98), that country be requested to sign the UN Convention on Statelessness as a way of seeking to resolve the problem of the Russian ethnic minority in that country indicates the foreign policy dimension of the mandatory visa question. Another example of such a political use of visas comes from the decision in the Second Pillar to exclude named persons from Serbia, starting with Mr Milošević, which Decision includes a prohibition on the issue of visas to the named persons.[34]

---

34 Common Position concerning additional restrictive measures against the Federal Republic of Yugoslavia: 07879/99 of 6.5.1999. Article 1:1. No visas shall be issued for President Milošević, his family, all Ministers and senior officials of the FRY and Serbian Governments, and for persons close to the regime whose activities support President Milošević.

The Schengen acquis regulates directly short stay visas, though there are consequences for long stay visas. The rules were designed around the grounds of mandatory refusal, their issue was left discretionary to the state concerned. By a requirement to aggregate all the grounds of refusal for all the participating Schengen states[35] before any one of them issued a visa, an immediate hardening of visa rules for all participants was one result of signing up to Schengen. The common blacklist of persons to be refused visas and admission, as contained in the Schengen Information System is the clearest manifestation of this exclusionary principle.

Further, the Schengen list of countries whose nationals require a visa consisted of three parts: a black list of countries whose national must obtain a Schengen visa (or a national visa in lieu); an implied white list of countries none of which appear on either the Schengen or national lists of mandatory visas, and thirdly a grey list: countries which do not appear on the black list but neither are they on the implied white list as some participating states require visas of their nationals. This grey list would prove to be a source of contention when it appeared in Community law. Even in the intergovernmental framework of Schengen it was a source of irritation and was finally abolished on 16 December 1998 by a Schengen Executive Committee Decision.[36] This decision would have unexpected consequences for the European Community with the incorporation of the Schengen acquis by virtue of the Amsterdam Treaty into the EC Treaty. Because the Schengen states decided to put their house in order before the incorporation, the result appears to be the abolition of the grey list for 12 of the 15, because the Schengen intergovernmental law has been transformed into Community law.[37] I will develop a little later the argument about the importance of the visa grey list in depriving the Community of a direct relationship with the individual. At that point it will be useful to remember the possibly unintended consequences of the Schengen incorporation.

At the international level European visa policy was beginning to spark questions about its compatibility with international human rights law. The increasingly exclusionary result of the mandatory visa lists coupled with the imposition of carrier sanctions on transporters which bring to the Member States persons not in possession of the required documents,[38] including visas,

---

35 T. Hoogeboom, Free Movement of non-EC Nationals; Schengen and Beyond, in H. Meijers, (ed.), *Schengen; Internationalism of Central Chapters of the Law on Aliens, Refugees, Privacy, Security and the Police*, Stichting NJCM, Leiden, 1992.

36 (98) 53 rev. Only Colombia continued to be treated inconsistently.

37 See K. Groenendijk, The Incorporation of Schengen: continuation of the democratic deficit or a fresh start? in A. Gormley, forthcoming.

38 Such sanctions were included as a requirement in the Schengen Implementing Convention 1990.

was subject to criticism.[39] By 1999, members of two international human rights committees were beginning to query the European mandatory visa system.[40]

8.2.   THE NEW IMMIGRATION REGIME IN THE EC TREATY

The Maastricht Treaty introduced into the EC Treaty two new and incongruous provisions in Article 100:[41] sub paragraphs (c) and (d). Article 100 had already evolved as a result of the Single European Act from its original form providing the constitutional mechanism whereby the Community could adopt legislation to give effect to the functioning of the Common Market[42] to something more detailed providing a number of sub-paragraphs to give a more specific legislative base to Article 14 EC. The Maastricht Treaty extended Article 100 further as regards migration related matters as follows:

Article 100c

"The Council, acting unanimously on a proposal from the Commission and after consulting the European Parliament, shall determine the third countries whose nationals must be in possession of a visa when crossing the external borders of the Member States.

However, in the event of an emergency situation in a third country posing a threat of sudden inflow of nationals from that country into the Community, the Council, acting by a qualified majority on a recommendation from the Commission, may introduce, for a period not exceeding six months, a visa requirement

---

39   F. Nicholson, Implementation of the Immigration (Carriers' Liability) Act 1987: privatizing immigration functions at the expense of international obligations? ICLQ 46:586, 1997; Danish Refugee Council, The Effects of Carrier Sanctions on the Asylum System, Copenhagen, 1991.

40   See M. Scheinen, member of the UN Human Rights Committee on the compatibility of carrier sanctions with Article 12 ICCPR; address given at the Åbo Academy, Turku Finland, 15 September 1999; also questions to the Austrian government on examination of the 1998 report on compliance with the UN Convention on the Elimination of All Forms of Racial Discrimination and the examination of the French government 2000.

41   Articles 100 (c) & (d) have been repealed by the Amsterdam Treaty. I will continue to refer to them by their numbers but these no longer correspond to the numbering of the EC Treaty.

42   "The Council, acting by means of a unanimous vote on a proposal of the Commission, shall issue directives for the approximation of such legislative and administrative provisions of the Member States as have a direct incidence on the establishment or functioning of the Common Market."
      "The Assembly and the Economic and Social Committee shall be consulted concerning any directives whose implementation in one or more of the Member States would involve amendment of legislative provision."

for nationals from the country in question. The visa requirement established under this paragraph may be extended in accordance with the procedure referred to in paragraph 1.

From 1 January 1996, the Council shall act by a qualified majority on the decisions referred to in paragraph 1. The Council shall, before that date, acting by a qualified majority on a proposal from the Commission and after consulting the European Parliament, adopt measures relating to a uniform format for visas.

In the matters referred to in this Article, the Commission shall examine any request made by a Member State that it submit a proposal to the Council.

This Article shall be without prejudice to the exercise of responsibilities incumbent upon the Member States with regard to the maintenance of law and order and the safeguarding of internal security.

This Article shall apply to other matters if so decided pursuant to Article K.9 of the provisions of the Treaty on European Union which relate to co-operation in the fields of justice and home affairs, subject to the voting conditions determined at the same time.

The provisions of the conventions in force between the Member States governing matters covered by this Article shall remain in force until their content has been replaced by directives or measures adopted pursuant to this Article."

Article 100d

"The Co-ordinating Committee consisting of senior officials set up by Article K.4 of the Treaty on European Union shall contribute, without prejudice to the provisions of Article 151, to the preparation of the proceedings of the Council in the fields referred to in Article 100c."

By Article 100c two legislative duties are placed on the Commission: to make a proposal for a uniform format for visas and to put forward a measure setting out a mandatory visa list before 1 January 1995. The Commission duly undertook its task proposing a Regulation on a common visa format[43] (which did not tangle itself up in legal proceedings) and then a Regulation on mandatory visa countries, both of which were adopted in 1995[44] but the second of which was annulled by the Court of Justice in 1997 for legislative failings (but with continuing effect of the contents).[45] Both of these requirements relate exclusively to third country nationals as there are no circumstances in which Com-

---

43 Council Regulation 1683/95 of 29 May 1995 laying down a uniform format for visas. OJ 1995 L 164/1.
44 Regulation 2317/95 OJ 1995 L 234/1.
45 C-392/95 *Parliament v Council* [1997] ECR 1-3213.

munity nationals may be required to obtain visas to enter a Member State other than that of their nationality.[46]

Article 100c is something of a Cinderella in the mainstream literature on the Maastricht Treaty. Some of the most well known Community law authors deal with all the other parts of the Treaty but not Article 100c or the Third Pillar, for example: Monar *et al.*,[47] and Dehousse.[48] Perhaps the significance of the Third Pillar was not yet apparent, though this excuse cannot apply to Dashwood writing in 1996.[49]

Cloos and others writing in 1993 do treat the issue briefly considering Article 100c to constituted a "victoire communautaire".[50] In their view Article 100c should be seen as encompassing three separate decisions responsibility for which accrues to the Community: (1) the determination of visa national countries; (2) the power to recommend introduction of a visa requirement for a limited period; (3) the visa format. In their view the most important aspect of Article 100c is the introduction of qualified majority voting from 1996.[51] This is a very institutional perspective, no doubt fuelled by their interest in whether the Maastricht Treaty actually made substantial progress towards the institutional reform some consider necessary before further enlargement. No doubt the fact the French Conseil Constitutionnel held that the introduction of qualified majority voting in this field required a constitutional amendment in France before the Treaty could be ratified also raised the importance of the question.[52] Kovar in his commentary on Article 100c sets out the issue but does not comment on what the consequences of the divided competence may be.[53]

---

46 Article 3(1) Directive 68/360.
47 J. Monar *et al.*, (eds.), *The Maastricht Treaty on European Union, Legal Complexity and Political Dynamic*, European Interuniversity Press, Brussels, 1993. There are two references to visa policy: one in a list of new competences, the second referring to the fact that qualified majority voting would be the rule in this area.
48 R. Dehousse, *Europe After Maastricht, An Ever Closer Union?* Law Books in Europe, Munich 1994. There is included a very interesting essay by J. H. H. Weiler on the three pillar structure in which he considers the separation of the Second and Third Pillars from the First Pillar. No specific chapter, however, considers the Third Pillar.
49 A. Dashwood, *Reviewing Maastricht, Issues for the 1996 IGC*, Sweet & Maxwell, London, 1996.
50 J. Cloos, G. Reinesch, D. Vignes & J. Weyland, *Le Traité de Maastricht, genèse, analyse, commentaires*, Bruylant, Brussels, 1993, p. 507.
51 J. Cloos, G. Reinesch, D. Vignes & J. Weyland, *Le Traité de Maastricht, genèse, analyse, commentaires*, Bruylant, Brussels, 1993, pp. 507-508.
52 J. Cloos, G. Reinesch, D. Vignes & J. Weyland, *Le Traité de Maastricht, genèse, analyse, commentaires*, Bruylant, Brussels, 1993, p. 508.
53 "Les autres aspects du régime de l'accès des étrangers non communautaires au territoire de la Communauté et de leur séjour appartiennent aux règles relatives à la coopération dans les domaines de la justice et des affaires intérieures... est possible suivant la

In respect of the three powers identified by Cloos, the second has never been exercised, but the first was, and caused the issue of the relationship of the Community with third country nationals to be explored. I will consider this in depth below but first I will set out the provisions which would be fundamental to the discussion.

The Commission introduced a Proposal for a Regulation based on Article 100c of the Treaty determining the third countries whose nationals must be in possession of a visa when crossing the external borders of the Member States on 10 December 1993.[54] The Maastricht Treaty had only just come into force on 1 November 1993 so the Commission's kick-off date for the proposal was prompt to say the least. The proposal accompanied another proposal of the Commission, and one of the few it would make in exercising its association with the Third Pillar until towards the commencement of the next intergovernmental conference in 1996: a Proposal for a Decision based on Article K.3 of the Treaty on European Union establishing the Convention on the crossing of the external frontiers of the Member States.[55] The salient points of the Commission's draft for a Directive under Article 100c which would be controversial are:

Article 1(2)

"Until 30 June 1996 Member States shall decide whether to require visas of nationals of third countries not listed in the Annex. Prior to that date the Council shall decide according to the procedure laid down in Article 100c either to add each of those countries to that list or to exempt its nationals from visa requirements."

In other words the list of visa countries would become definitive: a list of those countries whose nationals do require a visa to enter the territory of the Union and a list of those countries whose nationals do not require a visa to enter the territory of the Union. When finally adopted by the Council this had become:

Article 2(1)

"The Member States shall determine the visa requirements for nationals of third countries not on the common list."

This means a white list of nationals of countries who never require a visa would not come into existence.

---

procédure de l'article K 9 du traité de Maastricht." V. Constantinesco, R. Kovar & D. Simon, *Traité dur l'Union européenne, Commentaire article par article*, Economica, Paris, 1995, p. 226.

54 OJ 1994 C 11/15. I will refer to this as the Visa Regulation.

55 OJ 1994 C 22/6. I will refer to this as the draft External Frontiers Convention.

The Commission proposed:

Article 2

"A Member State shall not be entitled to require a visa of a person who seeks to cross its external frontiers and who holds a visa issued by another Member State, where that visa is valid throughout the Community."

There would be cross recognition of visas. Italy would not be entitled, for example, to refuse to recognise the validity for entry onto its territory of a person issued a visa by Germany. The Council eliminated this altogether.

The Commission proposed:

Article 3

"For the purposes of this Regulation, the following definitions shall apply: visa: any authorisation granted by a Member State which either:

– entitles a person to enter its territory, subject to other entry conditions being fulfilled, and is valid for a stay of no more than three months, or a number of stays not exceeding a total of three months in any six-month period commencing on the date of the first entry, or

– entitles a person to transit through its territory or through the transit zone of a port or airport, subject to other transit conditions being fulfilled, or

– entitles a person who is present on its territory to re-enter within a specified period."

A visa therefore would give an entitlement to enter the territory of the Union and would include transit or re-entry. Therefore this provision gives a right of entry to a third country national to any part of the territory of the Union when in possession of the common visa. The proposal did not include a provision permitting refusal of admission on the grounds of public policy, security or health (that right was proposed in the accompanying draft External Frontiers Convention and was wider than just these three grounds). The Council adopted:

Article 3

"For the purposes of this regulation 'visa' shall mean an authorisation given or a decision taken by a Member State which is required for entry into its territory with a view to:

– an intended stay in that Member State or in several Member States of no more than three months in all;

– transit through the territory of that Member State or several Member States, except for transit through the international zones of airports and transfers between airports in a Member State."

There is no longer a right of entry on presentation of a valid visa.

The Regulation was considered by the Parliament in 1994,[56] adopted by the Council duly amended in 1995,[57] annulled by the Court at the request of the Parliament in 1997,[58] and readopted by the Council in 1999.[59] I will look at length at each of these steps shortly.

The third power as discussed by Cloos was the common format visa. The Commission made a proposal which was adopted without excessive difficulty in the form of a regulation.[60] On the way it lost its uniformity: the Commission had proposed that it apply to all types of visas. The final version only requires that the uniform visa be designated for different types of visas.

In summary then, a power is included in the Treaty and a duty to implement legislation which involves movement of a class of persons whose movement has not previously been within the Community domain. These are third country nationals who have no connection of family or employment with a Community national (natural or legal). The question therefore arises, will the Community in the exercise of this new power create a new and direct relationship in law with this class of persons?

8.3.   VISAS AND COMMUNITY LAW

Until the entry into force of the Maastricht Treaty in 1993, the question of visas for third country nationals only arose in one situation in Community law and there by virtue of subsidiary legislation relating to the procedures under which Community national migrant workers and their family members of any nationality may exercise their free movement right.[61] Article 3(2) of Directive 68/360 permits the Member States to require a visa (or equivalent document) from third country national members of the family of a migrant Community national but requires the Member States to "accord to such persons every facility for obtaining any necessary visas." Therefore the existing provision was permissive not mandatory, allowing Member States to impose a visa requirement, but where they did require such a visa placing an obligation on the Member States in favour of the third country national to provide every facility

---

56 OJ 1994 C 128/350.
57 OJ 1995 L 234/1.
58 C-392/95 *Parliament v Council* [1997] ECR I-3213.
59 OJ 1999 L 72.
60 OJ 1995 L 164/1; for ease of reference I will refer to this as the Format Regulation.
61 R. Fernhout provides an excellent overview of the question of visas in the internal market context in his article The United States of Europe have Commenced, but for whom? Netherlands Quarterly of Human Rights, Vol. 11, No 3, 1993, pp. 249-266.

for the issue of such a visa. Further Article 9(2) of the Directive requires that such visas be issued free of charge.[62]

What does the third country national need to produce to obtain a visa? Article 3 of Directive 68/360 is silent on this point. It sets out a list of documents which the third country national family members need to produce after admission to the territory of the Member State in order to obtain a residence document[63] but not what needs to be produced to obtain the visa. According to one point of view, the issue of a visa for a family member cannot be made subject to more than evidence of the family relationship. So, for instance, a demand for evidence of means of support is not acceptable.[64] This reasoning is based on an extension of the argument accepted by the Court of Justice as to the powers of officials to check Community nationals crossing Community borders. The Court found that the only precondition to entry to the territory was the possession of a visa or identity card. Border officials therefore are not entitled to ask questions about the purpose and duration of the person's stay or about his or her financial resources even if that question is limited to determining their adequacy for the trip.[65] The check on eligibility for residence takes place not at a post abroad, nor indeed at the border crossing point but inside the territory when individuals apply for residence permits.

An alternative view on the issue of visas is that which UK entry clearance officers abroad adopt which is that they are entitled to the same evidence of eligibility for residence at the post abroad before the visa is issued as will be required after issue and entry when the person applies for a residence document. Even at the higher test, the only documents which may then be required are a document from the country of origin or the state whence they came proving their relationship, and if dependency is a prerequisite, a document issued by the competent authority of the state of origin or the state whence they came testifying that they are dependent on the worker or that they live under his/her roof in such country.[66]

---

62 This contrasts with the position in respect of visas for CEEC nationals seeking to exercise establishment rights in the Member States which I discussed in Chapter 6. Here the Community is leaving open to the Member States the question of which countries' nationals require a visa but limiting the scope for Member State action if a visa is required: though the specification of the grant of a visa. In the CEEC case, reference to visas is not found in the body of the agreement but implied through another provision, in the Poland Agreement Article 57. The lack of clarity which arises in respect of the Europe Agreements is not so apparent here.
63 Article 4(3) Directive 68/360.
64 D. Martin and E. Guild, *Free Movement of Persons in the European Union*, Butterworths, London, 1996, p. 160.
65 C-68/89 *Commission v Netherlands* [1991] ECR 1-2637.
66 Article 4(3) Directive 63/360.

The relative simplicity of determining the documents which must be produced to obtain a visa under Directive 68/360 comes from the fact that the underlying subject matter, the substantive right to entry and residence is clarified elsewhere: in Regulation 1612/68 on the right of residence of Community national workers and their family members.

For the purposes of the Visa Regulation under Article 100c, there is no clarification at all of what the individual must produce and therefore no indication of the limitations of the Member States, demands of the individual. What is missing from the framework is a second document setting out the rights attendant on the visa and the conditions of its issue.[67] Therefore, in terms of a structural change to the relationship between the Community, the Member State and the individual, the Regulation does nothing as regards obtaining visas as the necessary second part of the equation is missing. It is still a matter outside the Regulation implementing the visa list in Article 100c what can be required in order to obtain a visa. Further, as the second limb of the equation is missing, there is no check on Member States requiring completely different documentation from third country nationals seeking visas both in relation to one another and different third country nationals.

The reason for this is that the second half of the equation is to be found in the Third Pillar. Under Article K.1(2) "rules governing the crossing by persons of the external borders of the Member States and the exercise of controls thereon" are to be adopted in the intergovernmental pillar. In the Commission's first proposal under the Third Pillar it addressed this question within the logic of the Third Pillar. In the proposal for a decision establishing a Third Pillar Convention on the crossing of the external frontiers of the Member States[68] Article 19 provides for a uniform visa to be issued subject to procedural requirements only where the person meets the entry requirements of Article 7. These are that he or she presents a valid travel document which authorises the crossing of the frontier; if required is in possession of a visa valid for the length and purpose of the stay; he or she is not a threat to public policy, national security or international relations of Member States and in particular that his or her name does not appear on the joint list of inadmissible persons. The interests of the Member States appear to be cumulative. The relationship between the State and the convention is clear – the State must not issue a visa to an individual if another State objects. But no direct link is made with the individual who is the subject of the activity. He or she must rely on his or her relationship with the State. But that relationship has been changed by the

---

67 The structural basis for this second part is found in the Commission's proposal which accompanied the Visa Regulation: a Convention on the crossing of the external frontiers of the Member States COM(93) 684 final, Brussels, 10.12.93.

68 OJ 1994 C 11/6.

mandatory rules which apply to the State by virtue of the convention. The relationship between the State and the convention may bind the States hands to refuse a visa, but it does not create any right or remedy for the individual who is limited to his or her relationship with the State.

Next, what does the visa entitle the individual to do? The Visa Regulation defines a visa in terms of an authorisation to stay no more than three months out of every six within the territory of the Member States. However, nothing in the Regulation as adopted deals with any right to do so. There are two parts to this right, first the right to cross the border from outside the Union and secondly the right to stay for three months within the combined territory which presupposes a right to cross intra-Member State borders. The definition of a visa in the Regulation elides two aspects, a visa obtained abroad and a decision taken at a border crossing to give entry. It is either an "authorisation given" or "a decision taken". The Commission's original proposal made this clear, it only referred to an authorisation. Therefore, from the wording of the Regulation it is by no means apparent that a national of a third country on the list necessarily must obtain the visa at a post abroad. Article 1(1) of the Regulation requires that "nationals of countries on the common list in the Annex shall be required to be in possession of visas when crossing the external borders of the Member States." The temporal relationship between having the visa and crossing the border does not necessarily indicate that the visa must be held before the individual arrives at the border. A system where visas are issued at the border is, therefore consistent with the Regulation. Accordingly, the Regulation does not support a system of fines on carriers which extends to nationals of countries on the mandatory visa list who are in possession of valid travel documents but who have not yet, at the time of travel, obtained a visa abroad. This is because there is a power for the official to make a decision at the border. As he or she has the power to make a positive decision to issue a visa at the border the Regulation does not require that an airline be considered liable for fines for carrying a person who does not have a visa in advance of travelling.

Neither does the Regulation give a right to a person in possession of a common format visa to cross a border. Therefore, the individual is placed under a duty to obtain a visa as defined, possibly in the common format, but having done so, by virtue of Community law is no better off. He or she still has no right or, even according to the Regulation, presumption that he or she will actually be permitted to cross the external frontier of the Member States.

One right does exist: in the Format Regulation "an individual to whom a visa is issued shall have the right to verify the personal particulars entered on the visa and, where appropriate, to ask for any corrections or deletions to be made."[69] With the development of technology permitting machine readable information not apparent to the eye to be included on documents this right may be important though exactly what the legal consequences of a State's refusal to make corrections or deletions may be is uncertain.

Because the Commission interpreted Article 100c as conferring no power on the Community to establish common criteria for admission of third country nationals to the territory of the Member States, the power contained in the two Regulations is only capable of regulating activity of the Member States – what a visa is and what the common format visa should look like. With one noble exception, the individual, the object of these measures, is excluded from the framework.

Cruz argues that:

> "Now it should be quite obvious that granting the Commission competence over visa matters makes sense if and only if the Member States agree to common criteria and rules on checks at the external borders of the European Union and if the Commission is granted some competence over the issue of immigration of third country nationals ... Moreover, it would be unrealistic to dissociate a common visa policy from a common foreign and security policy, the so-called Second Pillar where competence has also been denied to Community institutions."[70]

Hailbronner looks in some depth at the development of the visa competence of the Community and concludes that the division between the First and Third Pillars "underlines the intention of the Member States to transfer only a limited part of their sovereign rights. On the other hand, the Community's powers must be interpreted in such a way as to enable the Community to discharge its legislative tasks and functions in a rational and effective way."[71] He goes on to consider the problem of white, black and grey lists. However, the same principle applies to all aspects of the Visa Regulation. Both Hailbronner[72] and d'Oliveira[73] note the relationship between the visa competence of the First Pillar and the Schengen visa competence which had already been exercised. The

---

69 Article 4(1) Regulation 1683/95.
70 A. Cruz, Visa Policy under the First Pillar: A Meaningless Compromise, in M. den Boer (ed.), *Schengen, Judicial Co-operation and Policy Co-ordination*, EIPA, Maastricht, 1997, pp. 218-219.
71 K. Hailbronner, Visa Regulations and Third Country Nationals in EC Law, CML Rev 31:969-995.
72 K. Hailbronner, Visa Regulations and Third Country Nationals in EC Law, CML Rev 31:969-995.
73 H. U. Jessurun d'Oliveira, Expanding External and Shrinking Internal Borders: Europe's Defence Mechanisms in the Areas of Free Movement, Immigration and Asylum, in P. Twomey & D. O'Keeffe, *Legal Issues of the Maastricht Treaty*, Chancery, London, 1994, pp. 261-278.

latter notes that the Schengen Executive Committee had been busy in mid December 1992, after the signing of the Maastricht Treaty, developing its list of third countries whose nationals would require visas, uniform visa formats and related matters all limited to short stay visas.

Was a wider competence on visas and their meaning denied to the Community? The provisions of the Treaty on European Union are "without prejudice to the powers of the European Community".[74] Therefore the hierarchy is clearly established, first come the powers of the Community and then the powers of the Third Pillar, the intergovernmental part of the Union. Only where there is not a power to the Community can the Third Pillar mop up responsibility for the field. Although an express provision was not included limiting the meaning of a visa to one valid only for a short stay, this appears to have been the assumption of all the participants. It has not been raised as regards the Visa Regulation mainly, it would appear, because both in the Schengen Implementing Convention and in the Commission's on draft external Frontiers Convention long stay visas were specifically defined as national visas.[75] Cruz does not appear to accept entirely that the limitation to a short term visas was necessary.[76] Hailbronner accepts the limitation as implicit from both the Member States intentions as evidence in the Schengen Implementing Agreement and the Commission's draft External Frontiers Convention.[77] In my view it is by no means so clear from the wording of Article 100c EC that it was limited to short term visas either as regards the countries whose nationals must obtain visas, nor as regards the common format visa. The immigration policy contained in the Third Pillar is compatible with such an extensive interpretation of the power to determine nationals of which countries must be in possession of visas and what those visas shall look like. However, the political concerns of the Member States – their determination to keep long stay visas within the Third Pillar made this legal argument rather beside the point.

Another legal analysis of the divided competence problem would entail rejecting the division of powers approach between the two Pillars in favour of a division between policy and law making which is co-extensive. "Common interest" which is the extent of the Third Pillar's involvement, may mean a

---

74 Article K.1 TEU (before amendment by the Amsterdam Treaty).
75 Article 25 draft External Frontiers Convention: "Visas for stays of more than three months shall be national visas issued by each Member State in accordance with its national rules."
76 A. Cruz, Visa Policy under the First Pillar: A Meaningless Compromise, in M. den Boer (ed.), *Schengen, Judicial Co-operation and Policy Co-ordination*, EIPA, Maastricht, 1997, pp. 218-219.
77 K. Hailbronner, Visa Regulations and Third Country Nationals in EC Law, CML Rev 31:969-995.

number of different things. Rather than being understood as a competence, it could just as easily mean that there is a forum outside the Community for the Member States to discuss and reach common agreement on policy without such a procedure impinging on the right of the Community to propose and adopt legislation in accordance with an expansive interpretation of Article 100c given the wide objective contained in Article 3 EC (discussed above). From the wording of the Treaty, the Third Pillar could have been treated as an intermediate framework to sort out differences among the Member States in sensitive areas in preparation for Community legislation under Article 100c. This then would make better sense of Article 100d EC which provided for the management committee of the Third Pillar (K.4 Committee) to contribute to the Council on measures proposed under Article 100c. Of course following the entry into force of the Amsterdam Treaty, this question has been resolved in the new Title IV EC.

8.4. INDIVIDUAL RIGHTS IN THE LIGHT OF WHITE, GREY AND BLACK LISTS

The Visa Regulation requires visas of nationals of the countries listed in its annex. The subject matter, the list of countries in the annex, was not the source of the difficulties which arose in respect of the Regulation. This list had been agreed to a large extent intergovernmentally in 1988 at the Copenhagen Council meeting. Additionally, under the Schengen system a list of countries had already been agreed and implemented among more than half of the Member States.[78] The problem in respect of this aspect of the Regulation was again the potential creation of a direct relationship between the individual and the Community.

All parties were agreed that nationals of countries on the common list had to have visas. But what about nationals of countries not on the list? This became a highly vexed question which led to the dispute between the Parliament and the Council before the Court of Justice. On the one hand there is a white list of countries which are neither on the list nor whose nationals are required by any Member State to have a visa. On the other hand there is a black list, contained in the Regulation's annex for which all Member States require a visa. Between the two is a grey list: countries which are not on the Visa

---

78 H. U. Jessurun d'Oliveira, *Expanding External and Shrinking Internal Borders: Europe's Defence Mechanisms in the Areas of Free Movement, Immigration and Asylum*, in P. Twomey & D. O'Keeffe, *Legal Issues of the Maastricht Treaty*, Chancery, London, 1994, pp. 261-278.

Regulation annex but whose nationals are required by some Member States to have a visa.[79]

Does Article 100c prevent more countries from being added to the grey list and does it require the abolition of the grey list altogether? In other words, does the purpose and intention of the provision to achieve harmonisation as regards the countries whose nationals must obtain visas prevent "backsliding" – the move away for convergence of lists by Member States unilaterally deciding to add to their national list of visa countries one which until then was part of the white list? If it does, then there is created at least in principle, a right to individuals, nationals of white list countries, to challenge any national requirement that they obtain a visa to gain admission to a Member State. Their right not to have to obtain a visa would be guaranteed by Community law irrespective of any national provision to the contrary.[80] The Commission's original proposal would have allowed a grace period to the Member States to sort out the countries which they agreed should be on the list and after that grace period the two lists would become definitive.[81] The relationship between the individual, Community and Member State would change in a graduated manner and with plenty of opportunity for the Member States to include on the list as many countries as they chose.

The Parliament agreed with the Commission regarding the effect of Article 100c but took the view that the change of relationship should happen more quickly. The Parliament proposed an amendment to the Regulation that the Member States should not be permitted to impose a visa requirement on countries which have, for fair and objective reasons, been excluded from the black list and shortened the period by which the mandatory white list had to be achieved. The Parliament's determination that Article 100c be implemented in such a way as to create a new relationship between the three actors was

---

79 The existence of black grey and white lists also bedevilled the Schengen acquis where similarly there was no agreement on all the countries. The problem was among the last to be settled by the Schengen Executive Committee before the hand over under the terms of the Schengen Protocol to the Amsterdam Treaty.

80 It could also be argued that the existence alone of a black list changes the relationships of the three as the Member State must institute a visa requirements on nationals of some countries and in theory at least nationals or those countries could insist on a visa requirement. However, visa requirements are obstacles to movement which no one willingly entertains. Perhaps there may be circumstances where a person would wish to insist on being under a duty to obtain a visa but these are difficult to imagine.

81 For a detailed analysis of the positions taken by all the participants in this discussion, including some of the lesser followed European Parliamentary Committees see A. Cruz, Visa Policy under the First Pillar: A Meaningless Compromise, in M. den Boer (ed.), Schengen, Judicial Co-operation and Policy Co-ordination, EIPA, Maastricht, 1997, pp. 218-219.

strengthened by its proposal to include provisions on the conditions for the issue of visas and a right of appeal in the event of refusal to grant a visa.

The Council, however, disagreed with the Commission and the Parliament. After the mandatory consultation with Parliament it inserted into the Regulation Article 2(1) "The Member States shall determine the visa requirements for nationals of third country not on the common visa list."[82] This provision has the effect of depriving the individual of the one real right[83] the Commission was willing to contemplate under Article 100c.

Further, the Council's interpretation of Article 100c(1) raises a question mark over the purpose of Article 100c(2): why would there need to be consultation and a Commission proposal to introduce a temporary visa requirement if there was a residual power to the Member States to do so unilaterally? If Article 100c(1) permits any Member State to introduce a visa requirement for any country on the white or grey list, then the possibility exists for the Member States acting together but outside the Council to add in practice more countries to the list without the intervention of the Commission or Parliament. They could individually all amend their national legislation to do so and thereby exclude the Commission from its role as guardian of the integrity of the Visa Regulation.

Hailbronner criticises the Council's position fiercely on a number of grounds. While he accepts that positive listing is not a necessary counterpart to negative listing he argues that a restrictive interpretation would deprive Article 100c EC of its effectiveness. He makes the argument of an implicit link between Article 100c and Article 14 EC. On this basis, with the abolition of border controls, the efficiency argument becomes stronger as third country nationals from a grey list country, if such is permitted to exist, will be able to enter one Member State where they are not on the national visa list and then travel without control to another Member State where they are on the visa list thereby frustrating the national visa list of the second country. He supports a proposal which is "close to the German system of visa regulation" and requires a white list. In his view "the abolition of internal border controls alone leads to the conclusion that a distinction between positive and negative listing cannot be maintained. It would

---

82 The UK, for instance has since the adoption of the Regulation unilaterally added Colombia to its mandatory visa list in June 1997 and on 8 October 1998 Slovakia. No consultation with the Commission was undertaken as regards the addition of these countries to the national list.

83 Leaving aside, for the moment, the right regarding information on the visa contained in the Format Regulation. This right does not impinge on the actual subject matter of Article 100c – is there a meaningful Community visa regime created upon which individuals can rely to cross borders?

be hard if not impossible to imagine how a system exclusively based on negative listing could function properly."[84]

It is not surprising, considering what was at stake, that the Parliament did not accept the Regulation as adopted by the Council. Amongst other points, the Parliament challenged the Council on the question of the grey list before the Court of Justice.[85] The Council's position, in the proceedings on the question as summarised in the judgment was as follows:

"The Council ... supported by the French Government, considers, first of all, that Article 2(1) of the regulation merely clarifies the scope of the Commission proposal, according to which, pending a Council decision as to the third countries not appearing in the annex, each Member State remains at liberty to decide whether or not to impose a visa requirement on nationals from those countries. The Council adds that the only difference existing in this regard between the proposal and the Regulation resides in the fact that the latter provides for a longer transitional period during which the Member States will remain free to regulate visa requirements concerning third country nationals whose countries are not on the common list."[86]

The only question before the Court was whether the text as adopted differed in essence from the text on which the Parliament had already been consulted. This is because the Parliament's attack was limited to the protection of its prerogatives (as indeed it had to be). The Court noted that the Council's adopted text allowed the Member States to maintain for an indefinite period their list of third countries not on the common list whose nationals are subject to visa requirements. For this reason the Court maintained that "those amendments go to the heart of the arrangements established and must therefore be described as substantial." On this ground alone the Court held that the Regulation must be annulled (though its effects were preserved) and it was not necessary to consider other arguments put forward by the Parliament.[87]

In my opinion, the essential difference between the two drafts was the question of the position of the individual *vis-à-vis* the Member State and the Community. The fundamental change of rights which would occur with a mandatory white list is the essence of the constitutional decision of the Court regarding the powers of the Parliament. A simple example illustrates this: if the Council acting by qualified majority voting, on a proposal from the Commis-

---

84 K. Hailbronner, Visa Regulations and Third Country Nationals in EC Law, CML Rev 31:969-995.
85 C-392/95 *Parliament v Council* [1997] ECR I-3213.
86 C-392/95 *Parliament v Council* [1997] ECR I-3213.
87 The Regulation was readopted by the Council 574/1999 OJ 1999 L 72/2. However, the same problems which arose the first time have reoccurred as regards consultation with the Parliament and respect for Parliamentary amendments.

sion decide to remove a country from the black list, could an aggrieved Member State who had voted against the proposal maintain visa requirements for that country on the basis that there is no white list? There is no right possible to the individual to avoid a visa requirement on the basis of Article 100c EC unless there is a white list. This may well have been the intention of the Member States in settling Article 100c: no rights should accrue. It is certainly the position which they put forward on the adoption of the Regulation and the one they defended before the Court. However, it is also the one which they abandoned in 1997 when the whole competence for visas moved into the First Pillar and when the Member States abolished the Schengen grey list in 1998 in anticipation of its assumption into EC law.

A second critical aspect of the Visa Regulation which would have changed the relationship of the individual, Member State and Community was the Commission's proposed Article 2:

> "A Member State shall not be entitled to require a visa of a person who seeks to cross its external frontiers and who holds a visa issued by another Member State, where that visa is valid throughout the Community."

This provision presupposes the adoption of a Community-wide equivalent of a Schengen visa. It relates to the second legislative duty placed on the Commission by Article 100c: the common format visa. The Regulation which was adopted does not contain an obligation of cross recognition.[88] Although the Format Regulation sets out the specifications of the visa and defines a visa consistently with the Visa Regulation (though with some changes), the consequences of having such a visa are nowhere spelled out.

Therefore in the implementation of the two Article 100c legislative duties, the result is a tension between, on the one hand, the Commission and Parliament and the Council on the other as to whether the transfer of this competence for visas will be allowed to change the relationship of the Community to a new group of foreigners: third country nationals who are neither family members of Community nationals nor associated with Community-based companies or privileged under agreements with their home state. The Commission and the Parliament favour legislation which will create such a change. The Council consistently blocks such a change of relationship, maintaining the *status quo* whereby the only effective relationship of the third country national is with the Member State. Community law is not permitted to extend any right to these third country nationals in the field.

The situation changed, however, with the incorporation of the Schengen acquis into the EC Treaty by virtue of the Schengen Protocol to the Amsterdam Treaty. Not only did the Schengen states arrange to abolish their

---

88 OJ 1995 L 164/2.

grey list in December 1998 before the entry into force of the Amsterdam Treaty but they participated in the creation of new confusion by adopting a new Community Visa Regulation which expressly permits the continuation of the grey list. A new conflict has been created, what law applies and what is the force of the Schengen acquis in comparison with standard Community measures? Is an individual entitled to rely on the Schengen list to establish a right against a Member State not to have a visa where his or her country is not on the Schengen list even though the country remains on the Community regulation's grey list? And if the individual's country of nationality is on the Schengen list does it give him or her a right to challenge in Community law any requirement by a Member State that he or she also obtain a national visa?

In my opinion, notwithstanding my arguments in general in favour of a direct relationship between the individual and the Community, in this case I am not sure that it is either legally correct or in terms of policy wise to prefer the force of the Schengen acquis over Community measures. Legally, it would seem to be that measures of secondary Community law duly adopted in accordance with the provisions of the Treaty must take priority over what is still, at the time of writing, a fairly amorphous mass of documents: the Schengen acquis. On the other hand, the cross recognition of residence permits for third country nationals living within the Schengen territory in the place of visas is particularly useful and has no Community counterpart. Accordingly, there does not appear to be any reason for it not to take effect in the Community regime for the Schengen 13. The legal consequences of bits of the Schengen acquis, in particular where in conflict with Community law need to be the subject of Community law amendment procedures. In terms of policy I would also be unwilling to promote a position on this question, which, while providing a right to individuals, gives away a key concern: the legitimacy of the Schengen process. Many non-governmental organisations criticised the Schengen system of adopting legislation as lacking democratic legitimacy. Their concerns were particularly valid as the fields of the Schengen acquis spread ever wider into areas of civil liberties, such as police co-operation. While the Community legislative process may not have all the elements of democratic accountability which some would like, it does enjoy substantially more authority on this ground than the Schengen acquis. Therefore as a matter of principle, in my view the Community provisions, even if flawed are preferable, but should be amended in accordance with the proper rules of Community legislative procedure as provided for now in Title IV EC which governs the Schengen immigration acquis. The most unsatisfactory solution would be two binding legal systems within Community covering the same legal territory but with different provisions.

Transit Visas

Article 100c EC also gave rise to the first dispute between the Commission and the Council on the scope of Community law under the new visa regime. The Visa Regulation adopted by the Council defines a visa as an authorisation or decision which is required for entry into the territory with a view to "transit through the territory of that Member State or several Member States, except for transit through the international zones of airports and transfers between airports in a Member State."[89] The Commission's original proposal for the Regulation expressly included transit through international zones at airports. The Council deleted this reference.

However, the Format Regulation defines a visa as an authorisation or decision which is required for entry into national territory *inter alia* with a view to "transit through the territory or airport transit zone of that Member State or several Member States".[90] There is a fundamental difference here between the two Regulations, one excludes for its purposes transit through an international zone at or between airports, the other could be interpreted as including transit through an international zone at an airport. So for the purposes of a common visa format, transit visas can be included in a measure adopted under Article 100c. But for the purposes of the list of countries whose nationals must have such a visa, transit is not included in the 100c measure. If the question of countries whose nationals must have visas for transit through international zones is not encompassed in Article 100c EC where would it lie? The answer, according to the Council, is within the Third Pillar. There was no question that the measures adopted in the Third Pillar lacked the possibility of direct effect. First they were outside the Community legal order, secondly they were agreed among the Member States in the Council in forms not known to Community law, thirdly they were worded in terms of inter-state obligations or action, and fourthly they were expressly stated to have no legally binding effect.[91]

So, anything which was going to take place within the ambit of the Third Pillar was not going to have a direct consequence for the structure of the relationship between the individual and the Member State and the individual and the Community.[92] However, the Third Pillar was specifically to be without prejudice to the powers of the European Community which must take preced-

---

89 Article 5 Regulation 2317/95.
90 Article 5 Regulation 1683/95.
91 An example which includes all of these features is the Resolution relating to limitations on the admission of third country nationals to the territory of the Member States for the purpose of self-employment: OJ 1996 C 274/7.
92 There is a change in the relationship between the Member States and the Community which is characterised by conflict as this case indicates.

ence over the Third Pillar.[93] The overlap between the First Pillar and the Third Pillar which resulted in the lack of comprehensiveness in the Visa Regulation is the source of confusion here as well.

The question came before the Court, when is a visa not a visa: and for the purposes of the Union there was no single definition, nor indeed was it clear whether a single definition was appropriate. On 4 March 1996 the Council adopted a Joint Action on the basis of Article K.3 of the Treaty on European Union on airport transit arrangements.[94] Although the heading rather delicately describes the matters as "arrangements" in fact the Joint Action is about transit visas and more specifically nationals of which countries must be in possession of such visas when entering the airports of the Union for transit purposes. To this extent, someone looking at the Joint Action and Regulation 2317/95 might well think that they dealt with the same issue and perhaps even might benefit from being consolidated.

This thought took legal shape in the form of an action by the Commission against the Council for adopting the Joint Action on the basis of Article K.3, in other words in the Third Pillar.[95] The concern was not simply that Union measures should be tidy. The reason the Commission took action was because it considered that the proper basis for the Joint Action was Article 100c. On this legal basis only the Commission has the power to propose legislation, the Parliament must be consulted and the Council adopts. The Commission had already included in its proposal for the Visa Regulation transit visas, and the Council had struck out this reference. The Council preferred to use the Third Pillar as the legal base for measures on transit visas. This meant that a Member State could propose a measure. The Parliament only had a right to be informed and although the Commission was fully associated in the Third Pillar, in practice this had meant the Commission had observer status at Third Pillar meetings. As has already been expressed, measures taken in the Third Pillar must not prejudice the First Pillar, and in the view of the Commission the adoption of a measure in the Third Pillar when its correct legal base is in the First Pillar (Article 100c) constituted a prejudice to the Community. Therefore the Joint Action on Transit Arrangements could not be accepted by the Commission.

---

93 "It is the task of the Court of ensure that acts which, according to the Council, fall within the scope of Article K.3(2) of the Treaty on European Union do not encroach upon the powers conferred by the EC Treaty on the Community" C -170/96 *Commission v Council* [1998] ECR I-2763. The same reasoning applies to the whole of the Third Pillar, not just Article K.3(2) (before amendment by the Amsterdam Treaty).

94 O J 1996 L 63/8.

95 C-170/96 *Commission v Council* [1998] ECR I-2763.

The relationship of the individual with the Member State as regards the application of the Joint Action excludes the Community as this is not Community law. Therefore the possibility of challenging the requirement of a transit visa for a person from a country not on the list on the basis of Community law does not arise.

According to the Joint Action itself, its purpose is to control:

> "the air route, particularly when it involves applications for entry or *de facto* entry, in the course of airport transit, [which] represents a significant way in with a view in particular to illegally taking up residence within the territory of the Member States".[96]

Therefore improvements to controlling that route are to be pursued by the harmonisation of a common list of countries whose nationals must obtain transit visas even where their sojourn in the territory of the Member States is only for the purpose of changing plane or indeed, waiting in the same plane on the tarmac.

In distinction from the Visa Regulation considered above, the transit visa "shall be issued by the consular authorities of the Member States". Accordingly there is no question that it may be obtained after arrival at the airport. However, it is to be in the format of the Format Regulation visa (1683/95). Article 2(2) of the Joint Action places the complete burden of proof on the applicant for the visa:

> "in all cases the consular services must ascertain that there is no security risk or risk of illegal immigration. They must above all be satisfied that the application for an airport transit visa is justified on the basis of the documents submitted by the applicant... "

The discretion, therefore granted to the consular officer considering a transit visa application is virtually absolute. It is sufficient for him or her to say that the visa was refused because he or she could not be entirely satisfied on the basis of the documents that the individual would not be a risk to security or to illegal immigration for the matter to be in compliance with the Joint Action. Only judicial interpretation of the Joint Action in such a way as to require, for instance, credible reasons for refusal, would limit the discretion. Measures adopted in the Third Pillar, however, like the Joint Action are outside the scope of the Court of Justice.

---

96 As the list of countries whose nationals require a transit visa is also a list of countries which by torturing and persecuting their citizens produce persons in need of international protection, the reference to "illegal" residence is distasteful. It might be more honest to refer to asylum seekers.

Therefore, in the Commission's challenge to the Council, the first issue to be resolved was that of the jurisdiction of the Court. The Court found that as it was responsible for ensuring that acts in the Third Pillar do not encroach on the First Pillar it must have a power to review the content of acts adopted in the Third Pillar and proceeded to do so. Therefore, the Court defined its jurisdiction to consider an act of the Third Pillar by reference to an exclusive division of powers between the First and Third Pillars. There is no question of complementarity as an alternative approach to the powers of the First and Third Pillars above.

On considering the merits of the Commission's case, both the Advocate General and the Court accepted that there are two aspects to border crossing: first that of "entering the territory of a country in the physical sense, without necessarily crossing a border control point; secondly that of entering the territory in the legal sense of crossing a border control point."[97] As the Advocate General explained regarding the legal crossing of a border as distinct from the physical crossing of a border: "If this is a fiction, then it is one of a legal character, that is, that the concept of crossing a border must be interpreted in accordance with legal and not necessarily geographical or physical, standards."[98]

The reasoning here sits very uncomfortably with the reasoning used by both the Advocate General and the Court to justify their jurisdiction as regards the case at all. If the Joint Action was properly within the Third Pillar then Article L of the Treaty on European Union excluded the Court entirely from considering the matter. However, both the Advocate General and the Court relied on the argument in favour of a reality test as opposed to a legal form test in that regard, as the Advocate General put it "In order for such an act to be excluded from review, it must still be determined whether having regard to its contents and all the circumstances in which it was adopted, the act in question is not in reality a decision of the Council."[99] Therefore the argument on *reality versus form* in jurisdiction goes in favour of reality, but when it comes to something as physical as actual presence on the territory, it goes in favour of form. I will come back to this point shortly when comparing the approach of the Court of Justice to persons actually on the territory with that adopted by the European Court of Human Rights.

Much prominence was given by both the Advocate General and the Court to the objective of Article 3(d) EC "measures concerning the entry and movement of persons" which in the light of their choice of a legal presence over a reality test led them to conclude the Joint Action was outside the scope of Article 100c. Additionally as pointed out by Oliveira, the insistence on a re-

---

97 Advocate General point 24; C-170/96 *Commission v Council* [1998] ECR I-2763.
98 Advocate General point 29; C-170/96 *Commission v Council* [1998] ECR I-2763.
99 Advocate General point 14; C-170/96 *Commission v Council* [1998] ECR I-2763.

strictive and conjunctive interpretation of Article 3(d) EC is not justified when considered in the light of the drafting history.[100]

Of further concern is the acceptance by the Advocate General of the Council's identified objective of the Joint Action:

> "as being to avoid the risk that nationals of certain third countries take advantage of their presence in the international zone of a Member State airport in order to submit abusive requests for asylum, or even enter the territory illegally by avoiding immigration control at a border post."[101]

First it is difficult to see how a third country national would find it easier to enter the territory of a Member State illegally by avoiding immigration control at an airport. Indeed, airports tend to have more effective immigration control procedures than roads or fields or indeed coastlines. Therefore this argument seems somewhat dubious. Of more concern, however, is the Advocate General's apparent acceptance of the *a priori* assessment of an asylum claim as abusive before it has even been made.

The Court also accepted the legal fiction test as opposed to the reality test in respect of third country nationals' presence on the territory. On considering the meaning of Article 3d "measures concerning the entry and movement of persons in the internal market" it held that:

> "Entry into and movement within the internal market by a national of a third country necessarily implies that that person is not only present on the territory of the Member State but also has been duly authorised to move within that territory. As regards entry into a Member State through an airport, that authorisation means that the person concerned is authorised to pass the border control point in the international area of the airport in that Member State."[102]

The Court found that the border between the First and Third Pillars as regards visas was whether the visa authorised the individual to have access to the territory of the internal market. The fact that the Visa Regulation does not provide any such right was irrelevant. The Court held:

> "It is not inconsistent with that interpretation that, as Community law now stands, a visa within the meaning of Article 100c of the Treaty, does not confer on its holder the right to move freely throughout the internal market and that the Member State issuing the visa is even permitted to restrict that right to movement within its own territory or, pursuant to agreements it has concluded

---

100 A. Oliveira, Case Note on Case C-170/96, *Commission v Council* in CLMRev 99: 149-155 (1999).
101 Advocate General point 36; C-170/96 *Commission v Council* [1998] ECR I-2763.
102 C-170/96 *Commission v Council* [1998] ECR I-2763.

with other Member States, within the entirety of their respective territories"[103] (a clear reference to the Schengen arrangements).

What the Court failed to add was that under the Visa Regulation, Article 100c does not even require the Member State issuing the visa to allow the third country national entry to its own territory. Community law has changed since that decision, not least by the incorporation of the Schengen acquis. It would appear that the cross recognition of residence permits at the very least under the Schengen rules gives a right of entry to the Schengen territory.

In concluding the Court held that as an airport transit visa does not authorise its holder to cross the external borders of Member States in the sense contemplated by Article 100c it does not fall within the ambit of that provision. The conclusion must then be that for the purposes of Community law, a third country national who is present at an airport in the "international zone" is not within the territory of the Member States for the purposes of the internal market. It would be interesting to know whether a third country national in that position would be within the territory of the Member States as regards other provisions of Community law. For instance, as a recipient of services, could service providers from other Member States rely on Article 49 EC?

8.5.   PHYSICAL PRESENCE AND LEGAL PRESENCE

The Court's position on transit visas contrasts with the position which the European Court of Human Rights has taken on the issue of "international zones" and physical versus legal presence. The ECtHR's geographic jurisdiction is clearly set out in Article 1 of the Convention: the jurisdiction of the High Contracting Parties. The responsibility of the ECtHR is to ensure the observance of the engagements of the parties under the ECHR.[104] Therefore the job of the two Courts is very different. However both were faced with the question of the status of persons within "international zones" of airports and the ECtHR directly with the status of a person who had never been admitted in law to a Member State though he was physically present at all times in the State with the knowledge and consent of its authorities.

The Court of Justice found that a third country national in "the international zone" was not within the internal market and further that "entry into and movement within the internal market implies that that person is not only present on the territory of a Member State but has also been duly authorised to

---

103 C-170/96 *Commission v Council* [1998] ECR I-2763.
104 Article 19 ECHR.

move within that territory."[105] This gives the legal presence test ascendance over the physical presence test. The ECtHR took a different approach. On considering the application of the duties which the ECHR places on member States as regards the protection of third country nationals, the ECtHR noted that:

> "even though the applicants were not in France within the meaning of the Ordinance of 2 November 1945, holding them in the international zone of Paris-Orly Airport made them subject to French law. Despite its name, the international zone does not have extraterritorial status."[106]

Therefore the full application of the rights contained in the ECHR had to be secured to persons in the international zone because physical presence is the decisive test irrespective of legal presence. In a second case this is even more clearly stated. The ECtHR had to resolve the second issue: *legal presence v physical presence* outside the international zone. The ECtHR held:

> "Regardless of whether he ever entered the United Kingdom in the technical sense it is to be noted that [D] has been physically present there and thus within the jurisdiction of the respondent State within the meaning of Article 1 of the Convention since 21 January 1993. It is for the respondent State therefore to secure to the applicant the rights guaranteed under Article 3 ... "[107]

The importance here to the question raised at the beginning of this chapter is that a physical presence test increases the personal scope of the treaty or convention and therefore increases the number of persons in different situations who can, at least potentially, rely upon it. It diminishes the possibility for the State through its categorisation of physically present persons as "not present in law" to exclude such persons from the benefits of a treaty or convention. The Court of Justice rejected the Member States' arguments that a national definition of "worker" must apply to Article 39 EC[108] because that would mean:

> "the Community rules on freedom of movement for workers would be frustrated, as the meaning of those terms could be fixed and modified unilaterally, without any control by the Community institutions by national laws which would this be able to exclude at will certain categories of persons from the benefit of the Treaty."[109]

However, when it comes to third country nationals and the internal market it is less clear that such an approach will be adopted. If it is not, then the Member

---

105 C-170/96 *Commission v Council* [1998] ECR I-2763.
106 *Amuur v France* ECtHR, 25 June 1996, 17/1995/523/609.
107 *D v UK* ECtHR, 2 May 1997, 146/1996/767/964.
108 See above, Part I Chapter 3.
109 53/81 *Levin* [1982] ECR 1835.

States will retain control over the categorisation which admits any third country national into the ambit of Community law and the direct relationship with the Community.

8.6. CONCLUSIONS

At the beginning of this chapter I asked the question: what is the Maastricht Treaty's resolution of the structural relationship in three areas. There are, as yet, only partial answers but these might be framed as follows:

The Community and the Member States

The establishment of the Third Pillar created a format within which the Community and the Member States could formally interact as regards immigration and asylum policy. It created a dynamic where Member States' policies on immigration and asylum could be pursued through the Third Pillar but were required to be aimed at achieving the goals of the Community, in particular the internal market. As interpreted, the Third Pillar was subordinate to the Community but that creation of a relationship of subordination caused friction and territorial disputes between the Community and the new forum of the Member States.

The Member State and the individual

The relationship between the Member State and the individual did not change substantially as a result of the Maastricht amendments. Not least because of the determination of the Member States within the Council, in the face of opposition from the Commission and the Parliament, that the implementation of the Community's powers in the field of immigration and asylum reserve the maximum continuing control at national level of all aspects of admission of third country nationals. The Member States retained the same degree of discretionary control as before the Maastricht amendments.

The Community and the individual

The Commission and the European Parliament clarified their intention to create a direct relationship between the individual and the Community as regards immigration. The dispute over the Visa Regulation showed the two institutions' will to change the dynamic of the Community and to encompass new rights. So far by this effort, the only substantive right which was gained for individuals was that relating to information contained in a common format visa contained in the Format Regulation. Another development as regards the relationship of the individual and the Community arises from the Court's decision on transit visas. Here the Court appears to be suggesting that the Member States will always retain control to determine who, among third country nationals, may benefit from the internal market by accepting a "legal presence" test for the market rather than an "actual presence" test.

In conclusion, the Maastricht Treaty created a space in the Third Pillar which allowed a forum for discussion among the Member States and some formulation of policy in the field of immigration and asylum. In doing so, it divided competences between the Community and the Third Pillar is a somewhat haphazard manner, for instance allocating visas and rules governing control of external borders to different frameworks. This set up a tension among the Union's institutions: Council, Commission, Parliament and Court which was not tenable in the long term. As regards the individual this meant very little change in the relationships which pre-dated the Maastricht Treaty, but the friction created by the Maastricht compromise meant there was a promise of further change before too long. That change took the form of the new intergovernmental conference which ended with the Amsterdam Treaty.

In the next chapter I will look at how the relationships of the Community, Member States and individual are changing or may change with the reallocation of powers which the Amsterdam Treaty has brought to the EC Treaty and the Treaty on European Union.

CHAPTER NINE

THE SEARCH FOR OBJECTIVES:
THE AMSTERDAM TREATY

9.1. INTRODUCTION

The Amsterdam Treaty which entered into force on 1 May 1999 has once again changed the balance and perspective of the Union regarding migration. It has amended both the Treaty on European Union and the EC Treaty on immigration and asylum, moving responsibilities from the former into the latter with important changes and provisos.

I will start by looking at what has happened as regards the competences and what the purpose of each change is. I will follow the drafting history of the new Title on immigration and asylum in the EC Treaty in search of clarity. Against the background of that drafting history, I will consider the purpose of the new powers. In order to understand those powers, I will examine the two measures which were produced by the Commission in the field at the time of the conclusion of the Amsterdam Treaty. These give a contemporaneous insight into what the Commission as guardian of the Treaties thought the new powers would entail and what the relationship with the individual would mean. To this end these are particularly relevant to the Conference's decision to give the Community those powers. I will end with some conclusions on the direction in which the new competences may be taken.[1]

The new immigration and asylum provisions of the Treaty are qualified in important ways by four Protocols. The Protocols of Denmark, Ireland and the UK specify that those countries are outside the scope of the Title as regards its application but have a right to request to opt in should they so decide (individually) subject to the consent of the participating States. The peculiar position of these three countries is historic. For Ireland and the UK it results from a combination of a free travel zone and a great attachment on the part of successive UK governments to the concept of border controls. For Denmark it is a matter of national definition of sovereignty. I will not consider these Protocols further. The Schengen Protocol provides that the Schengen acquis, as defined, becomes part of the law of the Union on the entry into force of the Treaty. I have already touched on some of the complexities of the incorporation of the Schengen acquis.

---

1 The full text of Title IV EC on immigration and asylum may be found in the Annex to this chapter.

9.2.   THE EC TREATY AND THIRD COUNTRY NATIONALS: AFTER AMSTERDAM

The EC Treaty has been amended to insert a new Title IV, Visas, Asylum, Immigration and Other Policies Related to Free Movement of Persons which follows on from Title III, Free Movement of Persons, Services and Capital. Title III contains the provisions on free movement of workers, the right of establishment and service provision which apply to nationals of the Member States and their family members of any nationality.[2] Here too is the base for movement of third country national employees of service providers sent by their employer to fulfil contracts for services in other Member States.[3] The new Title in part applies to Community nationals and third country nationals together and in part to third country nationals only. No attempt has been made to separate out third country nationals whose position is already regulated to a greater or lesser extent by agreements between the Community and third countries.

While Title III commences with the words: "Freedom of movement for workers shall be secured within the Community", Title IV is much less concrete. It commences: "In order to establish progressively an area of freedom, security and justice, the Council shall adopt". Two points deserve immediate attention. First, Title III is very clear about its objective. In the context of direct effect, each of its substantive provisions, Article 39 on workers, Article 42 on establishment and Article 49 on services has each been held to be sufficiently clear, precise and unconditional to regulate the relationship between the individual and the Member State directly without implementing legislation. Title IV is quite different. The objective, to which I will return shortly, can only be achieved by the adoption of legislation by the Council. There is a clear intention that here only through the intermediary of secondary legislation can the position of the individual and the Member State be regulated by Community law. Accordingly, direct effect does not appear to be the intention for any of the provisions which are found in this Title.

The concept of an area of freedom, security and justice does not appear anywhere else in the EC Treaty and no definition is given to it. Instead, Article 3, which sets out what activities the Community may pursue in achieving its task of establishing an internal market and Economic and Monetary Union (Article 2), has been expanded to include at (d) measures concerning the entry and movement of persons as provided for in Title IV. This means that in the

---

2   Articles 39-55 EC.
3   Article 49 EC; see in particular the Commission's proposals for implementation of the second paragraph, OJ 1999 C 167.

hierarchy of the objectives of the Community the establishment of an area of freedom, security and justice is somewhat anomalous. It is not specified as a task of the Community in Articles 2 or 3 directly. It applies only to the Title in which it appears. Its legitimacy in the Community order is based on the reference in Article 3(d) "as provided for in Title IV". It must therefore be interpreted as subject to the task of the Community contained in Article 2.[4] It is important to note that in the task of the Community, the benefits of its activities are not defined by reference to citizens of the Union. In the absence of such a limitation, the concept of, for example, "the raising of the standard of living and quality of life" should be understood as applying not only to citizens of the Union but to all persons resident within the Union.[5] I have already addressed the question of the application of other parts of the EC Treaty to third country nationals, contrasting the situation in the field of social policy to that in migration.[6]

The Drafting History

In a Presidency Introductory Note,[7] near the beginning of the intergovern-mental conference the following wording was proposed to start the new Title:

"In order to further develop an area of freedom, security and justice in which free movement of all persons is ensured, the Community shall adopt appropriate provisions as provided in this Title within the following areas: the removal of controls at internal borders and the crossing of external borders as provided for in Article B; asylum policy, immigration policy and policy regarding nationals of third countries within the Community as provided in Article C; coherent action in relation to the abuse of drugs as provided for in Article D;

---

4 "The Community shall have as its task, by establishing a common market and an economic and monetary union and by implementing common policies or activities referred to in Articles 3 and 4, to promote throughout the Community a harmonious, balanced and sustainable development of economic activities, a high level of employ-ment and of social protection, equality between men and women, sustainable and non-inflationary growth, a high degree of competitiveness and convergence of economic performance, a high level of protection and improvement of the quality of the environ-ment, the raising of the standard of living and quality of life, and economic and social cohesion and solidarity among the Member States."

5 There may be arguments in respect of the geographic scope of the task but these are not relevant to my thesis here.

6 See above chapter 1.

7 CONF/3976/96 of 11 November 1996.

strengthening co-operation between customs authorities as provided in Article
E."[8]

The reference is to *all* persons, and is not limited to Article 14 – the internal
market. These two aspects will be changed before the first public draft in December 1996.

Already at the time of the Presidency Note it was intended that "The
provisions of this Title shall be complemented by co-operation in the field of
justice and home affairs provided for in Title VI of the Treaty on European
Union." Stating that the Presidency Note had been circulated, the Conference
Secretariat whose task it was to manage the conference on behalf of the
Council, issued a Presidency paper on "An area of freedom and security: introduction of Community methods and procedures for certain aspects."[9]

The Note recalls that from the Turin Council meeting in March 1996
onwards there had been a continuous demand for adequate results in justice
and home affairs: "It is a constant feature that matters affecting our security
and individual freedoms are not at present being handled adequately. The
choice of forum of 'enhanced intergovernmental co-operation' has failed to
produce tangible results."[10] The Note proposes as the only realistic solution a
"clear break with a structure which is acknowledged to be unsuited, and the
definition of an approach which corresponds to the specific, frequently
normative nature of the subject matter. An approach of this type requires the
use of strong legal instruments which can ensure the application of law, the
establishment of an effective decision-making process based – ultimately at
least – on qualified majority voting, and the guarantee of democratic and
judicial review."[11] From this Note, it is clear that the Secretariat from the
beginning had accepted that root and branch change was needed. The
Secretariat was already working towards moving the area out of the Third Pillar
into the First which was the only part of the Union which would fulfil the
criteria of strong legal instrument with democratic and judicial review. The
acknowledgement that the area is "normative" meant the fact that this would
be a sensitive field.

---

8   The areas included with reference to immigration and asylum were: removal of controls
    at internal borders; the crossing of external borders, asylum policy, immigration policy
    and policy regarding nationals of third countries within the Community.
9   Note, Conference of the Representatives of the Governments of the Member States, 14
    November 1996.
10 Note, Conference of the Representatives of the Governments of the Member States, 14
    November 1996, para 2.
11 Note, Conference of the Representatives of the Governments of the Member States, 14
    November 1996, para 3.

On the specific question of the area of freedom, security and justice, the Note states:

"The idea of such an area is not new, or rather, not entirely new. First of all it follows on from the concept of a frontier-free area written into the EC Treaty by the Single European Act. The reference to Article 7A [14] of the EC Treaty ensures the 'acquis' already achieved in establishing the free movement of persons in maintained. However, the concept of an 'area of freedom, security and justice' is broader than just the free movement of persons: it means that this particular freedom must be underpinned by measures in the security and justice areas. Apart from the freedom to move around, in the widest sense of the term, the peoples and the States of Europe also want to guarantee security and justice for those living in the Union. Every person, whether or [not] benefiting from freedom of movement, expects to be protected effectively against threats such as drugs."

It is important to note here that from the outset it was intended that the area would include third country nationals, delicately put "whether or [not] benefiting from freedom of movement".

The Note described the intention of the allocation within the Treaty as follows "These two main objectives are specifically laid down in Article B of the Treaty on European Union and Article 3 of the EC Treaty (as amended)." Therefore there is an intentionality to the continued division between the two Pillars of the Union:

"The various indents under Article A list the areas in which the Community must act under this new Title. Indeed the articles that follow merely give an exhaustive list of areas where Community action is vital for the establishment of an area of freedom, security and justice."[12]

While the wording proposed indicates that the area is being developed, here further into the Note it is suggested that the area is in fact being established. It is important that from the beginning, the Secretariat had in mind that the area was something different from free movement of persons and the abolition of border controls. For this reason a reference would be required in the objectives of the Treaty.

The Dublin II draft was the first published text for the new Treaty. It was produced on 5 December 1996 under reference CONF 2500/96 and immediately published on the internet by members of the European Parliament. The issue of the area of freedom, security and justice was described as follows:

"The objective of furthering the development of the European Union as an area of freedom, security and justice shall be set out in Article B of the Treaty

---

12 Note, Conference of the Representatives of the Governments of the Member States, 14 November 1996, p. 2-3.

on European Union as proposed below. This objective should be addressed in
two principal ways: first, through the new Title on free movement of persons,
asylum and immigration which is proposed in Chapter 2 in the present Section
and, second, through the strengthened provisions (in Title VI of the Treaty on
European Union) on security and safety of persons as proposed in Chapter 3 of
the present Section."

The structure of the proposal resembles that of the Presidency Note, but there
is no longer the clear indication of where the new Title will be placed: in the
First or Third Pillars. Further, there is an important change to the wording of
Article A in the Dublin II draft in comparison with the Presidency Note: In
order to further the development of an area of freedom security and justice in
which the free movement of persons is ensured as provided for in Article 7a
[14], the Council shall: – the headings remain the same except that there is now
inserted "administrative co-operation, as provided for in Article D". Further an
explicit reference to law and order has been inserted at Article A(2) which will,
in the end, become Article 64(1). It mirrors, with only minor changes, the
wording of Article 100(c)(5) EC (repealed by the Amsterdam Treaty). As far as
I have been able to determine, that provision never found an independent life
in subsidiary legislation or in application. The Dublin II draft stressed the importance that clear objectives must be set in the field and target dates for their
achievement. It proposed 1 January 2001 as the date for completion of all the
measures required under the new Title. This wording and intention supports
the view that the Title would need to be in the First Pillar if it were to fulfil
these requirements.

The intergovernmental conference had been making its way through the
Dublin II draft bit by bit and by February it was ready to look again at justice
and home affairs. In a Non-Paper of 3 February 1997 the Conference Secretariat sought to concentrate the minds of the Member States on the area of
freedom, security and justice. The wording of the initial section setting out the
area had not changed. In the accompanying note, the Secretariat invited:

> "delegations to focus their attention on *the substance of draft Article A to F*, in the
> light of the need to give a clear definition and content to the objective of fur-
> thering the development of an area of freedom, security and justice, in which
> the free movement of persons would be ensured and underpinned by security
> for those living in the territory of the Member States. It should be stressed that,
> from the point of view of the thirteen Member States which are parties to the
> Schengen co-operation, the provisions which are being negotiated in this area
> could in no way represent a step back in respect of the achievements realized in
> the framework of that co-operation; and that appropriate flexibility arrange-

ments should be established with a view to allowing them to pursue that co-operation within the Union... "[13]

First, it is worth noting that the Secretariat is careful to refer to "security for those living in the territory of the Member States". There is no reference to citizens of the Union, even though the formulation is fairly unwieldy in English. It would be later that the provisions inserted into the Third Pillar would define the area for these purposes by reference to citizens.

By 19 February 1997 the opening wording had reached the stage it would have in the final version but the format had not: "In order to establish an area of freedom, security and justice in which the free movement of persons is ensured as provided for in Article 7a [14], the Council shall adopt appropriate measures in the following areas... "[14] Then by 19 March it had arrived at the form which would be included in the Treaty: "In order to establish progressively an area of freedom security and justice, the Council shall adopt: (a) – (e)".[15]

In the 19 February paper, the Secretariat was still seeking agreement on the content. By 19 March the Dutch Presidency came off the fence:

"The Presidency proposals in this area have a two-fold objective: creating a new Title in the TEC containing provisions on free movement of persons, asylum and immigration (Part B below) and strengthening the provisions on police and judicial co-operation in criminal matters in Title VI of the TEU (Part C below). This overarching objective is made explicit in a redrafted Article B, fourth indent (Part A below), which stresses the link between free movement of persons and flanking measures to ensure the safety of individuals."[16]

It was in the form of this 19 March paper that the new Title was inserted into the EC Treaty establishing an area of freedom, security and justice. Throughout the negotiating process the Secretariat had been careful to seek to ensure that the beneficiaries of the area should not be exclusively defined as citizens of the Union. This intention was reflected in Title IV EC though not in Title VI TEU. One of the striking points, though, about the final form of the Title was that the creation of the area had been cut free from the abolition of intra-Member State border controls. This was now a subsection of the area's objective. This change took place rather late in the drafting process appearing in the 19 March draft. As a result the provision rather lost its shape. On the one hand, by cutting off the reference to Article 14 and the abolition of intra-Member State

---

13 Non-Paper CONF/3811/97, Brussels 3 February 1997 which was published on the Internet by an MEP.
14 CONF/3823/97.
15 CONF/3849/97.
16 CONF/3849/97.

border controls from the opening paragraph and setting it out as one of the objectives to be achieved along with asylum and immigration policy, it could be argued that there is greater independence of the concept of the area from the context of control free movement across intra-Member State borders. On the other hand, it creates a contrast between objectives which are border control related and those which relate to the establishment of the area. The rationality of this division is not self-evident.

Another question which the establishment of an area raises is its relationship with the internal market. The geographical scope of the two appears to be the same. The internal market, however, having come into existence with the EC Treaty in 1957 predates the area. It was revitalised in 1987 with the SEA. It comprises "an area without internal frontiers in which the free movement of goods, persons, services and capital is ensured in accordance with the provisions of this Treaty." The internal market is an economic market which is structured around trade. The area of freedom, security and justice is about something else: it is about civil liberties, individual freedoms and security. However, it is a rather divided area as fundamental aspects of civil liberties, such as the right to citizenship and to vote are contained elsewhere in the Treaty: specifically in Part Two, Citizenship of the Union.

The assessment of the creation of the new area is now underway. The Parliament's Civil Liberties Committee produced a working document in November 1998 where it confirmed that in its view the creation of an area of freedom, security and liberty is critical to the new Treaty and is second in importance only to monetary union.[17]

Duff agrees with the Civil Liberties Committee that this is the biggest innovation of the Amsterdam Treaty: to substantiate the competences of the European Union in the field of civil liberties:

> "Between the time of Maastricht and Amsterdam the question of the rights of citizens, residents and aliens of the European Union emerged as a driving force of European integration. The Dutch government brought to the presidency their existing lively concerns about the efficacy of Schengen. The changes made at Amsterdam to the Maastricht settlement were in the event dramatic: visa, asylum and immigration were transplanted from the third pillar into the first... the Schengen Agreement was brought within the purview of the European Union... "[18]

The overwhelming concern of the Dutch Government was, in fact, to find a solution to the unstable framework of the Schengen co-operation which was resulting in inefficiency.

---

17 European Parliament, Working Document PE 228.961 6 November 1998.
18 A. Duff, The Amsterdam Treaty, Text and Commentary, Federal Trust, 1997, pp. 8-9.

The area of freedom, security and justice does have another home: in Title VI of the Treaty on European Union: provisions on police and judicial co-operation in criminal matters. At Article 29:

"Without prejudice to the powers of the European Community, the Union's objectives shall be to provide citizens with a high level of safety within an area of freedom, security and justice by developing common action among the Member States in the fields of police and judicial co-operation in criminal matters and by preventing and combating racism and xenophobia."

The limitation of the benefit of the objective to "citizens" raises a number of questions. Within Duff's framework of the development of civil liberties, traditionally these have been the settlement between the State and the citizen, the demarcation of powers and authority.[19] In the rights discourse on immigration and asylum within the Union, emphasis has been placed on fulfilling human rights standards as set out in the conventions and treaties encompassing them. This fits into the identification of aliens and refugees as inside the boundaries of human rights treaties but the inadvertent beneficiaries of civil liberties, the framework of citizens.

In December 1998 the Council and the Commission published a joint Action Plan on how best to implement the provisions of the Treaty of Amsterdam establishing an area of freedom, security and justice.[20] The two institutions are in agreement that there is a need to reflect on the general approach and philosophy inherent in the concept of an "area of freedom, security and justice". In their opinion "The three notions are closely inter-linked. Freedom loses much of its meaning if it cannot be enjoyed in a secure environment and with the full backing of a system of justice in which all Union citizens and residents can have confidence."[21] The Action Plan goes on to divide up the area into three and consider each part: freedom, security and justice separately. The intention, reflected through the negotiations of the Treaty that the area applies to all those resident in the Union is expressed here as well.

As regards an area of freedom the Action Plan notes:

"Freedom in the sense of free movement of people within the European Union remains a fundamental objective of the Treaty, and one to which the flanking

---

19 A. Giddens, *Modernity and Self-Identity: Self and Society in the Late Modern Age*, Stanford University Press, Stanford.
20 Action Plan of the Council and the Commission on how best to implement the provisions of the Treaty of Amsterdam establishing an area of freedom, security and justice, OJ 1999 C 19/1.
21 Action Plan of the Council and the Commission on how best to implement the provisions of the Treaty of Amsterdam establishing an area of freedom, security and justice, OJ 1999 C 19/1, para 5.

measures associated with the concepts of security and justice must make their essential contribution. The Schengen achievement has shown the way and provides the foundation on which to build. However, the Amsterdam Treaty also opens the way to giving "freedom" a meaning beyond free movement of people across internal borders. It is also freedom to live in a law-abiding environment in the knowledge that public authorities are using everything in their individual and collective power (nationally, at the level of the Union and beyond) to combat and contain those who seek to deny or abuse that freedom."[22]

The primacy of the objective of free movement of persons would appear to be accepted within the hierarchy of objectives and the other concepts of security and justice appear to be considered as flanking measures. Justice is termed a flanking measure of freedom. Further, it is not entirely clear what the concept of freedom means in general. Instead of it being the fundamental baseline in the relationship between the individual and the state according to the Action Plan it seems to have acquired a degree of horizontal effect. The idea upon which the European Convention on Human Rights is based that the power of the state must be limited or exercised so as to be consistent with the freedoms of the individual[23] appears no longer to be central. The Action Plan is suggesting that the power of the state must be exercised in order to regulate the division of freedoms between individuals.[24]

The form of the new area which provides powers to the Community in the field of immigration and asylum is fundamentally permissive. It permits action to be taken but in few cases specifies what sort of action must be taken. Therefore the implementing measures which are put forward are of great importance. They will give content to what is at the moment an empty shell. While the Member States share the right of initiative for the first five years after

---

22 Action Plan of the Council and the Commission on how best to implement the provisions of the Treaty of Amsterdam establishing an area of freedom, security and justice, OJ 1999 C 19/1.

23 For instance Articles 3 and 8 ECHR: first the state must not engage in torture, inhuman or degrading treatment – a freedom to the individual against the power of the state which obligation is absolute; secondly the state must not intervene with the private and family life of the individual but subject to specific provisos where such interference is permitted in order to achieve, *inter alia*, a balance between the freedoms of different individuals where those overlap.

24 For a general discussion on the nature of human rights see for instance P. van Dijk & Van Hoof, The Theory and the Practice of the European Convention on Human Rights, 2nd Edition, Kluwer Law and Tax Publishers, Deventer, 1990.

entry into force of the Amsterdam Treaty, it seems likely that the Commission will be expected to put forward proposals for measures.[25]

9.3.   THE INTERNAL MARKET AND AN AREA OF FREEDOM, SECURITY AND JUSTICE

In pursuit of the overarching objective of establishing the new area, a division occurs. First, there are measures which need to be adopted in order to secure free movement of persons in conformity with Article 14 (the internal market without controls on movement of persons). This object finds its clear validity in Article 3 EC, its subordination, therefore in Title IV to the area of freedom, security and justice, which only has tangential validity in the task of the Community is not satisfactory. Secondly, there are measures which are not attached to the completion of the internal market, but only to the creation of the new area. Each category of measures deserves attention separately.

Article 61 Title IV EC sets out the categories of measures which need to be adopted. However, these must be understood in the light of the Schengen Protocol to the Treaty. The Schengen experiment is now officially over – its fruits are inserted into the EC Treaty or the TEU depending on whether the content is immigration/asylum or policing/security oriented. The Protocol defines the Schengen fruit as an "acquis" which consists of the 1985 Agreement, the 1990 Convention and the decisions of the Executive Committee. Many parts of the Schengen acquis as defined cover the issue of abolition of intra-Member State border controls, flanking measures in the form of external border controls and importantly the Schengen Information System, which among other things contains the details of persons (third country nationals) who are *prima facie* inadmissible to the territory of the Schengen countries. Therefore a second source of implementing measures for Article 61 EC may be discerned.

Internal Market Measures

These are measures to give effect to Article 14 EC, the abolition of intra-Member State controls on persons "in conjunction with directly related flanking measures on external border controls, asylum and immigration". These are

---

25 See the reply on behalf of the Council to G. Hager MEP's question P-2933/98 (OJ C 135/140 of 14.5.1999. This is notwithstanding the fact that the first proposals under the new title were tabled by the Finnish Presidency in the second half of 1999 (a Directive form of the Eurodac Convention on fingerprinting asylum seekers; and some months later the Commission proposed a Directive on Family Reunion).

given specificity in Articles 62(1) as regards the principle and 62(2) and (3) and Article 63(1)(a) and (2)(a) on flanking measures. I will return shortly to the content of each of these. But reference is also made to the need for measures under Article 31(e) TEU "progressively adopting measures establishing minimum rules relating to the constituent elements of criminal acts and to penalties in the fields of organised crime, terrorism and illicit drug trafficking." A five-year time limit is placed on the adoption of such measures but it is unclear what penalty could result from failure to achieve agreement by that deadline.

Measures designed to implement free movement of persons

Article	Content
62(2)EC	Measures on the crossing of external borders including border procedures, visa rules and countries (including both white and black lists), formats and procedures for issue.
62(3)EC	Conditions under which third country nationals may travel within the Union for up to three months.
63(1)(a)EC	Criteria and mechanisms for determining which Member State is responsible for considering an application for asylum submitted by a third country national within the Union's territory.
63(2)(a)EC	Minimum standards for giving temporary protection to displaced persons from third countries who cannot return to their country of origin and for persons who otherwise need international protection.
31(e)TEU	Progressively adopting measures establishing minimum rules relating to the constituent elements of criminal acts and to penalties in the fields of organised crime, terrorism and illicit drug trafficking.

Article 62(2) requires the adoption of measures[26] on the crossing of the external frontier which establish:

(a) Standards and procedures to be followed by Member States in carrying out checks on persons at such borders.

This competence reflects the Commission's proposal in 1993 for an external frontier convention which remained unadopted.[27] Again this subject matter is

---

26 In the November 1996 Presidency Note this was referred to as "provisions".
27 OJ 1994 C 11.

covered by the Schengen acquis though exactly what that means is not entirely transparent. In the Presidency Note of 11 November 1996[28] the wording was almost identical: "standards and detailed procedures for carrying out checks at such borders". A slight amount of precision has been inserted after that draft, i.e. that it refers to checks on persons.

(b) Rules on visas for intended stays of no more than three months, including:

(i)   The list of third countries whose nationals must be in possession of visas when crossing the external borders and those whose nationals are exempt from that requirement. This provision now covers the disputed territory discussed in the last chapter: black, grey and white lists. The new competence indicates that the issue is now to be settled in the way in which both the Commission and the European Parliament requested: the creation of a right for nationals of some countries to resist a visa requirement proposed by a Member State relying on the right given to the individual by the Community. This indicates that at least to some extent a new personal relationship is intended between the individual third country national and the Community. However, as in respect of Community law provisions considered earlier, this relationship is again dependent on the nationality of the individual concerned. I have considered this question in some depth above in chapter 8. The fact that the Schengen acquis which has now been introduced by protocol into the EC Treaty already includes a visa list which is only "black" and "white" means that the individual relationship has already been established between the individual and the Community at least for 12 of the 15 Member States.

(ii) The procedures and conditions for issuing visas by Member States.
      This subject matter is covered by the Schengen acquis. However, one problem for the individual here is that the procedures and conditions for issuing visas to individuals in the Schengen acquis is based on the principle of refusal (another is the secrecy which surrounds the Schengen rules on the issue of visas). The Schengen Implementing Convention contains the list of reasons for refusing a visa but there is nowhere any mention of an entitlement to a visa. Therefore while rejection is mandatory through the SIS and permitted in exercise of discretion, no positive duty towards the individual arises. The issue of the visas remains a matter of discretion for the issuing authority. This creates a problem as regards the consistency which the Schengen acquis is supposed to have. While the negative consistency works, (the

---

28 CONF/3976/96.

individual is refused consistently a visa on the basis of the Schengen acquis) positive consistency does not exist: the grant of a visa depends on the national approaches and considerations of each issuing officer.

(iii) A uniform format for visas. This has already been the subject of Community legislation and was discussed in the preceding chapter in some depth. An important aspect here is that any information which is held on the visa must be verifiable by the individual with a right to have information corrected if it is inaccurate or irrelevant.

(iv) Rules on a uniform visa. This power holds the key to the importance of (ii) the procedures and conditions for issuing visas. Only under an approach where a uniform visa, once issued is valid for entry into the entirety of the territory, can the system actually work.

In the Presidency Note of November 1996, this list of activities on borders was substantially shorter. The list of third countries whose nationals require a visa was included, as were the procedures and conditions for issuing visas and the uniform visa. But also included were "the categories of visa and their territorial validity". By the Dublin II draft this had disappeared. However, the rules on the uniform visa did not enter the picture until the 19 March 1997 draft. No explanation was contained as to why the change had taken place. In my opinion it is not fundamental. It does no more than clarify that the rules on issue which could also be interpreted as included in procedures and conditions, are definitely covered.

Article 62(3) requires the adoption of measures setting out the conditions under which nationals of third countries shall have the freedom to travel within the territory of the Member States during a period of no more than three months. This issue has been the subject of a proposal by the Commission in 1995 which remains unadopted.[29] This proposal covers a wide group of persons: third country nationals resident in the Union and third country nationals who have just entered the territory on a uniform visa or otherwise. As regards third country nationals already resident in the Union, the basis for enjoying the right to travel is possession of a status evidenced by a document included in a list notified by each Member State to the Commission and other Member States.[30]

---

29 Proposal for a Council Directive on the right of third country nationals to travel in the Community, OJ 1995 C 306.

30 Article 3(4) of the Proposal for a Council Directive on the right of third country nationals to travel in the Community, OJ 1995 C 306 "Member States shall provide the Commission and the other Member States with a list of the documents they issue which are treated as equivalent to residence permits for the purposes of this Article, updating it as and when necessary."

As regards third country nationals visiting the Union, either admission to the territory of one of the Member States or a uniform visa is regarded as sufficient.

In the Presidency Note of November 1996, the wording was somewhat different: "provisions in relation to freedom of movement of nationals of third countries on the territory of the Union." This is a much wider formulation than that eventually chosen. In the Dublin II draft this has changed almost to the final wording except that the expression "free movement" is still included rather than the final wording "freedom to travel". Again it is the 19 March draft which includes the final wording. The incorporation of the Schengen acquis means that for 13 of the 15 Member States rules on freedom to travel for up to three months within the territory of the 13 are part of Community law. According to Articles 19-24 of the Schengen Implementing Convention 1990, the admission or Schengen visa must be valid throughout the Schengen States.[31]

Article 63(1)(a) moves to a rather different field: responsibility for asylum determination. It requires criteria and mechanisms to be adopted within five years for determining which Member State is responsible for considering an application for asylum submitted by a national of a third country in one of the Member States. This is the subject matter of the Dublin Convention 1990 which finally entered into force in September 1997.[32]

The only difference from the Presidency Note of November 1996 in respect of this provision is that the earlier proposal did not specifically refer to third country nationals. This did however appear by the time of the Dublin II draft. There are two sources for the change. First, it was inserted as part of the discussion about the Protocol limiting the right of asylum in the Union to third country nationals which was eventually included in a watered down form as a Protocol to the Treaty. This Protocol, which was insisted upon by the Spanish delegation was intended to limit if not exclude the possibility that a national of one Member State could seek or obtain asylum in another Member State. It was substantially criticised by UNHCR and a number of non-governmental organisations as incompatible with the Geneva Convention. This discussion is an example of the problem which arises in a Union which is less than a complete union but more than a Treaty: while it is acceptable that in the USA a resident of one state should not be able to seek asylum in another US state, the European Union has not reached the same level of integration, nor indeed is it clear that it will do so. Until the Community itself has become a party to the

---

31 House of Lords Select Committee on the European Communities, Incorporating the Schengen Acquis into the European Union, Session 1997/98, 31st Report, paras. 20 *et seq.*

32 OJ 1997 C 254/1.

relevant human rights conventions which protect displaced persons and refugees, this unity cannot be accepted for the purposes of defining refugees and displaced persons. The second source of the amendment is Article 1 of the Dublin Convention which defines asylum seekers as excluding nationals of the Member States.

Article 63(2)(a) requires the establishment of minimum standards for giving temporary protection to displaced persons from third countries who cannot return to their country of origin and for persons who otherwise need international protection. It is not entirely clear why minimum standards on temporary protection are required by Article 14 more than, for instance, minimum standards on reception of asylum seekers[33] or minimum standards on procedures with respect to qualification of nationals of third countries as refugees.[34] In more than one Member State there has been discussion about the need to reduce reception standards for asylum seekers in order to deter persons from coming to that State as opposed to some other Member State[35] while the courts in more than one Member State have been concerned about the lack of uniform minimum standards on procedures and appeal rights.[36] The problem of minimum standards on procedure is one of fairness and confidence. It is vital to the system of discouraging so called secondary movement by asylum seekers within the Union that it gives enough confidence to the asylum seeker to pursue his or her application in the country where he or she is rather than to seek to better his or her chances in another Member State. In my opinion a system of allocation of responsibility for asylum seekers among the Member States is flawed if it does not include an equivalent standard in all these areas. The establishment of minimum standards does not satisfy the legitimate demand of any asylum seeker, if he or she is to be excluded from the procedure in another Member State, that his or her treatment and the consideration of his or her claim for protection is subject to a standard equivalent

---

33 Article 63(1)(b) EC.
34 Article 63(1)(c) EC.
35 The UK has introduced a system of vouchers rather than social security payments for asylum seekers notwithstanding the fact that it is more expensive than admitting such persons to the social security system on the ground that it acts as a deterrent to asylum seekers, the Asylum and Immigration Act 1999. Similarly, the Dutch government has introduced a system of no social assistance to asylum seekers who are deemed to have arrived from another Member State as an incentive to them either not to come or to 'disappear' again.
36 S. Peers, Mind the Gap, Refugee Council and ILPA, London 1998; see also national jurisprudence in the UK on the safety of procedures in other Member States and the application of the Dublin Convention in A. Nicol QC and S. Harrison, Lessons of the Dublin Convention, European Journal or Migration and Law, Vol. 1, Issue 2, 1999.

to the highest in any Member State. So long as there is one Member State where the claim is more likely to be accepted than that where it is processed, the individual's right to protection arising from Articles 3 ECHR and the UN Convention Against Torture is not fully respected if he or she is excluded from making a claim in that State as a result of a negative decision by another Member State with only a "minimum" standard. Nevertheless, these issues, which might be considered of importance to the achievement of the abolition of intra-Member States border controls, are not designated as necessary to that end. Rather it is temporary protection which the Title states is necessary to the proper working of the internal market. These other considerations are necessary to the establishment of an area of freedom, security and justice.

There is no similar provision in the November 1996 draft. In the Dublin II draft there is included "rights of displaced persons from third countries who cannot be sent back to their country of origin". In the March 19 draft this has finally changed to "conditions for giving temporary protection to displaced persons from third countries who cannot return to their country of origin and to persons who otherwise need international protection." Again there is no mention in the commentary as to why the wording has changed.

9.4.   TEMPORARY PROTECTION: THE COMMISSION'S PROPOSAL DURING THE NEGOTIATIONS

The Commission proposed in March 1997 a Joint Action concerning temporary protection.[37] Although it predates the signing of the Amsterdam Treaty it was clearly adopted with a view to the new competence. Following discussion in the Council it was amended and republished in August 1998.[38] It deserves some attention as the opening statement by the Commission on its view of this part of the new powers and how they should be exercised. Two characteristics of the proposal deserve immediate attention: first, in comparison with the proposals put forward by the Member States on immigration and asylum, this one was very carefully prepared. It included a full explanatory memorandum with a detailed explanation of why the measure was being proposed and what it contained. Secondly, the proposal was almost immediately available in all the

---

37 Proposal to the Council for a Joint Action based on Article K.3(2)(b) of the Treaty on European Union concerning temporary Protection of displaced persons OJ 1997 C 106/13. This was subsequently amended and republished following discussions in the Council OJ 1998 C 268/13 and 268/22.

38 OJ 1998 C 268/13.

Community's official language to the Parliament[39] and from there to other interested parties. This represented a very substantial change from the practice of the Member States working within the Third Pillar where measures were only made public *after* adoption which limited the effectiveness of public discussion and debate on contents.[40]

The political agenda of the Member States had an important bearing on the shape of the Joint Action. By March 1997 the issue of temporary protection of displaced persons had become particularly hot in the Member States *not* as regards the admission of displaced persons but in respect of their return. The beginning of the civil war in the former Yugoslavia and Bosnia in particular took place before the coming into force of the Treaty on European Union. The Member States' response to that civil war and the admission of displaced persons from the region was almost entirely based on national considerations and political pressure.[41] The Member States agreed a Resolution on 1.6.1993 on Certain Common Guidelines as regards the Admission of Particularly Vulnerable Persons from the Former Yugoslavia[42] however it remains very unclear whether this Resolution had much, if any, impact on national admission policies. The Resolution was adopted under the Danish Presidency of the Union. There has been no published examination by the Council of the application of this measure.

The situation had changed dramatically by the winter of 1996 and spring of 1997. Some Member States, and Germany in particular, had reached the conclusion that following the Dayton Peace Accord it was time for the Bosnians to go back. Other Member States, however, were less committed to return of Bosnians, in particular those Member States which had not admitted very many

---

39 The proposal for a joint action based on Article K.3(2)(b) of the Treaty on European Union concerning temporary protection of displaced persons is *the first joint action* to be proposed by the Commission on which the European Parliament has been consulted in advance by the Council of Ministers". European Parliament, Draft Report on the proposal to the Council for a Joint Action based on Article K.3(2)(b) of the Treaty on European Union concerning temporary protection of displaced persons to Committee on Civil Liberties and Internal Affairs by Jan Kees Wiebenga MEP PE 222.716; DOC EN/PR/326/326339 para. 1.

40 A number of national parliaments had made arrangements with their administrations to have access to proposals under the Third Pillar before adoption, such as the House of Lords in the UK and the Tweede Kamer in the Netherlands, but such arrangements were specific to the national forum.

41 For a more complete consideration of the issue see J. van Selm-Thorburn, *Refugee Protection in Europe: Lessons of the Yugoslav Crisis*, Kluwer Law International, The Hague, 1998.

42 For text see: E. Guild & J. Niessen, *The Developing Immigration and Asylum Policies of the European Union*, Kluwer Law International, The Hague, 1996, p. 293.

Bosnians in the first instance .[43] The difference of treatment of Bosnians with temporary protection in the Member States was politically problematic, particularly for those states eager to encourage or enforce return. In particular, in the Netherlands, Belgium and Sweden where enforced return was not planned as in Germany, the possibility of a rush of asylum applications from Bosnians who had enjoyed temporary protection in Germany but were now under threat of expulsion was highly unwelcome. Clearly, if the Union was to have a credible policy on displaced persons some co-ordination on the treatment of persons had to be achieved.[44] Equally clearly, as the response to the civil war in Bosnia had been so different in the Member States this was an area where it was unlikely that any one Member State would be able to broker an agreement, therefore the room for manoeuvre for the Commission was particularly wide.

The proposal revolved around the concept of a "temporary protection regime". The preamble confirmed not only the duty under the TEU to comply with the Geneva Convention and specifically the duty of non-refoulement, but also the non-refoulement duty under the ECHR. The Council would be given the power to decide to establish a temporary protection regime on its own initiative.[45] In so doing it must consider two aspects when making the decision: first, is there a mass influx of persons in need of international protection? This is defined as "a significant number of persons" whose safe return under humane conditions is impossible. Guidance is given: this is intended to include persons who have fled armed conflict; who are at serious risk of human rights abuses including on a group basis, and persons otherwise presumed to need protection. Secondly, can adequate protection be found in the region of origin? No guidance was given on this.

The decision to establish a temporary protection regime must specify the groups of persons to whom it applies and its duration. The proposal acknowledged that people who are refugees in accordance with the Geneva Convention will be covered also by the temporary protection regime. However, as one

---

43 For example the UK recorded 5,635 asylum applications from the former Yugoslavia in 1992, 1,830 in 1993, 1,385 in 1994, 1,565 in 1995 and 1,030 in 1996 (Control of Immigration Statistics United Kingdom 1996, Cm 3737). On 18 July 1997 the UK announced that all Bosnians living in the UK with temporary refuge would not be required to return to Bosnia and would be allowed to settle in the UK (Statement: Immigration Minister Mike O'Brian MP 18.7.97). Also see J. Van Selm-Thorburn, *Refugee Protection in Europe: Lessons of the Yugoslav Crisis*, Kluwer Law International, The Hague, 1998.

44 According to the preamble of the Joint Action: "Whereas such a co-ordinated approach should demonstrate solidarity between the Member States and reflect Europe's humanitarian tradition, thus ensuring that all persons in need of international protection and within their jurisdiction are treated in conformity with human dignity;"

45 Article 3.

of the purposes of the measure is to deal with mass influxes where the national administration cannot cope with processing individual asylum applications the general protection of the regime takes priority.[46] Until a regime is to be phased out or in any event for a period not exceeding five years, Member States do not need to consider individual applications for asylum under the Geneva Convention from people enjoying temporary protection in accordance with a regime.

This has particularly important consequences as regards the rights which persons covered by a temporary protection regime are to be afforded. As the regime is intended to "displace" recognition under the Geneva Convention for a period of time at least if the persons covered by it are not entitled to rights equal to or at least approaching those guaranteed to refugees under the Geneva Convention, the whole system of regimes would risk falling into disrepute and be open to allegations of abuse as a means to deprive Geneva Convention refugees of rights to which they are entitled. For the non-governmental sector, the concern that temporary protection regimes may be used to reduce rights of refugees was the most consistent criticism.[47]

Rights for Persons Protected

According to the original proposal, therefore, persons covered by a temporary protection regime would be entitled to the following:[48]

(a) a residence authorisation for the duration of the regime;

(b) family reunification with spouses and minor and dependent children;

(c) access to engage in gainful activity which must include both employment and self-employment and equal treatment with refugees as regards social security;

(d) all necessary support in particular with regard to means of subsistence and medical care;

(e) access to public education under the same conditions as recognised refugees.

However, in respect of housing the Member States would only be under a duty to "endeavour to provide" housing facilities similar to those granted to

---

46 Article 10.

47 See for instance Briefing on the Proposal for a Joint Action on Temporary Protection from the European Council on Refugees and Exiles, and Justice Briefing July 1997.

48 According to the amended proposal these rights only apply after the person has received authorisation from the national authorities.

recognised refugees.[49] A saving provision was included that more favourable national treatment would not be affected by the minimum requirements of the Joint Action.[50]

In comparison with the Geneva Convention these rights include the most important which differentiate refugee status from humanitarian status in many European states. There are differences, in particular, the definition of family members who should be allowed to join a principal in a Member State falls below that recommended in the UNHCR Handbook.

Phasing Out a Regime

The procedure for phasing out a temporary protection regime would involve the following: first, the Commission must prepare a report at least once a year and in any event six months before the end of a temporary protection regime (the duration of the regime is set at the beginning when it is opened).[51] The Report must assess the situation in the country of origin, the application of the temporary protection regime and its financial implications. It is submitted to the Parliament and Council. Thereafter, the Council by qualified majority vote[52] at least three months before the end of the regime must decide: to revise the decision on the regime (i.e. extend its duration); or phase out the regime in which case the *Council* decides on the return of persons concerned and if the situation in the country of origin allows a safe return under humane conditions.[53]

While non-governmental organisations concerned with the protection of refugees and displaced persons supported the extension of common social rights to displaced persons under the proposal they were less enthusiastic about the power by qualified majority vote to determine whether the circumstances in a country of origin are such as to justify a decision to return refugees and displaced persons. Under the initial proposal if no decision was taken to phase out a regime within five years of its introduction "Member States should examine whether long-term measures should be introduced for beneficiaries of temporary protection".[54] This was very unclear and left people protected under a regime in a very insecure position potentially indefinitely. As the European Parliament's rapporteur put it "displaced persons must not be left in uncertainty for an indefinite period, as would be more or less the case as the joint action

---

49 Article 9(1).
50 Article 2(3).
51 Article 4.
52 Article 12.
53 Article 4.
54 Article 13.

stands. This would be inhuman. As time passes, after all, people gradually become used to or settle in the host country. They go to work, the children go to school, they learn the language, etc."[55]

As a first indication from the Treaty's guardian, the Commission, of its intentions under the new competences, what can be discerned as regards the relationship of the individual, Member State and Community from the proposal? First, between the Council and the Commission the division of power is that the Council alone may open, revise or phase out a scheme. It appears that it is for the Council to assess what a mass influx of persons is and which groups of persons should benefit from the scheme. The Commission is responsible for preparation of a report on the country of origin, the application of the scheme and financial implications. The Member States are under a duty to ensure the rights guaranteed to temporarily protected persons are accorded to them. As the rights to individuals are mandatory and their effect appears clear, precise and unconditional, they should give rise to direct effect. For instance, Article 7 in respect of family reunification: "Member States shall ensure that beneficiaries of a temporary protection regime have the right to family reunification with respect to their spouses and dependent children." Where a Member State refused to ensure such family reunion the individual beneficiary is likely to be able to rely directly on Article 7 against the Member State to require it to do so.

Therefore as regards the opening of a scheme and the definition of its beneficiaries, only the Council has power to decide. The Member States' relationship with the Community changes in that they must comply with the Council's decision[56] regarding a regime although this does not require any Member State actually to admit any person to cross the border, (leaving aside family reunification) it does require the Member States to act in certain ways towards persons already within their borders. Thus the relationship between the Member State and the individual changes: the individual would become entitled to various rights by virtue of an analogous measure adopted under Article 63(2)(a) EC upon which the person may rely in the event of the failure of the Member State to accord those rights. However, the individual also forfeits something: the "right" to have an application for asylum considered within a reasonable period of time. Article 10 permits the Member States to postpone

---

55 Report on the proposal to the Council for a Joint Action based on Article K.3(2)(b) of the Treaty on European Union concerning temporary protection of displaced persons (COM (97)0093 – C4-0247/97 – 97/0081 (CNS)) DOC EN/PR/326/326339; PE 222.716, 25 July 1997.

56 By qualified majority voting according to Article 12(1).

for five years[57] or until the end of the regime the consideration of asylum applications made under the Geneva Convention. No provision is made for postponement of applications made under Article 3 ECHR though as yet it is unclear whether this right extends beyond a right of non-refoulement. So the Community in its relationship with the individual in effect blocks the individual's right under an international human rights convention designed to protect him or her, the trade off being the extension of other rights which the Community the guarantees against the Member States.

Is the deferral of rights in international law by Community legislation lawful? If the rights in two categories are virtually the same does it matter if they are called by different names? A classic international law perspective would find this was the case as anything less than the standard agreed internationally will not engage the international protection. Therefore States which grant a status which is differently named to persons who are refugees under the Geneva Convention may in fact be depriving the individual of the recognition in international law to which he or she is entitled. Does this matter? In theory it is very important as it goes to the heart of the international solidarity which underlies the Geneva Convention – recognition in international law of the individual. In practice its initial consequences are no right to a refugee travel document, exclusion from the scope of the Community's regulation on co-ordination of social security (Regulation 1408/71) and inclusion in the proposal for a Directive on Eurodac regarding the fingerprinting of asylum seekers.

If regard is had to the approach of the UN Human Rights Committee in its supervisory role in respect of the ICCPR, state succession cannot have the effect of depriving an individual of rights addressed to him or her by an international human rights instrument.[58] If state succession cannot have that effect then it is unlikely that the transfer of power to regulate an area of fundamental human rights to a supra national body could have that effect either once exercised. In both cases what is at stake is the shift of responsibility from one body to another.

In the context of the European norms, the matter is even more pressing. The European Court of Human Rights following two decades or more of quiescence regarding the human rights consequences of Community law[59] has

---

57 In the revised version this time period is reduced to three years extendable for a further two years if the Council has adopted a measure to phase out a scheme.

58 UN Human Rights Committee's Decision on State Succession to the Obligations of the Former Yugoslavia under the International Covenant on Civil and Political Rights, (1993) 15 EHRR p. 233.

59 See D. Spielman, Human Rights Case Law in the Strasbourg and Luxembourg Courts: Conflicts, Inconsistencies and Complementarities, in P. Alston (ed.), *The EU and Human Rights*, Oxford University Press, Oxford, 2000.

recently opened the debate of the rights of individuals in the light of Community obligations. In a case regarding the right to vote in European Parliament elections of a British national resident in Gibraltar, the Court held that notwithstanding the transfer of competences to the European Community, Contracting States remained responsible for ensuring that ECHR rights were guaranteed. Contracting States were responsible under the Convention and its Protocols for the consequences of international treaties entered into subsequent to the applicability of the ECHR guarantees.[60] Accordingly if the level of protection in Community law does not fulfill the requirements of, for instance Article 3 ECHR, then the Member States will remain responsible for compliance with the ECHR duty irrespective of the Community rule. So long as the Community rules are no more than "minimum" standards, the Member States' adoption of higher standards to comply with their ECHR obligations does not undermine the Community legal order. However, such a situation would make a mockery of the Community's *soi disante* commitment to human rights standards *inter alia* as found in the ECHR.

In practice, the problem of temporary protection regimes is more likely to be the restrictions placed on entry and decisions on ending, either through the refusal of the Council to open a regime at all or by a very narrow definition of the persons entitled to protection under the regime. In neither of these cases is there scope for the individual to challenge the decision. While the individual could challenge a Member States' interpretation of the personal scope of a regime he or she could not challenge the Council's decision. So, where a person is outside a regime, there is no Community intermediary either between the individual and the Member State or between the individual and his or her right in international law.

I have now considered all the powers which the new Title IV EC gives to the Community in order to achieve free movement of persons within the internal market. In so doing I have analysed in some depth the fullest draft measure which had been produced with the new power in mind by the Commission in order to extract some indication of what the respective roles of the individual, Community and Member State may be once the powers are exercised. It is now time to turn to those powers which are given to the Community exclusively to achieve an area of freedom, security and justice.

---

60 *Matthews v UK.* 18.2.1999, 24833/94.

Freedom, Security and Justice Measures

The measures in relation to immigration and asylum the purpose of which is exclusively attached to the establishment of the area of freedom, justice and security are as follows:

Measures to implement an area of freedom, security and justice

Article	Content
62(1)	The absence of any controls on persons crossing internal borders.
63(1)(b)	Minimum standards on reception of asylum seekers.
63(1)(c)	Minimum standards with respect of qualification as a refugee.
63(1)(d)	Minimum standards on procedures for grant and withdrawal of refugee status.
63(2)(b)	Promoting a balance of effort between Member States in receiving and bearing the consequences of receiving refugees and displaced persons.
63(3)(a)	Measures on immigration policy including conditions of entry and residence, and standards on procedures for issue of long-term residence visas and residence permits including for family reunion.
63(3)(b)	Illegal immigration and illegal residence, including repatriation of illegal residents.
63(4)	Measures defining the rights and conditions under which nationals of third countries who are legally resident in a Member State may reside in other Member States.

I have already questioned whether the powers in relation to refugees and displaced persons can properly be ascribed to the new area of freedom, security and justice rather than the completion of the internal market. Similar questions also arise, *par excellence*, in respect of Article 62(1) the abolition of controls on persons moving between the Member States and Article 63(4) the rights of resident third country nationals. Surely the freedom to move and reside for them is intimately connected with the completion of the internal market. I shall now look at the provisions one by one, examining their scope.

Article 62(1): this is not specified as attaching to the internal market though it is the framework of the internal market. It must be considered then that as an implementing measure to the internal market, which too is in fact part of implementing the area of freedom, security and justice.

In the Presidency Note of November 1996, there was no division between the development of the area and the internal market provisions (see above on the meaning of the area). In that draft the wording was "provisions aimed at abolishing controls on people at internal borders". In the Dublin II draft, this had become "measures consistent with the best possible security conditions and in compliance with Article 7a [14], with a view to ensuring the absence of any controls on persons, be they citizens of the Union or nationals of third countries, when crossing internal borders". The final text first appears in the Presidency note of 19 February 1997.

Article 63(1)(b) minimum standards on reception: Discussion on this issue took place under the Spanish Presidency but no proposal was brought forward.[61] In the November 1996 Presidency Note the reference here was to "conditions under which asylum seekers are received". In my view there is no substantial change to the meaning by the change of wording. Some Member States have appeared to accept that reception standards are a factor which attracts asylum seekers. The resulting policy, for example in the UK or the Netherlands, is an unseemly rush to the bottom – to have the worst or most limited access to reception facilities possible. Some Member States' systems of protection do not include fully-fledged arrangements for reception: will the European measures, then, mean a drop to that level for the others? Clearly in the drafting of measures in this area, as in all the others where there is a minimum standard to be set a standstill clause will need to be inserted to protect the standard in the States from erosion. Further, while the level set by the Community is a minimum, nonetheless it should not fall to a level which could be attacked as inhuman or degrading treatment contrary to Article 3 ECHR.

Article 63(1)(c) refers to minimum standards with respect to the qualification of nationals of third countries as refugees. In the Presidency Note of November 1996 this is covered by "basic rules on the right of asylum". By the Dublin II draft it has become "common rules with respect to the qualification of third country nationals as refugees". The reference to minimum standards is very important as it allows a margin upwards only to the Member States in their treatment of refugees and the persons whom they recognise as such. Of course the principle is contrary to the idea that there is a single definition of who is a refugee under the Geneva Convention in Community law. However, the concept of minimum standards must always be accompanied by a standstill

---

61 S. Peers, Building Fortress Europe: The Development of EU Migration Law, CML Rev 35: 1235-1272, [1999].

clause which prevents the introduction of measures which would diminish the rights or position of refugees and asylum seekers and the widening of differences between the legal regimes of the Member States. Further, the qualification of minimum standards may, in the future, give rise to litigation before the Court of Justice, not only in search of the correct and definitive definition of a Geneva Convention refugee for the purposes of Community law. It may also arise if the Community sticks with the idea of the Dublin Convention that asylum seekers should go to the first Member State through which they passed. If that first Member State should happen to have a lower standard, even though meeting the minimum required by this provision than the Member State where the asylum seeker made the application then it is questionable whether it is fair for the asylum seeker to be sent there as his or her rights under the national law of the State where he or she applied for asylum will not be respected. [62]

Article 63(1)(d): standards on procedures in Member States for granting or withdrawing refugee status: this remained fairly consistent through the negotiations: the Presidency Note of November 1996 states "procedure for granting or withdrawing refugee status". The key to the fairness of asylum determination is the procedure of a Member State. If the procedures are inadequate there will always be the risk that someone entitled to international protection has not been accorded it. Then the expulsion of that person could result in refoulement contrary to the Member States' obligations under the Geneva Convention or the ECHR. By qualifying the requirement to "minimum" standards again the Treaty opens the discussion on the fairness to the individual and the compatibility with international obligations of applying a limitation of one procedural consideration for an asylum claim within the Union territory. So long as there is a real chance that the procedure of another Member State would result in the recognition of the right of protection to the individual it will be contrary to the Member States international obligations to block the individuals access to the procedure in that other Member State.

Article 63(2)(b) permits the adoption of a measure promoting a balance of effort between Member States in receiving and bearing the consequences of receiving refugees and displaced persons. There is no deadline for adoption of a measure under this heading. Further while minimum standards for giving temporary protection are a requirement of the internal market, burden sharing (as this is by another name) is not needed for that purpose but as part of the

---

62 For a fuller discussion of the issue of international standards and supremacy of Community law see the introduction to E. Guild & G Lesieur, *The European Court of Justice and the European Convention on Human Rights: Who said what when*, Kluwer Law International, London, 1998.

new area of freedom, security and justice. The Council and the Commission have produced a number of attempts at covering this issue.[63] Agreement on burden sharing has been blocked primarily by a difference of opinion between Germany on the one hand and France and the UK on the other about what is appropriate. Burden sharing was included in the Commission original proposal on temporary protection discussed above.

Article 63(3)(a) enters the territory of immigration policy. This is the central measure on conditions of entry and residence, and standards of procedures for the issue of long term visas and residence permits including for family reunion. In the Presidency Note of November 1996 the wording was generally the same "harmonisation of conditions of entry and residence, and of procedures for issuing residence permits, including those for the purpose of family reunion." A critical aspect is that the word "harmonisation" has disappeared. Instead the concept of immigration policy is the central feature. In the first proposal a more ambitious approach was floated; one in which there would be very substantial centralisation of immigration law through harmonisation. By the end of the negotiations what could be agreed was a general power to adopt measures on immigration policy. The use of the term "policy" suggests a power directed towards wide brush objectives rather than technical, legal provisions as would be required to achieve harmonisation.

The Commission presented a very detailed proposal which was developed at the time of the negotiations and which covers this issue. Subsequently, in December 1999 it introduced a detailed proposal on family reunification which is based substantially on that proposal confirming the role of the proposal introduced during the negotiations as a "trail blazer" for future action. I will deal with this in some detail below but first I will briefly finish with the powers in search of an area of freedom, security and justice.

Article 63(3)(b) creates a power in respect of illegal immigration and illegal residence. In the November 1996 Presidency Note this was much more extensive: "measures to combat illegal entry and residence on the territory of the Member States by nationals of third countries, including provisions for the return of illegal immigrants to the third country of origin or transit." This did not change substantially until the 19 March 1997 draft where it became "combating illegal immigration and illegal residence". Although a number of resolutions have been adopted on this subject in the Third Pillar, the fundamental problem of

---

63 96/198/JHA: Council Decision of 4 March 1996 on an alert and emergency procedure for burden-sharing with regard to the admission and residence of displaced persons on a temporary basis OJ 1996 L 063/10; Council Resolution of 25 September 1995 on burden-sharing with regard to the admission and residence of displaced persons on a temporary basis OJ 1995 C 262/1.

defining irregularity or illegality remains problematic notwithstanding a first effort in the proposal for a Eurodac Directive. For example in a number of Member States' legal systems a grey zone occurs between issue of a residence permit and expulsion. Third country nationals may, on account of family circumstances in the host State or civil war in the state of origin, be un-removable, yet at the same time not eligible for the issue of a residence permit. The Community's power to combat illegal residence, then needs also to require the issue of permits to persons who are not expellable either in law or practice. The reference to third countries has sparked off one of the first competence debates of the Title: is the Community exclusively competent for the settlement of readmission agreements with third countries?

Article 63(4) contains the power to adopt measures to define the rights and conditions under which third country nationals legally resident in one Member State may take up residence in another Member State. This started in the November 1996 Presidency Note as "provisions relating to the rights of nationals of third countries who are legally resident in a Member State, including their rights in other Member States." It then changed in the Dublin II draft to "measures defining the rights of nationals of third countries who are legally resident in a Member State, including their right of establishment and their right to seek employment in other Member States." In the 19 February 1997 draft this had become "including the conditions of their residence and seeking employment in other Member States". In the 19 March 1997 draft it had changed again to "measures defining the conditions under which nationals of third countries who are legally resident in a Member State may reside and have access to employment in other Member States." The final version suppressed any reference to economic activity, apparently at the insistence of the German Chancellor. Whether this deletion is significant is uncertain. A power to adopt measures regarding employment and third country nationals already exists in Article 137 EC, the former Social Chapter. In addition, the Court has always held that a right to work includes a right to reside,[64] though it is by no means clear that the contrary would apply – i.e. a right to reside implies a right to work. In the joint Action Plan of 1999 the Council and Commission declared their intention to adopt measures under this article within five years of the entry into force of the Amsterdam Treaty. The Treaty itself does not require adoption of implementing measures within any fixed time frame.

---

64 C-237/91 *Kus* [1992] ECR I-6781.

9.5. IMMIGRATION POLICY: THE COMMISSION'S PROPOSAL AT THE TIME OF THE NEGOTIATIONS

Article 63(3)(a) provides for measures to be adopted on immigration policy (without a time limit) on the conditions of entry and residence, and standards on procedures for the issue by Member States of long term visas and residence permits, including those for the purpose of family reunion. The history of Third Pillar measures in the fields of family reunion, admission for employment and self-employment, students and others has been well described elsewhere.[65] I will not repeat that now but rather turn again to the proposal of the Commission for a Convention on rules for the admission of third country nationals to the Member States.[66]

This proposal appeared just over a month after the signature of the Amsterdam Treaty. While clearly it had been in preparation for a substantial period before that date, its appearance, like that of its sister document the Joint Action on temporary protection indicated the intentions of the Commission in its new role as guardian[67] of the competence for third country nationals about to be inserted into the EC Treaty.

The draft convention takes a global approach to immigration policy. "The Commission believes that the European Union needs a comprehensive approach for dealing with migration policy issues. The purpose of the proposal presented here is to establish a set of common rules for the Member States of the European Union regarding immigration of third country nationals." It covers three distinct areas: admission of third country nationals for stays of more than three months (including family reunification), family reunion for citizens of the Union who have never exercised a Treaty free movement right[68] and rights of long-term resident third country nationals in the European Union. I will consider the two aspects of the draft which are tied to the new Title powers: admission of third country nationals for the first time – discretion to the Member States subject to overriding principles; treatment of third country nationals long resident in the Union – working towards assimilation of

---

65 S. Peers, Building Fortress Europe: The Development of EU Migration Law, CML Rev 35: 1235-1272, (1998). S. Peers, *EU Justice and Home Affairs Law*, Longman, Colchester, 2000.

66 OJ 1997 C 337.

67 The right of initiative is shared with the Member States for the first five years after entry into force of the Amsterdam Treaty, 1 May 1999, but becomes exclusive after that.

68 Such persons are therefore excluded from reliance on the family reunion rights contained in Regulation 1612/68 which are substantially more generous than those applicable in the national law of several Member States, for instance the UK and the Netherlands.

rights. The last category is the most important in practical terms but I shall treat it separately in section 6.

Admission of third country nationals for the first time – discretion to the Member States subject to guiding principles

The draft convention included clear guidelines on admission of migrants for employment, self-employment, study and training. They are drafted in such a way as to provide a detailed framework but do not exclude national discretionary powers which render migration such a risky business. As the Commission states in the preamble: "these common rules on admission, with the exception of those concerning family reunification as well as those applying to persons recognised as long term residents, confer no right of residence and the Member States retain their discretionary powers to take actual decisions as to the admission of nationals of non-member countries."

Authorisation of admission for employment remained discretionary at the Member State's choice. A third country national *may* be granted admission for paid employment where a job vacancy cannot be filled in the short term:

1. by a citizen of the Union; or

2. by a third country national who is legally resident in the Member State and already forms part of the regular labour market in that Member State; or

3. by a third country national who has been recognised as a long-term resident.

This was the first indication in the text of the draft convention of the importance of the new status of long term resident. In fact such persons are to be granted a labour market priority throughout the territory of the Union. However, this overlooks the Community's duty to give a second priority in access to the Community labour market to Turkish workers contained in Association Council Decision 1/80.

Again in the field of self-employment, the Commission's proposal leaves discretion in the hands of the Member States. The Member States *may* admit a third country national in this category. The requirements to be fulfilled are that the third country national has "sufficient resources to undertake in the relevant Member State, the activity for which they submit their admission application" and "the business generated by the person admitted will have, during the period of validity of the initial residence authorisation, a beneficial effect on the employment in the Member State". Both of these requirements are subjective. The first, as regards resources is, according to the Explanatory Memorandum, intended "to ensure that [the third country nationals] genuinely intend to engage in the activity for which they seek admission and have the economic capacity to do so".[69] Implementation measures were provided for under this provision.

As regards the "beneficial effect on employment" the Commission was fully aware of the difficult subjective nature of this requirement. It stated in the Explanatory Memorandum "The second purely economic condition is designed to ensure that the admission of third country nationals brings in value added for the economic capacity of the country where they settle. It should be seen in the most objective light possible. Consequently, if within the two years corresponding to the minimum residence authorisation available, at least one other person is recruited, whether full-time or part-time, or use is made of service companies (accounting, data-processing or maintenance services), or work is regularly given to subcontractors, there will be practical evidence for assessing value added in terms of employment."[70]

The draft did not make reference to the Community's obligations under the GATS[71] which provides a framework for movement of persons for service provision. Within the GATS definition of service provision is included the Community law concept of establishment (establishment of a commercial presence).[72]

9.6.   LEGALLY RESIDENT THIRD COUNTRY NATIONALS: A TESTING GROUND OF RIGHTS

The draft convention created a right for long-term resident third country nationals in the Union to move to any Member State to take employment and set out a catalogue of basic rights they would be entitled to enjoy in their host Member State. From the perspective of the relationship of the Community, Member State and individual, it is very important that the draft set out clearly and by reference to objective grounds the definition of who is a third country national for these purposes.[73] The foundation for the acquisition of rights of

---

69 Explanatory Memorandum, p. XII.
70 Explanatory Memorandum, p. XII.
71 Part of the World Trade Organisation Agreement.
72 See further on this E. Guild and P. Barth, GATS and the Union, European Foreign Affairs Review, October 1999 pp. 493.
73 Article 32: Third-country nationals shall be recognised as long-term residents in a Member State if they satisfy the following requirements:
     (a)   they shall have been legally resident on a regular basis in a Member State for at least five years; and

free movement for third country nationals is a minimum of five years actual residence and permission for a further five years residence. However, the provision was worded in terms that where a person had completed ten years' residence even if that had been on the basis of residence permits renewed on a six-monthly basis the person still qualified for the Community right. This included a right to a residence permit which was either indefinite or valid for ten years and automatically renewable.

No mention is made in the Explanatory Memorandum to the Council of Europe's Convention on Establishment. However, the periods of five and ten years as benchmarks for the acquisition of secure residence rights is contained in that Convention at Article 12. The status, according to the Commission's proposal entitled the individual to a wide range of work and residence rights in the territory of the host Member State.[74] It also included the right to apply for employment on offer in another Member State coupled with a duty on the new host Member State to admit the individual and issue the relevant permits. This right also extended to studies.

In Chapter 5, I compared the Community measures which pre-dated the end of the transitional period on free movement of workers with the subsidiary legislation of the Turkey Agreement as regards the protection of workers. I concluded that there is a strong parallel in the development of the rights of Community workers and those of Turkish workers under the agreement. Now it is time to compare the development evidenced in respect of those classes of workers with that of third country nationals within the Union.

This comparison is important to the question which I am looking at: the relation of the Community, Member State and individual. So far in the development of Community law, rights which have been acquired by individuals have been on the basis of a wide concept of reciprocity. They devolve on individuals because of their nationality. Other conditions may be imposed as well, but nationality has so far been the *sine qua non*. Now, however, the Commission was proposing to treat third country nationals undifferentiated on the basis of nationality. Any rights which they may acquire are unrelated to any promise which their country of nationality may have given as regards the treatment of Community nationals. The defining characteristic of these third country nationals is the fact of their residence within the Union. Can the principles of the Community's immigration law apply on this basis or is "reciprocity"

(b)   they shall hold an authorisation which permits residence for a total period of at least ten years from their first admission.

74 Article 34. These include: access to the entire territory; authorisation to engage in all economic activities; residence authorisation; increased protection from expulsion; equal treatment with own nationals on access to economic activities, vocational training, trade union rights, the right of association, access to housing, social welfare and schooling.

fundamental to the treatment of individuals within the Community immigration sphere? In the earlier chapter I examined seven areas covered by the measures on Community and Turkish workers:

1. recitals which set out the objectives;

2. access to the labour market;

3. extension of permission to work;

4. calculation of time periods;

5. the presence and scope of equal treatment provisions;

6. the treatment of family members;

7. standstill clauses.

The two Community measures which predate 1968 are Regulations 15/61 and 38/64. The EEC Turkey subsidiary legislation is Decision 2/76 and 1/80. I will take each of the two together as the provisions proposed for third country nationals telescope to some extent the development of rights which took place as regards Community nationals and Turkish workers.

In the Community measures, the purpose is to achieve abolition of discrimination and obstacles for free movement; in the Association Council Decisions the objective is to achieve access to the labour market for Turkish workers. In the Commission's proposal there is virtually no explanation for the inclusion of these rights: "Considering that the common rules should also define the rights of third-country nationals residing legally in a Member State, especially those who are resident on a long term basis, and the conditions under which they may enjoy those rights in a Member State other than the Member State where they have acquired the status of long-term residents". No reference is made to the need to achieve equal treatment. However, at the special European Council meeting in Tampere Finland, October 1999 on the questions of justice and home affairs, the Council clarified its commitment to assimilating, as far as possible, the rights of legally resident third country nationals to those of Community nationals. In giving precision to the implementation of the new area of freedom, security and justice, the Council stated in its conclusions "The European Union must ensure fair treatment of third country nationals who reside legally on the territory of its Member States. A more vigorous integration policy should aim at granting them rights and obligations comparable to those of EU citizens."

As regards access to the labour market, in the Community Regulations, first Member States were allowed to impose a three-week waiting period before they had to admit a worker from another Member State who had a job offer. This waiting period disappeared in the second measure. Thereafter, Community workers were entitled to continue employment, change employment within the sector after three years and free access to the labour market after five years. In the second Community measure the worker was only in exceptional circumstances subject to a limitation on free access to the labour market *ab initia* For Turkish workers, free access to the labour market was delayed first for five years then reduced to four, but after the first year of employment the worker's right to continue employment was guaranteed. First access to the labour market is limited to a priority over other third country nationals except in the case of admitted family members of a Turkish worker who enjoy access to employment after either a period of residence or completion of studies.

The Commission's proposal places no limitation on first access to the labour market for third country nationals. The individual is not required to have an employment history in the first host Member State though the individual does need to have a history of legal residence of five years minimum extended for a further five years. Employment activity is the first basis upon which a right to move to another Member State is founded. To this extent it mirrors the early Community measures, free access to employment once the individual has moved appears to be delayed for two years[75] though this is inconsistent with the right to move to take up any employment. To this extent it comes closer to the second Community measure than to the other three. A further basis for movement however, is added: education. Only Community nationals have the right to move from one Member State to another for the purpose of study the rules in respect of which were only laid down by Directive in 1990.

Extension of permission to work, while an issue for the first Community measure and for both of the Association Council Decisions is not an issue for third country nationals under the proposal. The new host Member State is under a duty to issue the necessary authorisations. However, the individual is entitled to recognition of qualification as a long-term resident third country national in the new host Member State after two years residence. The calculation of time periods was carefully dealt with in both the Community measures and the Association Council measures. The Commission proposal is silent on this aspect. However, acquisition and scope of equal treatment rights is covered.

In the Community measures, the right to equal treatment as regards conditions of work and employment, remuneration and dismissal were included from the beginning. In the second Regulation it was extended to access to employment, housing and employment services. The wider right to equal treatment in social and tax advantages was not included for Community workers until 1968

---

75 See Article 34 in conjunction with Article 35(2) of the proposal.

in Regulation 1612/68.[76] For Turkish workers, notwithstanding the agreement provision and that in the additional protocol guaranteeing them equal treatment in working conditions and remuneration,[77] a similar provision was not inserted into the subsidiary legislation until 1980. In the Commission's proposal, the right to equal treatment with own nationals extends to: (1) access to employment or self-employment; (2) vocational training; (3) trade union rights; (4) the right of association; (5) access to housing; (6) social welfare; (7) schooling.[78]

These rights are acquired when the individual is recognised as long-term resident in the host Member State. As recognition of long term residence status by the new host Member State is delayed for a period of two years according to the Commission proposal, these equal treatment rights appear also to be delayed. They are still guaranteed to the individual in the former host Member State for the first two years, though that may be of little use as the person will normally be living and working in the new host Member State.

As regards family members, under the Community Regulations, from the beginning Community migrant workers were entitled to family reunion with spouses and children under 21 or dependent immediately and subject only to a housing requirement. Admitted family members were entitled to take employment on the same conditions as applicable to the principal. The Association Council Decisions are silent on the admission of family members. The first one only referred to children's education. The second Decision permits admitted family members economic rights after three and five years, and for children, additionally, after completion of vocational training.

The Commission's proposal follows a substantially different approach. The rights of long-resident third country nationals to family reunion are not differentiated from those applicable to other third country nationals. This means that they only apply after the individual has been legally resident in the Member State for one year.[79] The category of family members eligible for admission are limited to spouses and children below the age of majority in the host Member State. The Member State is under a duty to give favourable consideration to dependent relatives in the ascending and descending lines provided there is sufficient accommodation and means of support.[80] Generally, family members will not be permitted to engage in economic activities for the first six months of residence.

---

76 Article 7(2) Regulation 1612/68.
77 Article 9 Turkey Agreement and Article 37 Additional Protocol.
78 Article 34.
79 Article 24 of the Commission's proposal.
80 Articles 26 and 28 of the Commission's proposal.

The final item which I considered as regards the Community and Association Council measures was standstill clauses to protect the position of persons already resident and working in the host Member State. No such provisions appear in the Commission's proposal. The incremental development of rights in the three cases is consistent. In respect of third country nationals, the basis for a Community right of residence and movement is set at a high threshold – five years' lawful residence and permission to reside for a further five years. Only the right to move on a long-term basis for employment to another host State is regulated by the individual's capacity as a worker. While the elements of the treatment of third country nationals in the Commission proposal differ somewhat from those which appeared first in the Regulations and Association Council Decisions, still a parallel is clearly discernible. The structure is maintained, the contents are varied, perhaps most surprising as regards the equal treatment right.

The Community's approach to the treatment of third country nationals where there is no reciprocal agreement with their country of nationality divides, then, into two categories: those third country nationals who are defined as belonging to the Community and those who do not. Those third country nationals who belong to the Community are given rights both in their first host Member State and *vis-à-vis* other Member States which are clear, precise and unconditional. They are capable of direct effect and place these third country nationals in an analogous position to Community national migrant workers. Under the Commission's proposal the Community would create a direct relationship with third country nationals as regards the conditions of their residence, economic activity[81] and treatment throughout the Union after a period at the latest of ten years residence in the Union. As in the case of Community nationals, the effect of Community law would be to give the choice to the third country national to move or engage in economic activity at his or her election and to oblige the Member State authorities to recognise and respect that choice.

The Powers and The Two Commission Proposals

In general, the Member States, under the Commission's proposals, remain the gatekeepers as regards which third county nationals are permitted to cross the threshold into Community rights. First as regards temporary protection, the Council is entitled to choose whether to open a scheme or not. If such a scheme is opened, only then is it possible that the protected person may rely on Community law rights regarding his or her treatment. Again, it is for the

---

81 And education.

Council to choose whether to close a scheme. Although the decision is taken on the basis of a Commission report it is not limited to any recommendation of the Commission in that report. As yet it remains unclear how individual rights to international protection will be dealt with. Nevertheless, indirectly the Community becomes the guardian of the Member States' obligations in international law to provide protection to persons in need under the powers of the new Title IV. Thus the Community is responsible for ensuring compliance with the international law duty to give rights to individuals. The preparation of Community legislation to exercise those powers must respect the right of the individual to protection.

It is for the Council to decide whether to keep a protection scheme open for ten years, in which case its recipients, under the proposal on third country nationals would acquire the status of long-term resident third country nationals and be entitled to security of residence and access to employment across the Union. Similarly, if a protection scheme is kept open for five years, followed by a successful individual application for international protection which gave rise either to a five year residence right or a continuing residence right which ultimately is renewable up to the ten year mark, such a person would also come within the Community's sphere of rights for long-resident third country nationals.

When considering the Community's powers in respect of persons in need of international protection on an individual basis, the objective must be ensuring observance of the Member States' human rights duties in a border-free Europe. To this end "minimum" standards must, in my view, be the highest available in any Member State, otherwise the Member State which finds itself constitutionally bound by a higher international standard will be in difficulties fulfilling its obligation to respect the supremacy of Community law. During the transitional period while such a position is being achieved, all Community measures in this area should include a standstill clause which prevents changes to national legislation to the detriment of third country nationals. This would also have the effect of limiting the risk of further divergence among the Member States' laws and of bringing national legislation, to some extent within the scope of interpretation of Community law as well as protecting the position of the individual *vis-à-vis* the national settlement.

As regards the admission of third country nationals for economic or study purposes, the Community's power is to provide measures on *immigration policy*. This infers a co-ordination of objectives rather than specific rights. Under the Commission's proposal this intention is respected. The Member States retain their status as gatekeepers with discretionary power to decide whether to admit or refuse a particular third country national. This power is limited, however, as regards third country national family members. Once a third country national has been admitted, the Member State retains control over his or her continued economic or other activity for a period of five years but extendable to ten years at which point the individual acquires automatically a Community based right of residence and economic activity.

Structurally, the system is more or less coherent from the perspective of division of discretion and rights. Where a discretion exists it is left to the Member States to exercise subject to strong guidelines in Community law. Where a Community power is created as regards persons, its exercise is proposed to be in such a way as to limit Member States' discretion without the substitution of a Community discretion. Rather a right is created which leaves it to the individual to choose whether to exercise that right or not. What is less coherent is the variety of different categories of persons whose rights differ depending on their country of origin, their length of residence, their relationship to a Community national or enterprise etc.[82] As yet, little attempt appears to have been made to reduce the number of different categories – an exercise which would only be possible with a levelling up of rights in view of the interest of third countries to the protection of their nationals through bilateral agreements.

It is curious that the Community, which began its engagement with immigration exclusively on the basis of regulating the movement of persons for economic activities, has arrived now at the place where it must regulate the movement of all persons into and within the Union. However, the main category of persons from which it is excluded, in principle at least, from exercising direct regulation are third country nationals coming to the Union for economic activities. The Community is directly responsible for regulating crossing of internal and external borders, issue of visas and the treatment of third country nationals within the Union. It is also responsible for ensuring the engagements under third country agreements and the GATS but it is only in respect of these agreements that it has responsibility for directly regulating access to economic activities by third country nationals outside the Union within the Union. Only after the Member State have exercised their control over first access to the territory and economic activities, and permitted these for five years plus five years (according to the Commission's proposal), does the Community take responsibility for regulating the rights of these persons.

---

82 This incoherence is accentuated by the variation which has occurred in the new Title as regards access to the Court of Justice. Article 68 limits the right to ask preliminary questions of the Court to those tribunals against whose decisions there is no judicial remedy under national law but at the same time it gives a power to the Commission, Council or a Member State to seek an interpretative ruling on any part of the Title. It also purports to oust the jurisdiction of the Court in respect of any decision or measure taken as regards the crossing of an internal border on the grounds of the maintenance of law and order and the safeguarding of internal security.

9.7. CONCLUSIONS

The objective of the new powers of the Community is the creation of an area of freedom, security and justice. In order to achieve that objective the internal market must be completed at least for the time being including, finally, the free movement of persons within the combined territory of the Union (with the exception of those three Member States which opted out of the Title). It is apparent, and reinforced by the conclusions of the European Council Meeting in Tampere, that freedom in this context is wider than freedom of movement alone. But what more is it to include? My argument in this chapter has been that freedom must include the guarantee of rights which can be enjoyed by third country nationals and Community nationals alike in this field. Without the creation of a framework of rights which can be accessed by individuals, it is difficult to comprehend what freedom might mean as there is no clear check on State discretion. In the context of the ECHR this freedom is clearly defined as the enjoyment of rights contained in the Convention which must be respected by the member States, and increasingly in the discussion about those rights, in certain circumstances places an obligation on the member States to take positive steps to ensure those freedoms. Thus in giving effect to the powers of the Community in the field of immigration and asylum the only starting point consistent with the creation of the area of freedom security and justice is the same one which the Community adopted when legislating immigration rights for Community nationals: rights of movement, economic activity and family reunion so that those rights can be exercised in dignity. As in respect of the Community's approach in the subsidiary legislation to the Turkey Agreement and the free movement right of the Europe Agreements, it may not be appropriate to legislate as wide a scope of rights for third country nationals outside the Union at least, as for Community nationals and third country nationals already resident in the Union. However, the framework should be consistent.

Secondly, the area must be one of security. Again, security has many faces and it is important to consider how best to interpret the concept as regards migration. The drafters of the provision clearly had in mind a concept of security which encompasses crime and criminal procedures. From the perspective of this book, the relationship of rights between the Community, the individual and the Member State, security must include clarity of the division among the three parties of their rights and obligations. As I have shown in the previous chapter, the failure to provide such clarity during the period between the Maastricht and Amsterdam Treaties set the Community institutions and Member States on a collision course which ended before the Court of Justice. Such events evidence a lack of security for the parties of their powers, roles, duties and obligations. From the perspective of the individual, security must be as regards his or her present and future. For the migrant, security is the legal framework which clarifies his or her duties and rights *vis-à-vis* the State and supra-national body. He or she is entitled to know what is permitted and to be able to plan his or her life accordingly. This approach of the Community as regards its own nationals fits well into the creation of an area of security for third country nationals as well. Security has another face as well: security from being forced to return to a country where there is a serious risk of persecution or torture. This security is one of the duties of the Member States towards third country nationals expressed in the Geneva Convention as well as Article 3 ECHR.

Finally, an area of justice expresses itself in a number of ways. First the rights which form the subject matter of the freedom and the clarity which provides an area of security must be underwritten by individual access to justice to enforce the rights and enjoy the security set out. The legal expression of freedom and security must encompass the individual if this is also to be an area of justice. However, there is another aspect to the creation of an area of justice. To achieve an area of justice worthy of the name, it must also uphold, at the very least, the minimum thresholds set by international human rights treaties which touch upon the area. Justice for migrants as expressed in the jurisprudence of the European Court of Human Rights regarding the protection of family life guaranteed by Article 8 ECHR means protection from expulsion where the circumstances of the individual and his or her family outweigh other interests of the state. It also finds voice in the judicial protection of third country nationals from return to a country where there is a serious risk of persecution or torture through procedures and appeal rights which provide effective control of administrative decision making for the individual. This protection must at least meet the international standards contained in the Geneva Convention and elsewhere if the implementation of an area of justice is to be achieved.

The Community has set itself a task of creation of an area of freedom, security and justice. In doing so and in giving effect to the powers which the Member States have transferred to it, the Community must not fail the individual who is the object of those powers by withholding from him or her freedom, security and justice. It also must not fail itself by falling below internationally recognised standards to which the Member States have adhered.

ANNEX

Title IV EC

Visas, Asylum, Immigration and Other Policies Related to Free Movement of Persons

Article 61

In order to establish progressively an area of freedom, security and justice, the Council shall adopt:

(a) within a period of five years after the entry into force of the Treaty of Amsterdam, measures aimed at ensuring the free movement of persons in accordance with Article 14, in conjunction with directly related flanking measures with respect to external border controls, asylum and immigration, in accordance with the provisions of Article 62(2) and (3) and Article 63(1)(a) and (2)(a), and measures to prevent and combat crime in accordance with the provisions of Article 31(e) of the Treaty on European Union;

(b) other measures in the field of asylum, immigration and safeguarding the rights of nationals of third countries, in accordance with the provisions of Article 63;

...

Article 62

The Council, acting in accordance with the procedure referred to in Article 67, shall, within a period of five years after entry into force of the Treaty of Amsterdam, adopt:

(1) measures with a view to ensuring, in compliance with Article 14, the absence of any controls on persons, be they citizens of the Union or nationals of third countries, when crossing internal borders;

(2) measures on the crossing of the external borders of the Member States which shall establish:

(a) standards and procedures to be followed by Member States in carrying out checks on persons at such borders;

(b) rules on visas for intended stays of no more than three months, including:

    (i)   the list of third countries whose nationals must be in possession of visas when crossing the external borders and those whose nationals are exempt from that requirement;

    (ii)   the procedures and conditions for issuing visas by Member States;

    (iii) a uniform format for visas;

    (iv) rules on a uniform visa;

(3) measures setting out the conditions under which nationals of third countries shall have the freedom to travel within the territory of the Member States during a period of no more than three months.

Article 63

The Council, acting in accordance with the procedure referred to in Article 67, shall, within a period of five years after the entry into force of the Amsterdam Treaty, adopt:

(1) measures on asylum, in accordance with the Geneva Convention of 28 July 1951 and the Protocol of 31 January 1967 relating to the status of refugees and other relevant treaties, within the following areas:

    (a) criteria and mechanisms for determining which Member State is responsible for considering an application for asylum submitted by a national of a third country in one of the Member States,

    (b) minimum standards on the reception of asylum seekers in the Member States,

    (c) minimum standards with respect to the qualification of nationals of third countries as refugees,

    (d) minimum standards on procedures in Member States for granting or withdrawing refugee status;

(2) measures on refugees and displaced persons within the following areas:

    (a) minimum standards for giving temporary protection to displaced persons from third countries who cannot return to their country of origin and for persons who otherwise need international protection,

    (b) promoting a balance of effort between Member States in receiving and bearing the consequences of receiving refugees and displaced persons;

(3) measures on immigration policy within the following areas:

(a) conditions of entry and residence, and standards on procedures for the issue by Member States of long term visas and residence permits, including those for the purpose of family reunion,

(b) illegal immigration and illegal residence, including repatriation of illegal residents;

(4) measures defining the rights and conditions under which nationals of third countries who are legally resident in a Member State may reside in other Member States.

Measures adopted by the Council pursuant to points 3 and 4 shall not prevent any Member State from maintaining or introducing in the areas concerned national provisions which are compatible with this Treaty and with international agreements.

Measures to be adopted pursuant to points 2(b), 3(a) and 4 shall not be subject to the five year period referred to above.

Article 64

1. This Title shall not affect the exercise of the responsibilities incumbent upon Member States with regard to the maintenance of law and order and the safeguarding of internal security.

2. In the event of one or more Member States being confronted with an emergency situation characterised by a sudden inflow of nationals of third countries and without prejudice to paragraph 1, the Council may, acting by qualified majority on a proposal from the Commission, adopt provisional measures of a duration not exceeding six months for the benefit of the Member States concerned.

...

Article 67

1. During a transitional period of five years following the entry into force of the Treaty of Amsterdam, the Council shall act unanimously on a proposal from the Commission or on the initiative of a Member State and after consulting the European Parliament.

2. After a period of five years:

   - the Council shall act on proposals from the Commission; the Commission shall examine any request made by a Member State that it submit a proposal to the Council;

...

3. By derogation from paragraphs 1 and 2:

   - measures referred to in Article 62(2)(b)(I) and (iii) shall, from the entry into force of the Treaty of Amsterdam, be adopted by the Council acting by a qualified majority on a proposal from the Commission and after consulting the European Parliament;

   - measures referred to in Article 62(2)(b)(ii) and (iv) shall, after a period of five years following the entry into force of the Treaty of Amsterdam, be adopted by the Council acting in accordance with the procedure referred to in Article 251.

Article 68

1. Article 234 shall apply to this Title under the following circumstances and conditions: where a question on the interpretation of this Title or on the validity or interpretation of acts of the institutions of the Community based on this Title is raised in a case pending before a court or tribunal of a Member State against whose decision there is no judicial remedy under national law, that court or tribunal shall, if it considers that a decision on the question is necessary to enable it to give judgment, request the Court of Justice to give a ruling thereon.

2. In any event, the Court of Justice shall not have jurisdiction to rule on any measure or decision taken pursuant to Article 62(1) relating to the maintenance of law and order and the safeguarding of internal security.

3. The Council, the Commission or a Member State may request the Court of Justice to give a ruling on a question of interpretation of this Title or of acts of the institutions of the Community based on this Title. The ruling given by the Court of Justice in response to such a request shall not apply to judgments of courts or tribunals of the Member States which have become *res judicata.*

CHAPTER 10

CONCLUSIONS

> "The aim is an open and secure European Union fully committed to the obligations of the Geneva Refugee Convention and other relevant human rights instruments and able to respond to humanitarian needs on the basis of solidarity. A common approach must also be developed to ensure the integration into our societies of those third country nationals who are lawfully resident in the Union."

With this expression of intention the European Council at Tampere, Finland, October 1999, set out its objectives for the implementation of the new powers on immigration and asylum given to the Community by the Amsterdam Treaty.

The future is not possible to construct without some knowledge of the past, no matter how short or long that past may have been. When faced with the new challenge of a general competence in the fields of immigration and asylum, the first step for the Community must be to look at how it has used the powers provided to it already in these fields and draw conclusions from those experiences. In this book, I have sought to spell out those steps, analysing the development of Community law from the perspective of the migrant and his or her rights and possibilities. The perspective of the migrant must always be informed by what the law permits or prohibits him or her from doing. In the field of immigration, the question is one of the possibility to move, reside, exercise economic activities and enjoy protection from discrimination and expulsion. For the migrant the first thing which he or she wants to know is whether there is a right to move, a right to reside and a right to engage in economic activities. The starting point is the relationship between the migrant and the State: is this one of rights to the individual or discretion to the State? Within the context of the European Community another actor came into the equation: the Community itself as a law-making body. So, from the beginning of this study, I took as the framework for investigation the triangular relationship between the individual and the Member State, the Member State and the Community and the individual and the Community. Along all three sides of the triangle there is a relationship of rights and duties which extend with the competences of the Community and their exercise.

The Tools of Community Law

The initial immigration law of the Community was founded on the realisation of the objective of the abolition of obstacles to the free movement of persons within the territory of the Community. This was given particularity as regards workers, the self-employed and service providers and recipients. The Community chose to define its legal order by reference to a direct relationship between the individuals resident within it and Community law without, necessarily, the intermediary of national law.[1] Further, it established the supremacy of Community rules which seek uniformity of result in their application across the diverse territory of the Union, over contrary national rules. When applying this legal framework to the objective of free movement of persons, the Community legal order created a system based on a right of choice to the individual, supported by the full power of Community law, taking precedence over national rules or the exercise of national discretion.

What then were the keys which the original Treaty gave to or required of the individual to exercise free movement rights? First and most importantly was the need for the individual to exercise an economic activity in order to access the movement right. In the definition of economic activity and its adequacy or otherwise for the purpose of accessing the right, the Community ring-fenced the defining capacity as one reserved to the Community itself and not available to the Member States. The reasoning for this was not only to ensure that persons in similar situations anywhere in the Union would be able to enjoy the same right defined in a consistent manner, but also expressly to avoid the risk of Member State attempts to limit the rights of individuals and make them subject to more narrow national rules. The specified economic activities were work, self-employment or service provision or receipt. The legislator intentionally included the first three, the Court found the last implicit in the third. By so doing, the right of movement and residence extended to both active and passive economic activity. In one interpretation, as everyone is a service recipient in one way or another almost all the time, there is not a moment when a person is not exercising a right which is a prerequisite to free movement.[2] The second criterion, which is more questionable, was the application of a nationality

---

1   And in those cases where such an intermediary was necessary the Community defined for itself the remedies for the individual against the failure of the national authorities to give definition in national law.

2   By extension then, the creation of a right of free movement for three categories of economically "inactive" persons – students, pensioners and the self-sufficient – in June 1990 did no more than give legislative voice to a pre-existing right.

requirement on the exercise of the free movement right. An individual was entitled to access the right of free movement in his or her capacity as an economic actor provided that he or she also held the nationality of one of the Member States. This development occurred almost inadvertently during the early stages of the Community's development, at least in so far as workers were concerned. In respect of the self-employed and service providers a clear Treaty limitation to nationals of the Member States was included, though as the Court of Justice has indicated this does not exclude the power to extend the rules to third country nationals.

In my view, the nationality limitation to free movement of workers was a false step which has created confusion as regards the creation of the internal market in labour. While in the field of goods and capital the Community has developed its law on the basis that once a product enters the Community market from a third country it becomes subject to the Community's rules on free movement of goods, in the field of workers, once a thid country national worker has lawfully entered the Community labour market in one Member State he or she remains trapped by Community law in that first host State and is not treated as belonging, for the purpose of free movement, to the Community labour market. This undoubtedly creates a distortion and unnecessary differentiation between fields of Community competence. It has also created, in my view a false differentiation between the considerations relevant to movement of goods and services and those relevant to workers. For instance, because of the exclusion of third country nationals from free movement of workers in Community law, a Community employer is entitled to send its third country national staff to carry out service provision across Community borders exercising Community law rights, but the individual so sent is excluded from rights deriving from free movement of workers, such as the right to family reunion.[3]

Therefore, in the development of the Community's original immigration law the first step was to consolidate the law-making power, the relationship of that lawmaking power with national law and the right to define its constituent parts. In so doing it created clear rules giving a right to the individual to choose whether to exercise a movement right based on economic activity. The discretionary control of the Member States over the treatment of aliens, at least those who held the nationality of another Member State, was excluded. A margin was left open to them only as regards the assessment of a risk to public policy, security and health, the only permitted ground for expulsion of Community nationals, but even that discretion

---

3   This is the combined effect of C-230/97 *Awoyeri* [1999] ECR I-6781 and C-43/93 *Van der Elst* [1994] ECR I-3803.

become, over time, highly circumscribed. The Community concept of good faith then provided the necessary tool for application and remedies. In enforcing the rights of the individual, the mechanisms the Community developed to ensure State obedience, often deriving from other fields of activity, had the consequence of making available to the migrant worker first the concept of direct effect of the Community rights for the benefit of the individual against contrary Member State action, then liability in damages where the Member State failed to recognise the right conferred by Community law.

Securing Free Movement: Non-Discrimination and Obstacles

Among the powerful tools which the Community brought to the individual in safeguarding his or her right to chose to move, reside, exercise economic activities or not were the concepts of non-discrimination and obstacles. By the first, the Community gave a wide meaning to the concept of discrimination including both direct discrimination and indirect discrimination but on a very narrow ground: nationality only. The comparator was defined as the national of the host Member State. It extended the scope of the application of the right to non-discrimination from matters directly related to the exercise of an economic activity to a wider field of issues: social and tax advantages. Finally, the concept of non-discrimination was extended out to all fields: the objective to achieve perfect equality.[4] The duty to ensure non-discrimination extended not only to emanations of the State but also to private parties.[5]

Non-discrimination, no matter how widely interpreted was not sufficient to ensure the free exercise of the right of movement. For that to be achieved the abolition of obstacles to movement had to be ensured. In pursuit of this objective, for example, family reunion rights for migrant workers were created.[6] Similarly, obstacles such as in the form of transfer payments between football clubs which hindered the athlete's movement were found contrary to Community law.[7]

As the scope of non-discrimination became more developed, and the concept of obstacles received clarification, the differences between the rights migrant nationals of the Community enjoyed in comparison with those who stayed at home became apparent. The more liberal legal regime of the Community towards its migrant workers gives them the right to

---

4   C-43/95 *Data Delecta* [1996] ECR I-4671.
5   C-350/96 *Clean Car* [1997] ECR I-2521.
6   Article 10 Regulation 1612/68.
7   C-415/93 *Bosman* [1995] ECR I-492.

choose to move and exercise rights with only minor discretion to the Member State authorities. The unacceptable conundrum came into existence which has yet to be solved that a Community migrant worker may enjoy more rights in a State other than that of his or her nationality than at home.[8] The Community's legal rule of excluding from the benefit of Community free movement rights any situation which appears to be wholly internal to a Member State is having the consequence of distorting free movement patterns as people move exclusively in order to enjoy a right derived from Community free movement law which they could not enjoy at home.[9]

Even with the development of a Community immigration law which aimed at abolishing all obstacles to the movement of persons within the Union, some areas remained unaddressed, for instance the need for a durable residence right for spouses after the death, divorce or departure the Community national spouse from the host State. The issue of compliance with Community law by national authorities in a timely and consistent manner has also continued to be a problem throughout the development of Community free movement rights.

The development, then of the Community's immigration law was based on the creation of a relationship of rights between the individual and the Community which allowed the individual the choice of movement or not. As extended by the legislator and interpreted by the Court the individual was increasingly able to move in confidence, given the right to counter discrimination against him or her on the basis of nationality and seek to enjoy all the benefits of the host State in which he or she found him or herself. The Member States' duty of good faith to the Community included the obligation to give effect to the choices of the individual and to provide remedies for any failure to secure equal treatment. In this regime of easy circulation with rights and guarantees extending even to access to social security benefits, in a Community of 15 Member States including States with development levels as different as Greece and Denmark what has the result been? Only 1.4 to 1.5% of the population of the Member States consists of nationals of other Member States. While many people move across the Union on holiday, for business, for a short trip, very few people actually stay and exercise a longer-term economic and residence right. What

---

8 For example in the areas of family reunion: C-370/90 *Singh* [1992] ECR I-4265; and of course footballers as regards transfer payments which are only illegal as regards inter-State transfers.

9 This has been particularly so in the Netherlands and the UK where harsh family reunion rules have encouraged British and Dutch nationals to exercise their free movement rights to go to other Member States in order to enjoy family reunion in accordance with the more liberal Community rules.

might seem a perverse result of the right of free movement of persons and the increasingly complete regime to encourage migration within the Community is the fact that fewer people use their right than when there were greater controls pre-1968 (the end of the transitional provisions on free movement of workers in the EC Treaty). It would appear that movement of persons in the European Union is not affected by legal measures designed to make movement easier. It must then be asked whether legal measures designed to make movement more difficult are in fact different in their result.

We live in a political world which is convinced that legal measures on migration are critical to the decisions people make about whether or not to move and if so where. This extends from the political justification for visa requirements that there are too many unwanted people coming from a country and thus they should be made subject to such rules, to the statement that asylum seekers are influenced by the harshness or otherwise of the asylum determination regime in the choices they make of where to seek asylum. We also live in an actual world in which the evidence of where nationals of the Member States move within the Union appears unaffected by the increasing liberalisation of the immigration rules around it. Similarly, differences in unemployment rates, benefit levels and wages seem to have a surprisingly small effect bearing in mind the low mobility rate within the Union. However, it is also the case that for those who do move, small in number though they may be, the Community's rules permit them to go about their affairs with a degree of dignity uncontemplated in the national regimes of the Member States regarding third country nationals.

Extending the Community's Immigration Regime: Third Country Agreements

From as early as 1961 the European Community was extending the rules of its internal immigration regime to third country nationals. In doing so it used exactly the same structural tools as it had done in respect of Community nationals. The categorisation of persons remained constant – workers, self-employed and service providers and recipients. The approach remained constant: the creation of rights accessible to individuals to make choices about the migratory patterns of their lives to the limitation of the exercise of discretion by the Member State authorities. What differed was the scope of the provisions. In only one case were full free movement rights secured for third country nationals on the basis of a multilateral agreement between the Community and the states of origin.[10]

---

10 The EEA Agreement.

The regime developed in a somewhat haphazard manner, but in general was characterised by the extension of some immigration related rights to nationals of states on the borders of the Community. The first agreements were with Greece and Turkey, called Association Agreements, intended to lead to accession of those states. In the agreements workers, the self-employed and service providers were all permitted various levels of protection within the Community territory. The most important rights which I have looked at are those of Turkish workers under the subsidiary legislation of that agreement. Here a ladder of rights based on length of work within the Community gives these workers security of residence both for themselves and their family members limited to their host Member State. The legislator who designed the subsidiary legislation of the Turkey Agreement followed closely the development of the Community's legislation on workers during the transitional period and followed very similar steps towards the liberalisation of movement. Of course free movement of Turkish workers has not been achieved. On the other hand, Greece joined the Union and thereby secured full free movement for its nationals. Although the importance of the agreements for workers from these states did not become apparent until the late 1980s and early 1990s, once they did, there was no change in the policy of the Community towards the use of such agreements to regulate migratory pressure. Indeed, there was an intensification of such use once the full value of the agreements was felt.

The second group of agreements to enjoy provisions on workers were the Maghreb Agreements from 1976. These rights were more limited, providing non-discrimination in social security and working conditions for nationals of those countries. While the concept of working conditions in these agreements cannot extend to a right to extension of a residence permit, it can impede a Member State's action on expulsion in the event that the national of the Maghreb has an existing work permit. These agreements have been recently renegotiated and the rights for workers not only confirmed but (minimally) extended. Similar protection to that provided for Maghreb workers also appears in an annex to the Lomé IV agreement with 69 countries of Africa, the Caribbean and Pacific though it remains unclear whether, as a result of its weak legal form, it can actually provide some protection to those workers. This is most undesirable as it creates differences in levels of protection of migrant workers without reasonable justification.

The approach of the Court of Justice in interpreting the provisions designed to protect persons in these agreements has been consistent with its jurisprudence on the EC Treaty's provision on Community migrants. Without exception the Court has brought to bear on these provisions the same tools of interpretation and enforcement which it has made available to nationals of the Member States. First it has confirmed its right to interpret the agreements. Secondly, it has applied the same concept of direct effect and the same qualifying criteria to the provisions of third country agreements on persons as it has applied to Community legislation. Thirdly, it has so far used the same interpretative tools for the concepts of third country agreements as it has for concepts of Community law, most importantly the concept of "worker" in the Turkey Agreement.[11]

What then has been the Community legislator's response to the recognition of rights in third country agreements and thereby the creation of an immigration law for the Community independent of the derived rights of some third country nationals which in any event are dependent on their relationship to a Community national principal? The legislator appears to have recognised the value of this immigration law and used the technique to develop a new series of immigration rights for nationals of the Central and Eastern European countries, the Baltic states and Slovenia. In the negotiation and settlement of agreements with these states from 1991 to the present, the Community has consistently included provisions on workers which promise, at least, non-discrimination in working conditions. Further, they have included in all the agreements provisions creating a right of self-employment for nationals of those states, whether natural or legal persons, in the Member States. This right, worded similarly to Article 43 EC the right of establishment for Community nationals, provides a mechanism to permit lawful migration for economic purposes from countries on the borders of the Community and from which, particularly during the period 1990-1994, were perceived as source of substantial migration flows into the Community. The Court of Justice has yet to interpret these agreements. Four references have been made to it, three from UK courts and one from a Dutch court. All the referring courts accept that there is a right of establishment for nationals of the relevant countries under the agreements. However, it is the means for the implementation of that right which is worrying them.

In the UK, the Member State accepts the principle that the establishment provision of the agreements has direct effect but it disputes whether that means that a national from one of those states who has been unlawfully residing in the State is entitled to rely on the self-employment provision to resist an expulsion decision. In so arguing the UK relies on provisions of the agreements which in rather vague terms appear to indicate a contrary intention to the rights which appear to be granted by the establishment provision. If the Court follows its jurisprudence on the EC Treaty it could find useful the tool of the duty to abolish obstacles to free movement. All

---

11 C-1/97 *Birden* [1998] ECR I-7747.

the agreements include a provision which prohibits measures which would have the effect of nullifying or impairing the exercise of the rights thereunder. Such a provision may well be considered as prohibiting, then, administrative obstacles to the right's exercise.

The expansive use of third country agreements has extended the immigration law of the Community into the regulation of third country nationals both within the Member States and seeking extensions of their work and residence permits as in the case of Turkish workers, as regards a right to non-discrimination in fundamental fields of life such as working conditions and social security in the Maghreb Agreements and has been extended in a number of different cases to a right to economic activity and residence on the territory of the Member States, such as the EEA Agreement and the Europe Agreements. Of course those third country nationals who enjoy a right of entry by virtue of a third country agreement, also enjoy a right of entry to any Member State which means in effect a right to move within the territory of the Member States for the purposes permitted under their country's agreement with the Community.

The Community has used the same tools in the development of its internal immigration law and its extension towards the outside world. It has created a relationship between the individual and the Community and given the choice of activity to the individual. The scope of the rights is more limited in some agreements than in others. But the quality of the rights remains constant, these are rights worded in the light of the Community Treaty equivalents, interpreted in the light of the same and designed for the individual. In no case have the rights granted under third country agreements resulted in a substantial change in migration patterns from the countries of origin, though of course only under some of the agreements is there a right of entry to natural persons. If a conclusion can be drawn, it would appear that third country nationals behave in a similar manner to Community nationals *vis-à-vis* the creation of legal regimes on migration. Beneficial regimes which give them rights and guarantee non-discrimination do not appear to result in increased flows of persons. Indeed, in respect of the CEECs, after the settling of agreements with those countries all of which include a legal route for economic activity in the Union it appears that actual numbers have decreased substantially.[12]

---

12 The total numbers of persons coming to the Member States from the CEECs appears to have dropped substantially over the period in question. One argument is that the *de facto* exclusion of CEEC nationals from the asylum procedures in some Member States (i.e. Germany's law on safe country of origin) has resulted in the change. Another is that the abolition of mandatory visas for short visits took the pressure off the border control system for all but those few CEECs which remain

Co-ordination outside the Community

From 1985 to 1999 the Member States indulged in a variety of attempts at
co-ordination of immigration and asylum policy outside the structures of
the European Community. The moves were at least nominally associated
with the decision to complete the internal market and to abolish intra-
Member State controls at borders on the movement of persons. This
objective caused consternation in a number of ministries in the Member
States, particularly those engaged in the control of aliens. The prospect that
other Member States' unwanted aliens would come to their country over
"open" borders raised doubts which found popular voice in many Member
States. One immediate result was new pressure for the involvement of
security services in the Member States in the internal market project as
regards the movement of aliens (an explicit provision to this effect was only
deleted at a very late stage in the drafting of the Schengen Implementing
Convention 1990). Another was the political decision to seek to co-ordinate
if not harmonise some aspects of external border control in order to
achieve the abolition of internal border controls. The overt co-ordination of
external border control measures became the overwhelming concern of the
Member States in the face of a wider border control free area. Out of this
determination, some Member States proceeded more quickly through the
creation of the Schengen Agreement 1985 and the Schengen Implementing
Agreement 1990. These two agreements together with the UK's refusal to
participate in the frontier control free area ensured that the fields of border
controls, internal and external including visa policy remained within an
intergovernmental sphere at first for 5 of the Member States and by May
1999 13 of the 15 Member States. As an intergovernmental regime ruled by
international law, no common interpretation of the project by a supra-
national court was possible.

At the same time the Member States began co-ordination of their
substantive immigration and asylum law first through international conventions settled exclusively among themselves such as the Dublin Convention,
and then through rather ill-defined instruments called resolutions, recommendations and conclusions. These developments were the subject of substantial and well-justified public criticism on grounds of lack of transparency, democratic legitimacy and uniform judicial supervision. These
intergovernmental activities were brought within the scope of the Union
with the Maastricht Treaty which established a new venue, the Third Pillar,

---

subject to such restrictions. Eurostat Migration Statistics 1994, 1995 and 1996,
Luxembourg 1994, 1995 and 1996 respectively.

for co-ordination of activity in the fields of immigration and asylum. Both the Schengen experiment and the Third Pillar provided venues for the Member States to discuss and approximate ideas about immigration and asylum. However, the result was not the achievement of co-ordination, though some argue that it provided at least a venue to make the first steps towards this. The division contained in the TEU which created a Community competence for visas – their form and the countries whose nationals must have them – and the underlying immigration and border policy which was placed in the Third Pillar highlighted the problematic relationship created not only within the Union – dividing the Council, Commission and Parliament in separate legal actions before the Court of Justice – but also between the position of the individual the subject of the measures and the Community. The direct relationship which had character-ised Community law in its relationships in immigration was no longer in sight.

The experiments were of qualified success. By the time of the next inter-governmental conference the Member States (with notable exceptions) were ready to change the mechanisms and grant substantial powers to the Euro-pean Community in the field of immigration and asylum.

Implementing the Amsterdam Powers

The Community has now been granted extensive powers in the fields of immigration and asylum by the new Title IV EC. The question arises, how should these new powers be exercised, and what lessons should be learned from the Community's engagement with immigration so far? The first lesson I would suggest that the Community has learned is that the limitation of discretion is a value to be ignored at high cost.

The benefits of a rights-based approach rather than one based on discretion may be summarised as follows:

1. Clarity of rights reduces administrative delay and cost as the rules are clear and simple and do not require senior officials to weigh up dis-cretionary elements in order to reach decisions;

2. The individual alone can regulate his or her life in accordance with clear rules with a degree of security as to the consequences of any particular choice or action;

3. The alien and the society benefit from security as to who is and who is not entitled to reside, leave, return and exercise economic activities;

4. The suspicions of the host society that the alien is "abusing" the
    immigration laws should be diminished by the application of trans-
    parent rules agreed by the Member States.

The disadvantage of the elimination of discretion is perhaps a reluctance of
Member States to concede progress on rights for third country nationals. As
has been seen in the context of the Third Pillar it is easy to agree rules
which one does not intend to apply. In order to make the move from
national discretionary control to Community rules easier, it may help to use
the traditional tool of Community law, the standstill clause which eases the
transition. Standstill clauses are to be found liberally in the original EC
Treaty as an interim step towards harmonisation. They prohibit changes to
national law which would reduce the rights of the actors in areas which are
undergoing harmonisation. They allow Member States to maintain national
provisions subject to minimum requirements at Community level. Thus
standstill clauses permit a margin of appreciation to the Member States but
prevent a widening of differences in national law which would be contrary
to the goal.

The first field which needs to be regulated on a rights-based approach is
that of free movement rights for third country nationals lawfully resident in
the Union. The failure of the Community to include this part of the labour
force in its interpretation of Article 39 EC now needs to be remedied. The
position of these persons needs to be assimilated to the free movement
rights of Community nationals. This is also necessary in order to bring into
line the rights of nationals of third countries protected under different
agreements. The upward harmonisation of the rights of all third country
nationals resident in the Union is the fairest and most equitable way to
implement this new power in Article 63(4) EC. The second category which
needs urgent implementation is family reunion rights. If the rights of Europe's third country nationals are to be assimilated to the position of Community nationals the same rules of family reunion should apply without the
requirement of the exercise of a free movement right. Remaining then in
the immigration field, the development of a primary immigration law for
Europe should respect the rules of liberalization of trade which the Community has so fervently promoted. In particular a genuine reduction in the
protectionism which is manifested by harsh primary immigration laws to
keep out migrant workers should be a feature of the Community's policy. It
is not acceptable to seek to force other countries to open up their frontiers
to permit European consultants and workers access to their markets yet
retain closed access to Europe. Building on the existing Community and
international framework to develop the Community's new immigration laws
will be the easiest route and the most politically acceptable. It will also
impose the least new administrative burdens on the Member States.

This perspective also needs to inform the common rules on visas and crossing of borders. The administrative discretion which currently renders it such a time-consuming and degrading activity to seek a short-stay visa to come to the Schengen territory (or indeed increasingly to any Member State) needs to be limited and made subject to clear rules. Where a person does not come within the list of clear reasons for refusal of a short stay visa then there should be a presumption in favour of its issue. In this way the increasing and unfortunately also accurate characterisation of the European Community as suspicious of outsiders other than those coming from the developed (white) world can be dispelled.

In the field of asylum the most important perspective for the Member States is that the transfer of competence to the Community has been deemed necessary in order to ensure the full implementation and application of the Member States human rights commitments including the Geneva Convention, in a Europe without internal borders. Therefore measures which purport to reintroduce borders for asylum seekers alone, such as those applicable in the Dublin Convention, are inappropriate and counter-productive. The recognition of refugees and persons in need of protection as regards reception, procedures, determination and rights should ensure that the highest standard in any Member State is the minimum standard for the Community as a whole. If there is the possibility that an applicant's application for protection would have succeeded in one Member State while it has been rejected in another then the system is open to criticism as to its fairness to the individual. Further, the Member State where protection would have been granted may be in breach of its international commitments if it does not consider such an application if made to it. Where national courts have applied an anxious scrutiny to the decisions of the administration on protection of individuals at risk of persecution or torture, their commitment to the Community framework can only be secured by an upwards harmonisation of the interpretation of the protection commitments of Europe. The constitutional balance of the Community and the loyalty of the constitutional courts of the Member States can only be assured where they are satisfied that the human rights standards of the Community as regards the protection of individuals is sufficiently high as to ensure that a different result would not have obtained in another Member State. Only then can the principle of the Dublin Convention, that there should be only one consideration of an application for protection within the territory of the Union, be accepted.

The respect for international commitments, both in trade and human rights must be the best way for the Community to found the exercise of its new powers in immigration and asylum. The Community has already proven to itself that a regime of relative freedom of movement does not result in waves of migrants. Human rights abuses abroad, the needs of the European economy and demographic changes are the real sources of movements of persons to and within Europe. The lesson which the European Community's history of regulating immigration teaches is that the benefits of the adoption of clear, easily implemented rules which allow the individual dignity and freedom in the choice of movement do not necessarily come with a high price of mass movement of persons. Further, only a system which builds on the Community's own history of regulating migration among the Member States will enable the Union to realise its objective of an area of freedom, security and justice: freedom to move, reside and engage in economic activities, security from unjustified interference with those rights and justice in the creation of rights recognised and upheld by Community law and its judiciary both at national and supranational level.

BIBLIOGRAPHY

Amphoux, J., Cour de Justice des Communautés européenes et Tribunal de première instance, *Cahiers de droit européen*, 1994.

Barnard, C., The Principle of Equality in the Community Context: P, Grant, Kalanke and Marshall: Four Uneasy Bedfellows, *Cambridge Law Review*, July 1998, Volume 57.2, p. 352.

Baun, M., *An Imperfect Union: The Maastricht Treaty and the New Politics of European Integration*, Westview Press, Oxford, 1996.

Bell, M., *EU Anti-Discrimination Policy: From Equal Opportunities Between Women and Men to Combating Racism*, European Parliament, Brussels/Luxembourg LIBE 102 EN02-1998.

Bigo, D., The Landscape of Police Co-Operation, in E Bort and R. Keat, (eds.) *The Boundaries of Understanding*, ISSI, Edinburgh, 1999.

Bigo, D., Frontiers and Security in the European Union: The Illusion of Migration Control, in M. Anderson and E. Bort, *The Frontiers of Europe*, Pinter, London, 1998, pp. 148-164.

Bigo, D., *Polices en Reseaux*, Presses de Sciences - Po, Paris, 1996.

Boeles, P., *Fair Immigration Proceedings in Europe*, Martinus Nijhoff, The Hague, 1998.

Boer, M. den, *Schengen's Last Days? The Incorporation of Schengen into the New TEU, External Borders and Information Systems*, EIPA, Maastricht, 1998.

Boer, M. den, *Taming the Third Pillar: Improving the Management of Justice and Home Affairs Co-operation in the EU*, EIPA, Maastricht, 1998.

Böhning, W. R., *The Migration of Workers in the United Kingdom and the European Union*, OUP, London 1972.

Brauw, P. J. W. de, La Libéralisation de la profession d'avocat en Europe après la directive emise par le Conseil des Ministres des Communautés européenes du 22 mars 1977, *Cahiers de droit européen*, 1978.

Burca, G. de, The Role as Equality in European Community Law, in A. Dashwood and S. O'Leary (eds.), The Principle of Equal Treatment in E.C. Law, Sweet & Maxwell, London, 1997.

Cappelletti, A., T. Seccombe and J. H. H. Weiler, A General Introduction, in A. Cappelletti, T. Seccombe and J. H. H. Weiler, *Integration Through Law*, Vol. 1, Book 1, De Gruyter, Leiden, 1986.

Castles, S., The Guestworker in Western Europe, *International Migration Review* 1986, Vol. 20, No. 3.

Castles, S. and G. Kosack, The Function of Labour Immigration in Western European Capitalism, in P. Braham, *Discrimination and Disadvantage in Employment; the experience of black workers*, Harper & Row, London 1981.

Cecchini, P., *The European Challenge, 1992, The Benefits of the Single Market*, Gower, London, 1998.

Cloos, J, G. Reinesch, D. Vignes and J. Weyland, *Le Traité de Maastricht, genèse, analyse, commentaires*, Bruylant, Brussels, 1993

Cohen, R., *The New Helots*, Ashgate, Aldershot, 1987.

Costonis, J., The Treaty-Making Power of the European Economic Community: the Perspectives of a Decade, *CMLRev* 1966/67.

Cremona, M., The New Associations: Substantive Issues of the Europe Agreements with the Central and Eastern European States, in S. Konstantinidis, *The Legal Regulation of the European Community's External Relations After the Completion of the Internal Market*, Aldershot, 1996, p. 141.

Cruz, A., Schengen, *Ad Hoc Immigration Group and other European Intergovernmental bodies in view of a Europe without internal borders*, Briefing Paper No 12, Churches Committee for Migrants in Europe, Brussels 1996.

Cruz, A., Visa Policy under the First Pillar: A Meaningless Compromise, in M. den Boer, *Schengen, Judicial Co-operation and Policy Co-ordination*, EIPA, Maastricht, 1997, pp. 213-239.

Dal, G. A., Observations: droit de libre éstablissement et equivalence des diplomes, *Cahiers de droit européen*, 1978.

Decaux, E., Jurisprudence, *Revue trimestrielle de droit européen* 23 (4) oct-dec 1987, p. 707-716.

Dehousse, F., *Les resultats de la Conference intergovernmentale*, CRISP, Brussels 1997.

Dehousse, R., *Europe After Maastricht, An Ever Closer Union?*, Law Books in Europe, Munich 1994.

Desoire, G., Observations, *Cahiers de droit européen*, 1990, 1-2 pp.453-464.

Dijk, P. van and G. J. H. van Hoof, *Theory and Practice of the European Convention on Human Rights*, 2nd Edition, Kluwer Law and Taxation Publishers, Deventer, 1990.

Dinan, D., The Commission and the Reform Process, in G. Edwards and A. Pijpers (eds.), *The Politics of European Treaty Reform: the 1996 Intergovernmental Conference and Beyond*, London, 1998, pp. 326-339.

Dobson-Mack, M., Independent Immigration Selection Criteria and Equality Rights: Discretion, Discrimination and Due Process, *Les Cahiers de Droit* 34, pp. 549-572 (1993).

Dollat, P., *Libre circulation des personnes et citoyenneté: enjeux et perspectives*, Bruylant, Brussels, 1998, pp. 360-364.

Dubois, A., L'association de la Tunisie et du Maroc à la Communauté, *Revue du Marché Commun* (1969), p. 355.

Due, O., *Conférence Robert Schuman sur le Droit Communautaire*, à Forence, le 17 juin 1991.

Duff, A., *The Amsterdam Treaty, Text and Commentary*, Federal Trust, 1997.

Elsen, C., Schengen et la coopération dans les domaines de la justice et des affaires intérieures. Besoin actuels et options future, in M. den Boer, *The Implementation of Schengen: First the Widening, Now the Deepening*, EIPA, Maastricht, 1997, p. 5.

Essen, J. L. F. van, La Convention Européene d'Établissement, NTIR, 1956.

European Commission, *Research on the "Cost of Non-Europe" – the Completion of the Internal Market: A Survey of European Industries' perception of the likely effects*, Brussels, 1988.

European Commission, *Abolition of Border Controls*, Communication to the Council and to Parliament, SEC(92) 877 final.

Evans, A., *European Union Law*, Hart, Oxford, 1998.

Fernhout, R., Justice and Home Affairs: Immigration and Asylum Policy from JHA co-operation to communitarisation, in J. de Winter *et al.* (eds.), *Reforming the Treaty on European Union, The Legal Debate*, Kluwer Law International, The Hague, 1995, pp. 377-398.

Fernhout, R., The United States of Europe have Commenced, but for Whom?, *Netherlands Quarterly of Human Rights*, Vol. 11, No 3, 1993, pp. 249-266.

Flaesch-Mougin, C., Le Traité Maastricht et les competence externes de la communauté européenne: à la recherche d'une politique externe de l'union, *Cahiers de droit européen*, 1993, No. 1-2.

Flynn, L., Joined Cases C-92/92 and C-326/93 Collins, *CMLRev* 32: 997-1011, (1995).

Gacon, H., *Dictionnaire Permanent du Droit des étrangers*, no 60, étude Accords CE/Etats tiers, June 1999.

Gautron, J. Cl., De Lomé I à Lomé II: La Convention ACP-EC du 31 octobre 1979, *Cahiers de droit européen*, 1980.

Gerven, W. van, The Right of Establishment and Free Supply of Services within the Common Market, *CMLRev* (66.67).

Giddens, A., *Modernity and Self-Identity: Self and Society in the late Modern Age*, Stanford University Press, Stanford, 1991.

Groenendijk K. and R. Hampsink, *Temporary Employment of Migrants in Europe*, Reeks, Recht & Samenleving No 10, GNI, Nijmegen, 1995.

Groenendijk, K., *Case note Rechtspraak Vreemdelingenrecht 1997, Nr. 94*, Ars Aequi Libri, Nijmegen, 1998, p. 344.

Groenendijk, K., E. Guild and H. Dogan, *Security of Residence of long-term migrants: a comparative study of law and practice in European countries*, Council of Europe, Strasbourg, 1998.

Groenendijk, K., *Jurisprudentie Vreemdelingrecht 1999*.

Groenendijk, K., Regulation of ethnic immigration: the case of the Aussiedler, *New Community* 23(4) 461, 1997.

Groenendijk, K., The Incorporation of Schengen: continuation of the democratic deficit or a fresh start? in A. Gormley, forthcoming.

Groenendijk, K., Strategien zur Verbesserung des Rechtsstatus von Drittstaatsangehöriger, in K. Barwig, G. Brinkmann, L. Huber, K. Lorcher and C. Schumacher, *Vom Ausländer zum Bürger: Problemanzeigen in Ausländer-, Asyl- und Staatsangehörigkeitsrecht*, Nomos Verlagsgesellschaft, Baden-Baden, 1994.

Guild, E., *A Guide to the Right of Establishment in the Europe Agreements*, ILPA/BS&G, London, 1996.

Guild, E., The Constitutional Consequences of Lawmaking in the Third Pillar of the European Union, in P. Craig and C. Harlow, *Lawmaking in the European Union*, Kluwer Law International, London, 1998, pp. 65-88.

Guild, E., *The European Convention on the Legal Status of Migrant Workers (1977). An analysis of its Scope and Benefits*, Council of Europe, Strasbourg, 1999.

Guild, E., The Right to Travel: three new directives from the European Commission, *I&NL&P* (1996), Vol. 10/2, p. 5.

Guild, E., Waltzing towards Accession: the Case of the Central and Eastern European Countries, *European Business Law*, 1998, p. 34.

Guild, E. and P. Barth, The Movement of Natural Persons at the GATS: A UK Perspective and European Dilemmas, *European Foreign Affairs Reviews*, Autumn 1999.

Guild, E. and G. Lesieur, *The European Court of Justice and the European Convention on Human Rights: Who said what when*, Kluwer Law International, London, 1998.

Guild, E. and J. Niessen, *The Developing Immigration and Asylum Policies of the European Union*, Kluwer Law International, The Hague, 1996.

Gutmann, R., *Die Assoziationsfreizügigigkeit türkisher Staatsangehöriger, Ihre Entdeckung und ihr Inhalt*, 2. Auflage, Nomos Verlag, Baden-Baden, 1999.

Gutmann, R., Discrimination against own nationals: a brief look at European and German immigration law, *Immigration and Nationality Law and Practice*, Vol. 9 No 3, 1995.

Haberland, J, Die Entschliessungen der Justiz- und Innenminister der Europäischen Union im Bericht der Aufname, *ZAR* 1/1996, p. 3.

Hailbronner, K., *Asyl- und Einwanderungsrecht im europäischen Vergleich*, Band 1 Schriftenreihe der Europäischen Rechtsakademie Trier, Bundesanzeiger Verlagsges. GmbH, Cologne, 1992.

Hailbronner, K., Die europäische Asylrechtsharmonisierung nach dem Vertrag von Maastricht, *ZAR* 1/1995, p. 3

Hailbronner, K., Visa Regulations and Third Country Nationals in EC Law, *CMLRev* 31:969-995.

Hall, S., *Nationality, Migration Rights & Citizenship of the Union*, Martinus Nijhoff, The Hague, 1995.

Hartley, T., The Commission as Legislator under the EEC Treaty, *European Law Review*, 1988, pp. 122-125.

Hedemann-Robinson, M., Third-County Nationals, European Union Citizenship, and Free Movement of Persons: a Time for Bridges rather than Divisions, 16 *YEL* (1996), p.321.

Heide, H. ter, The Free Movement of Workers in the Final Phase, *CMLRev* (68/69).

Heldmann, H., Familiennachzug für Türken in Deutschland, in H. Lichtenburg, G. Linne, H. Gümrükcü (Hrsg), *Gastarbeiter – Einwanderer – Bürger?*, Nomos Verlag, Baden-Baden, 1994.

Henson, P. and N. Malhan, *Domestic Politics and Europeanisation in the German Migration Debate: The Elusive Search for a European Migration Policy*, Third ECSA-World Conference, Brussels, 19-20 September 1996.

Jackson, J., *The World Trading System, Law and Policy of International Economic Relations*, 2nd Edition, The MIT Press, Cambridge Massachusetts, London, 1997.

Jacque, J-P. and J. H. H. Weiler, On the Road to European Union – A New Judicial Architecture: An Agenda for the Intergovernmental Conference, *CMLRev* 27:185-207 (1990).

Johnston, E. and D. O'Keeffe, From Discrimination to Obstacles to Free Movement: Recent Developments Concerning the Free Movement of Workers 1989-1994, *CMLRev* 31:1313, (1994).

Keohane, R. and S. Hoffmann, *The New European Community Decision-Making and Institutional Change*, Westview Press, Boulder, 1991.

Labayle, H., *Coopération dans les domaines de la justice et des affaires intérieures*, Rép. communautaire Dalloz, mai 1998 p. 1.

Laursen, F. and S. Vanhoonacker, *The Intergovernmental Conference on Political Union. Institutional Reforms, New Policies and International Identity of the European Community*, EIPA, Maastricht, 1992.

Lenaerts, K., Légalité de Traitement en droit communautaire – un principe unique aux apparence multiple, *Cahier de droit européen*, 1991.

Lepoivre, M., Le domaine de la justice et des affairs intérieures dans le perspective de la conférences intergouvernementale de 1996, *Cahiers de droit européen*, 1995, No. 1-2, pp. 323-349.

Lewin, L., The Free Movement of Workers, *CMLRev* (64/65), pp. 300-324.

Lobkowicz, W. de, Quelle libre circulation des personnes en 1993?, *Revue du marché commun*, No. 334, Février 1990, pp. 93-102.

Louis, J. V., Droit et politique des relations exterieures des communautés européenes, *Cahiers de droit européen*, 1971.

Macdonald, I., *Immigration Law and Practice*, 2nd Edition, Butterworths, London, 1987, chapter 8.

Macleod, I., I. Hendry and S. Hyett, *The External Relations of the European Communities*, Clarendon Press, Oxford 1996.

Majone, G., *Regulating Europe*, Routledge, London 1997.

Mancini, G. F., The Making of Constitution for Europe, *CMLRev* 26:595 (1989).

Mancini, G. F., The Free Movement of Workers in the Case-Law of the European Court of Justice in Constitutional Adjudication, in D. Curtin and D. O'Keeffe (eds.), *European Community and National Law, Essays for the Hon. Mr Justice T.F. O'Higgins*, Butts, Dublin, 1992.

Maresceau M. and E. Montaguti, The Relations Between the European Union and Central and Eastern Europe: A Legal Appraisal, *CLMRev* 32: 1327-1367, 1995.

Marshall, T. H., Class, *Citizenship and Social Development*, Doubleday, Garden City, NY, 1964.

Martin, D. and E. Guild, *Free Movement of Persons in the European Union*, Butterworths, London, 1996, p. 290.

Martin, D., Association Agreements with Mediterranean and with Eastern Countries: Similarities and Differences, in Antalovsky, Konig, K., Perchinig, B., Vana, H., *Assoziierungsabkommen de EU mit Drittstaaten*, 1998, p. 23.

Martin, D., "Discriminations" "entraves" et "raisons impérieuses" dans le traité CE: trois concepts en quête d'identité, *Cahiers de droit européen*, 1998, vols. 5-6, p. 561.

Marx, R., The German Constitutional Court's Decision of 14th May 1996 on the concept of Safe Third Countries - A Basis for Burden-Sharing in Europe?, *IJRL* 8 (1996) p. 419.

McGoldrick, D., *International Relations Law of the European Union*, Longman, London 1997.

Monar, J., *Cooperation in the Fields of Justice and Home Affairs: Progress, Deficits and the needs for Reform*, TEPSA Seminar 7-8 November 1996.

Monar, J. et al. (eds.), *The Maastricht Treaty on European Union, Legal Complexity and Political Dynamic*, European Interuniversity Press, Brussels, 1993.

Moravcsik, A., Negotiating the Single European Act, in R. Keohane and S. Hoffmann, *The New European Community, Decision-Making and Institutional Change*, Westview Press, Boulder 1991.

Much, W. and J. Cl. Séché, Les droits de l'etranger dans les communautes européenes, *Cahiers de droit européen*, 1975 p. 267.

Nanz, K-P., Free Movement of Persons According to the Schengen Convention and in the Framework of the European Union, in A. Pauly, *De Schengen à Maastricht: voie royale et course d'obstacles*, EIPA, Maastricht, 1996 pp. 61-79.

Nicholson, F., Implementation of the Immigration (Carriers' Liability) Act 1987: privatizing immigration functions at the expense of international obligations?, *ICLQ* 46:586, 1997.

Nicol, A. QC and S. Harrison, Lessons of the Dublin Convention, *European Journal on Migration and Law*, Vol. 1 Issue 3, winter 2000 (forthcoming).

Noll, G., The Non-Admission and Return of Protection Seekers in Germany, *International Journal of Refugee Law*, Vol. 9, 1997, pp. 415-452.

O'Keeffe, D., Practical Difficulties in the Application of Article 48[39] of the EEC Treaty, *CMLRev* 19:35-60 (1982).

O'Keeffe, D., A Critical View of the Third Pillar, in A. Pauly, *De Schengen à Maastricht, voie royale et course d"obstacles*, EIPA, 1996, pp. 1-16.

O'Keeffe, D., Union Citizenship, and C. Closa, Citizenship of the Union and Nationality of the Member States, in D. O'Keeffe and P. Twomey (eds.), *Legal Issues of the Maastricht Treaty*, Chancery Law Publishing, Chichester, 1994.

O'Leary, O., Employment and Residence for Turkish Workers and their Families: Analogies with the Case-law of the Court of Justice on Article 48 [39] EC, in *Scritti in onore di Guiseppi Federico Mancini*, Vol. II, Guiffre editore, 1998.

O'Leary, S., *Nationality Law and Community Citizenship: A Tale of Two Uneasy Bedfellows*, (1992) 12 Yearbook of European Law.

O'Leary, S., Putting Flesh on the Bones of European Union Citizenship, *European Law Review*, 1999, Vol. 24, No. 1 p.86-79.

O'Leary, S., *The Evolving Concept of Community Citizenship: From the Free Movement of Persons to Union Citizenship*, Kluwer Law International, The Hague, 1996.

O'Leary, S., The Principle of Equal Treatment on Grounds of Nationality in Article 6[12] EC: A Lucrative Source of Rights for Member State Nationals?, in A. Dashwood and S. O'Leary (eds.), *The Principle of Equal Treatment in E.C. Law*, Sweet & Maxwell, London, 1997.

Oliveira, J. d', Expanding External and Shrinking Internal Borders: Europe's Defence Mechanisms in the areas of Free Movement, Immigration and Asylum, in D. O'Keeffe and P. Twomey (eds.), *Legal Issues of the Maastricht Treaty*, Chancery, London, 1994, pp. 261-278.

Ooik, R. H. van, Het verkeer van personen volgens de Europa akkoorden, *Migrantenrecht*, 98/10.

Papademetriou, D., *Coming together or pulling apart? The European Union's struggle with immigration and asylum*, Carnegie Endowment for International Peace, New York, 1996.

Peers, S., *EU Justice and Home Affairs Law*, Longman, Colchester, 2000.

Peers, S., Building Fortress Europe: The Development of EU Migration Law, *CMLRev* 35:1235-1272, (1999).

Peers, S., An Ever Closer Waiting Room? The Case for Eastern European Accession to the European Economic Area, *CMLRev* 32: 187-213, (1995).

Peers, S., Living in Sin: Legal Integration Under the EC Treaty – Turkey Customs Union, 7 *EJIL* (1996).

Peers, S., *Mind the Gap*, Refugee Council and ILPA, London 1998.

Peers, S., Towards Equality: Actual and Potential Rights of Third-Country Nationals in the European Union, *CMLRev* 33: 7-50, (1996).

Pescatore, P., The doctrine of 'Direct Effect': An Infant Disease in Community Law, *ELRev* 8:155 (1983).

Phinnemore, D., *Association: Stepping-Stone or Alternative to EU Membership*, Sheffield Academic Press, Sheffield 1999.

Piore, M., *Birds of Passage: Migrant Labour and Industrial Societies*, CUP, Cambridge, 1979.

Plender, R., *Basic Documents on International Migration Law*, 2nd Ed., Martinus Nijhoff, The Hague, 1997.

Raepenbusch, S. van, La Jurisprudence de la Cour de justice des Communautés européennes vis-à-vis des ressortissants des pays tiers, in M. den Boer, *The Implementation of Schengen: First the Widening, Now the Deepening*, European Institute of Public Administration, Maastricht, 1997.

Reermann, O., Ministerialdirigent, Bundesministerium des Innern, Bonn, Grundzüge des geltenden Asyl- und Einwanderungsrechts, in K. Hailbronner, *Asyl- und Einwanderungsrecht im europäischen Vergleich*, Band 1 Schriftenreihe der Europäischen Rechtsakademie Trier, Bundesanzeiger Verlagsges. GmbH, Cologne, 1992, p.16.

Report of the High-Level Panel on the Free Movement of Persons, chaired by Mrs Simone Veil, European Commission, 18 March 1997.

Report of the House of Lords Select Committee on the European Communities 1992: Border Control of People, Session 1998-9, 22nd Report (HL Paper 90).

Rittsteig, H., Anmerkung El Yassini, *InfAusIR* 5/99.

Rittsteig, H., Anmerkung zum Beschluss des Bundesverwaltungsgerichts vom 23.12.1993 - 1 B 63.93, *InfAusIR* 170.

Rogers, N., Case Note El Yassini, *EMJL*, Vol. 1, Issue 3.

Salt, J., *Temporary migration for employment and training purposes, Report and Guidelines*, Council of Europe, Strasbourg, 1996.

Schermers, H. G., *Free Movement of Persons in Europe, Legal Problems and Experiences*, Martinus Nijhoff, The Hague, 1993.

Schermers, H. G., The Effect of the Date of 31 December 1992, *CMLRev* 28:275-298 1991.

Schockweiler, F., Les conséquences de l'expiration du délai imparti pour l'établissement du marché intérieur, *Revue du Marché Commun de l'Union européen*, 1991, pp. 882-886.

Selm-Thorburn, J. van, *Refugee Protection in Europe: Lessons of the Yugoslav Crisis*, Kluwer Law International, The Hague, 1998.

Shapiro, M., The European Court of Justice, in P. Craig and G. de Burca, *The Evolution of EU Law*, Clarendon, Oxford, 1998.

Simmonds, K., *CMLRev* 52: 177-200 (1988).

Snyder, F., The Effectiveness of European Community Law: Institutions, Processes, Tools and Techniques, *MLR* 56:19 (1993).

Spielman, D., Human Rights Case Law in the Strasbourg and Luxembourg Courts: Conflicts, Inconsistencies and Complementarities, in P. Alston (ed.), *The EU and Human Rights*, Oxford University Press, Oxford, 2000.

Stangos, P., Les ressortissants d'états tiers au sein de l'ordre juridique communautaire, *Cahiers de droit européen*, 1992, p. 305.

Staples, H., *The Legal Status of Third County Nationals Resident in the European Union*, Kluwer Law International, The Hague, 1999.

Testa, G., L'intervention des états membres dans la procedure de conclusion des accords d'association de la communauté economique européene, *Cahiers de droit européen*, 1966.

Timmermans, A., Free Movement of Persons and the Division of Power between the Community and its Member States, in H. G. Schermers, *Free Movement of Persons in Europe, Legal Problems and Experiences*, The Hague, Martinus Nijhoff 1993 p. 352-368.

Toledano Laredo, A., L'Union Européenne, l'ex-Union Sovietique et les pays de l'Europe centrale et orientale: un aperçu de leurs accords, *Cahiers de droit européen*, No 1-2 1994.

Toth, A., The Legal Status of the Declarations annexed to the Single European Act, *CMLRev* (1986).

Touret, D., Le Tarif Duanier Commun de la CEE et les problèmes posés par son application, *Cahiers de droit européen*, (1974) p. 323.

Waelbroek, M., Le Role de la Cour de Justice dans la mise en oeuvre de l'Acte unique européen, *Cahiers de droit européen*, 1989, p. 41.

Weber, A., Einwanderungs-und Asylpolitik nach Maastricht, *ZAR* 1/1993, p. 11.

Weber, C., *Der assoziationsrechtliche Status Drittstaatsangehöriger in der Europäischen Union*, Peter Lang, Frankfurt am Main, 1996.

Weiler, J. H. H., Neither Unity nor Three Pillars – The Trinity Structure of the Treaty on European Union in J. Monar *et al.*, *The Maastricht Treaty on European Union: Legal Complexity and Political Dynamic*, European Interuniversity Press, Brussels, 1993.

Weiler, J. H. H., Thou Shalt Not Oppress a Stranger: On the Judicial Protection of the Human Rights of Non- EC Nationals, 3 *EJIL* (1992) 65.

Weiss, W., Zur Wirkung des arbeitsrechtlichen Gleichbehandlungsgebot in den Assoziations-abkommen der EG mit Drittstaaten insbesondere auf Auslanderklauseln, *InfAuslR* 7/8/98.

Widgren, J., The Need to Improve Co-operation of European Asylum and Migration Policies in K. Hailbronner, *Asyl- und Einwanderungsrecht im europäischen Vergleich*, Band 1 Schriftenreihe der Europäischen Rechtsakademie Trier, Bundesanzeiger Verlagsges. GmbH, Cologne, 1992.

Wiener, A., *European Citizenship Practice: Building Institutions of a Non-State*, Westview Press, London, 1997.

Wihtol de Wenden, C., *CERI, Paris, Les obstacles à une politique communautaire de l'immigration*, Third ECSA-World Conference, Brussels 19-20 September 1996.

Wyatt, A. D. and A. Dashwood, *European Community Law*, 3rd ed., Sweet & Maxwell, London, 1993.

Zlotnick, H., Identification of Migration Systems, in M. Kritz, L. Lean Lim and H. Zlotnik, *International Migration Systems: A Global Approach*, Clarendon Press, Oxford 1992.

INDEX

admission, 8, 12, 28, 34, 35, 47, 48, 51, 118, 126, 129, 138, 140, 141, 142, 148, 154, 160, 166, 168, 195, 207, 240, 252, 260, 263, 265, 266, 267, 272, 274, 277, 280, 292, 309, 312, 324, 325, 326, 330, 332

Algeria, 66, 89, 96, 111, 112, 114

area of freedom, security and justice, 296, 297, 299, 300, 301, 302, 303, 305, 311, 318, 319, 320, 322, 336

Association Agreement, 28, 45, 65, 86, 88, 217

Association Council, 74, 75, 83, 84, 87, 88, 92, 93, 95, 100, 105, 115, 116, 125, 126, 129, 133, 136, 183, 325, 328, 329, 330, 331

asylum, 12, 18, 30, 168, 178, 179, 180, 181, 214, 215, 216, 217, 218, 219, 220, 222, 232, 233, 241, 242, 244, 245, 246, 247, 248, 251, 255, 256, 258, 260, 289, 292, 293, 295, 297, 300, 301, 302, 303, 304, 305, 306, 309, 310, 311, 313, 314, 316, 319, 320, 321, 336, 337, 341, 346, 350, 351, 353

Austria, 81, 218

authorised to join, 87, 140, 141, 155, 157, 158

Belgium, 38, 39, 50, 57, 69, 167, 196, 215, 313

Benelux, 8, 98, 222

border controls, 14, 17, 214, 215, 217, 218, 220, 222, 223, 224, 226, 229, 231, 232, 233, 241, 242, 243, 244, 245, 246, 253, 262, 281, 295, 299, 301, 305, 311, 336, 350

Bulgaria, 176, 180, 181

CEECs, 173, 174, 175, 177, 178, 180, 182, 186, 194, 195, 198, 207, 208, 209, 217, 266, 349

child, 19, 59, 109, 139, 142, 152, 160, 161, 202

citizenship, 14, 20, 22, 23, 24, 25, 26, 49, 50, 68, 70, 109, 170, 232, 302

Competence, 67, 78, 233, 265

Cooperation Council, 92, 100

Czech Republic, 175, 176

declaratory effect, 28

Denmark, 295, 345

Direct Effect, 82, 86, 88, 89, 92, 195, 198

Discretion, 21, 121, 240

Dublin Convention, 216, 246, 259, 309, 310, 321, 350, 353

EEA, 38, 39, 177, 346, 349

Egypt, 97, 116

Establishment, 11, 27, 35, 124, 181, 190, 192, 327

Estonia, 175, 176, 266

European Convention on Human Rights, 26, 304

Expulsion 11, 28, 29, 34, 46, 47, 48, 49, 54, 58, 60, 67, 88, 99 112, 156, 161, 162, 178, 204, 313, 321, 323, 341, 343, 347, 348 external borders, 226, 229, 241, 244, 246, 247, 255, 268, 271, 275, 276, 277, 290, 293, 297, 306, 307, 333, 336, 337

family member, 55, 75, 140, 141, 156, 158, 266, 274

Finland, 218, 233, 328, 341

France, 8, 38, 39, 56, 98, 109, 111, 113, 179, 180, 181, 215, 224, 233, 270, 291, 322

Free Movement of Workers, 38, 40, 47, 48, 124, 182

GATS, 9, 115, 116, 326, 333

Geneva Convention, 178, 309, 313, 314, 315, 317, 320, 321, 337, 353

Germany, 8, 24, 27, 38, 39, 49, 57, 59, 75, 98, 113, 124, 126, 131, 143, 154, 157, 160, 164, 166, 179, 180, 181, 182, 183, 201, 215, 216, 218, 234, 260, 272, 312, 322

good faith, 20, 25, 26, 30, 32, 33, 34, 35, 71, 81, 91, 258, 344, 345

Greece, 39, 50, 65, 66, 95, 97, 101, 102, 103, 104, 117, 118, 127, 216, 218, 345, 347

housing, 37, 134, 139, 140, 142, 154, 156314, 329, 330

human rights, 73, 74, 75, 96, 105, 251, 267, 303, 310, 313, 317, 332, 341, 353

Hungary, 175, 176

Iceland, 38

Indirect Discrimination, 45, 51

integration, 37, 38, 56, 61, 117, 127, 131, 138, 145, 154, 155, 160, 161, 169, 177, 214, 219, 220,

237, 239, 248, 259, 302, 309, 341

internal borders, 214, 228, 232, 249, 297, 304, 319, 320, 336, 353

Internal Market, 213, 219, 305

Ireland, 39, 59, 232, 233, 262, 295

Israel, 96, 97, 110, 116

Italy, 8, 25, 38, 39, 51, 164, 185, 272

Jordan, 96, 116

judicial control, 250

Justice and Home Affairs, 242, 247, 256

labour market, 14, 26, 34, 35, 50, 60, 86, 99, 118, 126, 128, 129, 130, 131, 134, 135, 137, 141, 144, 148, 152, 153, 158, 161, 182, 183, 227, 236, 325, 328, 329, 343

Latvia, 176

Lebanon, 97, 116

Legal Presence, 290

Lithuania, 176

Lomé, 65, 66, 67, 96, 104, 105, 106, 107, 108, 110, 117, 118, 173, 347

Loss of Status, 161

Luxembourg, 38, 41, 45, 65, 173, 197, 215, 350

Macedonia, 116, 118

Maghreb Agreements, 65, 85, 89, 96, 97, 100, 101, 104, 106, 108, 110, 114, 116, 119, 174, 184, 347, 349

Minimum standards, 306, 319

monetary union, 217, 248, 302

Morocco, 66, 85, 86, 89, 96, 97, 108, 110, 111, 112, 119, 153, 174, 184, 187, 198, 202

Nationality, 21, 24, 40, 42, 45, 68

Netherlands, 30, 67, 113, 143, 168, 179, 181, 201, 208, 215, 232, 313, 320

Norway, 38, 218

Obstacles, 38, 55, 56, 201, 344

parent, 139, 142, 143, 161

Physical Presence, 290

Poland, 175, 176, 180, 183, 184, 185, 186, 188, 190, 196, 197, 198, 199, 201, 204, 207, 217

Policy, 45, 161, 162, 247, 324

Portugal, 39, 127, 214, 218

Pressure to Emigrate, 178

public health, 29, 46, 47, 49, 113, 162, 192, 236

public security, 29, 46, 47, 48, 49, 113, 162, 192, 235, 236, 343

refoulement, 313, 317, 321

remuneration, 29, 31, 40, 41, 45, 89, 104, 112, 132, 133, 139, 140, 145, 146, 147, 149, 151, 183, 187, 193, 329

residence permit, 28, 46, 49, 113, 148, 150, 152, 157, 158, 161, 165, 167, 168, 187, 207, 228, 323, 327, 347

right of residence, 14, 49, 148, 156, 157, 167, 168, 178, 195, 228, 275, 325, 333

Romania, 176, 180, 181

Schengen, 180, 215, 216, 218, 222, 231, 232, 233, 234, 240, 242, 261, 263, 264, 265, 266, 267, 277, 278, 279, 283, 284, 290, 295, 300, 302, 304, 305, 307, 308, 309, 350, 351, 353

self employment, 22, 31, 35, 131, 174, 207, 208, 314, 324, 325, 330, 342, 348

service provision, 27, 77, 95, 110, 116, 122, 194, 296, 326, 342, 343

Slovakia, 176

Slovenia, 116, 175, 176, 348

social security, 22, 49, 52, 57, 81, 89, 93, 99, 101, 106, 111, 112, 114, 118, 119, 140, 145, 153, 164, 166, 169, 174, 183, 185, 186, 202, 209, 314, 345, 347, 349

Spain, 39, 97, 127, 214, 218, 225, 233

spouse, 54, 58, 68, 128, 140, 147, 154, 155, 156, 157, 158, 159, 181, 345

standstill clause, 86, 104, 135

State Obedience, 32

subordination, 146, 193, 292, 305

Sweden, 39, 43, 218, 313

Switzerland, 218

Temporary Protection, 311

Turkey, 25, 28, 45, 65, 66, 71, 73, 74, 84, 85, 86, 88, 89, 90, 91, 92, 95, 97, 98, 99, 100, 101, 102, 103, 104, 105, 106, 114, 117, 118, 121, 122, 123, 124, 125, 126, 127, 129, 131, 133, 136, 140, 143, 144, 147, 148, 149, 153, 155, 161, 162, 163, 166,

169, 171, 173, 174, 183, 184, 188, 198, 327, 328, 347, 348

Turkish worker, 73, 87, 88, 128, 131, 135, 140, 147, 148, 149, 151, 152, 155, 157, 158, 159, 160, 161, 162, 165, 166, 167, 169, 170, 329

United Kingdom, 39, 91, 134, 225, 242, 291

Visa, 275, 276, 277, 278, 279, 281, 283, 284, 285, 286, 287, 289, 290, 292

Visas, 231, 262, 263, 265, 266, 273, 296, 336

work permit, 113, 130, 148, 168, 169, 187, 347

Worker, 145

working conditions, 11, 16, 45, 60, 89, 99, 104, 106, 111, 112, 118, 133, 139, 140, 183, 184, 185, 186, 187, 188, 189, 190, 202, 236, 237, 238, 239, 330, 347, 348, 349

Yaounde, 96, 105

Yugoslavia, 65, 66, 96, 97, 116, 117, 118, 312

Immigration and Asylum Law and Policy in Europe

1. E. Guild and P. Minderhoud (eds.): *Security of Residence and Expulsion.* 2000
   ISBN 90-411-1458-0
2. E. Guild: *Immigration Law in the European Community.* 2001 ISBN 90-411-1593-5

Kluwer Law International – The Hague / London / Boston